P9-CND-778

TOURO COLLEGE LIBRARY
Kings Hwy

Online Collaborative Learning: Theory and Practice

Tim S. Roberts
Central Queensland University, Australia

TOURO COLLEGE LIBRARY
Kings Hwy

WITHDRAWN

 **Information Science Publishing**
Hershey • London • Melbourne • Singapore

KH

Acquisition Editor:	Mehdi Khosrow-Pour
Senior Managing Editor:	Jan Travers
Managing Editor:	Amanda Appicello
Development Editor:	Michele Rossi
Copy Editor:	Heidi Hormel
Typesetter:	Jennifer Wetzel
Cover Design:	Lisa Tosheff
Printed at:	Integrated Book Technology

Published in the United States of America by
Information Science Publishing (an imprint of Idea Group Inc.)
701 E. Chocolate Avenue, Suite 200
Hershey PA 17033
Tel: 717-533-8845
Fax: 717-533-8661
E-mail: cust@idea-group.com
Web site: http://www.idea-group.com

and in the United Kingdom by
Information Science Publishing (an imprint of Idea Group Inc.)
3 Henrietta Street
Covent Garden
London WC2E 8LU
Tel: 44 20 7240 0856
Fax: 44 20 7379 3313
Web site: http://www.eurospan.co.uk

Copyright © 2004 by Idea Group Inc. All rights reserved. No part of this book may be repro-
duced in any form or by any means, electronic or mechanical, including photocopying, without
written permission from the publisher.

Library of Congress Cataloging-in-Publication Data

Online collaborative learning : theory and practice / Tim S. Roberts,
editor.
    p. cm.
 ISBN 1-59140-174-7 (hardcover) -- ISBN 1-59140-175-5 (ebook) -- ISBN
1-59140-227-1 (pbk.)
 1. Group work in education. 2. Education, Higher--Computer-assisted
instruction. I. Roberts, Tim S., 1955-
 LB1032.O55 2003
 378.1'76--dc22
                                2003014957

British Cataloguing in Publication Data
A Cataloguing in Publication record for this book is available from the British Library.

All work contributed to this book is new, previously-unpublished material. The view expressed in
this book are those of the authors, but not necessarily of the publisher.

10/25/04

Online Collaborative Learning: Theory and Practice

Table of Contents

Preface

Online collaborative learning is an idea whose time has come.

The desire by students to undertake programs and courses via the Internet and access resources online is forever altering the nature of formal education. Many institutions and educators have been caught largely unprepared for the radical changes forced upon them. Research into teaching and learning techniques that are effective in the online environment is therefore both urgent and · important.

The educational changes necessitated by the new computing and communication technologies are profound. The new environment is one in which students are more likely to come from a diverse range of backgrounds, have differing levels of technical and language abilities and have the desire to study at times and in places of their own choosing. Thus research into paradigms beyond those traditionally associated with universities, where students are often obliged to attend classes on-campus, sit through lectures and attend face-to-face tutorials, is long overdue. One such paradigm that holds significant promise is that of online collaborative (or group) learning.

Collaborative learning itself is hardly a new idea. Indeed, it seems likely that people have been learning informally in groups for thousands of years. It is interesting to observe therefore that almost all formal learning today, particularly at university level, still takes place in an environment in which students are expected to learn individually. Despite this, students often form their own informal study groups to assist their learning.

As Gaillet (1994, p. 94) has pointed out, collaborative learning methods were experimented with, and found to be successful, at least as early the late 18th century, when George Jardine employed them for his philosophy classes at the University of Glasgow. He came to believe that "the teacher should move to the perimeter of the action. ...and allow the students freedom to...learn from one another." An up-to-date review of the research and the long history of peer/collaborative learning can be found in Gaillet (1994).

The Russian psychologist Vygotsky (1978) was foremost amongst the pioneers who explored the causal relationships that exist between social interaction and individual learning. Piaget (1929) pointed out that collaborative learning and constructive cognitive development often go hand-in-hand, and conducted research more than six decades based on a framework that he termed "genetic epistemology," perhaps more appropriately translated today as "developmental theory of knowledge." For the American psychologist Bruner (1986), learning is an active, social process in which students construct new ideas or concepts based on current knowledge. In this version of constructivist theory, the learner "selects and transforms information, constructs hypotheses, and makes decisions, relying on a cognitive structure to do so" (Kearsley, 2000). More recently Lave and Wenger (1991) have stressed the importance of the environment, both physical and social, to the learning process. New theories of cognition and learning, many of them stressing the importance of interaction, continue to be put forward and vie for acceptance.

Today the benefits of collaborative learning are widely known but rarely practiced, particularly at the university level. Panitz (1997) has listed 67 distinct benefits — academic, social and psychological — that can be expected from the use of group work. These include such factors as building self-esteem, reducing anxiety, encouraging understanding of diversity, fostering relationships and stimulating critical thinking.

In particular, research has suggested that group work tends to advantage below-average students. Webb et al. (1997) reported that amongst groups with above-average students, the higher level of discussion translated into an advantage in the achievement tests for the below-average students in those groups, both when they were tested on a group basis and individually. On the other hand, high ability students performed equally well in heterogeneous groups, homogeneous groups, and when they worked alone. Both of these results have also been shown in different contexts by others (Azmitia, 1988; Dembo & McAuliffe, 1987; Hooper & Hannafin, 1998).

Many researchers have stressed that collaborative learning can also have disadvantages. Salomon (1992) among others has pointed out that despite the mass of literature praising collaborative learning, teams frequently do not work well, and lists as common problems the "free rider" effect (Kerr & Brunn, 1983), the "sucker" effect (Kerr, 1983), the "status sensitivity" effect (Dembo & McAuliffe, 1987) and the "ganging up on the task" phenomenon (Salomon & Globerson, 1987).

The use of collaborative learning techniques specifically within certain topic areas has not received much attention, though definite benefits have been found, for example, with their use in the teaching of a computer science curriculum (Wills, Deremer, McCauley, & Null, 1999), and for the teaching of electronic commerce (Roberts, Jones, & Romm, 2000; Romm & Taylor, 2000). Such examples tend to rely heavily on learner-learner interaction, with students working asynchronously in groups and with minimal traditional instruction being provided by the course facilitator.

Many other cases of successfully utilizing collaborative techniques within an online environment have been reported in the literature. Thus, the field is not devoid of systematic empirical investigation. However, the difficulties of control and replication are substantial. Rarely is it possible to compare circumstances where variables such as class size, student background, curriculum and even the level of enthusiasm of the instructor are effectively controlled. This may be one reason why many educators remain unconvinced of the potential benefits of group learning.

Another reason that may be cited for a general lack of enthusiasm is inertia. It is clearly easier for practitioners to follow accepted methodologies, than it is for them to risk the wrath of superiors, colleagues and students that may be incurred by attempts to introduce what many view as still unproven methods of instruction.

Further research into online collaborative learning therefore needs to build on existing research in related areas, and ask further questions: how can groups with shared goals work collaboratively using the new technologies? What problems can be expected and what are the benefits? In what ways does online group work differ from face-to-face group work? And what implications are there for both educators and students?

This present volume attempts to go some way toward answering these questions by presenting a range of views and case studies from researchers and practitioners working at the forefront of this important area.

In Chapter 1, Sue Bennett, a researcher at the University of Wollongong, provides an excellent point from which to start exploring these issues. In "Supporting Collaborative Project Teams Using Computer-Based Technologies," she describes the successes and challenges experienced by students working in an online collaborative learning environment. The case study offers many insights for those relatively new to the field, including the importance of properly organized class discussion forums, and the need for the instructor to take on the role of facilitator.

In Chapter 2, "Computer-Mediated Progressive Inquiry in Higher Education," Hanni Muukkonen, Kai Hakkarainen and Minna Lakkala describe the theoretical background of a pedagogical model that has been implemented within the structure of a collaborative learning environment. They argue convincingly that three metaphors of learning — acquisition, participation and knowledge creation — together constitute a broad base for envisioning the future skills and competencies to be developed by higher education. They caution that simply introducing a collaborative environment is not enough because productive changes will often require a realignment of epistemic, pedagogical and institutional goals.

Some of the benefits and implications of learner-centered online learning are outlined in Chapter 3, "Moderating Learner-Centered E-Learning: Problems and Solutions, Benefits and Implications," by Curtis J. Bonk, Robert A. Wisher and Ji-Yeon Lee. They focus particularly on the stresses and strains placed on the instructor. In this brave new world, they suggest that traditional teaching ability is likely to have to be redefined to include social, technical, pedagogical and managerial skills. Will the future of online collaborative learning see a leading role played by artificially intelligent electronic agents?

Most educators who have had firsthand experience with teaching online would agree that timely feedback to students is an essential factor of most successful courses. In Chapter 4, "Supporting Distributed Problem-Based Learning: The Use of Feedback Mechanisms in Online Learning," Joerg Zumbach, Annette Hillers and Peter Reimann examine the effect of providing feedback about group member's interactions, as well as their problem-solving processes; as they readily admit, research in this area is till very much in its infancy, and a large amount more could be done in this area.

Even with appropriate skills and good intentions on the part of the instructor, sufficient resources provided by the institution and timely feedback to students, online learning courses may still fail to provide effective learning environments that cater effectively for the needs of all participants. Chapter 5, "Online Collaborative Learning in Mathematics: Some Necessary Innovations," by Rod Nason and Earl Woodruff, looks at knowledge-building communities within the sphere of mathematics, and identify problems and possible solutions, and in particular the advisability of including model-eliciting mathematical problems and comprehension modelling tools within the online environment. They argue persuasively that such innovations are necessary for students to achieve in mathematics the kind of sustained, progressive knowledge building that can occur in other subject areas.

Pasta may not be the first thing that comes to mind when one thinks about online collaborative learning, but that is the analogy used by John M. Dirkx and Regina O. Smith in Chapter 6, "Thinking Out of a Bowl of Spaghetti: Learning to Learn in Online Collaborative Groups" to describe the group dynamics that can occur when students are faced with the prospect of learning in online groups without proper preparation. Pulling no punches, they state categorically what many practitioners already know: that group members may find the team dynamics, the decision-making processes and the need for at least a certain level of consensus less than satisfying. They suggest that to create a space in which effective collaborative learning can take place, specific strategies need to be employed that help the learners to move from a subjective and individualistic sense of identity to one in which they can reconstruct themselves as group members.

In Chapter 7, Lesley Treleaven presents "A New Taxonomy for Evaluation Studies of Online Collaborative Learning," identifying three principal categories: phenomenographic, instructional method and sociocultural studies. As with the introduction of any new taxonomy, this very valuable and innovative contribution to the literature is likely to assist many and stir debate among others. The chapter also provides a very welcome reintroduction to the communicative model of collaborative learning, or CMCL (Cecez-Kecmanovic & Webb, 2000), which takes as its theoretical basis that communication and language acts are central to the social interaction through which collaborative learning takes place.

Charles R. Graham and Melanie Misanchuk outline critical differences between learning groups and work groups, and further explore the benefits and challenges associated with using group work in an online environment in Chapter 8, "Computer Mediated-Learning Groups: Benefits and Challenges to Using Groupwork in Online Learning Environments." They stress that to ensure the maximal chance of success in the creation of an online environment in which effective collaboration can occur three factors must be addressed: group creation, including size and homogeneity; the design and implementation of structured learning activities and appropriate facilitation of group interaction.

In any field of endeavor, the same terminology can suggest different concepts to different people, even to those brought up within similar academic cultures. Similarly, different terminology can sometimes have meanings that can easily be conflated. Talking at cross-purposes to colleagues can result in misunderstandings, frustration and an enormous wasting of time and effort. Chapter 9, "Collaborative or Cooperative Learning?" by Joanne M. McInnerney and Tim S. Roberts, looks at the differences between these two terms. Are the differences significant? And do the benefits, problems and challenges outlined by other authors in this volume and elsewhere critically depend upon which type of learning is being studied?

Albert L. Ingram and Lesley G. Hathorn agree that drawing a distinction between collaboration and cooperation is important, and provide their own version of the important differences in which collaboration is seen as the more complex of the two. The central theme of their Chapter 10, "Methods for Analyzing Collaboration in Online Communications," is the development of coding procedures for content analysis that can be used to examine the various factors that may play a vital role in any successful collaborative learning exercise.

The anthropologist, social scientist and cyberneticist Gregory Bateson conceptualized learning as a transcendence of levels of reflection taking place within different hierarchical layers of context (Bateson, 1979). In Chapter 11, Elsebeth Korsgaard Sorensen uses a Batesonian perspective as the basis for her chapter, "Reflection and Intellectual Amplification in Online Communities of Collaborative Learning," in which she suggests that new didactic and instructional methods need to be developed in order to fully realize the potential that online collaborative learning has to offer. Scaffolding, in the normal sense as it is related to the decomposition of learning content, is not enough — rather, attention should be directed towards helping the learner to navigate through different meta-cognitive levels.

In Chapter 12, "Do Online Collaborative Groups Need Leaders?," Agnes Kukulska-Hulme explores the value and strategies of online group leadership. What are the appropriate roles for the instructor, the group leader and other group members, and what sets of skills do they require?

Finally, a return to evaluation in Chapter 13, "Drawing on Design to Improve Evaluation of Computer Supported Collaborative Learning: Two Complementary Views." John B. Nash, Christoph Richter and Heidrun Allert examine scenario-based design and program theory in the evaluation of computer support for online collaborative learning, describe the similarities and differences between these two approaches and suggest ways in which both can be used to evaluate and improve online courses.

As all of the chapters in this volume indicate, the next few years hold enormous potential for further work in this area, by both researchers and practitioners alike. Whether or not online collaborative learning replaces the traditional lecture as the predominant paradigm, those of us with interest or expertise in this field seem bound by the ancient Chinese curse — We live in interesting times.

For researchers interested in the evolution of research into collaborative learning, an excellent starting point is Dillenbourg, Baker, Blaye and O'Malley (1996). For practitioners interested in introducing collaborative learning into their classes, an excellent list of practical strategies and tips is given by Davis (1999). For everyone interested in online collaborative learning in higher education, an extensive list of books, articles, journals and other resources related to this topic can be found at Roberts, McNamee and Williams (2001).

REFERENCES

Azmitia, M. (1988). Peer interaction and problem solving: When are two heads better than one? *Child Development, 59*, 87-96.

Bateson, G. (1979). *Mind and Nature: A Necessary Unity*. New York: E. P. Dutton.

Bruner, J. S. (1986). *Acts of Meaning*. Cambridge, MA: Harvard University Press.

Cecez-Kecmanovic, D. & Webb, C. (2000). A critical enquiry into web-mediated collaborative learning. In A. K. Aggarwal (Ed.), *Web-Based Learning: Opportunities and Challenges* (pp. 307-326). Hershey, PA: Idea Group Publishing.

Davis, B. G. (1999). Collaborative learning: group work and study teams. In *Tools for Teaching*. Retrieved on March 10, 2001 from the University of California at Berkeley web site: http://teaching.berkeley.edu/bgd/collaborative.html.

Dembo, M. H. & McAuliffe, T. J., (1987). Effects of perceived ability and grade status on social interaction and influence in cooperative groups. *Journal of Educational Psychology, 79*, 415-423.

Dillenbourg, P., Baker, M., Blaye, A., & O'Malley, C. (1996). The evolution of research on collaborative learning. In E. Spada & P. Riemann (Eds.), *Learning in Human and Machine: Towards an Interdisciplinary Learning Science* (pp. 189-211). Oxford, UK: Elsevier.

Gaillet, L. L. (1994). An historical perspective on collaborative learning. *Journal of Advanced Composition, 14*(1), 93-110.

Hooper, S. & Hannafin, M. J. (1988). Cooperative CBI: The effects of heterogeneous versus homogeneous grouping on the learning of progressively complex concepts. *Journal of Educational Computing Research, 4*, 413-424.

Kearsley, G. (2000). *Explorations in learning & instruction: The theory into practice database.* Retrieved July 24, 2003 from the web site: http://tip.psychology.org/.

Kerr, N. L. (1983). Motivation losses in small groups: A social dilemma analysis. *Journal of Personality and Social Psychology, 45*, 819-828.

Kerr, N. L. & Bruun, S. E. (1983). Dispensability of member effort and group motivation losses: Free rider effects. *Journal of Personality and Social Psychology, 44,* 78-94.

Lave, J. & Wenger, E. (1991). *Situated Learning.* Cambridge, UK: Cambridge University Press.

Panitz, T. (1997). Collaborative versus cooperative learning: A comparison of two concepts which will help us understand the underlying nature of interactive learning. Retrieved on July 24, 2003 from http://home.capecod.net/~tpanitz/tedsarticles/coopdefinition.htm.

Piaget, J. (1929). *The Child's Conception of the World.* New York: Harcourt, Brace Jovanovich.

Roberts, T., Jones, D., & Romm, C. T. (2000). Four models of on-line delivery. *Proceedings of the Technological Education and National Development (TEND2000) Conference,* CD-ROM.

Roberts, T., McNamee, L., & Williams, S. (2001). *Online collaborative learning in higher education.* Retrieved on November 14, 2002 from the web site: http://musgrave.cqu.edu.au/clp.

Romm, C. T. & Taylor, W. (2000). Thinking creatively about on-line education. In M. Khosrow-Pour (Ed.), *Challenges of Information Technology Management in the 21st Century* (pp. 1167-1169). Hershey, PA: Idea Group Publishing.

Salomon, G. (1992). What does the design of effective CSCL require and how do we study its effects? *SIGCUE Outlook, 21*(3), 62-68.

Salomon, G. & Globerson, T. (1987). When teams do not function the way they ought to. *International Journal of Educational Research, 13*, 89-100.

Vygotsky, L. S. (1978). *Mind in Society: The Development of Higher Psychological Processes.* Cambridge, UK: Harvard University Press.

Webb, N.M., Nemer, K., Chizhik, A., & Sugrue, B. (1998). Equity issues in collaborative group assessment: Group composition and performance. *American Educational Research Journal, 35*(4), 607-651.

Wills, C., Deremer, D., McCauley, R., & Null, L. (1999, August). Studying the use of peer learning in the introductory computer science curriculum. *Computer Science Education, 9*(2), 71-88.

Acknowledgment

This book is the work of many people. I would particularly like to thank all of the authors of the individual chapters for their excellent contributions, and all of the reviewers, without whose support the project could not have been satisfactorily completed. Special mention in this regard must go to Sue Bennett, Herman Buelens, Dianne Conrad, Thanasis Daradoumis, John Dirkx, Richard Ferdig, Charles Graham, Simon Heilesen, Albert Ingram, Aditya Johri, William Klemm, Agnes Kukulska-Hulme, Alexandra Lilavati, Sebastian Loh, Joanne McInnerney, Antonio Santos Moreno, Hanni Muukkonen, John Nash, Rod Nason, Trena Paulus, Celia Romm, Sabita d'Souza, Elizabeth Stacey, Valerie Taylor, Lesley Treleaven, Raven Wallace, Leigh Wood and Ke Zhang.

A further special note of thanks is due to the staff at Idea Group Inc., whose assistance throughout the whole process has been invaluable, and to Central Queensland University, which provided me with the very necessary time and resources to see the book through to completion.

Finally, I would like to thank my wife Jane, and my children Rickie-Lee and Mitchell. Their love, patience and support throughout the project made the book possible.

Tim S. Roberts
Central Queensland University, Australia
June 2003

Chapter I

Supporting Collaborative Project Teams Using Computer-Based Technologies

Sue Bennett
University of Wollongong, Australia

ABSTRACT

This chapter considers computer-supported collaborative learning within the context of a technology-supported project-based subject offered to advanced-level students in a postgraduate education program. The subject was the focus of a qualitative case study investigation that revealed how student teams worked together on an authentic project task and the role online tools play in supporting their collaboration. This chapter discusses the research and conceptual literature that informed the design of the learning environment, the nature of the research study and the relevant findings, and some of the practical implications for teachers and designers in selecting online tools to support collaborative learning.

Copyright © 2004, Idea Group Inc. Copying or distributing in print or electronic forms without written permission of Idea Group Inc. is prohibited.

INTRODUCTION

The study presented in this chapter investigated learners' experiences of a technology-supported learning environment in which they worked in small teams on authentic project tasks to develop a multimedia product for a real client. The students were enrolled in an advanced-level subject in a Master of Education program, with most studying part time, often at a distance from the main campus. The researcher collected data in the form of assignment work, discussion records and interviews. Analysis of the data revealed the challenges experienced by the students as they worked on their group projects, the teamwork issues that arose and the strategies adopted in response.

The purpose of this chapter is to describe a particular implementation of a computer-supported collaborative learning environment and the students' experiences within it. The findings presented in this chapter focus on the role of online tools and their effectiveness in supporting collaboration. While these findings are of greatest relevance to the particular subject from which they were derived, teachers and designers interested in using online technologies to support collaborative learning will find the practical implications relevant to their own teaching situations.

The following sections describe: the background of the study in terms of the relevant literature; the design and implementation of the subject, including the nature of the collaborative task and the theoretical underpinnings; the details of the research study; a summary of the relevant findings and a discussion of the implications for the subject and beyond.

BACKGROUND

Developing Collaborative Skills through Authentic Learning

Helping students develop the interpersonal skills that underpin collaboration is an essential part of preparation for the world of work. A capacity for and understanding of teamwork, along with critical thinking, adaptability and self-evaluation is one of the generic skills that a university education should develop (Candy, Crebert, & O'Leary, 1994). This belief is reflected in the attributes that universities aim for their graduates to acquire (see, for example, Griffith University, n.d.; University of Canberra, n.d.; University of Wollongong, n.d.). While learning through small group tutorials and laboratory work in pairs has long been part of university study, traditional pedagogical approaches in tertiary education have tended to decontextualize knowledge and skills in ways that remove the links to real-world application (McLoughlin, 2002). This situation presents a challenge for many educators as they seek to develop group-based

Copyright © 2004, Idea Group Inc. Copying or distributing in print or electronic forms without written permission of Idea Group Inc. is prohibited.

activities that encourage meaningful collaboration within environments that support teamwork.

Authentic activities that reflect the ways in which knowledge and skills are used in practice provide learners with experience in real-world collaboration. The rationale for authentic activities comes from the assumption that "people transfer learning with difficulty, needing both context and content learning," and therefore "skills and knowledge are best acquired within realistic contexts" (Grabinger, 1996, p. 667). Thus, authenticity is derived from the real-world relevance of a task, and so the learning context within which the activity is set should reflect the characteristics and complexity of the real world setting (Barab & Duffy, 2000). As collaboration is commonly a feature of the work environment, it must also be reflected in the design of authentic activities. Working with others helps students build a deep understanding that takes account of multiple perspectives, reflects the way practitioners work and reflects the ways in which knowledge is shared within communities of practice (Brown, Collins, & Duguid, 1989; Duffy & Cunningham, 1996; Lave & Wenger, 1991).

Case-, problem- and project-based learning have been advocated as specific instructional strategies to support authentic activities (see for example, Duffy & Cunningham, 1996; Jonassen, Mayes, & McAleese, 1993; Savery & Duffy, 1995). Such approaches encourage collaboration through:

- Collective problem solving (Barrows, 1994; Jonassen et al., 1993; Herrington & Oliver, 1997),
- Group project work (Blumenfeld, Soloway, Marx, Krajcik, Guzdial, & Palincsar, 1991; Cognition and Technology Group at Vanderbilt, 1997), and
- Discussion of rich descriptions of realistic cases (Ertmer & Russell, 1995; Stepich, Ertmer, & Lane, 2001).

These approaches are thought to offer a wide range of benefits to students by distributing knowledge and workload among group members, providing motivational support, and bringing learners into contact with alternative interpretations and views.

Furthermore, the adoption of authentic activities represents a shift towards incorporating collaboration into realistic contexts that develop skills learners can transfer to the real world.

Collaboration in the Online Environment

In the past, collaborative learning activities have been restricted to full-time students in on-campus settings because of the logistical difficulties in finding time and space for students to work together (Kimball, 2001). However, the advent of Internet-based communication technologies has transformed higher education for both teachers and learners (Collis, 1996). The introduction of more flexible

Copyright © 2004, Idea Group Inc. Copying or distributing in print or electronic forms without written permission of Idea Group Inc. is prohibited.

approaches to learning and greater use of online tools offer new opportunities for student collaboration and new challenges for teachers supporting group work (Bonk, Malinkowski, Angeli, & Supplee, 1998; Palloff & Pratt, 1999). The course management systems that have been widely adopted in the university sector, such as WebCT and Blackboard, incorporate tools for synchronous and asynchronous online communication and student presentations. Distance learners, who previously had little contact with other students, can now take part in discussion forums and group activities. Support for learning "any time, any where" has also changed patterns of on-campus attendance at many institutions, meaning that students come to class irregularly, infrequently or not at all. These changes challenge instructors to provide opportunities and support for collaboration amongst learners, studying in different locations at different times.

Computer-Supported Collaboration in Authentic Activities

The study described in this chapter investigated the experiences of learners engaged in computer-supported authentic activities that relied on collaboration among team members. The learning experience was centered on a project activity in which students worked in small teams on a design and development task for a real client. This task sought to mimic characteristics of a real-life instructional design problem as complex and ill-structured, and provide students with an opportunity to experience the kind of team-based approach typical of real-life multimedia production. As most of the students were enrolled part time and many lived away from campus, online support tools were an essential component of the learning environment. This study provides insights into how learners used the technology tools to support their collaboration.

DESIGN OF THE
LEARNING ENVIRONMENT

The research study was set within the context of a graduate-level subject in which students worked in collaborative teams. The purpose of the collaboration was to provide students with an authentic project experience in which they could take on particular roles and responsibilities in the process of developing an educational multimedia product for a real client. The teamwork aspects of the project reflect the "decidedly unindividualistic" nature of multimedia design and development (Blum, 1995, p. 54). The aim of the task was to encourage learners to "think like practitioners" and so develop expertise by learning in a realistic context (Honebein, Duffy, & Fishman, 1993; Jonassen et al., 1993). The learning supports for these activities were developed using Jonassen's (1999) model for

Copyright © 2004, Idea Group Inc. Copying or distributing in print or electronic forms without written permission of Idea Group Inc. is prohibited.

Figure 1: Model for a Constructivist Learning Environment (Adapted from Jonassen, 1999)

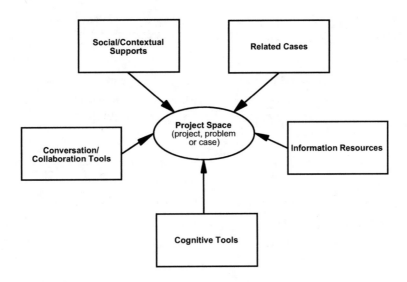

a constructivist learning environment. The key elements of the model are represented diagrammatically in Figure 1.

The model is based around an authentic activity, which may be a project, problem or case that the learner must solve or resolve. This activity should reflect the types of ill-structured and complex tasks undertaken by real-world practitioners in the discipline. For this subject the focal activity was the collaborative project task described above. The model suggests a range of resources, tools and supports that should be provided within the learning environment to assist learners throughout the task. Table 1 explains the role of each feature in the learning environment and describes its implementation in the subject.

A key feature of Jonassen's (1999) model is the inclusion of related cases within the learning environment. The case materials developed for this subject illustrate the ill-structured and ill-defined nature of multimedia design problems. The two cases detail the development of "Exploring the Nardoo" and "StageStruck" — educational CD-ROM products developed at the University of Wollongong (see Harper, Hedberg, & Wright, 2000, for more detail). The cases trace the progress of the projects from the early discussions with the clients through to the distribution of the final versions. Each case includes an overview,

Copyright © 2004, Idea Group Inc. Copying or distributing in print or electronic forms without written permission of Idea Group Inc. is prohibited.

Table 1: Resources, Tools and Supports Provided

Role of feature	Implementation in this learning design
Related cases describe solutions to past problems similar in nature to the focal challenge that learners can draw on to develop their own solution.	Richly detailed case materials describe two real-life multimedia design projects from inception to completion from the perspectives of the designers.
Information resources help learners develop an understanding of concepts and principles relevant to their task.	Information resources include suggested readings from the academic and popular literature, technical documentation, templates and examples.
Cognitive tools assist learners in representing the problem, their knowledge and ideas, and/or automating low-level tasks.	Software tools were made available to assist learners in representing their project ideas through text and graphics, and organising their content.
Conversation and collaboration tools allow learners to share their ideas and interpretations, and aid group negotiation and organization.	Online tools were provided for interpersonal, small group and whole class communication. Server space was available to all groups for file storage.
Social/contextual supports are tailored to suit the physical, social, cultural, organizational and technical characteristics of the learning context.	Face-to-face sessions and access to computer labs and meeting rooms provided social support and were tailored to the particular needs of the class.

a timeline, interviews with the key designers, original project documents, product reviews and research papers. The materials provide a rich set of resources that allow learners to explore the multiple perspectives and issues that are part of a real-life project. Such resources serve to illustrate the ambiguities and contingencies that are part of multimedia design and development.

Jonassen (1999) suggested that learners be engaged in activities that help them to analyze and explore the problem situation, articulate their solution and then reflect on the outcomes and their experiences. These three stages are the basis for the sequence of learning activities developed for this subject as represented in Figure 2.

Copyright © 2004, Idea Group Inc. Copying or distributing in print or electronic forms without written permission of Idea Group Inc. is prohibited.

Figure 2: Representation of the Learning Sequence

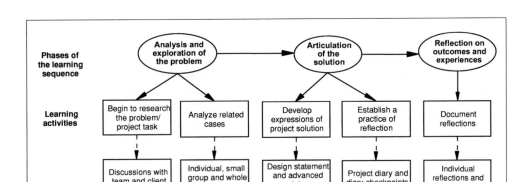

The learning sequence begins with a class meeting during which the students form project teams and select a project. Students can choose from a number of projects identified by the instructor prior to the session or they may seek out their own. The condition is that each project must involve a real client who requires a solution to an education or training problem. This process of negotiation encourages students to develop ownership over their projects (Honebein et al., 1993). The students then begin the process of analyzing and exploring their project problems. This process has two aspects. The first is researching their project through discussions with the client and among the team members, while negotiating the distribution of work and responsibilities among the team members.

The second aspect of the process is analyzing the related cases. To guide their exploration of the cases, learners are given a series of analysis questions and asked to prepare individual responses. This allows learners to develop their own interpretations of the cases (Duffy & Cunningham, 1996; Hazard, 1992) and an understanding of the specifics of the situations (Christensen, 1987; Miller & Kantrov, 1998). Learners enhance their understanding further through participation in small group and whole class discussions that encourage them to share their ideas. This brings learners into contact with alternate views (Carlson, Quintero, & Karp, 1998; Levin, 1995). As part of the analysis process, discussion activities also encourage learners to relate their understanding of the cases to their own

Copyright © 2004, Idea Group Inc. Copying or distributing in print or electronic forms without written permission of Idea Group Inc. is prohibited.

experiences, concepts they have encountered in the literature and their initial ideas about their own projects. These activities are important for helping learners move beyond the context of the cases to consider issues more broadly (Miller & Kantrov, 1998).

In the second phase of the learning sequence, students begin to concentrate on their collaborative tasks by preparing a design statement that details their proposed solution and then developing an advanced prototype of the product that demonstrates their design ideas. Working in a team environment with a client on a realistic design problem requires the student teams to attend to a range of design and management issues relevant to the corresponding real-world context. It is through engaging in authentic activities such as these that learners face cognitive challenges similar to those present in practice (Savery & Duffy, 1995). During this phase the reflective process is also established with learners encouraged to keep a project journal and contribute brief progress reports in the form of diary checkpoints to the class discussion forum.

In the final phase of the sequence, learners are prompted to evaluate and reflect on the outcomes of the project and their experiences. The reflective task has two components: an individual response to a series of focus questions and the preparation of a collaborative case that "tells the story" of the project. These two activities encourage learners to develop both their own understanding and a shared meaning (Rowland, 1992). The reflective process also helps learners to move beyond the context of their own project experiences and consider better or more general solutions that might be of use in future situations (Schön, 1987).

The design of the learning environment and sequence was evaluated through pilot testing with two groups of students. The results of these evaluations were used to refine the final version of the subject materials and activities. A more detailed description of the learning design can be found in Bennett (2002).

THE RESEARCH STUDY

A qualitative case study approach was used to undertake an in-depth investigation of the learners' experiences of the subject. This approach allowed the researcher to consider the complexity of the situation, the interplay of factors inherent in the real-life context and focus on the perspective of the participants (Glesne & Peshkin, 1992; Stake, 1995; Yin, 1994). As an in-depth examination of a particular situation, the case study captured detailed information using a range of data sources in the form of student assignment work, discussion list transcripts, class observation notes, student interviews, instructor comments and the researcher's reflections. This rich data set provided complementary and confirmatory information. The author's role in the subject was as researcher and instructor.

Copyright © 2004, Idea Group Inc. Copying or distributing in print or electronic forms without written permission of Idea Group Inc. is prohibited.

Table 2:   Research Study Participants

2000 class	2002 class
Group A: Kath, Lynn, Margaret & Steve Project: A CD-ROM training package on stock management and promotion for franchisees of a national dairy foods company.	**Group D**: Alex, Mike & Yvonne Project: An educational CD-ROM package to teach upper primary school students about government, developed for a local school.
Group B: Anna, Ian, Sheryl & Barbara Project: A CD-ROM training package for heavy vehicle drivers on the safe transport of dangerous goods, developed for an international manufacturing and resources company.	**Group E**: Brian, Mark & Jacqui Project: A CD-ROM training package to prepare hospitality workers in the responsible service of alcohol, developed for the author of the existing print materials.
Group C: Joanne, Liz, Rod & Simon Project: An educational CD-ROM package to support secondary school visual arts students, developed for the local art gallery.	**Group F**: Carolyn, Leslie & Sophie Project: An educational Web site for primary level students unable to attend the school environment because of illness, developed for a hospital school.

The data set was drawn from two classes of students enrolled in a graduate-level education class offered on the Wollongong University campus in 2000 and 2002. The classes followed the same learning sequence with identical tasks and resources. The students formed teams with three or four members. A summary of the composition of the teams and a brief description of their projects is provided in Table 2. Pseudonyms have been used to protect the identity of the participants.

Approximately half of the participants were K-12 classroom teachers, with the remaining half involved in adult education and training. All participants had knowledge of educational technology and instructional design principles, and had developed Web and multimedia authoring skills through previous classes in the program. More than half of the students lived outside of the Wollongong local area, and thus the teams tended to be geographically dispersed. The majority of the students studied part time, with only two of the 21 students enrolled full time.

Copyright © 2004, Idea Group Inc. Copying or distributing in print or electronic forms without written permission of Idea Group Inc. is prohibited.

The qualitative data analysis process involves reducing and interpreting the data to identify patterns, categories and themes (Merriam, 1998; Stake, 1995). For this study, analysis began with reading and memoing to identify a preliminary set of issues emerging from the data. The issues were classified into a hierarchy, and units of text from each data source were coded with the aid of qualitative data analysis software. The coding process revealed new issues and suggested adaptations to the categories. Refinements made through iterations of this process led to the development of the final coding scheme.

Data reduction and display techniques from Miles and Huberman (1994) were used to develop concepts maps, tables and interpretive descriptions of the data. These were examined to identify patterns and themes, which were summarized and presented with quotes from the data. This process allowed the researcher to draw "naturalistic" generalizations that others can learn from (Creswell, 1998), presented in this chapter as implications for practice. The researcher used a number of verification measures to improve the trustworthiness of interpretations of the data including: prolonged engagement and persistent observation, triangulation using multiple sources, peer review and debriefing, member checking, and rich description (Creswell, 1998; Merriam, 1998; Stake, 1995).

The results of the study yielded insights into how the learners worked in their teams to develop their products and how they used the supports and the resources provided within the learning environment. The findings relevant to the perspective of this chapter are presented in the next section.

KEY FINDINGS

Although it included a number of individual tasks, the basis of the subject was collaborative project work. Issues related to working together arose throughout the session, from the formation of the teams during the first class meeting through to the completion of the group reflective case. Analysis of the data from student work, observations and interviews revealed the key issues that the students identified as impacting on collaboration. The findings presented in this section focus specifically on the role of online tools in supporting collaboration. The emergent themes are discussed below and supported by direct quotes from the students. Pseudonyms have been used to protect the identities of the participants in the study. Minor editing of the quotes has been undertaken to improve readability, with any changes represented by the usual conventions.

Open Communication was Critical to Team Success

The students identified a range of factors that influenced team success and, although the specifics of these varied according to the experiences of the

Copyright © 2004, Idea Group Inc. Copying or distributing in print or electronic forms without written permission of Idea Group Inc. is prohibited.

different teams, common conclusions emerged. One of these was the observation that open communication had to be established and maintained for the team to succeed:

Having effective communication with the client and within the team is vital. If all parties are well informed on decisions things will run smoother than otherwise... Team cohesion develops through lots of communication, feedback and predetermined goals, which is a great asset for developing a multimedia package. (Group D reflective case)

For most teams this meant managing communication among members working in different locations and at different times. This proved to be a significant challenge:

After reading the case studies, I knew that good communication practices between team members was going to be essential to the success of the project. I realized from the outset that communication was going to be a challenge because of the different geographical locations of the other members. (Leslie, Group F)

Our group was isolated geographically, particularly with myself in Bowral and other members down [on] the south coast. Although we commenced our project on a stable footing with regular meetings, life soon encroached on our teamwork and the client. As a consequence we failed to create an active group environment. (Steve, Group A)

Students observed that many aspects of teamwork were reliant on good communication. For example, coming to an understanding about roles and responsibilities required negotiation and discussion, as did developing a shared vision of the project.

We applied the consensus approach (Visscher-Voerman, Gustafson, & Plomp, 1999) throughout the design and development processes of our project. According to Visscher-Voerman et al.'s communicative paradigm, the social part of the development process receives considerable attention. "Establishing a shared frame of reference and reaching consensus among all those involved are important elements." The consistent communication between each team member as well as our client worked out very well and all the major decisions have been made by consensus. (Liz, Group C)

Good communication was also essential for coordinating the individual efforts of the team members to support the production effort, particularly in

Copyright © 2004, Idea Group Inc. Copying or distributing in print or electronic forms without written permission of Idea Group Inc. is prohibited.

managing the collection of resources, the development of media elements and construction of the prototype product. Regular reporting is one example of a strategy developed to help manage the project:

The weekly progress reports, which we established earlier on in our project, were very useful to keep everyone informed of what is going on, what tasks have been completed and what is still outstanding, and who is responsible for each task. (Group C reflective case)

A Range of Tools and Strategies was Needed to Support Teamwork

Each of the teams used a range of tools and strategies that supported group work, including face-to-face meetings and computer-based communication tools to enable discussion, and e-mail attachments and FTP spaces to share files. They chose these from the range of supports made available to them within the learning environment, according to the needs of the team. The following quotes describe the approaches used by several teams:

As all members of the group were geographically apart and had different commitments, communication was mainly done online through WebCT, e-mail, the FTP site and by phone. (Jacqui, Group E)

The team process used by our group included a mixture of face-to-face meetings and electronic (mainly e-mail) communication. Face-to-face meetings were more prevalent in the early stage where it was beneficial to toss ideas around in a way that cannot easily be done online. Electronic communication was used more for keeping each other up-to-date and for discussion of minor issues. (Rod, Group C)

We decided to use a group e-mail configuration where all members received copies of all e-mails. This method was chosen as all members had access to e-mail both at work and at home. It was assumed that all members would regularly read e-mail and reply when necessary. (Margaret, Group A)

All of the teams made use of asynchronous online communication tools. The most popular form was e-mail, which was used by all teams. Some teams also made use of private discussion forums set up within WebCT. Asynchronous tools were effective in keeping communication going when the team members couldn't meet face to face:

Copyright © 2004, Idea Group Inc. Copying or distributing in print or electronic forms without written permission of Idea Group Inc. is prohibited.

Between meetings we used a[n e-mail] list serve for communication. This proved to be an excellent way to keep up to date with [the] progress of the project and with the work being completed by each individual. (Sheryl, Group B)

Such strategies enabled team members to participate in discussions and make contributions independent of time and place. This flexibility was particularly important given that nearly all the students were part time and team members were geographically dispersed.

The WebCT discussion forums also provided a full record of contributions, which could be revisited at a later time. This provided a means for the teams to document their progress, for example, through the diary checkpoints and meeting reports and to share and store documents as attachments:

...the WebCT discussion space was satisfactory, since we had a private forum set up for our discussions, and we could attach documents along with comments. (Group F reflective case)

The ability to communicate in real time was also considered important by students. Many commented that being able to meet face-to-face was critical to teamwork, and that some types of discussion were better conducted when the team members could meet in person:

Arranging meeting times when everyone could be together [was important]. Frequent, face-to-face team meetings are essential. (Ian, Group B)

It was essential to meet face-to-face on a regular basis to develop our project. I preferred this arrangement and felt that it was the best way to collectively generate our ideas and make decisions however, it was difficult to keep the regular meetings because team members were busy with other commitments. (Joanne, Group C)

The students did recognize, however, that online communication was necessary and many concluded that such tools helped them to make the most of their time together. They were able to plan meetings in advance and follow up by distributing notes. This added structure to the development process and helped some of the groups formalize their plans.

Only one team made use of synchronous online communication, but they had limited success due to technical difficulties:

Copyright © 2004, Idea Group Inc. Copying or distributing in print or electronic forms without written permission of Idea Group Inc. is prohibited.

After our first class meeting we decided to use the live chat facility to set up future meetings and "check in" with each other. Barbara had some technical issues getting access to the chat room, however, so this was not a success. We did try again using a chat room Barbara could access. Unfortunately since this was a busy public chat room (in Germany!) this was a very frustrating experience and we did not achieve anything. After that we abandoned live chat as a communication option. (Sheryl, Group B)

Although the difficulties alluded to above were due to incompatibility between the chat tool and some operating systems, the 2002 class did not make use of chat either. The telephone was the preferred tool used for distant synchronous communications, with one team setting up a teleconference to bring the team members and the client together.

These and other comments from the students make some of the strengths and weaknesses of computer-supported communication tools apparent. It seems that finding the right balance of tools and strategies to suit the team's particular needs was critical:

Asynchronous online communication through e-mail, WebCT and the FTP site provided greater flexibility for our group as we were separated geographically and had varying work and family commitments. This also gave us time to reflect and learn from others and so improve our contributions [to the] final product. However, at times synchronous communication by phone was the only way to clarify and solve problems and to provide solace and support. (Group E reflective case)

There Were Particular Challenges to Good Communication Using Online Tools

Despite the advantages of using online tools, team members found some difficulties in initiating and maintaining communication. Messages sent by e-mail or posted on the discussion forum were more easily ignored because they lacked the immediacy of a face-to-face conversation. For one group this was a particular problem from the beginning of the project since one team member being unresponsive:

All members agreed that e-mail would be the major means of communicating, as owing to geographical diversity, it was difficult for the team to get together for ad-hoc meetings. Initially we had problems with access to e-mail, as one member was off-line for several weeks at the beginning of the project. A successful team project relies on all members of the team reading and responding to e-mails in a timely fashion. This did not occur with one

Copyright © 2004, Idea Group Inc. Copying or distributing in print or electronic forms without written permission of Idea Group Inc. is prohibited.

member of the team, who also did not return phone messages, so at times the rest of the team were oblivious as to how things were progressing. (Lynn, Group A)

Switching to a discussion forum as an alternative means of group communication did not alleviate the problem for the team either:

In order to address problems we were having with e-mail, the team established an area within the discussion on [WebCT], so that all members could access team communications from any networked computer, without relying on logging in to e-mail. This was no more successful than individual e-mail, as the same person did not respond to confirm that they had been able to access the site. (Lynn, Group A)

These and other comments from the students express the common conclusion that team members who did not read and respond to messages jeopardized the collaborative process. Even when communication did not break down as dramatically as it did for Group A, keeping in touch still proved to be a challenge for most teams:

Maintaining communication between members of our project team was a challenge. Not everyone attended all our scheduled meetings and some important e-mails weren't read or replied to. It was difficult to organize the regular meeting times because team members have other work and family commitments. Several times we had to call someone at home or work to get an update or keep them updated because we hadn't heard from them for a while. I felt that there wasn't a 100% commitment from the whole team. In the real world you can't afford to [have] team members not contributing as it would be costly to the project. You would most likely be removed. (Joanne, Group C)

A lack of response from some team members wasn't the only barrier to good communication. For some students, technical problems caused communication to break down:

Initially, we had decided to communicate via e-mail. After our first meeting, we exchanged e-mail addresses and went our separate ways. However, this proved to be difficult as two of the members used Hotmail accounts that were unreliable. They could communicate with me, but I was sending them e-mails, and having them "bounce" back to me as undeliverable. I constantly had this feeling of being "left out of the loop" and out of the decision

Copyright © 2004, Idea Group Inc. Copying or distributing in print or electronic forms without written permission of Idea Group Inc. is prohibited.

making circle. T[he other t]eam members believed that because I was not (seemingly) communicating with them, I was disinterested in the project. (Leslie, Group F)

For this group, moving to a WebCT discussion forum was an effective solution to the problem of unreliable e-mail contact. These types of experiences demonstrated to teams the importance of exploring a number of communication alternatives in order to find the right tool or tools. This experience is described in the following comment:

[We explored] various technical means so that if one avenue failed, then another would serve the purpose. Circumventing my later problems with the FTP server by e-mailing smaller stack portions was one example. (Brian, Group E)

The nature of asynchronous communication as a written interaction involving the exchange of messages over a period of time also created opportunities for miscommunication among team members. This was an issue for one group in particular, for which the misinterpretation of written communication created conflict. This became sufficiently serious that the lecturer chose to intervene to facilitate a resolution to the situation. The students in the team commented that the formality of written communication and the inability to immediately verify the meaning of another person's statement, as is possible in face-to-face discussions, meant that extra care needed to be taken with the wording of a message.

Teams Needed to Adapt Their Communication Patterns Throughout the Project

The teams also found that their communication needs, and therefore the patterns of communication, changed throughout the session. In the early stages of the project most groups met at least once per week as they got to know each other and the project requirements. At this stage discussion focused on exchanging and developing the design ideas that would become the basis of the team's design statement. Having all the team members participate in this process was considered important:

I was pleased that the team appeared to share the vision of the project. We all agreed on the scope of the product and worked together on the overall design of the interface. The successful collaboration in writing the design statement ensured we all had a sense of ownership in the project and a say in any decision making. (Margaret, Group A)

Copyright © 2004, Idea Group Inc. Copying or distributing in print or electronic forms without written permission of Idea Group Inc. is prohibited.

Two main strategies were used to develop the design statement document. Some teams assigned their instructional designer the job of collating the team's ideas and coordinating the development of the document by distributing a series of drafts. Other teams distributed the workload, with each person preparing a few sections of the document and then sending these to the instructional designer to be consolidated into a final version. Online communication assisted in the drafting and feedback stages by allowing the easy exchange of documents between team members. Teams that were successful in this form of collaboration produced written documents that were coherent and complete. Teams less successful in collaborative writing submitted design statements that were disjointed and segmented, with a collection of individual contributions, rather than a collective effort as the final outcome.

As the projects progressed, team members began to take on more specialized tasks within their roles as instructional designers, graphic designers, content researchers, media developers and programmers. At this stage the teams met less frequently as individual team members worked separately to produce components of the package. Towards the end of production, some teams found they needed to meet and work on the project together. Many students felt that these face-to-face meetings provided critical support during the production phase, even if not all the team members were present:

Once the design statement and specifications were prepared team members worked for a significant part of the project independently using the specifications as a basis for programming and media production. As we got further into the project the need for face-to-face meetings became more apparent. Given our locations (Northern suburbs of Sydney to Wollongong) these were not as frequent as they could have been. We certainly made more immediate decisions and worked more creatively in solving problems when we got together. Most often only two or three of the four of us met at any one time. (Anna, Group B)

For Group A, the team not able to communicate effectively online, the reduction of face-to-face meetings in the production phase led to a complete communication breakdown and resulted in some members being excluded from the production phase:

As the instructional designer I felt it was important that I worked together with the programmer to develop the instructional tasks. I did not feel I was able to contribute at all during the final stages. My role was relegated to conducting testing and passing on the feedback from the testing to the programmer. I found this to be a frustrating task as I had no control of how

Copyright © 2004, Idea Group Inc. Copying or distributing in print or electronic forms without written permission of Idea Group Inc. is prohibited.

the test results would be applied. I felt I had no control of the quality of the final product once the second prototype was developed. (Margaret, Group A)

In the final stage of the class, online communication again became important in supporting collaborative writing as the teams began preparing the reflective cases. Again, asynchronous tools were used to distribute versions of the documents and coordinate contributions from each of the team members.

Online Tools Were Used for Managing and Organizing the Project

In addition to using asynchronous communication tools to keep in contact with other team members and plan meetings, the ability to store versions of the project on an FTP site, and publish and share documents on the Web also helped teams manage their projects. As most of the teams chose to develop media-rich CD-based packages, the FTP site provided a space to store files. Team members who were responsible for content development would create media elements and make these available to the programmer on the server. The server was also a repository for project management documentation, such as the design statement and meeting records. This allowed all team members to review documentation at any stage of the project, and ensured that everyone had access to the same versions.

Reading the cases prompted some teams to take a proactive approach and establish protocols for file storage, version control and backups at the beginning of their project:

[The] StageStuck [team] had problems with version control and file backups which was very important to note. It was at the right time when we started using the FTP server. It meant that version control was maintained and the programmer was able to make changes without any problems. All team members could access these files in a central location from anywhere and know that they have the most updated version. (Joanne, Group C)

However, some students understood the wisdom of adopting such strategies only after they experienced the problems first hand:

File management complications were an issue that I personally encountered. The other group members understood the importance of a file management system from the outset. Sheryl developed an effective system that allowed everyone to know the name, location, and version of each element of our project. I failed to follow the system and this resulted in problems for the

Copyright © 2004, Idea Group Inc. Copying or distributing in print or electronic forms without written permission of Idea Group Inc. is prohibited.

group. In the end, Sheryl assisted me in getting my files in order —
according to the system. (Ian, Group B)

One group used the Web publishing space, which was part of each team's FTP site, to support collaboration. This allowed the team members to share project documentation and review the various stages of their prototype web site:

The server allowed me to upload the images and code allowing the other
team members to see the changes I was making on a daily basis. It allowed
better version control, as I was the only one contributing to the actual Web
site files. All other files from other members were uploaded into different
[folders on] the server, so then all I needed to do was download them,
incorporate them into the existing pages, and then upload them to the server
again. (Leslie, Group F)

Online Tools Supported Interaction with the Whole Class and the Instructor

In addition to supporting communication among the team members, asynchronous communication tools enabled students to interact as a class group and with the instructor. The whole class discussion forum in WebCT provided a space for students to ask general questions about the subject, as well as share observations through their small group case discussion summaries and diary checkpoint contributions. This meant that students could follow the progress of other teams and feel that they were a part of a larger group.

The lecturer could also make contributions to this forum, allowing clarification of issues and continuation of discussion between the class meetings. Discussion postings made by the students provided the lecturer with an indication of each team's progress and, in some cases, the difficulties they were experiencing at the time. This allowed the lecturer to provide prompts and general advice to help teams stay on track. Students also contacted the lecturer individually by e-mail, which allowed them to receive responses to more personal questions. This was important in further revealing some of the problems teams were experiencing, and allowing the lecturer to intervene or provide additional support as necessary.

SUMMARY

The themes and issues that emerge from the data collected in this study provide insights into the use of online tools to support collaboration on the group project task. Comments from the students about their successes and failures

Copyright © 2004, Idea Group Inc. Copying or distributing in print or electronic forms without written permission of Idea Group Inc. is prohibited.

indicate that online technologies played a critical role in supporting the collaborative process among team members, many of whom were studying part time and living away from the Wollongong campus. A range of online tools was provided, allowing teams to choose a mix of strategies to support communication, according to the changing demands of their own projects. Asynchronous communication tools were used to complement face-to-face interaction, maintain contact over time and share group documents. Access to the FTP site allowed support for project production by enabling teams to manage and organize individual contributions. Online tools provided opportunities for multiple levels and forms of interaction, from one-to-one, small group and whole class. Each of these supported the collaborative process.

DISCUSSION OF FINDINGS

Qualitative case studies of the kind described in this chapter enable the researcher to draw conclusions about the particular situation and consider how the lessons learned might be applied more widely (Merriam, 1998; Creswell, 1998). As an in-depth study of a particular situation, this research study provides insights into a specific implementation of computer-supported collaborative learning, and as such has implications for the design of the class.

The findings show that the students in the class saw open and regular communication as the foundation of successful collaboration, and recognized that online tools played a critical role in supporting teamwork. Many groups began the session with discussions about how they would communicate and with expectations of participation by all team members. For some groups, a lack of responsiveness on the part of some team members meant that communication broke down, sometimes dramatically. Issues of non-participation in student group work are not new, and, in some ways, the experiences of these student teams mirror those typical of face-to-face groups (Jacques, 1991). However, it appears that reliance on online communication can exacerbate teamwork issues because without the immediacy of face-to-face interaction students may find it easier to opt out. Furthermore, non-participation is less obvious and may take time to become apparent. Team members may assume that everyone in the group is reading the messages sent to them and keeping track of the project's progress, only to discover later that this is not the case. A lack of response can also be misinterpreted as a lack of interest, if technical problems or unreliable e-mail addresses result in undelivered messages. The students' experiences show that it is sometimes possible for teams to overcome such difficulties through negotiation among the members. However, it may also be necessary for the instructor to intervene if problems become serious.

Copyright © 2004, Idea Group Inc. Copying or distributing in print or electronic forms without written permission of Idea Group Inc. is prohibited.

The students' comments also indicate the importance of face-to-face communication. They placed a high value on being able to meet in person and identified particular aspects of collaboration, such as debating design ideas and solving problems, as being best achieved through face-to-face interaction. This preference reflects arguments made in the literature for the particular strengths of spoken discourse (Koschmann, Kelson, Feltovich, & Barrows, 1996). Students also found particular uses for online tools. Asynchronous communication through e-mail and discussion lists allowed interaction to continue between face-to-face meetings. This kept the momentum going and helped teams maintain motivation. Collaborative writing tasks were also facilitated through the ability to exchange successive drafts online quickly and easily. Remote access to space on the FTP server also provided an essential support. The FTP space was used as a repository for documents, allowing all team members access to project documentation. It also provided a place for students to upload their individual contributions to be incorporated into the package by the programmer, and allowed team members to access prototype versions for review and testing. Teams made use of the tools available in a variety of ways according to the task at hand. Variations in the patterns of use demonstrate the need for flexible and adaptable supports within the learning environment.

The use of an authentic activity for the basis of this class provided a relevant context in which learners gained skills in the use of technology. The choice of tools and their use depended on the particular demands of the project and the needs of the team. The communication challenges were realistic ones as it is common for multimedia projects to involve large teams working in multiple locations. Through the experiences of their own project team and through those reported by other teams in the class, the students developed a sophisticated understanding of how online tools could support collaboration.

IMPLICATIONS FOR PRACTICE

In considering broader application of the findings researchers, designers and teachers should consider the similarities and differences between the learning context described in this chapter and their own situations. While the experiences of the students described in this chapter may be familiar to experienced online teachers, the findings of the study offer validation of claims found in the conceptual literature and set these within an actual context of use. The findings suggest implications for the design of this particular subject, which may also be applicable to other forms of group work in which there are limited opportunities for students to meet. The following suggestions drawn from the study are provided for consideration by instructors and designers.

Copyright © 2004, Idea Group Inc. Copying or distributing in print or electronic forms without written permission of Idea Group Inc. is prohibited.

Include a Variety of Opportunities for Collaboration

Include a variety of opportunities to collaborate in the design of the learning experience. Consider how working with others reflects real-world practice in the discipline and help learners understand the nature of collaboration in context. Analyze the requirements of the task and ensure you have provided the necessary supports. Encourage students to participate in a variety of activities relevant to the task, including small group and whole class discussions, collaborative writing and team production. Where possible, design group activities that build on one another or towards a larger goal, are integrated into assessable components and encourage appropriate use of technology tools. This allows learners to practice with the tools and fosters skill development and confidence building in context.

Provide an Array of Tools and Allow Students to Choose

Provide an array of online tools within the learning environment and make students aware of these at the beginning of the class. Allow them to choose the tools they need and how they will use them. Be ready to support students in setting up the tools and learning how to use them. Expect different groups to have different needs and be prepared to accept that not all groups will use all the tools offered. Encourage learners to monitor their use of the tools and be prepared to help them explore alternatives if an option fails. This approach goes beyond making tools available and providing technical support. It requires the teacher to model and scaffold the use of the tools.

Help Students to Develop Effective Online Communication Skills

Develop students' awareness of the particular advantages and limitations of online communication. Prepare them for communicating in the online environment through discussion about potential problems and strategies they might consider. Include this as a discussion topic for project teams. Encourage teams to continuously evaluate the effectiveness of their communication, and help them diagnose problems and develop solutions. Be ready to mediate if there is a dramatic communication breakdown. Even though the students may be engaged in an authentic project task, there is still a role for the teacher in facilitating group interaction by offering appropriate levels of support throughout the subject.

Encourage a Mix of Face-to-Face and Online Communication

Provide opportunities for both face-to-face and online communication within the design of the subject. Also encourage students to think about when teams need to meet and how members will contribute to the project when they are apart. When there are limited opportunities to meet, be strategic about face-to-face time and help the students do the same. Use face-to-face time for

Copyright © 2004, Idea Group Inc. Copying or distributing in print or electronic forms without written permission of Idea Group Inc. is prohibited.

brainstorming and debating ideas and for whole class discussion. Use asynchronous communication tools to maintain interaction and support continuous collaboration. A balance between the two forms of communication supports interaction while also giving learners their own time to think.

These comments have been derived from a study of advanced-level students who have already developed significant conceptual knowledge and skill in the discipline. These students were also confident and competent computer users. Additional supports may be needed when applying the ideas to undergraduate classes or students with less well-developed computer skills.

CONCLUSION

This chapter describes the successes and challenges experienced by students working in a computer-supported collaborative learning environment. In this case, students had limited opportunities to meet in person because most studied part time and lived away from the campus, so online tools became an essential support for collaboration. Comments from the students indicate that they found complementary uses for face-to-face interaction and online communication, balancing the strengths and limitations of each.

The findings from this study highlight the benefits of designing authentic project tasks, set within a learning environment that incorporates an array of online support tools from which learners can choose and adapt to suit their needs. The teacher takes on the role of facilitator in this process, encouraging learners to analyze their needs, select tools and develop strategies for their use. In addition, class discussion forums (face-to-face and online) play an important role in enabling learners to share problems, strategies and successes. The teacher also needs to consider how group activities might be included in the learning sequence to best support learners. Incorporating a variety of collaborative activities into work towards a larger task gives learners an opportunity to practice and develop skills with the technology. This type of learning design allows learners to explore a range of tools within a context of realistic, meaningful collaboration, and helps them to develop an understanding of how to use such tools to best advantage.

The students in this subject developed a sophisticated understanding of the conditions for successful teamwork, and of the role online tools can play in supporting collaboration among team members distributed in place and time. The data collected enabled the researcher to develop a better understanding of the how student teams worked in this particular learning context, and informed more general suggestions for the support of learners in similar situations.

Copyright © 2004, Idea Group Inc. Copying or distributing in print or electronic forms without written permission of Idea Group Inc. is prohibited.

ᐣACKNOWLEDGMENTS

Some of the data analyzed for this paper was collected as part of the author's doctoral study. The author would like to acknowledge the support she received from her supervisors, Professors Barry Harper and John Hedberg, and through an Australian Postgraduate Award.

REFERENCES

Barab, S. A. & Duffy, T. (2000). From practice fields to communities of practice. In D. H. Jonassen & S. M. Land (Eds.), *Theoretical Foundations of Learning Environments* (pp. 25-55). Mahwah, NJ: Lawrence Erlbaum Associates.

Barrows, H. (1994). *Practice-Based Learning: Problem-Based Learning Applied to Medical Education.* Springfield, IL: Southern Illinois University School of Medicine.

Bennett, S. (2002). *Learning about design in context: an investigation of learners' interpretations and use of real-life cases design to supported authentic activities within a constructivist learning environment.* Unpublished doctoral dissertation, University of Wollongong, Australia.

Blum, B. (1995). *Interactive Media: Essentials for Success.* Emeryville, CA: Ziff-Davis Press.

Blumenfeld, P., Soloway, E., Marx, R., Krajcik, J., Guzdial, M., & Palincsar, A. (1991). Motivating project-based learning: sustaining the doing, supporting the learning. *Educational Psychologist, 26*(3/4), 369-398.

Bonk, C. J., Malikowksi, S., Angeli, C., & Supplee, L. (1998). *Holy COW: Scaffolding case-based conference on the Web with preservice teachers.* Paper presented at the annual meeting of the American Educational Research Association, San Diego, California, USA.

Brown, J. S., Collins, A., & Duguid, P. (1989). Situated cognition and the culture of learning. *Educational Researcher, 18*(1), 32-42.

Candy, P., Crebert, G., & O'Leary, J. (1994). *Developing Lifelong Learners Through Undergraduate Education.* Canberra, Australia: Australian Government Publishing Service.

Carlson, H. L., Quintero, E., & Karp, J. (1998). Interdisciplinary in-service at the university: a participatory model for professional development. *Teaching in Higher Education, 3*(1), 63-78.

Christensen, C. R. (1987). *Teaching and the Case Method.* Boston, MA: Harvard Business School Publishing.

Cognition and Technology Group at Vanderbilt. (1997). *The Jasper Project.* Mahwah, NJ: Lawrence Erlbaum Associates.

Copyright © 2004, Idea Group Inc. Copying or distributing in print or electronic forms without written permission of Idea Group Inc. is prohibited.

Collis, B. (1996). *Tele-Learning in a Digital World: The Future of Distance Learning*. London: International Thomson Publishing.

Creswell, J. W. (1998). *Qualitative Inquiry and Research Design*. Thousand Oaks, CA: Sage.

Duffy, T. M. & Cunningham, D. J. (1996). Constructivism: Implications for the design and delivery of instruction. In D. H. Jonassen (Ed.), *Handbook of Research for Educational Communications and Technology,* pp. 170-198. New York: Macmillan Library Reference.

Ertmer, P. A. & Russell, J. D. (1995). Using case studies to enhance instructional design education. *Educational Technology, 35*(4), 23-31.

Glesne, C. & Peshkin, A. (1992). *Becoming Qualitative Researchers: An Introduction*. New York: Longman.

Grabinger, S. (1996). Rich environments for active learning. In D. H. Jonassen (Ed.), *Handbook of Research for Educational Communications and Technology* (pp. 665-692). New York: Macmillan Library Reference.

Griffith University (n.d.). *What skills does a Griffith graduate need?* Retrieved March 13, 2003, from the web site: http://www.gu.edu.au/centre/gihe/griffith_graduate/frameset7.html.

Harper, B., Hedberg, J. G., & Wright, R. (2000). Who benefits from virtuality? *Computers and Education, 34*(3/4), 163-176.

Hazard, H. (1992). *Teaching, learning and the case method* (MINT, No 7, INT). Copenhagen, Denmark: Copenhagen Business School.

Herrington, J. & Oliver, R. (1997). Multimedia, magic and the way students respond to a situated learning environment. *Australian Journal of Educational Technology, 13*(2), 127-143.

Honebein, P. C., Duffy, T. M., & Fishman, B. J. (1993) Constructivism and the design of learning environments: context and authentic activities for learning. In T. M. Duffy, J. Lowyck, & D. H. Jonassen (Eds.), *Designing Environments for Constructive Learning* (pp. 87-108). Berlin, Germany: Springer-Verlag.

Jacques, D. (1991). *Learning in Groups*. London: Kogan Page.

Jonassen, D. (1999). Designing constructivist learning environments. In C. M. Reigeluth (Ed.), *Instructional Theories and Models* (2nd ed., pp. 215-239). Mahwah, NJ: Lawrence Erlbaum Associates.

Jonassen, D., Mayes, T., & McAleese, A. (1993). A manifesto for a constructivist approach to uses of technology in higher education. In T. M. Duffy, J. Lowyck, & D. H. Jonassen (Eds.), *Designing Environments for Constructive Learning* (pp. 231-247). Berlin, Germany: Springer-Verlag.

Kimball, L. (2001). Managing distance learning: New challenges for faculty. In R. Hazemi, S. Hailes, & S. Wilbur (Eds.), *The Digital University: Reinventing the Academy* (pp. 25-38). Berlin, Germany: Springer Verlag.

Copyright © 2004, Idea Group Inc. Copying or distributing in print or electronic forms without written permission of Idea Group Inc. is prohibited.

Koschmann, T., Kelson, A. C., Feltovich, P. J., & Barrows, H. S. (1996). Computer-supported problem-based learning: A principled approach to the use of computers in collaborative learning. In T. Koschmann (Ed.), *CSCL: Theory and Practice of an Emerging Paradigm*, pp. 83-124. Mahwah, NJ: Lawrence Erlbaum Associates.

Lave, J., & Wenger, E. (1991). *Situated Learning: Legitimate Peripheral Participation*. Cambridge: Cambridge University Press.

Levin, B. (1995). Using the case method in teacher education: The role of discussion and experience in teacher's thinking about cases. *Teacher Education and Training, 11*, 63-79.

McLoughlin, C. (2002). Computer supported teamwork: An integrative approach to evaluating cooperative learning in an online environment. *Australian Journal of Educational Technology, 18*(2), 227-245.

Merriam, S. B. (1998). *Qualitative Research and Case Study Applications in Education*. San Francisco, CA: Jossey-Bass.

Miles, M. B. & Huberman, A. M. (1994). *Qualitative Data Analysis: An Expanded Sourcebook*. Thousand Oaks, CA: Sage.

Miller, B. & Kantrov, I. (1998). *A Guide to Facilitating Cases in Education*. Portsmouth, NH: Heinemann.

Paloff, R. H. & Pratt, K. (1999). *Building Learning Communities in Cyberspace: Effective Strategies for the On-Line Classroom*. San Francisco, CA: Jossey-Bass.

Rowland, G. (1992). What do instructional designers actually do? An initial investigation of expert practice. *Performance Improvement Quarterly, 5*(2), 65-86.

Savery, J. R. & Duffy, T. M. (1995). Problem based learning: An instructional model and its constructivist framework. *Education Technology, 35*(5), 31-58.

Schön, D. A. (1987). *Educating the Reflective Practitioner*. San Francisco, CA: Jossey-Bass.

Stake, R. E. (1995). *The Art of Case Study Research*. Thousand Oaks, CA: Sage.

Stepich, D. A., Ertmer, P. A., & Lane, M. M. (2001). Problem-solving in a case-based course: Strategies for facilitating coached expertise. *Educational Technology Research and Development, 49*(3), 53-69.

University of Canberra (n.d.). *Generic skills and attributes of University of Canberra graduates from undergraduate and postgraduate coursework courses*. Retrieved March 13, 2003, from the web site: http://wasp.canberra.edu.au:80/secretariat/council/generic.html.

University of Wollongong (n.d.). *Attributes of a Wollongong graduate*. Retrieved March 13, 2003, from the web site: http://www.uow.edu.au/student/attributes.html.

Copyright © 2004, Idea Group Inc. Copying or distributing in print or electronic forms without written permission of Idea Group Inc. is prohibited.

Visscher-Voerman, I., Gustafson, K., & Plomp, T. (1999). Educational design and development: An overview of paradigms. In J. van den Akker, R. M. Branch, K. Gustafson, N. Nieveen, & T. Plomp (Eds.), *Design Approaches and Tools in Education and Training* (pp. 15-28). Dordrecht, The Netherlands: Kluwer Academic Publishers.

Yin, R. K. (1994). *Case Study Research: Design and Methods*. Thousand Oaks, CA: Sage.

Copyright © 2004, Idea Group Inc. Copying or distributing in print or electronic forms without written permission of Idea Group Inc. is prohibited.

Chapter II

Computer-Mediated Progressive Inquiry in Higher Education

Hanni Muukkonen
University of Helsinki, Finland

Kai Hakkarainen
University of Helsinki, Finland

Minna Lakkala
University of Helsinki, Finland

ABSTRACT

With the introduction of new learning technology into universities, schools and classrooms, there is the potential to change educational practices in the direction of collaborative knowledge advancement. Yet, fundamental change in educational practices necessitates re-examining the foundations and goals of the prevailing learning culture in higher education. This chapter will describe the theoretical background of a pedagogical model of progressive inquiry and provide an overview of how this model has been implemented in the structure of a collaborative learning environment, the Future Learning Environment (FLE). We will take a brief look at studies of implementation of the model of progressive inquiry in university education. In conclusion, we discuss the challenges of changing educational settings

Copyright © 2004, Idea Group Inc. Copying or distributing in print or electronic forms without written permission of Idea Group Inc. is prohibited.

and students' study practices, how they may be encouraged to go beyond using individualistic knowledge acquisition skills, towards employing metaskills that are central in academic literacy, knowledge creation and developing expertise.

INTRODUCTION

We start this chapter by presenting two episodes that represent collective experiences in our university studies. We have either personally participated in or observed the processes in question although some details have been altered.

Jaana arrived late to the second lecture of one of her introductory courses. Fortunately, the lecturer was late as well. Jaana found a place beside her friend Maria. "Can you give me your notes of this lecture?" she asked hurriedly. "I have another course to take simultaneously. Besides, I am not so interested in this subject matter anyway, but I need to get the credit units." "All right, no problem," answered Maria. "I can give you my notes. ...By the way, do you know anyone from the Monday's subject-level course? Perhaps you could help me to get notes from that course in return." They agreed quickly to exchange notes, and Jaana slipped from the course just before the lecturer came.

At the end of the semester, they successfully passed the course examinations that focused on assessing how much of the course content they had acquired. Both of them received more than satisfactory scores. They accumulated a couple more credit units needed for graduation, but forgot most of the issues studied rather quickly after the examination.

The above description represents a more or less common episode in studies at Finnish universities, and is also likely to be true of undergraduate studies elsewhere. A traditional explanation for such study practices is that students tend to take surface-level approaches to learning. The students in question apparently did not engage in in-depth processing of knowledge. However, some researchers encourage investigators to take another perspective for understanding the described study processes. Such study practices are proposed to be signs of the students' ingenious — and economical — adaptation within a learning environment where depth of understanding is not highly valued (Scardamalia & Bereiter, 1996). In this perspective, it is assumed that the practices in question do not so much represent specific characteristics of Jaana's and Maria's individual cognition, but represent a socio-culturally formed agency concerning practices of taking university courses (Ratner, 2000; Wertsch, Tulviste, & Hagstrom, 1993). Characteristic of this type of agency is that the teachers of the courses

Copyright © 2004, Idea Group Inc. Copying or distributing in print or electronic forms without written permission of Idea Group Inc. is prohibited.

carry the responsibility for practically all higher-level processes, whereas students' engage only in an impoverished and narrow educational activity focused on remembering and reconstructing the content of course material. Accordingly, the agency was distributed between the participants and the social system of their learning environment, rather than carried out by the students alone (c.f., Lemke, 2001). Another episode provides evidence of an emergent type of agency in the course of Jaana and Maria's university studies:

Simultaneously with their second-year courses, Jaana and Maria got involved in a very interesting project. They participated in designing a supported open-house project for students suffering from moderate mental disturbances (non-institutional social care called NYYTI). Toward this end, they needed to understand the mechanisms of various mental disorders and their cultural and social causations as well as possibilities of rehabilitation. They went together to the library and hardly succeeded in carrying home all the relevant books and articles that they needed to process in a short period of time, in order to create a well-justified and plausible plan for the project. While working with the plan, they participated in some meetings with health care experts and administrators, as well as visited a local residential home of mentally disturbed people. A great deal of effort was invested, and, finally, as they got their report ready, they felt they understood the problems involved in the design of the supported housing project much more deeply than before. In the end, Jaana and Maria's report affected initiation of the NYYTI open-house social care project. Moreover, they were able to use parts of the report in one of their compulsory study courses.

The above episode provides indications of a different type of agency. Jaana and Maria were not only studying to assimilate isolated pieces of knowledge in order to get their credit units. They engaged in a personally meaningful study project that involved a rich social and cultural context, and included interaction with communities external to the university; further, the project was focused on bringing about a real world change. Moreover, it involved a great deal of joint planning and organizing, as well as pursuit of principal epistemic activities, such as generating questions and explanations about issues personally relevant to them. By taking cognitive responsibility for their own inquiry, the students demonstrated, for the first time in their studies, genuine epistemic agency (Scardamalia, 2002). Characteristic of this kind of agency is that the students themselves manage how to advance their knowledge. They coordinate their personal ideas with others' and also monitor how their collaborative efforts are proceeding. These tasks require them to employ cognitive strategies for collaborative problem solving (Scardamalia, 2002). Rather than subsuming their thinking

Copyright © 2004, Idea Group Inc. Copying or distributing in print or electronic forms without written permission of Idea Group Inc. is prohibited.

under the teachers' cognitive authority, Jaana and Maria, in this case, took responsibility for their own thinking and problem solving.

The epistemic agency did not arise from the psychological make up of the participating students, but emerged through their participation in the socio-cultural activities in question. We propose that a principal goal of university education is to encourage and facilitate emergence of such genuine epistemic agency. That emergence is dependent on appropriate learning experiences. The problem to be pursued in the present chapter is whether innovative pedagogical approaches and advanced learning technologies could be used to facilitate the type of epistemic agency that characterized Jaana and Maria's personal study project. The issues of learning and agency will become clearer if we first examine them in relation to three metaphors of learning.

Practices of higher education may be productively examined, in respect of epistemic agency, through three metaphors of learning: acquisition, participation and knowledge-creation metaphors (Paavola, Lipponen, & Hakkarainen, 2002). Sfard (1998) has proposed two metaphors of learning: learning as acquisition of knowledge and learning as participation in community's work or activity. The acquisition metaphor represents a traditional view according to which learning is mainly a process of acquiring desired pieces of knowledge. Therefore, learning is a matter of individual construction and acquisition, and such outcomes are realized through a process of transfer. It consists in a person's capability to use and apply knowledge in new situations (Paavola et al., 2002; Sfard, 1998). Jaana and Maria's experiences from their course work (first episode) focused almost entirely on acquiring a pre-determined body of knowledge that was measured in terms of mastery of content in the end of their courses. There simply was no space for the students' own epistemic agency; it would have required exceptional efforts from Jaana and Maria themselves to generate their own meaningful learning agenda. Although their personal study project likewise involved extensive accumulation of knowledge, the acquisition perspective captures only a single aspect of their activities.

Second, learning may be seen as a process of participating in various cultural practices and shared learning activities. According to the participation metaphor, knowledge does not exist either in a world of its own or in individual minds, but is an aspect of participation in cultural practices (Brown, Collins, & Duguide, 1989; Lave & Wenger, 1991). Cognition and knowing are distributed over individuals and their environments, and learning is "located" in these relations and networks of distributed activities of participation (Paavola et al., 2002). The participation processes involved in Jaana and Maria's course work were rather narrow and impoverished. The personal study project, in contrast, involved strong ownership, continuous dialogue with heterogeneous voices that they identified with and a repeated crossing of boundaries between their academic studies and expert communities. Jaana and Maria's learning involved

Copyright © 2004, Idea Group Inc. Copying or distributing in print or electronic forms without written permission of Idea Group Inc. is prohibited.

profound changes in their way of understanding mentally vulnerable people. Epistemic agency arises naturally in the context of solving these kinds of meaningful and complex problems.

The acquisition and participation metaphors of learning do not, however, address the essential aspects of Jaana and Maria's personal study project. In pursuing their project, they were not only acquiring prevailing knowledge, but creating and building new knowledge by synthesizing results of their inquiries. Rather than just trying to store knowledge mentally, they were jointly working for the advancement of a knowledge artifact — their joint project plan for a mental health facility — that was commented on, discussed about and further elaborated with their entire social network and, finally, implemented in practice (in conjunction with other reports and plans). To represent such a process, Paavola et al. (2002) have proposed that a third metaphor is needed, the knowledge-creation metaphor, which addresses processes of deliberate building and creation of knowledge and corresponding collective social practices. In the knowledge-creation approach, learning is treated as analogous to innovative processes of inquiry where something new is created and initial knowledge is either substantially enriched or significantly transformed during the process (Bereiter, 2002; Paavola et al., 2002). Epistemic agency is facilitated through learning processes in which there are aspects of all three metaphors of learning: acquisition of existing knowledge, a variety of ways of participating in cultural practices and joint creation of new ideas and thoughts.

Even if the two episodes described above represent pedagogically very different learning processes, there are certain similarities. Typical of Jaana and Maria's courses was that each student wrote her own notes. Although these notes were copied from one to another student, there was hardly any discussion between the students about the ideas presented. Processes of thoughtful learning that occurred while preparing for an examination remained private and, in the outcome, invisible to the teacher and fellow students. Interestingly, the same phenomenon also characterizes Jaana and Maria's study project. They discussed a great deal about it between themselves, but their own intellectual efforts, constant struggles for understanding and going beyond information given are nowhere visible in the final product — their report.

A central argument of this article is that collaborative technologies, if embedded in appropriate social and pedagogical infrastructures (Bielaczyc, 2001; Lipponen, 2002) may at least partially change this situation of invisibility. Suppose students participating either in course work or a larger study project were established in a networked learning environment that provided each student with access to a shared database for making their notes, posing their questions, explicating their conceptions and sharing their reflections either during or between face-to-face meetings. This kind of "mediated agency" (Wertsch et al., 1993) would likely transform the students' educational activity. The argument

Copyright © 2004, Idea Group Inc. Copying or distributing in print or electronic forms without written permission of Idea Group Inc. is prohibited.

here is not that the collaborative technology should replace lectures — lectures have a valuable role in university education — but that it is necessary to profoundly transform the one-directional flow of information to a collaborative building of knowledge.

Marlene Scardamalia and Carl Bereiter, who have been doing groundbreaking research in this field, propose that these kinds of networked learning environments, when properly designed, help to facilitate epistemic agency by moving students' own ideas into the center rather than the periphery of discussion (Scardamalia, 1999). They have developed and investigated a pedagogical approach — knowledge building framework — that guides educators in providing scaffolding for sharing ideas and thoughts within networked databases, thereby making these "objects" available for others to work on and further elaborate. These researchers have designed the CSILE (Computer Supported Intentional Learning Environments) and Knowledge Forum (e.g., Scardamalia & Bereiter, 1993) environments in order to provide an environment and the technological and procedural facilities for knowledge-building communities.

Collaborative technologies may be considered as new tools that provide students a "space for authoring themselves" (Holland, Lachicotte, Skinner, & Cain, 1998, p. 169). What characterizes successful knowledge building communities is that they establish socio-cognitive norms and values that all participants are aware of and work toward (Scardamalia & Bereiter, in press). These norms include contributing to collective knowledge advances, constructive and considerate criticism and continual seeking to improve and develop knowledge objects, such as theories, plans, designs and ideas.

As the three metaphors of learning draw attention to different aspects of learning, new pedagogical models are also required that would support these processes as parts of knowledge-building efforts. In the literature on educational research, one finds several models for scaffolding the processes of inquiry in primary and secondary education. A number of them have been developed to model and facilitate inquiry in natural sciences, e.g., scientific visualization technologies to support inquiry-based learning in the geosciences (Edelson, Gordin, & Pea, 1999), project-based science and laboratory work (Krajcik, Blumenfeld, Marx, Bass, Fredricks, & Soloway, 1998), laws of force and motion (White & Frederiksen, 1998) and concepts of growth and development (Zuckerman, Chudinova, & Khavkin, 1998). It may be argued that an inquiry process in well-defined scientific fields takes different forms and calls for different scaffolding focuses than in ill-defined domains. In the former, the problem-setting, hypothesis testing, systematic data collection and analysis practices demand more attention. In the latter, ill-defined scientific domains — such as social sciences or philosophy — efforts at theory building, conceptual clarification, argumentation and critical evaluation are more often the focus of scaffolding.

Copyright © 2004, Idea Group Inc. Copying or distributing in print or electronic forms without written permission of Idea Group Inc. is prohibited.

To facilitate epistemic agency in university-level education, the present investigators had to first develop a theoretical framework; it is based on the model of progressive inquiry. The model involves, in a compressed form, those key epistemic activities that Jaana, Maria and other pursuers of knowledge advancement undertake during their inquiry processes. The idea is to provide pedagogical guidelines for a teacher or tutor and participating students in the critical goals of knowledge-advancing inquiry. This model is intended to provide a heuristic framework for the key activities of a knowledge building community, and model the processes in which the community is involved. Notice that the epistemic activities were actually present in Jaana and Maria's own study project described in the second episode; the problem was that these activities, and corresponding expert-like practices of working with knowledge, generally fell outside the institutionalized part of their curriculum. Accordingly, the idea presented here is not to bring completely new activities into university studies, but to focus on activities critical to the development of epistemic agency.

THE MODEL OF PROGRESSIVE INQUIRY

Progressive inquiry is a heuristic framework for structuring and supporting students' epistemological advancement and development of epistemic agency and related skills. The model of progressive inquiry has been developed by Hakkarainen and his colleagues (Hakkarainen, 1998; Hakkarainen, Lonka, & Lipponen, 1999; Muukkonen, Hakkarainen, & Lakkala, 1999) as a pedagogical and epistemological model for representing principal features of scientific collaborative inquiry. It is primarily based on theories of knowledge building (Bereiter & Scardamalia, 1993), the interrogative model of scientific inquiry (Hintikka, 1985; Hakkarainen & Sintonen, 2002) and concepts of distributed expertise in a community of learners (Brown & Campione, 1994). The progressive inquiry model says that to arrive at a deeper understanding of phenomena and problems in science, one has to take part in a deepening question-explanation process. Original, often vague questions are based on students' initial understanding of the issues. As summarized by Otero and Graesser (2001), research in question asking has provided evidence that generation of questions is triggered by clashes between world knowledge and the materials or stimulus at hand, such as contradictions, anomalous information, obstacles to goals, uncertainty or obvious gaps in knowledge. In the progressive inquiry process, the initial questions are generally found, during the process, to consist of several subordinate questions, which, in turn, become the focus of students' inquiry (Hakkarainen & Sintonen, 2002). Ideally, the original questions are answered in this progressive process, but it might also turn out that the initial questions are such that science, at present, is not able to provide one single answer, but rather offers multiple competing theories.

Copyright © 2004, Idea Group Inc. Copying or distributing in print or electronic forms without written permission of Idea Group Inc. is prohibited.

Figure 1: Elements of Progressive Inquiry

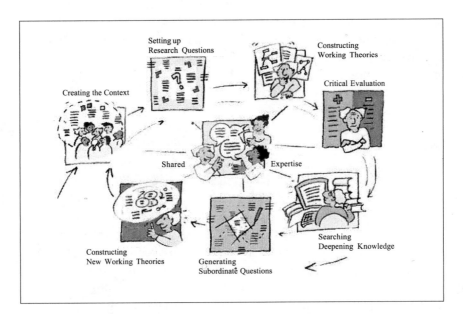

As depicted in Figure 1, the following elements have been placed in a cyclic, but not step-wise process, to describe the progressive inquiry process (Hakkarainen, 1998; Hakkarainen et al., 1999; Muukkonen et al., 1999):

a. *Creating the Context.* In the beginning of the process, the teacher or tutor creates, together with students, a context in order to anchor the problems being investigated to central conceptual principles of the domain or complex real-world problems. The learning community is established by joint planning and setting up common goals. It is important to create a social culture that supports collaborative sharing of knowledge and ideas that are in the process of being formulated and improved.

b. *Setting Up Research Questions.* An essential aspect of progressive inquiry is generating students' own problems and questions that direct the inquiry. Explanation-seeking questions (Why? How? What?) are especially valuable. The learning community should be encouraged to focus on questions that are knowledge-driven and based on results of students' own cognitive efforts and the need to understand (Bereiter, 2002; Scardamalia & Bereiter, 1994). It is crucial to see studying as a problem-solving process that includes addressing problems in understanding the theoretical constructs, methods and practices of scientific culture.

c. *Constructing Working Theories.* A critical condition for developing conceptual understanding is generation of students' own hypotheses, theories or interpretations of the phenomena being investigated. At the

Copyright © 2004, Idea Group Inc. Copying or distributing in print or electronic forms without written permission of Idea Group Inc. is prohibited.

beginning of the inquiry process, it is important that phenomena be explained with existing background knowledge, before using information sources. This serves a number of goals: first, to make visible the prior (intuitive) conceptions of the issues at hand; secondly, trying to explain to other students is an effective way of testing the coherence of a student's own understanding and it makes the gaps and contradictions in his or her own knowledge more apparent (e.g., Hatano & Inakagi, 1992; Perkins, Crismond, Simmons, & Under, 1995; Schank, 1986). Wells (1999) has highlighted the role of others in one's learning: "by contributing to the joint meaning making with and for others, one also makes meaning for oneself, and in the process, extends one's own understanding" (p. 108). Thirdly, it serves to create a culture in which knowledge is treated as essentially involving objects and artifacts that can be improved (Bereiter, 2002). Consequently, thoughts and ideas presented are not final and unchangeable, but rather utterances in an ongoing discourse (Wells, 1999).

d.   *Critical Evaluation.* Critical evaluation addresses the need to assess strengths and weaknesses of theories and explanations that are produced, in order to direct and regulate the community's joint cognitive efforts. It holds a constructive evaluation of the inquiry process itself, placing the process as the center of evaluation and not only the end result. Again, rather than focusing on individual students' productions, it is more fruitful to evaluate the community's productions and efforts, and give the student participants a main role in this evaluation process. Critical evaluation is a way of helping the community to rise above its earlier achievements, by creating a higher-level synthesis of the results of inquiry processes.

e.   *Searching Deepening Knowledge.* Looking for and working with explanatory scientific knowledge is necessary for deepening one's understanding (Chi, Bassok, Lewis, Reiman, & Glaser, 1989). A comparison between intuitive working theories produced and well-established scientific theories tends to make explicit the weaknesses and limitations of the community's conceptions (Scardamalia & Bereiter, 1994). The teacher of a course must decide how much of the materials should be offered to the students and how much they should actually have to search out for themselves. Questions stemming from true wonderment on the part of the students can easily extend the scope of materials beyond what a teacher can foresee or provide suggestions for. On the other hand, searching for relevant materials provides an excellent opportunity for self-directed inquiry and hands-on practice in struggling to grasp the differences between various concepts and theories.

f.   *Generating Subordinate Questions.* The process of inquiry advances through learners transforming the initial big and unspecified questions into subordinate and frequently, more specific questions, based on their evalu-

Copyright © 2004, Idea Group Inc. Copying or distributing in print or electronic forms without written permission of Idea Group Inc. is prohibited.

ation of new knowledge. Formulation of subordinate questions helps to refocus the inquiry (Hakkarainen, 1998; Hintikka, 1985). Directing students towards returning to previously stated problems, making more subordinate questions and answering them are ways to procedurally scaffold the inquiry.

g.   *Developing New Working Theories.* New questions and scientific knowledge that the participants attain give rise to new theories and explanations. The process includes publication of the summaries and conclusions of the community's inquiry. If all productions shared with the database in a collaborative environment have been meaningfully organized, all participants should have easy access to prior productions and theories, making the development of conceptions and artifacts a visible process.

h.   *Distributed Expertise.* A progressive inquiry model intends to engage the community in a shared process of knowledge advancement and to convey simultaneously the cognitive goals for collaboration. Diversity in expertise among participants, and interaction with expert cultures, promotes knowledge advancement (Brown, Ash, Rutherford, Nakagawa, Gordon, & Campione, 1993; Dunbar 1995). Acting as a member in the community includes sharing cognitive responsibility for the success of inquiry. This responsibility can be explained in terms not only of delivering tasks or productions on time, but also of learners taking responsibility for discovering what needs to be known, goal setting, planning and monitoring the inquiry process (Scardamalia, 2002). Salomon and Perkins (1998) argue for the importance of developing students' (and experts') social metacognition — students learning to understand the cognitive value of social collaboration and gaining the capacity to utilize socially distributed cognitive resources.

Lehtinen and colleagues (Lehtinen, Hakkarainen, Lipponen, Rahikainen, & Muukkonen, 1999) have concluded, in a review article on computer-supported collaborative learning (CSCL), that the use of collaborative technologies is associated with improved performance in a considerable number of studies. In terms of cognitive development, these improvements are linked to the existence of a collaborative community that provides multiple zones of proximal development (Brown & Campione, 1994; Vygotsky, 1978). Therefore, by drawing upon a larger collective memory and the multiple ways in which knowledge can be structured among individuals working together, groups could attain more success than individuals working alone (Bruer, 1993; Palincsar, 1998). Further, when other students, tutors, teachers or experts participate in an inquiry process, they demonstrate forms of self-reflection, explications of understanding, engagement in problemsetting and re-definition. Such processes can serve as a model for less experienced students in their knowledge-building efforts.

Copyright © 2004, Idea Group Inc. Copying or distributing in print or electronic forms without written permission of Idea Group Inc. is prohibited.

The best practices in the CSCL paradigm have several features in common: Consideration, in an interrelated manner, of the development of technological applications, timely pedagogical models and new understandings of human thinking and social learning. These practices seek to bring an individual into a collaborative community that shares goals, tools and practices for taking part in an inquiry process.

Collaborative technologies can potentially offer tools for collaborative knowledge creation, and the development of epistemic agency. One key aspect is the functionality that can be embedded in the technology that supports an inquiry process. It includes built-in structures or software tools in the technology environments for structuring and directing students' work. The main benefit in functionality and tools should be that it provides support that enables students to deal with more challenging tasks, than they could otherwise handle without the technology or working on their own (Lakkala, Muukkonen, & Hakkarainen, 2003; Reiser, 2002).

PROGRESSIVE INQUIRY EMBEDDED IN THE FUTURE LEARNING ENVIRONMENT

The Future Learning Environment (FLE) is an asynchronous groupware system developed by the Media Laboratory, University of Art and Design Helsinki, in collaboration with the Centre for Research on Networked Learning and Knowledge Building at the Department of Psychology, University of Helsinki. It is designed to support collaborative knowledge building and progressive inquiry in educational settings (Leinonen, Raami, Mielonen, Seitamaa-Hakkarainen, Muukkonen, & Hakkarainen, 1999). FLE is an open source and free software, and the development of the system continues (see http://fle3.uiah.fi).

The pedagogical model of progressive inquiry is embedded in the FLE design (Muukkonen et al., 1999). The environment provides each student with a Virtual WebTop for storing and sharing documents. The working space has direct links to the WebTops of the other members of the study group. The WebTops were used to a small extent during the investigated course for sharing study materials, articles and editable documents. The Knowledge Building module (KB module) provides a shared space for working together to solve problems and develop participants' ideas and thoughts (see Figure 2, a snapshot from FLE version 3). In the KB module, the sent messages are organized in threads under the *starting problems* of the course, which are constructed together with the participants. The notes are visible to all members in the same study group. The KB module of the environment includes built-in scaffolds for progressive inquiry, similar to those in the CSILE (Scardamalia & Bereiter, 1994). In the KB module, progressive inquiry is promoted by asking a user, who

Copyright © 2004, Idea Group Inc. Copying or distributing in print or electronic forms without written permission of Idea Group Inc. is prohibited.

Figure 2: My Explanation Note in the Knowledge Building Module of FLE

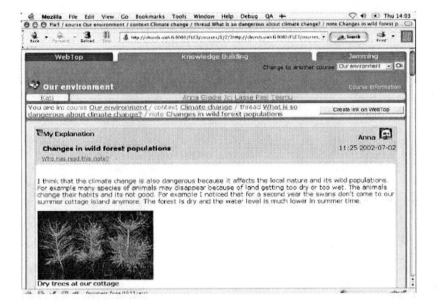

is preparing a message, to categorize the note by choosing a category of inquiry-scaffold corresponding to the progressive inquiry model. The default categories are Problem, My explanation, Scientific explanation, Evaluation of the process and Summary. These scaffolds are intended to help the students to move beyond simple question-answer discussion and elicit practices of progressive inquiry. Teachers may also develop their own inquiry scaffolds to suit their pedagogical goals.

A third major module is the Jam Session module, which enables the graphic presentation of knowledge artifacts, such as pictures, video or sketches. It can be used to import the drafts, design, pictures or other productions into the collaborative environment. These artifacts can then be picked up and further elaborated on by the co-collaborators. In FLE version 2 this module was not available. Otherwise, the major functionality of the environment has remained the same throughout versions 1 and 2, and the current version 3.

CASES OF PROGRESSIVE INQUIRY PROCESSES IN HIGHER EDUCATION

Two cases of implementing the progressive inquiry process in higher education are now presented. The first case is an example from a cognitive psychology course, and the second case is a collaborative design process. Both courses used earlier versions of FLE (versions 2 and 1, respectively).

Copyright © 2004, Idea Group Inc. Copying or distributing in print or electronic forms without written permission of Idea Group Inc. is prohibited.

Progressive Inquiry in Cognitive Psychology Course

A study was conducted by Muukkonen, Lakkala and Hakkarainen (2001) to test the implementation of the progressive inquiry model in a cognitive psychology course with the use of the FLE-environment. In this course, the students attended weekly lectures, and all 80 participants were offered the use of the FLE environment to scaffold their progressive inquiry process. About a fourth of the students decided to use the environment. They formed three groups, and each group had a tutor to facilitate their collaboration. All the students were guided during the first two lectures to formulate research problems. Initially, they individually produced these formulations. They continued by discussing their research problems with a peer and, finally, within a small group, selecting the most interesting questions to pursue. These questions were then presented to all the participants in the class. After this initial problem setting, the technology-mediated groups were instructed to continue their inquiry processes between the weekly lectures in the FLE environment. The tutor-facilitators took part in the FLE environment, whereas the teacher conducted the weekly lectures without participating in the database discourse.

The students not using the FLE environment were expected to keep learning logs on the contents covered in the lectures and write essays at the end of the course. They were also asked to read at least two learning logs written by other students and to provide written feedback to them. The students in the technology-mediated groups were expected to participate actively by posting their own writings, as well as reading and commenting on productions of other members of their group. They were also expected to write a summary of their own contributions and learning process at the end of the course. Overall, for both settings, emphasis in the evaluation was given to demonstrating an understanding of the theoretical concepts of the course as well as explaining their knowledge of recent research on learning.

A qualitative analysis of the written productions was performed to examine whether the two settings produced different progressive inquiry processes. The writings were segmented and each segment coded to represent either a problem, a working theory, a scientific explanation, a metacomment, a quote of another participant's idea or a reference to lecture (as described in detail in Muukkonen et al., 2001).

A comparative analysis of the materials provided evidence that the technology-mediated groups were more engaged in problem setting and redefining practices. Further, they reflected on the process they had undertaken, with respect to the collaboration and their individual efforts. In the groups who had not used collaboration tools, the social and communal aspects of inquiry and knowledge building did not appear at all in their learning logs, although they were engaged in collaboration during the lectures. The type of the comments they provided to two of the learning logs written by other members of their group were

Copyright © 2004, Idea Group Inc. Copying or distributing in print or electronic forms without written permission of Idea Group Inc. is prohibited.

very general, and they concentrated mainly on evaluating the level of writing, not on advancement of ideas. However, many of their learning logs were conceptually well developed and integrated. It appeared to us that while the students were commenting on the learning logs, they evaluated the whole process of learning rather than being engaged in a dialogue with the ideas presented in the learning logs. Discourse interaction within the FLE environment was different in terms of the participants sometimes engaging in extensive dialogues with ideas presented by fellow students. This phenomenon was not systematically investigated, but there were clear indications that these two types of dialogues differed in several characteristics. Figure 3 presents the percent of coded segments that was allocated to each of the coding categories.

The results of this study and a study by Muukkonen et al. (1999) reported that students used only a limited number of external sources in trying to explain and deepen their understanding of the studied phenomena, although the progressive inquiry model emphasized the search of deepening knowledge. Overcoming this limitation appears to be a further challenge in developing implementation of the progressive inquiry model.

Progressive Inquiry in Design Course

Two studies carried out by Seitamaa-Hakkarainen and her colleagues (Seitamaa-Hakkarainen, Lahti, Muukkonen, & Hakkarainen, 2000; Seitamaa-Hakkarainen, Raunio, Raami, Muukkonen, & Hakkarainen, 2001) analyzed a

Figure 3: Distribution within Coding Categories for the FLE Groups' and the Comparison Groups' Learning Logs

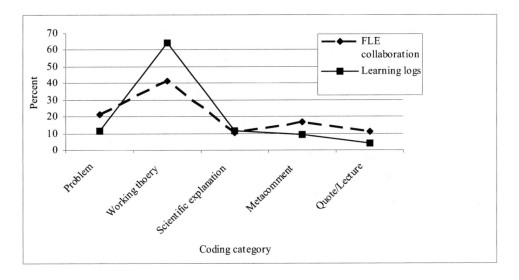

Copyright © 2004, Idea Group Inc. Copying or distributing in print or electronic forms without written permission of Idea Group Inc. is prohibited.

Figure 4: Jam Session and Design Products

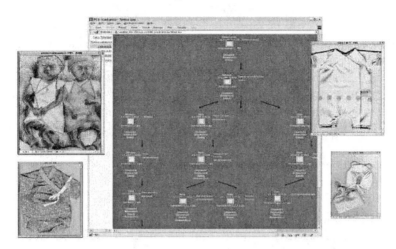

collaborative design process as it occurred in a complex and authentic design task of designing clothing for premature babies. The framework of the studies was based on evidence from cognitive research on expertise, which indicated that novices in design tend to generate solutions without engaging in extensive problem structuring; experts, by contrast, focus on structuring and restructuring the problem space before proposing solutions (Glaser & Chi, 1988). The studies described in this case were designed to examine whether an expert-like engagement in the design process would be supported in the FLE environment. In the KB module, a set of Design-thinking-tool labels (i.e., Design Problem, Working Idea, Comment, Deepening Knowledge, Summary and Metacomment) was composed to encourage the users to engage in expert-like designing. Further, the Jam Session module was employed to enable graphic presentation of the knowledge artifacts. It was used to import students' drafts and prototypes into the collaborative environment and to develop multiple versions of the designs.

During the collaborative design course, the students were first guided to find out information about the constraints of their design task — such as the size of the babies, special needs for the usability of the clothing and about the materials — and post it to the KB module of the environment. Then they were asked to produce their own sketches and work in small groups to share design ideas and develop their designs in the Jam Session module (Figure 4). Following this development, each group produced a prototype, which was tested by actual end users in hospital. Feedback and suggestions were then used to develop advanced design ideas.

In these studies of designing with the support of a networked collaborative environment, Seitamaa-Hakkarainen and her colleagues found that a key aspect

Copyright © 2004, Idea Group Inc. Copying or distributing in print or electronic forms without written permission of Idea Group Inc. is prohibited.

of these environments is to provide tools for progressive discourse interaction between the designers and users of the future products. Further, the environments can offer shared spaces and tools to elaborate on conceptual and theoretical knowledge related to the design problem. The collaborative technology (FLE1 in their studies) made design thinking more explicit and accessible to fellow designers and enabled participants to share their ideas and construct a joint understanding of design problems and solutions. Collaborative technology enabled the users to rely on socially distributed intellectual resources embedded in the learning community while conducting various projects (Seitamaa-Hakkarainen et al., 2000).

Tutors' Role and Activity in the Progressive Inquiry Process

A special question in implementing progressive inquiry and knowledge-building practices in higher education is the teachers' or tutors' role in supporting and guiding students' collaborative inquiry. In progressive inquiry, the traditional role of a teacher as an expert who delivers the essential information by lecturing is radically changed: The important role of the teacher and the facilitators of collaboration is to create the context for collaboration and provide anchors between the theoretical representations, world knowledge and the real-life experiences that students report. It is also necessary for the teacher to structure and scaffold the process, keep it active and in focus during the progression of the course and to help students to gradually take upon themselves the responsibility of these higher-level cognitive processes (Scardamalia, 2002).

The term "scaffolding" has been used to describe the experts' role in student-centered learning activity: giving support which enables a learner to carry out a task that would not be possible without that support and which gradually allows the student to succeed without the support in the future (Guzdial, 1994; Wood, Bruner, & Ross, 1976). In addition to providing the students with the conceptual framework of progressive inquiry and collaborative technology that supports the pedagogical model, it is necessary to construct the organizational and process-level scaffolding and tutoring accordingly (Lakkala et al., 2003; Mercer & Fischer, 1993; Wells, 2000). *Organizational level* refers to the initial "framing," or organizing, of the learning community's activities, or structuring the task according to the pedagogical approach. In the above-described courses, this framing was actualized by defining the goals, tasks and activities of the whole course, following the elements and principles of progressive inquiry. *Process level*, on the other hand, refers to coaching, situation-specific guidance, and expert participation during the inquiry process. Teachers, with whom we usually collaborate in developing the practices of progressive inquiry, frequently tell us that they feel rather insecure when deciding how to contribute to the students' collaborative inquiry process, especially in the

Copyright © 2004, Idea Group Inc. Copying or distributing in print or electronic forms without written permission of Idea Group Inc. is prohibited.

technology-mediated discourse. They see many possible ways of participation: as active question producers, initiators and directors of the process; passive followers and evaluators, who participate only when necessary; equal participants and co-inquirers; procedural guides; content experts or commentators.

The teachers' or tutors' role in the newer approaches has been described by other investigators as that of an *expert participant* in the process: co-inquirer (Wells, 2000) or an *expert model*, as in the concept of cognitive apprenticeship (Collins, Brown, & Newman, 1989). On the other hand, the teacher or tutor has the role of facilitator or guide in supporting the students' advancement. This role is strongly related to the conceptions of scaffolding. In the knowledge-building framework (e.g., Scardamalia, 2002), it has been emphasized that the teacher or tutor should explicitly aim at coaching the students gradually to take upon themselves responsibility for higher-level aspects of inquiry and fostering the development of students' metacognitive competencies.

In the above-described course of cognitive psychology, each of the three technology-mediated student groups (four to seven students) had a tutor (postgraduate student) who participated to the discourse in FLE. In another study (Lakkala, Muukkonen, Ilomäki, Lallimo, Niemivirta, & Hakkarainen, 2001; Lakkala et al., 2003), we analyzed in detail the tutors' participation to the inquiry and ways of scaffolding technology-mediated discourse. First, we evaluated the tutors' activity as participants in the inquiry by analyzing their postings, using the same progressive inquiry categories as were applied to the students' written productions. In the analysis we observed that, more frequently than the students, the three tutors' used the inquiry-scaffold Metacomment. Their productions also included a relatively greater number of metacomments (i.e., ideas that included assessment of one's own learning process or understanding, advancement of the discourse or group process, functionality of FLE or planning the future work) and a smaller number of explanations within their notes. We concluded, on the evidence, that the tutors acted more like metalevel process organizers and evaluators than equal participants in the process.

Second, a re-analysis of the tutors' contributions using a scaffolding-oriented coding scheme revealed that 37% of the tutors' scaffolding was *asking explanation-seeking questions*, including both the tutors' own wonderment and requests for the students to clarify their explanations, which indicates, apparently, that the tutors tried to model and promote the practices of question-driven inquiry. Of the tutors' productions, 23% was content-related *experts' explanations*, either explicating the tutor's own understanding or referring to scientific theories and studies. Similarly, about 25% of the contents in the tutors' notes was *reviewing and evaluating* the discourse, such as referring to previous discourse, making summaries or giving positive feedback. Only 16% of the ideas were *recommendations of study practices*, mostly rather general suggestions for further actions. Most of the recommendations for study practices and the review and evaluation styles showed a quite traditional coaching style,

Copyright © 2004, Idea Group Inc. Copying or distributing in print or electronic forms without written permission of Idea Group Inc. is prohibited.

in which the tutor takes the cognitive responsibility. The recommendations did not, on the present evidence, draw the students' attention to the higher-level metacognitive tasks of planning, monitoring and evaluating the inquiry process themselves.

There was an interesting difference between the one less experienced tutor and two more experienced tutors (all female). The less experienced tutor produced longer notes and relatively more starting notes, and the proportion of problem statements in her notes was greater than in the notes of the other tutors. In addition, her notes got plentiful replies from the students in her group. Her scaffolding concentrated more on asking content-related questions and less on giving recommendations to students for advancing their inquiry themselves. We may conclude that the less experienced tutor acted more as an initiator of new wonderment in the inquiry process, rather than a supporter of the students' process. She kept for herself a portion of the cognitive responsibility by generating a lot of questions and discourse openings herself; hence, she partly directed the content of the inquiry. The two other more experienced tutors, who were also more acquainted with the theories behind the progressive inquiry model than the third tutor, could be interpreted as trying to move from their own active participation to fostering students' inquiry; they attempted to assign the cognitive responsibility of the inquiry to the students. However, their scaffolding partly concentrated on very general study recommendations, and they also produced a rather great number of experts' explanations to the discourse. Hence, it could be argued that the more experienced two tutors were in the intermediate position between acting like a traditional tutor, who still controls the process, and an inquiry-oriented tutor who tries to promote advancement of students' own metacognitive skills and knowledge building practices.

CHALLENGES OF CHANGING EDUCATIONAL SETTINGS AND STUDENTS' STUDY PRACTICES

Lemke (2001) has analyzed how human activity self-organizes across multiple timescales. He argued that while analyzing human activity, investigators should always look at one level down from the level in which we are mostly interested, in order to understand the constituent sub-processes that give rise to it, as well as one level up in order to understand how characteristics of the environment constrain the activity in question. Researchers interested in learning processes taking place within a university course usually do not have problems of "zooming" in to analyze micro-processes of individual learning. The real challenge is to zoom out to the larger spatial and temporal structures of the learning environment and examine co-evolution of individuals and their learning

Copyright © 2004, Idea Group Inc. Copying or distributing in print or electronic forms without written permission of Idea Group Inc. is prohibited.

communities across extended periods of time. Our discussion of Jaana and Maria's personal project indicated that even relatively short learning processes may have long-standing effects on socio-cognitive development; the methods and focuses of many learning researchers — including our own approach — tend to leave these kinds of processes unexamined.

Correspondingly, Fjuk and Ludvigsen (2001) argued that when analyzing the outcomes of inquiry processes (as in Muukkonen et al., 1999), investigators should also consider whether the curriculum design and the settings of the courses are such that learners will find a truly deepening search for understanding to be cognitively economical. In the Finnish higher education system, students take part in about eight courses with equally numerous topics within a semester, even at the graduate level. This obviously limits the time available per course, and in-depth inquiry into one field calls for a particular commitment, perhaps at the expense of other courses. Therefore, as Fjuk and Ludvigsen (2001) also pointed out, in order to change the educational settings, it is necessary to develop awareness of the contradictions and possible conflicts between pedagogical, institutional and individual goals and practices. Any sustainable developments thus call for changes in curriculum design; they would not be easy to apply at a single course level.

Lemke (2001) proposes that investigations across extended timescales are beneficial because they may help one to understand long-standing changes in meaning making or attitudinal dispositions. It appears to us that the development of epistemic agency is a transformation that should take place throughout university education. Whether this really is the case depends on the structures of educational activities in which students are asked to take part across their academic studies. The three metaphors of learning — acquisition, participation and knowledge creation — examined above appear to provide valuable heuristic resources for designing education intended to facilitate the development of genuine epistemic agency. One way of trying to elicit the development of skills and competencies of knowledge creation is to facilitate explorative processes from the beginning of education; for teachers to instruct students not only how to find answers to pre-existing questions, but also how to set up new questions and to search for knowledge that may be new both for them and their teachers (Hakkarainen, 1998; Hakkarainen & Sintonen, 2002). This is a special challenge for the present educational system that has traditionally been designed to transmit pre-existing and well-specified knowledge to new generations of students.

Systematic knowledge advancement is an important part of knowledge work, and present-day students are expected to engage in deliberate knowledge advancement when they enter the workforce. In order to facilitate the development of corresponding skills, it is important that students learn to work with knowledge in the same transformative way as do the experts (Hakkarainen, Palonen, Paavola, & Lehtinen, 2002). Taking part in a collaborative, progressive

Copyright © 2004, Idea Group Inc. Copying or distributing in print or electronic forms without written permission of Idea Group Inc. is prohibited.

inquiry process has been shown to encourage practices of reflection on one's own and shared advancements in understanding, organizing and evaluating collaborative knowledge building; it promotes an approach to learning tasks as problem-solving processes (Muukkonen et al., 2001; Seitamaa-Hakkarainen et al., 2001).

One important research finding regarding higher-level expertise has been that an individual's ability to develop his or her content-specific knowledge and apply it in different situations often co-evolves with the development of general thinking skills and metacognitive strategies (Davidson & Sternberg, 1998). The present investigators argue that even if learners' expertise is bound to a specific field of inquiry, there are many skills, competencies and aspects of expertise that are, at least to a certain extent, generalizable and provide intellectual resources for managing new problem-solving situations. Higher-level skills that emerge through epistemic agency and sustained efforts of advancing knowledge may be called *metaskills* (Hakkarainen et al., 2002). We argue that such skills include epistemic skills related to mastery of principal categories and processes of inquiry. Further, these skills involve academic literacy (Geisler, 1994), i.e., an ability to critically examine implicit inferences or rhetorical aspect of texts. One particularly important category of these generalizable skills is metacognitive skills, which are related to planning, monitoring, and regulating comprehension-related activities.

The development of expertise has a cumulative characteristic so that human cognition becomes continuously transformed when a person gets sufficient support and cultural resources for starting to pursue an expert career. From a sustained process of progressive problem solving emerges expertise in learning, doing inquiry, working with knowledge and collaborating that appears to be generalizable, at least to some extent. These higher-level skills allow one to solve increasingly complex problems, acquire correspondingly even more complex skills and give impetus to sustained cognitive growth (Bereiter, 2002). Such cognitive transformations are, however, very difficult to study because the development of these competencies takes many years, and it is usually difficult to separate these skills from changes in academic and professional expertise (Hakkarainen et al., 2002). A significant challenge nevertheless remains in developing curricula that support students in acquiring deep understanding in their area, and anchoring the scientific problems they are studying to authentic problems of the various professional fields.

CONCLUSION

This chapter has taken the three metaphors of learning — acquisition, participation and knowledge-creation — as fundamentally different dimensions of learning. We have argued that together they could constitute a broad base for

Copyright © 2004, Idea Group Inc. Copying or distributing in print or electronic forms without written permission of Idea Group Inc. is prohibited.

envisioning the future skills and competencies to be developed by higher education. A principal goal of university education, we propose, should be to encourage and facilitate emergence of genuine epistemic agency. The emergence of epistemic agency appears to be dependent on appropriate learning experiences. The problem pursued in the present chapter has been whether innovative pedagogical approaches and advanced learning technologies may be used to facilitate the development of epistemic agency. It would appear that the pedagogical model of progressive inquiry could be used as a basis for the development of such agency, metacognitive skills and corresponding practices within the computer-mediated collaboration. Simply introducing a collaborative environment into courses is unlikely to achieve any lasting changes. Further, introducing a pedagogical model that is congruent with the scaffolds and tools of a collaborative environment is a good start, but may nevertheless be opposed by students, if inquiry activities planned for the course do not correspond to students' conceptions of learning processes or to their abilities and willingness to take part in such processes. Such situation may develop if the pedagogical model is introduced in a new environment where studying is traditionally teacher directed or a culture of competition prevails over a culture of collaboration. Therefore, productive changes, we have argued, would require an alignment of epistemic, pedagogical, institutional and technological goals and actions.

ACKNOWLEDGMENT

The work of the first author has been supported by a grant from The Finnish Cultural Foundation.

REFERENCES

Bereiter, C. (2002). *Education and Mind in the Knowledge Age.* Hillsdale, NJ: Erlbaum.

Bereiter, C. & Scardamalia, M. (1993). *Surpassing Ourselves: An Inquiry into the Nature and Implications of Expertise.* Chicago, IL: Open Court.

Bielaczyc, K. (2001). Designing social infrastructure: The challenge of building computer-supported learning communities. In P. Dillenbourg, A. Eurelings, & K. Hakkarainen (Eds.), *European Perspectives on Computer-Supported Collaborative Learning.* Proceedings of the First European Conference on Computer-Supported Collaborative Learning (pp. 106-114). Maastricht, The Netherlands: Maastricht McLuhan Institute.

Brown, A. L., & Campione, J. C. (1994). Guided discovery in a community of learners. In K. McGilly (Ed.), *Classroom Lessons: Integrating Cognitive Theory & Classroom Practice* (pp. 229-287). Cambridge, MA: MIT Press.

Copyright © 2004, Idea Group Inc. Copying or distributing in print or electronic forms without written permission of Idea Group Inc. is prohibited.

Brown, A. L., Ash, D., Rutherford, M., Nakagawa, K., Gordon, A., & Campione, J. (1993). Distributed expertise in the classroom. In G. Salomon (Ed.), *Distributed Cognitions: Psychological and Educational Considerations* (pp. 188-228). Cambridge, UK: Cambridge University Press.

Brown, J. S, Collins, A., & Duguide, P. (1989). Situated cognition and the culture of learning. *Educational Researcher, 18,* 32-42.

Bruer, J. T. (1993). *Schools for Thought. A Science of Learning in the Classroom.* Cambridge, MA: MIT Press.

Chi, M. T. H., Bassok, M., Lewis, M. W., Reiman, P., & Glaser, R. (1989). Self-explanations: How students study and use examples in learning to solve problems. *Cognitive Science, 13,* 145-182.

Collins, A., Brown, J. S., & Newman, S. E. (1989). Cognitive apprenticeship: teaching the crafts of reading, writing, and mathematics. In L. B. Resnick (Ed.), *Knowing, Learning, and Instruction. Essays in Honor of Robert Glaser* (pp. 453-494). Hillsdale, NJ: Erlbaum.

Davidson, J. E. & Sternberg, R. J. (1998). Smart problem solving: How metacognition helps. In D. J. Hackeer, J. Dunlosky, & A. C. Graesser (Eds.), *Metacognition in Educational Theory and Practice* (pp. 47-68). Mahwah, NJ: Erlbaum.

Dunbar, K. (1995). How scientist really reason: Scientific reasoning in real world laboratories. In R. J. Sternberg & J. Davidson (Eds.), *Mechanisms of Insight* (pp. 365-395). Cambridge, MA: MIT Press.

Edelson, D. C., Gordin, D. N., & Pea, R. D. (1999). Addressing the challenges of inquiry-based learning through technology and curriculum design. *Journal of the Learning Sciences, 8,* 391-450.

Fjuk, A. & Ludvigsen, S. (2001). The complexity of distributed collaborative learning: Unit of analysis. In P. Dillenbourg, A. Eurelings, & K. Hakkarainen (Eds.), *European Perspectives on Computer-Supported Collaborative Learning.* Proceedings of the First European Conference on CSCL (pp. 237-244). Maastricht, The Netherlands: Maastricht McLuhan Institute.

Geisler, C. (1994). *Academic Literacy and the Nature of Expertise.* Hillsdale, NJ: Erlbaum.

Glaser, R. & Chi, H. T. M. (1988). Overview. In H. T. M. Chi & M. Farr (Eds.), *The Nature of Expertise* (pp. xv-xxviii). Hillsdale, NJ: Erlbaum.

Guzdial, M. (1994). Software-realized scaffolding to facilitate programming for science learning. *Interactive Learning Environments, 4*(1), 1-44.

Hakkarainen, K. (1998). *Epistemology of inquiry and computer-supported collaborative learning.* Unpublished doctoral dissertation, University of Toronto, Ontario, Canada.

Hakkarainen, K. & Sintonen, M. (2002). Interrogative model of inquiry and computer-supported collaborative learning. *Science & Education, 11,* 25-43.

Copyright © 2004, Idea Group Inc. Copying or distributing in print or electronic forms without written permission of Idea Group Inc. is prohibited.

Hakkarainen, K., Lonka, K., & Lipponen, L. (1999). Tutkiva oppiminen: älykkään toiminnat rajat ja niiden ylittäminen [Progressive inquiry: How to overcome limitations of human intelligent activity]. Helsinki, Finland: WSOY.

Hakkarainen, K., Palonen, T., Paavola, S., & Lehtinen, E. (2002). *Networked expertise: Professional and educational perspectives.* Unpublished manuscript.

Hatano, G. & Inagaki, K. (1992). Desituating cognition through the construction of conceptual knowledge. In P. Light & G. Butterworth (Eds.), *Context and Cognition: Ways of Knowing and Learning* (pp. 115-133). New York: Harvester.

Hintikka, J. (1985). True and false logic of scientific discovery. In J. Hintikka & F. Vandamme (Eds.), *Logic of Discovery and Logic of Discourse* (pp. 3-14). New York: Plenum.

Holland, D., Lachicotte, W., Skinner, D., & Cain, C. (1998). *Identity and Agency in Cultural Worlds.* Cambridge, MA: Harvard University Press.

Krajcik, J., Blumenfeld, P .C., Marx, R. W., Bass, K. M., Fredricks, J., & Soloway, E. (1998). Inquiry in project-based science classrooms: Initial attempts by middle school students. *The Journal of the Learning Sciences, 7,* 313-350.

Lakkala, M., Muukkonen, H., & Hakkarainen, K. (2003). Patterns of scaffolding in technology-mediated collaborative inquiry. Manuscript submitted for publication.

Lakkala, M., Muukkonen, H., Ilomäki, L., Lallimo, J., Niemivirta, M., & Hakkarainen, K. (2001). Approaches for analysing tutor's role in a networked inquiry discourse. In P. Dillenbourg, A. Eurelings, & K. Hakkarainen (Eds.), *European Perspectives on Computer-Supported Collaborative Learning.* Proceedings of the First European Conference on CSCL (pp. 389-396). Maastricht, The Netherlands: Maastricht McLuhan Institute. Retrieved from the web site: http://www.mmi.unimaas.nl/euro-cscl/Papers/99.doc.

Lave, J. (1988). *Cognition in Practice.* Cambridge, MA: Cambridge University Press.

Lave, J. & Wenger, E. (1991). *Situated Learning: Legitimate Peripheral Participation.* Cambridge, UK: Cambridge University Press.

Lehtinen, E., Hakkarainen, K., Lipponen, L., Rahikainen, M., & Muukkonen, H. (1999). *Computer supported collaborative learning: A review of CL-Net project* (The J.H.G.I. Giesbers Reports on Education No. 10). Nijmegen, The Netherlands: University of Nijmegen.

Leinonen, T., Raami, A., Mielonen, S., Seitamaa-Hakkarainen, P., Muukkonen, H., & Hakkarainen, K. (1999). FLE – tools prototype: A WWW-based learning environment for collaborative knowledge building. In E. Rämö (Ed.), *Proceedings of ENABLE99 (Enabling Networked-Based Learn-*

Copyright © 2004, Idea Group Inc. Copying or distributing in print or electronic forms without written permission of Idea Group Inc. is prohibited.

ing). Espoo, Finland: Espoo-Vantaa Institute of Technology. Retrieved on July 29, 2002 from http://www.enable.evitech.fi/enable99/papers/leinonen/leinonen.html.

Lemke, J. (2001). The long and the short of it: comments on multiple timescale studies of human activity. *The Journal of the Learning Sciences, 10,* 17-26.

Lipponen, L. (2002). Exploring foundations for computer-supported collaborative learning. In G. Stahl (Ed.), *Computer-Support for Collaborative Learning: Foundations for a CSCL Community.* Proceedings of the Computer-Supported Collaborative Learning 2002 Conference (pp. 72-81). Hillsdale, NJ: Erlbaum.

Mercer, N. & Fisher, E. (1993). How do teachers help children to learn? An analysis of teachers' interventions in computer-based activities. *Learning and Instruction, 2,* 339-355.

Muukkonen, H., Hakkarainen, K., & Lakkala, M. (1999). Collaborative technology for facilitating progressive inquiry: Future learning environment tools. In C. Hoadley & J. Roschelle (Eds.), *Proceedings of the Computer Support for Collaborative Learning (CSCL) 1999 Conference* (pp. 406-415). Mahwah, NJ: Erlbaum. Retrieved from the web site: http://kn.cilt.org/cscl99/A51/A51.HTM.

Muukkonen, H., Lakkala, M., & Hakkarainen, K. (2001). Characteristics of university students' inquiry in individual and computer-supported collaborative study process. In P. Dillenbourg, A. Eurelings, & K. Hakkarainen (Eds.), *European Perspectives on Computer-Supported Collaborative Learning.* Proceedings of the First European Conference on CSCL (pp. 462-469). Maastricht, The Netherlands: Maastricht McLuhan Institute. Retrieved from the web site: http://www.mmi.unimaas.nl/euro-cscl/Papers/117.doc.

Otero, J. & Graesser, A. C. (2001). PREG: Elements of a model of question asking. *Cognition and Instruction, 19,* 143-175.

Paavola, S., Lipponen, L., & Hakkarainen, K. (2002). Epistemological foundations for CSCL: A comparison of three models of innovative knowledge communities. In G. Stahl (Ed.), *Computer Support for Collaborative Learning: Foundations for a CSCL Community.* Proceedings of the Computer-supported Collaborative Learning 2002 Conference (pp. 24-32). Hillsdale, NJ: Erlbaum. Retrieved from the web site: http://newmedia.colorado.edu/cscl/228.html.

Palincsar, A. S. (1998). Social constructivist perspectives on teaching and learning. *Annual Review of Psychology, 49,* 345-375.

Perkins, D. A., Crismond, D., Simmons, R., & Under, C. (1995). Inside understanding. In D. N. Perkins, J. L. Schwartz, M. M. West, & M. S. Wiske (Eds.), *Software Goes to School* (pp. 70-87). Oxford, UK: Oxford University Press.

Copyright © 2004, Idea Group Inc. Copying or distributing in print or electronic forms without written permission of Idea Group Inc. is prohibited.

Ratner, C. (2000) Agency and culture. *Journal of the Theory of Social Behavior, 30,* 413-434.

Reiser, B. J. (2002). Why scaffolding should sometimes make tasks more difficult for learners. In G. Stahl (Ed.), *Computer Support for Collaborative Learning: Foundations for a CSCL Community.* Proceedings of CSCL 2002 (pp. 443-452). Hillsdale, NJ: Erlbaum. Retrieved from the web site: http://newmedia.colorado.edu/cscl/281.html.

Salomon, G. & Perkins, D. N. (1998). Individual and social aspects of learning. Review of *Research of Education 23,* 1-24.

Scardamalia, M. (1999). Moving ideas to the center. In L. Harasim (Ed.), *Wisdom & Wizardry: Celebrating the Pioneers of Online Education* (pp. 14-15). Vancouver, British Columbia, Canada: Telelearning Inc.

Scardamalia, M. (2002). Collective cognitive responsibility for the advancement of knowledge. In B. Smith (Ed.), *Liberal Education in a Knowledge Society* (pp. 67-98). Chicago, IL: Open Court.

Scardamalia, M. & Bereiter, C. (1993). Technologies for knowledge-building discourse. *Communications of the ACM, 36,* 37-41.

Scardamalia, M. & Bereiter, C. (1994). Computer support for knowledge-building communities. *The Journal of the Learning Sciences, 3,* 265-283.

Scardamalia, M. & Bereiter, C. (1996). Adaptation and understanding: A case for new cultures of schooling. In S. Vosniadou, E. De Corte, R. Glaser, & H. Mandl (Eds.), *International Perspectives on the Psychological Foundations of Technology-Based Learning Environments* (pp. 149-163). Mahwah, NJ: Erlbaum.

Scardamalia, M. & Bereiter, C. (in press). Knowledge building. In *Encyclopedia of Education* (2nd ed.). New York: Macmillan.

Schank, R. (1986). *Explanation Patterns*. Hillsdale, NJ: Erlbaum.

Seitamaa-Hakkarainen, P., Lahti, H., Muukkonen, H., & Hakkarainen, K. (2000). Collaborative designing in a networked learning environment. In S. A. R. Scrivener, L. J. Ball, & A. Woodcock (Eds.), *Collaborative Design: The Proceedings of CoDesigning 2000* (pp. 411-420). London: Springer.

Seitamaa-Hakkarainen, P., Raunio, A. M., Raami, A., Muukkonen, H., & Hakkarainen, K. (2001). Computer-support for collaborative designing. *International Journal of Technology and Design Education, 11,* 181-202.

Sfard, A. (1998). On two metaphors for learning and the dangers of choosing just one. *Educational Researcher, 27,* 4-13.

Vygotsky, L. S. (1978). *Mind in Society: The Development of Higher Psychological Processes.* Cambridge, MA: Harvard University Press.

Wells, G. (1999). *Dialogic Inquiry: Towards a Sociocultural Practice and Theory of Education.* Cambridge, UK: Cambridge University Press.

Copyright © 2004, Idea Group Inc. Copying or distributing in print or electronic forms without written permission of Idea Group Inc. is prohibited.

Wells, G. (2000). Dialogic inquiry in education: Building on the legacy of Vygotsky. In C. D. Lee & P. Smagorinsky (Eds.), *Vygotskian Perspectives on Literacy Research: Constructing Meaning through Collaborative Inquiry* (pp. 51-85). Cambridge, MA: Cambridge University Press.

Wertsch, J., Tulviste, P., & Hagstrom, F. (1993). A sociocultural approach to agency. In E. Forman, N. Minick, & C. A. Stone (Eds.), *Context for Learning: Sociocultural Dynamics in Children's Development* (pp. 336-356). Oxford, UK: Oxford University Press.

White, Y. B. & Frederiksen, J. R. (1998). Inquiry, modeling, and metacognition: Making science accessible to all students. *Cognition and Instruction, 16,* 3-118.

Wood, D., Bruner, J. S., & Ross, G. (1976). The role of tutoring in problem solving. *Journal of Child Psychology and Psychiatry, 17,* 89-100.

Zuckerman, G. A., Chudinova, E. V., & Khavkin, E. E. (1998). Inquiry as a pivotal element of knowledge acquisition within the Vygotskian paradigm: Building a science curriculum for the elementary school. *Cognition and Instruction, 16,* 201-233.

Copyright © 2004, Idea Group Inc. Copying or distributing in print or electronic forms without written permission of Idea Group Inc. is prohibited.

Chapter III

Moderating Learner-Centered E-Learning: Problems and Solutions, Benefits and Implications

Curtis J. Bonk
Indiana University, USA

Robert A. Wisher
US Department of Defense, USA

Ji-Yeon Lee
The University of South Carolina, USA

ABSTRACT

In response to the changes taking place in collaborative online learning environments, this chapter discusses how the simultaneous emergence of collaborative technologies and the learner-centered movement impacts the role of the online instructor. As part of this review, research related to online moderation and facilitation of learning is summarized. It is suggested that online instructors need to facilitate student generation and sharing of information, while assuming the role of learning coach or mentor to provide needed leadership and guidance. Finally, ten key benefits and implications of e-learning, as well as ten potential problems and solutions, are summarized to assist e-learning decision makers and instructors. Among the benefits include the permanence of the online text, the availability of online mentors, and the fostering of student idea generation. Some

Copyright © 2004, Idea Group Inc. Copying or distributing in print or electronic forms without written permission of Idea Group Inc. is prohibited.

consistent online learning problems include learner confusion, lack of justification of student reasoning, and difficulties in grading online content. Instructors are provided with guidelines on how to take advantage of the benefits while limiting or overcoming the problems.

INTRODUCTION

Teaching in an online world is a relatively new and often uncertain event. With popular technologies and instructional trends coming and going, distance learning practice and policies are constantly changing. No matter how careful one may be in selecting an online course management system, he or she may be forced to drop it in favor of an inferior and untested courseware shell that was developed internally and adopted by university administrators or training managers solely because it was free. Adding to the confusion, technology trade shows as well as teaching and learning conferences continue to change their annual themes so that they all start sounding alike: "e-Learning," "Online Learning," "Asynchronous Learning Conference," "Collaborate East," "Collaborate West," "WebNet" or "Training and Learning," to name a few. Of course, the associated terminology also swiftly changes and evolves. One year "online learning" spews off the tongues of supposed distance learning experts. The following year everyone is clamoring to know more about "Web-based learning." At the time of this writing, the latest buzz word from the gurus is "e-learning[1]." What's next? It is no small wonder that many professors, administrators and corporate trainers are habitually nervous about each new wave of distance learning technology.

Despite the anxiety caused by the many uncertainties and the accelerating pace of change, teaching online is fast becoming an expected part of one's daily scholarly endeavors or, at the very least, a legitimate practice of one's colleagues and home institution. A June 2000 report from the National Education Association (NEA) (2000) indicated that while only 10% of NEA members taught a distance learning course, 90% were in institutions that offered distance learning courses, 44% of which were Web based. The report also revealed that such courses were widely distributed across fields and types of institutions. More importantly, those teaching online displayed fairly positive attitudes about these experiences and the training with which they were provided. Not surprisingly, most widespread is the use of online technologies to supplement instruction in a *blended learning* format (Ganzel, 2001; Laster, 2003; Mantyla, 2001), combining online and face-to-face instruction. While such formats may appear costly, many argue that there is significant return on investment for blended e-learning (Barbian, 2002).

Among many benefits are opportunities to create online learning communities rich in collaborative learning and to assist the learning process of adults who can now share work-related experiences around the globe (Bonk & Kim, 1998).

Copyright © 2004, Idea Group Inc. Copying or distributing in print or electronic forms without written permission of Idea Group Inc. is prohibited.

Clearly adult learners enrolling in online courses are expecting more inquiry activities and learner-centered approaches than in the past (Rogers, 2000). As Web-based instruction continues to expand, understanding how to facilitate or moderate student learning in virtual spaces has become an important issue. Online instructors must create situations where students are building knowledge and sharing it with experts and peers who, in turn, offer authentic evaluation and timely feedback.

In response to these issues and trends, this chapter begins with a discussion of the learner-centered movement followed by brief descriptions of team centered and collaborative environments. Next, possible roles for online instructors are suggested; in particular, the role of instructor as moderator of learning (Salmon, 2000). Recent research on the various roles of the online instructor will be also discussed. Finally, ten key benefits and implications of e-learning as well as 10 associated problems and potential solutions are highlighted based on our own research. This final section is meant to provide insights for administrators making decisions about e-learning tools and systems, as well as practical guidelines for college instructors, military trainers and corporate human resource personnel embedded in the e-learning trenches.

Learner-Centered Psychological Principles

During the early 1990s, the American Psychological Association (APA) announced a set of 14 Learner-Centered Psychological Principles (LCPs) (Alexander & Murphy, 1994; APA, 1993) (see Table 1). These principles were derived after an APA presidential task force reviewed previous research on learning and instruction, motivation, and development since the emergence of cognitive psychology in the 1970s and 1980s. While the initial guidelines met with some resistance, the final set of psychological principles, published a couple of years later ("Learner-Centered Psychological Principles Revised," 1996), have been widely accepted and assisted many school reform and restructuring efforts. The LCPs address areas such as fostering curiosity and intrinsic motivation, linking new information to old in meaningful ways, providing learner choice and personal control, nurturing social interaction and interpersonal relations, promoting thinking and reasoning strategies, constructing meaning from information and experience, and taking into account learner social and cultural background.

According to Barbara McCombs (personal communication, Nov. 5, 2002), one of the key leaders of the task force, the principles have direct relevance to online learning where the autonomy, self-determination and choice of learners become critical for their success. Our previous reports also indicate that the LCPs hold great promise for Web-based instruction (Bonk, Appelman, & Hay, 1996; Bonk & Cummings, 1998; Bonk & Reynolds, 1997). For instance, Bonk and Cummings (1998) document a dozen recommendations for designing Web-based instruction from a learner-centered perspective. Their guidelines describe the need for psychologically safe online environments, changes in the instructor

Copyright © 2004, Idea Group Inc. Copying or distributing in print or electronic forms without written permission of Idea Group Inc. is prohibited.

Table 1:   Learner-Centered Psychological Principles Revised

Cognitive and metacognitive factors

1. **Nature of the learning process.** The learning of complex subject matter is most effective when it is an intentional process of constructing meaning from information and experience.
2. **Goals of the learning process.** The successful learner, over time and with support and instructional guidance, can create meaningful, coherent representations of knowledge.
3. **Construction of knowledge.** The successful learner can link new information with existing knowledge in meaningful ways.
4. **Strategic thinking.** The successful learner can create and use a repertoire of thinking and reasoning strategies to achieve complex learning goals.
5. **Thinking about thinking.** Higher order strategies for selecting and monitoring mental operations facilitate creative and critical thinking.
6. **Context of learning.** Learning is influenced by environmental factors, including culture, technology and instructional practices.

Motivational and affective factors

7. **Motivational and emotional influences on learning.** What and how much is learned is influenced by the learner's motivation. Motivation to learn, in turn, is influenced by the individual's emotional states.
8. **Intrinsic motivation to learn.** The learner's creativity, higher order thinking and natural curiosity all contribute to the motivation to learn. Intrinsic motivation is stimulated by tasks of optimal novelty and difficulty, relevant to personal interests, and providing for personal choice and control.
9. **Effects of motivation on effort.** Acquisition of complex knowledge and skills requires extended learner effort and guided practice. Without the learner's motivation to learn, the willingness to exert this effort is unlikely without coercion.

Developmental and social factors

10. **Developmental influences on learning.** As individuals develop, there are different opportunities and constraints for learning. Learning is most effective when differential development within and across physical, intellectual, emotional and social domains is taken into account.
11. **Social influences on learning.** Learning is influenced by social interactions, interpersonal relations and communication with others.

Individual differences

12. **Individual differences in learning.** Learners have different strategies, approaches and capabilities for learning that are a function of prior experience and heredity.
13. **Learning and diversity.** Learning is most effective when differences in learners' linguistic, cultural and social backgrounds are taken into account.
14. **Standards and assessment.** Setting appropriately high and challenging standards and assessing the learner as well as learning progress -- including diagnostic, process and outcome assessment -- are integral parts of the learning process.

For a full text of the principles listed as well as additional rationale and explanation, refer to the APA web site at http://www.apa.org/ed/lcp.html or write to the APA for the December 1995 report "The Learner-Centered Psychological Principles: A Framework for School Redesign and Reform." Permission to reproduce this list has been granted by APA. This document is not copyrighted.

role from sage to moderator or facilitator of learning, the emergence of new electronic mentoring practices and other related ideas. In a nutshell, the LCPs provide a backdrop for thinking about the benefits and implications as well as the problems and solutions of online instruction, some of which are detailed at the end of this chapter.

Along these same lines, many educational technologists are advocating the need to shift from teacher-centered to learner-centered approaches (Bracewell, Breuleux, Laferrière, Benoit, & Abdous, 1998; Hannafin & Land, 1997; Harasim, 1990). Learner-centered pedagogy asks what students need to learn, what their

Copyright © 2004, Idea Group Inc. Copying or distributing in print or electronic forms without written permission of Idea Group Inc. is prohibited.

learning preferences are and what is meaningful to them, not just what is considered basic knowledge in a given discipline or what instructors want to teach. In this regard, Web-based instruction provides a unique opportunity for learning materials, tasks and activities to fit individual learning styles and preferences. Networks of learning information are available to stimulate student interests and ideas. Such environments also provide access to more authentic learning communities than typically found in conventional teacher-centered educational environments.

In accordance with the learner-centered movement, online tools provide opportunities to construct knowledge and actively share and seek information (Harasim, 1990). Similarly, Hannafin and Land (1997) offer a detailed look at the examples, functions and supporting research for technology-enhanced learner-centered environments. There is mounting evidence that online course activities enable learners to generate a diverse array of ideas as well as appreciate multiple perspectives (Chong, 1998). Oliver and McLoughlin (1999) note that online environments allow learners to take ownership over the learning process, engage in social interaction and dialogue, develop multiple modes of representation and become more self aware. In many online settings, there are opportunities to pose problems to others online as well as solve them with authentic data. Using virtual classroom or synchronous presentation tools, such as WebEx, NetMeeting, Placeware or Centra, learners can now construct meaning with their peers with application sharing, online surveys, real-time chats, collaborative writing ex-changes and live content presentations. Simply stated, technology-rich environments support learner engagement in meaningful contexts, thereby increasing ownership over their own learning (Chung, Rodes, & Knapczyk, 1998). As a result, instructors need to configure their new roles as moderators of e-learning tools. Doherty (1998) noted that that emergence of hypermedia technology combined with *asynchronous learning* networks provides greater opportunity for learners to take control over their own learning. She argued that learner control is the most dominant characteristic of this new form of instruction. Clearly, the "learn anytime, anywhere, by anyone" mentality will foster additional expectations for greater learner control and learning options. In online settings, learners can decide when to explore additional resources or progress to more complex concepts or modules. With the proliferation of information and fast-changing job roles, there are increasing expectations that learners will soon be guiding much of their own learning. Consequently, instructors need to develop pedagogical strategies and employ technological tools that foster self-directed student inquiry and investigation (Bonk, Kirkley, Hara, & Dennen, 2001). In such environments, tools and tactics for student discovery and manipulation of information, generation of artifacts and sharing of knowledge are highlighted (Hannafin & Land, 1997). In addition, students can examine problems at multiple levels of complexity, thereby deepening their understanding.

Copyright © 2004, Idea Group Inc. Copying or distributing in print or electronic forms without written permission of Idea Group Inc. is prohibited.

The *open-ended learning environments* (OELEs) described by Hannafin, Hill and Land (1997) corroborate the benefits of student-centered learning. In OELEs, knowledge evolves as understanding is modified and tested, while learners begin to evaluate their own learning needs. Basically, the focus is on relevant and meaningful problems linked to everyday experiences. In accordance with the vision of student-centered environments, OELEs support self-regulated learning, enable novices to negotiate through complex problems, showcase knowledge interrelationships, anchor concepts in real world events and nurture various problem-solving processes. Clearly, these are complex but powerful learning environments.

Advances in interactive and collaborative technologies are forcing instructional designers and technology users to confront and envision learner-centered instruction as well as their role in it (Doherty, 1998). Fortunately, the Web is emerging as a viable teaching and learning platform for learner-centered instruction at the same time that there is a call for incorporating learner-centered approaches in education. It is difficult to tell whether this will lead to serendipitous or tremulous events or both. What is clear, however, is that there currently is a dearth of pedagogical tools and ideas for Web-based instruction (Bonk & Dennen, 1999; Oliver & McLoughlin, 1999; Oliver, 1999). Consequently, most Web tools available today fail to transform or revolutionize education.

As John Stephenson (2001) recently pointed out, online learning has the potential to give learners power and control over their own learning. One can now access experts for advice, download relevant documents, self-assess progress and collaborate with others around the planet. Too often, however, online courseware is simply meant to facilitate course administration and registration procedures. Given the growth of course management systems, such as WebCT and Blackboard, it is clear that many universities, colleges and other educational institutions are finding these tools valuable (Olsen, 2001). However, these tools by themselves do not guarantee quality learning. They do not foster student reflection, metacognition, interdisciplinary learning, collaborative knowledge building or higher-order thinking. As a result, many online learners are being warehoused on the Web, instead of engaging in rich case experiences and interactive simulations as has been promised by e-learning vendors and other zealots. It is as though online learning tool designers have forgotten to consider learner and instructor's needs. The key question Stephenson (2001) argued is not whether online learners will be granted more responsibility for their own learning in the future, but how much they are going to be offered. Of course, the amount offered depends on the tools that are afforded, the pedagogical activities that are designed and used, and the general acceptance and promotion of any new tools and approaches within the online teaching community.

The current situation facing many online learners and instructors is not surprising, since most course management systems emanate from a behavioral learning model (Firdyiwek, 1999). Most systems are embedded with tracking and

Copyright © 2004, Idea Group Inc. Copying or distributing in print or electronic forms without written permission of Idea Group Inc. is prohibited.

controlling devices for student learning, rather than innovative ways to nurture student ownership and progress for learning. At the same time, there are emerging instructional techniques related to teaching on the Web, some for student creativity and others for student critical thinking, and they hold great promise for fostering student learning in online environments (Bonk, Hara, Dennen, Malikowski, & Supplee, 2000; Bonk & Reynolds, 1997). Levin and Waugh (1998) detailed approaches such as Web resource searching and evaluation, project generation and coordination, and student publication of work. Such techniques emphasize individual exploration as well as small group collaboration and sharing. Oliver and McLoughlin (1999), moreover, argued for the development of tools for course simulations, information exchange, parallel problem solving, database creation and case-based reasoning. Such tools empower learners to construct knowledge and share or debate it with others.

Still, a myriad of learner-centered tools are needed in online environments. For instance, Wood (1999) pointed to new instructional opportunities to locate information (i.e., scavenger hunts), conduct research, analyze data, take part in virtual tours, exchange and publish information and solve problems. The possibilities exist, therefore, for rich electronic learning. Unfortunately, for the most part, pedagogically sound and exciting Web courseware tools have yet to be developed to take advantage of such opportunities. There are no tools to create a gallery tour of student work in these platforms. There are no tools for a debate or role play activity. There are no concept mapping tools for displaying student understanding of content. Instead, as indicated, most e-learning technology remains focused on behavioral models, rather than learning models derived from the LCPs presented in Table 1. So while learning theory has moved toward a more active and learner-centered perspective, the tools developed for online learning remain stuck in a teacher-centered past.

So how might courseware, such as WebCT and Blackboard, be enhanced to address this dilemma? We suggest developing templates for creativity, critical thinking and cooperative learning that instructors and students might select for different course activities (Bonk & Dennen, 1999). In effect, if an instructor would like to include learners in a brainstorming or mind mapping activity, she could select the requisite template and alter it for her particular needs. Glimpses of such tools currently may be available as stand-alone packages, but are typically not embedded in course management software.

Some might argue that educators simply do not know how to utilize emerging Web technologies. In effect, the pace of change is so fast that pedagogical models are needed to help create and understand Web tools from a constructivist or learner-centered perspective (Bracewell et al., 1998). As Salomon (1998) noted, for the first time in history, technologies are outpacing pedagogical and psychological rationale. Online learning tools may afford us opportunities to extend our theories as well as connect them in ways currently unfathomable. As

Copyright © 2004, Idea Group Inc. Copying or distributing in print or electronic forms without written permission of Idea Group Inc. is prohibited.

indicated, students can now make predictions or interpretations about text, video or animations encountered online. As tools afford innovative forms of inquiry and project-based learning (Barab, MaKinster, & Scheckler, in press), there is a need for training instructors (and their supervisors) in the task structuring required to guide knowledge exploration and communication among learning participants (Bracewell et al., 1998). Bourne (1998), for instance, provided a model of potential shifts in faculty instructional roles with more time projected for online mentoring and less time required for testing.

Some new models look at the degree to which the Web is embedded or integrated into a course (Bonk, Cummings, Hara, Fischler, & Lee, 2000; Mason, 1998), as well as the forms and directions of interaction utilized by such Web courses (Cummings, Bonk, & Jacobs, 2002). At the same time that such model building is taking place, researchers like Ron Oliver and Betty Collis are reacting to the lack of pedagogical tools for the Web by building specific tools for team projects, critical thinking, mentoring, online debates, URL postings, reflection, concept mapping, student surveying and electronic discussion (Oliver, 1999, 2001; Oliver & McLoughlin, 1999), as well as course management shells with similar opportunities (Collis & De Boer, 1999). Similarly, Bonk (1998) responded to the current void by creating interactive tools for online portfolio feedback, profile commenting and Web-linked rating (see http://www.indiana.edu/~smartweb). In step with the learner-centered movement, these camps are focused on building constructivist tools that foster active and authentic learning, goal setting, student articulation, social interaction on collaborative tasks and metacognitive reflection.

Clearly additional experimentation with online instructional strategies and approaches is needed. Just what types of tools work in what situations? What pedagogical strategies foster student engagement online? With continuation of such efforts, the coming decade may witness a growth spurt in pedagogically based e-learning technologies. It may simultaneously give rise to a myriad of instructor sharing tools and resources. Already instructor resources and portals, such as CourseShare.com, MERLOT.org and the World Lecture Hall, have arisen.

Trends in pedagogy are beginning to converge with the emergence of Web-based technologies that allow for greater learner control, personal responsibility and collaboration. In part, this convergence has been brought about because e-learning settings tend to attract self-directed learners who want meaningful and engaging activities, as well as instructors willing to experiment with a variety of techniques and practices to individualize learning (National Center for Education Statistics (NCES), 1999; Wagner & McCombs, 1995). Fortunately, e-learning is a unique context wherein *learner-centered principles* are particularly relevant, since students become the center of the learning environment. In successful online courses, for example, students might assume significant instructional roles

Copyright © 2004, Idea Group Inc. Copying or distributing in print or electronic forms without written permission of Idea Group Inc. is prohibited.

(e.g., offering instructional tips and constructing new knowledge) that were once the domain of the instructor (Harasim, 1993). In addition to student self-directed learning and learning ownership, Levin and Ben-Jacob (1998) predict that a key component of learning in higher education at the start of this millennium will be collaborative learning. Certainly student-centered e-learning environments will be composed of many team learning and peer mentoring opportunities.

Learning-Team Centered

Both IBM and the Lotus Institute have published white papers that address the need to extend learner-centered approaches proposed by APA (1993) in the early 1990s to "learning team centered" approaches (Kulp, 1999; Lotus Institute, 1996). According to these reports, not only do Web-based learning environments offer opportunities for actively interpreting, challenging, testing and discussing ideas, but they also provide a means to collaboratively create and share new knowledge. While these white papers typically do not extensively detail (or sometimes even acknowledge) the research and theory on which the principles are based (e.g., Brown, Collins, & Duguid, 1989; Tharp & Gallimore, 1988; Vygotsky, 1978), it is clear that many training personnel in corporate settings now grasp the importance of being learner-centered on the Web.

The role of the instructor in such an environment is to facilitate student generation of information as well as the sharing of that information, not to control the delivery and pace of it. A key goal of team-based learning activities, therefore, is to apply expertise and experience of the participants to a group problem solving situation or research project that helps participants accomplish something that they could not achieve individually. Other objectives of such activities include the fostering of teamwork, communication and good listening skills (Lotus Institute, 1996). While Kulp (1999) admitted that small team electronic collaboration requires significantly more time and effort than traditional learning environments, it can generate new knowledge, attitudes and behavior. To foster learner interaction and accountability, he recommended the use of roles such as coordinator, resource investigator, summarizer, encourager, implementer and specialist in these team-based learning environments. The following section will shed some light on how an instructor effectively assumes and assigns such roles.

New Role for Instructors Online

In many ways, e-learning is an entirely new type of education requiring a redesign of instructor roles, responsibilities and commitments (Besser & Bonn, 1997), as well as timely support and training for those agreeing to teach online (Lawrence, 1996-1997). Not surprisingly, then, the wealth of online instructional roles might seem daunting to newcomers. As student-centered activities are increasingly facilitated by emerging technology, the role of the faculty member

Copyright © 2004, Idea Group Inc. Copying or distributing in print or electronic forms without written permission of Idea Group Inc. is prohibited.

or instructor shifts to facilitator, coach or mentor who provides leadership and wisdom in guiding student learning (Dillon & Walsh, 1992; Doherty, 1998). Of course, until instructors feel comfortable and gain experience in this new role, online courses may experience higher than expected student dropout rates (Carr, 2000).

To lessen attrition, instructors have a number of roles they can assume online. For instance, in any given online session, the instructor might be a chair, host, lecturer, tutor, facilitator, mediator of team debates, mentor, provocateur, observer, participant, co-learner, assistant, community organizer or some combination of these (Salmon, 2000). From one perspective, a good moderator is like a successful host or hostess; he or she must know how to connect guests at the party with similar interests and bring those hiding on the fringes into the community (Rogan & Denton, 1996). From another perspective, it might be important for the instructor to act as a co-learner or co-participant in online activities. Rice-Lively (1994) found that the online instructor must be flexible in constantly shifting roles between the roles of instructor, facilitator and consultant. This is not particularly easy. Fortunately, many of these instructional roles can be assigned to learners, outside experts and teaching assistants (Paulsen, 1995; Selinger, 1999). At the same time, instructors must create an ethos of mutual support and community so that students with limited technology experience can perform well in these environments (Ross, 1996).

The assignment of teams is not always easy, however. Some learners may have minimal collaborative learning experience, while others will rely on teammates to do the majority of the work. Consequently, the guidance and moderating skills of the instructor are vital for online team success.

Researchers have suggested various guidelines for online facilitation. For instance, Cummings (2000) offered a set of steps to be used within a virtual debate (see Table 2). Here, the instructor first selects controversial topics based on input from the class. Next, the instructor assigns students to pairs or groups for the virtual debate(s). While not depicted in the sequence of steps from Cummings, during the debate, the instructor has a critical role in encouraging student participation, providing additional evidence, asking questions, providing counter examples and nudging students toward compromise. Certainly, templates like this are valuable guides for instructors who are new to online teaching and learning. Dozens more are now needed.

Also of value are descriptions of potential teacher roles online. Mason (1991) advocated three key roles of the online instructor: organizational, social and intellectual. The organizational role entails setting the agenda, objectives, timetable and procedural rules for posting and interaction. Recommendations for instructors here include patience, avoiding lecturing, inviting guest speakers and addressing unanticipated activities or problems. They should also find ways to entice learners into discussions and participation in the online class. Without the

Copyright © 2004, Idea Group Inc. Copying or distributing in print or electronic forms without written permission of Idea Group Inc. is prohibited.

Table 2:   Sequence of Steps Within a Virtual Debate (Cummings, 2000)

Virtual debate steps
1.   Instructor selects controversial topic with input from class.
2.   Instructor divides class into subtopic pairs.
3.   Instructor assigns subtopic to each pair, one as critic and one as defender.
4.   Critic and defender pairs post initial position statements.
5.   Students review all initial position statements.
6.   Students reply to at least two position statements of other groups with comments or questions.
7.   Each student rebuts the opposing initial statement from the individual in his/her pair.
8.   Based on a review of all statements, comments and questions, students formulate personal positions.
9.   Students post personal position statements in private forums.

organizational role, many online learners would lack the necessary support structures and would likely flounder. How many or what percentage would struggle remains an open question.

In contrast, the social role involves sending welcoming messages, thank you notices, prompt feedback on student inputs and a generally friendly, positive and responsive tone. Instructional caveats concerning the social role include reinforcing good discussion behaviors and inviting students to be candid about the way the course is going. In effect, the social role sets the tone for the class. A positive, nurturing environment is typically recommended (Bonk et al., 2001).

Of the three roles Mason (1991) describes, the intellectual role is the most crucial since it includes high-level activities such as asking questions, probing responses and refocusing discussion. It also entails setting goals, explaining tasks and overlooked information, weaving disparate comments, synthesizing key points raised, identifying unifying themes, directing discussion and generally setting and raising the intellectual climate of the online course or module. This is where teaching skill takes over. High quality online instruction requires knowing when to push groups or individuals for additional information, when to provide hints or help with knowledge construction, when to ask for visual representations of ideas, when to summarize an activity, when to let the learning activity continue unabated and when to provide evaluation on student products. One must also have a feel for when to expose conflicting opinions as well as when to request comments on specific issues. Summarization and weaving of comments should occur when discussion becomes lengthy, but such responses may only be needed every week or two. Given the critical nature of these skills, it is not too surprising that online pedagogy is currently a key component of many instructor training programs.

A report from a yearlong faculty seminar on online teaching and learning at the University of Illinois (The Report of the University of Illinois Teaching at an Internet Distance Seminar, 1999) recommended that when attempting to facilitate online collaborative learning, instructors should be patient, flexible, responsive and clear about expectations and norms for participation. Online instructors might focus their facilitation on collaborative processes as well as final team

Copyright © 2004, Idea Group Inc. Copying or distributing in print or electronic forms without written permission of Idea Group Inc. is prohibited.

products. Of course, process facilitation requires that they limit lecturing, while monitoring and prompting student participation, organizing student interactions and writing integrative or weaving comments every week or two. Furthermore, instructors need to find ways for individuals and small groups to assume teaching-related roles from time to time. Instructors also need to become adept at promoting interaction, addressing multiple learning styles, performing needs assessments and projecting a friendly image (Thach, 1993).

The presence of the instructor in online environments is felt in numerous ways. For example, the instructor might:

- Determine appropriate goals, standards, facts and skills to be taught;
- Provide access to relevant tools and resources;
- Arrange the pedagogical activity or process;
- Supply help and advice regarding online technology that is used to support the online learning process; and
- Assure fair, valid and authentic assessment.

Both Berge (1995) and Ashton, Roberts and Teles (1999) suggest that categorizing the online acts of instructors into four categories — pedagogical, managerial, technical and social — might be helpful in understanding the role of the instructor in collaborative online environments. In helping explicate these duties, Bonk, Kirkley et al. (2001) provided specific online course examples of each of the four roles.

In similarity to the intellectual role described by Mason (1991), pedagogical actions include feedback, providing instructions, giving information, offering advice and preferences, summarizing or weaving student comments and refer-ring to outside resources and experts in the field. In effect, the pedagogical role relates to direct instructor involvement in class activities. The online instructor must have knowledge of when to foster student-student interaction or have students listen to guest experts. Will multiple viewpoints be encouraged and expressed online? How will debatable or controversial issues be addressed? Will mentors be brought into the virtual class to prompt or provoke these? What about the use of heterogeneous collaborative groups? What pedagogical activities foster group effectiveness? Clearly, instructor consideration of the overall learning environment is vital.

Similar to Mason's (1991) organizational role, Bonk, Kirkley et al. (2001) indicated that online managerial actions involve overseeing task and course structuring. Managerial actions include explaining assignments, assigning part-ners and groups, setting task due dates and extensions, and coordinating receipt of student work. Task clarifications might occur via e-mail or in a specific discussion thread or topic. For collaborative groups, assignments might be posted within team workspaces or on team specific distribution lists. In addition to assignment management, a good online manager knows how to structure

Copyright © 2004, Idea Group Inc. Copying or distributing in print or electronic forms without written permission of Idea Group Inc. is prohibited.

discussions. These actions include pointing students to other messages, commenting about posting length or format, defining the audience, noting on and off task participation and directing students to different topics and folders for posting. In a blended course (Barbian, 2002), which, as noted earlier, involves both online and face-to-face components, the instructor might even print out weekly discussion transcripts as a means to legitimize the experience as well as foster student reflection. And when using cross cultural or cross-institution collaboration, the instructor will need to be sure that everyone has access to the forums they will be participating in. Do their passwords work? Are there internal firewalls that will interfere with global partnerships and collaboration? Finally, there are overall course management activities, such as explaining the relevance of the course, setting office hours, organizing meeting times and places, defining grade distributions, correcting course materials and discussing potential course revisions. Grades on collaborative group work, for instance, might be specifically posted to a team's workspace or sent via private e-mail to each group member.

According to Bonk, Kirkley et al. (2001), technical actions relate to helping with user or system technology issues. Support here might include orientation sessions or online tutorials and help systems. If technical issues remain unresolved, those students will be disadvantaged in collaborative group activities. As expected, a recent study of blended learning in a military setting found that student technical issues or problems actually decreased over time (Orvis, Wisher, Bonk, & Olson, 2002).

Finally, as detailed earlier, social actions might include instructor empathy, interpersonal outreach (e.g., welcoming statements, invitations and apologies), candid discussions of one's own online experiences and humor. Such social activities directly impact the effectiveness of online collaboration. Collaborative teams or communities of practice might show their identity through group names, banners or slogans. They might also share work or family experiences and problems in an online café or forum. Sharing personal experiences among group members will help in binding the team as well as in solving course-related problems.

Ashton et al. (1999) suggested that future research look at the role of the instructor in these roles from the start to end of an online course, across instructors, across different offerings of the same course and across different courses. In collaborative environments, research might explore the role of the instructor in building, facilitating and responding to teams. Just how does the instructor manage these four roles — pedagogical, managerial, technical and social — and others so as to foster effective group functioning? Researchers also might explore how different technologies and pedagogical strategies change the collaboration patterns and help promote community building. Such issues are addressed in later sections of this manuscript as well as in Bonk and Wisher (2000).

Copyright © 2004, Idea Group Inc. Copying or distributing in print or electronic forms without written permission of Idea Group Inc. is prohibited.

Both Bonk and Cummings (1998) and Bailey and Luetkehans (1998) provided several tips for online instructors to create learner-centered environments. Each camp mentioned the need to develop psychologically safe learning environments where there is extensive student interaction and elaboration. Reduction of cyber-stress must be one of the key initial goals. To accomplish this, the instructor's expectations must be clear and prompt. In addition, online learning teams should be assembled according to the tasks involved and available talent and interests. Students in small groups work best when they are offered open-ended problems with some degree of choice, though timely instructional support and feedback is needed when students are struggling to reach consensus or make decisions. Moreover, student assignments should build on their experiences and prior knowledge, while allowing students to find ways to utilize the Web resources and share them with team members. The instructor, for instance, might intervene to indicate where the group members have found some common ground.

In addition to prompt task structuring and feedback, instructors should take advantage of both public and private forms of feedback, as well as online questioning techniques and facilitation that can stimulate student reflection and processing of information. Along these same lines, instructors should make attempts to utilize the Web for social interaction with peers and experts beyond one's class in student collaborative projects. Online peers and experts might also offer useful mentoring and advice. Students can be electronically apprenticed with timely insights and suggestions from other instructors and students located anywhere in the world (Bonk, Angeli, Malikowski, & Supplee, 2001). Finally, in student-centered e-learning environments, instructors should create an atmosphere wherein participants avoid quick judgment and overall negative criticism or personal attacks on one another's projects.

Online Moderator Research

While guidelines such as those above may be useful, what do online instructors prefer? Research indicates that online instructors tend to rely on simple tools, such as e-mail, static or dynamic syllabi, Web links to course material, posting lecture notes online and accepting student work online, while significantly fewer use online chat rooms, multimedia lectures, online examinations, animation and video streaming (Peffers & Bloom, 1999). However, more sophisticated Web-based instruction looms on the horizon. Already, tools such as Groove and SiteScape Forum, offer increasing opportunities for the development of shared document workspaces and idea exchange for learning teams. Naturally, the tools one selects will change as the Internet II and other technologies raise available bandwidth and increase the number and location of possible online participants. Nevertheless, the tendency to select less complex tools has an impact on how instructional time becomes allocated and vice versa.

Copyright © 2004, Idea Group Inc. Copying or distributing in print or electronic forms without written permission of Idea Group Inc. is prohibited.

A study by McIsaac, Blocher, Mahes and Vrasidas (1999) indicated that instructor time could be apportioned to numerous tasks and subtasks. In that study, online instructors divided their time into planning and preparation (10%), online teaching (17%), administration (15%), interaction with peers (21%), interaction with students (15%) and interaction with content (22%). Keep in mind, this was just one study. Still, McIsaac et al. (1999) conclude that online instructors tend to be more concerned with encouraging student participation and the quality of interaction than might be expected in traditional settings. As a result of this change in role, Web courses require significant amounts of time for instructors to create and coordinate (Gaud, 1999). To help instructors meet these requirements, they need assistance and advice both in the development and delivery of Web courses (Lawrence, 1996-1997).

In an attempt to provide such guidance, Dennen's (2001) recent exploration of nine online classes at seven different colleges or universities distinguished good and poor online instruction. For instance, more effective online instructors posted qualitative and quantitative criteria for weekly discussions as well as timely feedback on student work. These instructors tended to embed more relevant activities, personal anecdotes and overall structure. They also provided personal models of high quality discussion for their students and encouraged the sharing of multiple perspectives.

In contrast, the less successful instructors in Dennen's (1991) study did not have a sense of how to foster discussion and were less clear in their guidance. Their discussion prompts were often factual or knowledge-based questions (e.g., "Who invented the phonograph?," "When did the Spanish-American War occur?," etc.) where one response is typically all that is necessary. Along these same lines, less successful instructors would often post their lecture notes and dominate discussion, thereby placing students into more a passive or receptive mode, and reducing their sense of course ownership and overall level of participation or contribution. In addition, some failed to value or assign grades to student participation or online activities, thereby further reducing student participation. In addition, ultimate deadlines, which were used more often by the less effective online instructors, encouraged students to post, while simultaneously reducing student interactions and collaborations.

Online Moderator Summary

As is clear from the information above, *online moderation* is a complex and vital skill. While the moderating talents of online environments are not easily explained and understood and online success stories are not pervasive, some guidelines are emerging. According to Selinger (1997), successful moderation tends to include student system familiarity, encouraging introductory messages, clear guidelines and sense of purpose, online guests and intermittent summaries and refocusing of discussion. To be successful, therefore, moderators should

Copyright © 2004, Idea Group Inc. Copying or distributing in print or electronic forms without written permission of Idea Group Inc. is prohibited.

identify their preferred forms of moderation or facilitation and pedagogical styles (Paulsen, 1995).[2] They should also know how to move between different roles or styles of instruction. As online roles evolve, researchers need to investigate just how much student autonomy and interaction they will promote. Researchers might also inquire about how often instructors, using different roles, intervene to offer advice and feedback in student discussions and activities. Some initial research has begun to answer these questions.

Significant teaching and learning changes are underway due to the emergence and popularity of e-learning. For instance, e-learning supports a more social constructivist learning environment wherein students negotiate meaning and are involved in extensive dialogue and interaction. Instructors can offer many forms of learning assistance in such environments including questioning students, coaching them on their progress and providing varied layers of task structuring for the highly anxious (Bonk & Kim, 1998). As online assistance has become increasingly understood and acknowledged, the role of the instructor has shifted from learning director or controller to facilitator or moderator of learning (Salmon, 2000; Selinger, 1999). In adding fuel to this movement, electronic learners are more autonomous and independent in their own learning than their traditionally taught counterparts. E-learners also have greater opportunities for interacting with other learners, their instructor and outside experts. Clearly, teaching and learning takes on a more collaborative feel in an e-learning environment where learners have greater opportunities for reflection and exploration, thereby expanding ideas about when and where learning in a course actually takes place.

E-Learning Benefits and Implications

While the research literature on moderating learner-centered e-learning environments is important, many instructors and administrators desperately seek specific and practical information. In response to these needs, Table 3 outlines 10 benefits and implications of online instruction[3]. For instance, since low participators and shy students tend to participate more online than they do in traditional environments (Bonk & King, 1998; Chong, 1998; Cooney, 1998), instructors might consider computer conferences, expert chats and Web explorations as supplements or adjunct tools to live instruction. Such blended learning models of live and online instruction are already fairly common in training environments (Barbian, 2002; Hoffman, 2001; Orvis et al., 2002) as well as in higher education (Bonk, 2001; Harasim, 2003). In particular, blended formats might be highly successful in graduate courses with one or more foreign students who need additional time to reflect on course content and then can use an online forum or Web conference to discuss and debate ideas. Blended learning can also create online access to lecture notes, collaborative team drafts and final documents and case problems and solutions.

Copyright © 2004, Idea Group Inc. Copying or distributing in print or electronic forms without written permission of Idea Group Inc. is prohibited.

Table 3:   Benefits and Implications of E-Learning (Bonk & King, 1998)

Benefits	Implications
1. Low participants and shy students sometimes open up.	Use computer conferencing for course discussions in traditionally taught classes, especially with international students.
2. There are minimal off-task behaviors.	While this is typically a good sign in terms of student learning, and perhaps unexpected given the expectations of students being lost in cyberspace, students are often so task oriented online that they fail to interact with peers or form online learning communities. As a result, instructors may need to create socially oriented tasks and opportunities to share personal stories.
3. Delayed collaboration is more extensive and rich than real time; real time is more immediate and personal.	Utilize *asynchronous collaboration* for article discussions, reactions and debates, while synchronous tools should be used for online experts and assignment assistance and teamwork.
4. Students can generate tons of information or case situations on the Web.	Structure student content generation activities, perhaps limiting the amount and type of postings. Force reflection on and integration of comments as well as interactive questioning as a way to focus students on the content.
5. Minimal student disruptions and dominance.	There may be times when the instructor needs to foster critical commentary and debate as well as help students take sides on issues.
6. Students are excited to publish work.	When students produce something of extremely high quality, ask permission to post it to the Web as examples for current and future students. Publishing student work helps form a classroom legacy as well as an archive of successful products.
7. Many forms of online advice are available. Practitioner, expert, instructor and student online feedback are all valuable and important.	Find experts, practitioners, colleagues and peers who might offer your students online advice and mentoring. Look at the Web as an opportunity to develop expertise within their chosen field.
8. With the permanence of online forum postings, one can print out discussions and perform retrospective analyses and other reflective activities.	Find ways to foster reflection and metacognitive commenting on student posts. Instructors might have students discuss concepts embedded in their posts for a particular discussion thread or week. Additionally, they might have students pull out and discuss the key issues, questions or themes in a discussion.
9. Discussion extends across the semester and creates opportunities to share perspectives beyond a particular course or module.	Have students revisit and rethink their earlier postings. Also, try to find colleagues in other universities and countries teaching similar topics who want to collaborate and get involved in online mentoring. Have students reflect on apparent cultural differences in their posts. Perhaps arrange a day wherein students can meet in a live videoconferencing or online chat situation.
10. E-learning encourages instructors to coach and guide learning.	Reflect on the online activities employed as an instructor and try to incorporate some of them in a traditional class. Have learners print out their online posts and analyze them for the type of interaction or form of learning assistance embedded in the post (e.g., questioning, feedback, pushing students to explore, explanations, task structuring, etc.). A similar activity could be conducted during the training of online instructors.

An associated benefit of e-learning is that students generally love generating new knowledge and publishing their work for others to read. They like the authenticity of their online audiences. Consequently, instead of relying on a few scattered nuggets of instructor wisdom or a smattering of recycled jokes, online

Copyright © 2004, Idea Group Inc. Copying or distributing in print or electronic forms without written permission of Idea Group Inc. is prohibited.

instructors should allow students to generate ideas, cases, anecdotes or potential test questions. Students can also receive countless comments or insights from mentors, tutors, peers and online guests instead of, or in addition to, the instructor. In fact, many "ask-an-expert" forums and mentoring services are free on the Web (for a few online mentoring examples, see http://www.indiana.edu/~tickit/ resourcecenter/resource3.htm). At the same time, e-learning also opens up opportunities for team teaching and collaboration with instructors from other universities and countries. Perhaps, more importantly, students can begin to understand the importance of different terms and concepts from the vantage point of distant peers in places such as Korea, Peru or Finland (Bonk, Angeli et al., 2001). As suggested by the learner-centered movement, embedding comments from practitioners and real world experts will foster student social interaction and dialogue.

With such tools and forums available on demand, the online instructor has many opportunities to become a moderator or facilitator of student learning. For instance, he or she can question, encourage, push to explore or otherwise nudge student learning. And when appropriate, the online instructor also can assume a more traditional direct instruction approach. Understanding when to facilitate the interactions of students and when to provide lecture notes and organizational aids is critical for online success.

Interestingly, the permanence of online discourse offers a new window into the mix of strategies utilized by students and instructors. It opens up new vistas on student writing skill and idea negotiation. Additionally, it affords opportunities for shared document workspaces and team products (Bonk & King, 1998). With text permanence, teams can more easily argue and discuss points, draft white papers, and label their thinking (Duffy, Dueber, & Hawley 1998). If writing is thinking, then such online forums and shared workspaces should be powerful allies in the assessment of student understanding of key course concepts. This permanence of the online environments also can foster student self-reflection on their conceptual learning as well as instructor evaluation of the effectiveness of various online teaching techniques.

Another benefit of e-learning is reduced off-task behaviors of students. Cooney (1998) and others (Bonk, Hansen, Grabner-Hagen, Lazar, & Mirabelli, 1998; Bonk & King, 1998) discovered that students in computer conferencing environments stay on task more than 90% of the time. Students in these studies were so task driven that they often failed to interact beyond basic task requirements. To nurture student interpersonal skills and knowledge, therefore, instructors might consider using tools that foster socially related interactions, such as coffee houses and icebreaking activities. In contrast to the above asynchronous learning studies, a recent study of student synchronous training in the military found that students were off-task about 30% of the time (Orvis et al., 2002). These findings, in fact, approximated what had been the norms of face-to-face training.

Copyright © 2004, Idea Group Inc. Copying or distributing in print or electronic forms without written permission of Idea Group Inc. is prohibited.

A related benefit of e-learning is that students are seldom disruptive to or destructive of each other's work. However, the first author has found that returning adult students tend to take more liberty in making comments in jest or poking fun of their peers. Somewhat surprisingly, the dominant or disruptive student is sometimes the one whom peers rush to read and respond to (Bonk, Hansen et al., 1998).

Perhaps instructors will simply need to embed tension or conflict in their online activities. They might consider different ways to foster debates, role play and critical commentary. Ron Oliver (1999), for instance, has developed an online debate tool to explore topics or interest areas, defend or refute arguments and generally be exposed to a range of alternative viewpoints or perspectives. Arguments can be recorded online for other students to peruse and reflect upon. There are many ways to involve students in online debates or critical reviews. For instance, as noted below, the use of devil's advocate roles and "critical friend" activities might give license to students to take alternative sides on arguments. Oliver and McLoughlin (1999) argue that posting online journals fosters student reflection and metacognition, searching authentic or real-world databases enhances student motivation, posting works in progress to the Web forces students to articulate and negotiate their ideas and exploring and comparing online resources promotes critical thinking (Oliver, 2001). In effect, instructors should consider all the benefits of e-learning and find ways to take advantage of them in their teaching, as well as promote them to colleagues.

E-Learning Problems and Solutions

In addition to the benefits and implications of e-learning, as detailed in Table 4, instructors face many serious problems and potential solutions when teaching online. First of all, there is a need for clarity and structure in teaching online. Without some online guidance and direction, student confusion and complaints will significantly interfere with learning. Displaying prior student work samples online as well as specifying exact due dates and time requirements will limit student confusion. Moreover, establishing posting expectations in terms of both quality and quantity is also helpful to novice online learning students. Additionally, assigning e-mail pals or Web buddies to keep each other informed of weekly course events and due dates helps students stay on task and understand course requirements.

Another serious e-learning problem is that students too often fail to justify or back-up their claims in face-to-face settings (Halpern, 1999; Paul, 1995) as well as online ones (Angeli, Valanides, & Bonk, 2003; Bonk, Angeli et al., 2001; Duffy et al., 1998). Instead, they often rely on personal opinions and anecdotes (Bonk, Malikowski, Angeli, & East, 1998). What can be done? First of all, instructor modeling as well as prior student work may establish general expectations or standards. In addition, clear instructional aids and explanations of

Copyright © 2004, Idea Group Inc. Copying or distributing in print or electronic forms without written permission of Idea Group Inc. is prohibited.

Table 4: Problems and Solutions of E-Learning (Bonk & King, 1998; Murray, 2000)

Problems	Solutions
1. Online learning tasks can quickly overwhelm students who lack experience in this area.	Have an initial training day for students. Plan and streamline the course discussions and activities so that students have a clear sense of what is due and when. Require something due early in the course so that the students have an opportunity to test both their equipment and the courseware system. Check to see if all students are experiencing the same technological problem(s) that a few students might be experiencing.
2. Even students with extensive technology experience can become confused and lost on the Web.	Students need some structure and guidance online. For example, computer conferencing and online discussion, as well as any other online tasks, must include explicit expectations and perhaps some samples of prior students' Web work. Assigning specific times and dates when postings are due tends to help limit confusion. Suffice it to say, effective online instruction requires extensive planning and forethought.
3. Students are too nice to one another on the Web, perhaps because they have minimal face-to-face interactions and limited shared histories.	Develop controversies and conflict perhaps by assigning some students to particular roles such as devil's advocate, bloodletter, pessimist, idea squelcher and watchdog. Such roles also can spur discussion when it is lacking. At the same time, instruct students in how to appropriately debate or discuss ideas without directly criticizing or insulting the other person. Instructors must guide such interactions and help students take on different roles in an online debate. Also, they might build ways to form shared histories and a safe environment to take risks online.
4. Students' comments too often lack justification or examples that connect their online comments to specific course concepts. Moreover, they sometimes simply tell stories unrelated to the class. While off-task behavior is rare online, students still may not realize that they are supposed to justify their reasoning.	Train students how to back up their claims and link concepts from their discussion postings to pages and ideas from their textbook or other course materials. Posting prior student work might serve as examples for new or prospective students. The instructor might also model the types of answers and argument support expected by citing theories, studies or concepts. Frame questions and prompts in terms of key concepts or issues for a particular unit. In addition, assigning international collaboration projects with rich cross-cultural feedback provides incentives for students to look competent to their foreign peers. Foreign peers also might provide useful role models related to justifying one's comments.

objectives also tend to help. For instance, think sheets or question guides that encourage text references might foster student reflection. Such tools might also assist peers in knowing what to focus on when they mentor each other. Brescia's (2001) study of a nonprofit management course found that mentoring includes nourishing good ideas as well as championing lost ideas. It also entails challenging hypotheses, modeling good analyses, summarizing learner ideas and asking for clarification when warranted. Based on his research, Brescia (2001) created an initial telementoring taxonomy. Many such online mentoring advice guides and forums will likely emerge during the next few years.

Copyright © 2004, Idea Group Inc. Copying or distributing in print or electronic forms without written permission of Idea Group Inc. is prohibited.

Table 4: Problems and Solutions of E-Learning (Bonk & King, 1998; Murray, 2000) (continued)

Problems	Solutions
5. It is tough to electronically teach and not preach. In our research, we often find some verticality or authoritativeness in instructor or expert mentoring (i.e., "You need to remember to do…" or "The concept that is key here is"). Horizontal or collegial interactions are not as pervasive as learner-centered theory would suggest.	To limit instructor dominance, find ways to encourage students to take the lead role. For instance, the instructor might require students to take turns starting or summarizing discussion.
6. Peer online mentoring is not as thoughtful as instructor feedback.	Provide students with tip sheets and guides on how to provide peer feedback. In addition, instead of directly teaching information, create lists of sample responses that assist in the learning process.
7. Communities of learners are difficult to form, in part, because students are extremely task, not discussion, oriented. This is also partially due to the limited social cues and trust building activities of most e-learning environments. Often peer camaraderie is lacking.	Encourage social and informal types of interactions such as in cafes, coffee houses and quotes of the week. Create forums for students to hang out as well as to post personal introductions. One might assign online buddies to help respond to pressing needs. Also, the instructor might embed a few key initial events or postings wherein students get to know each other early in the course. In effect, one might create a more open-ended environment wherein students could come back from time-to-time. For example, have students post a set number of times per semester instead of per week.
8. Too much data and information to read and to respond to all of it.	To avoid becoming overwhelmed, instructors should establish set times each week in which they participate in the online discussion (with options for additional participation). They might also assign learners as e-mail pals, Web buddies or critical friends to give each other weekly feedback on their work. With such peer feedback, the instructor can be more strategic and selective in response strategies.
9. It is time consuming to grade student online discussions.	Perhaps assign some points simply for task completion and timeliness. Other times, the instructor might assign points for interacting concisely with others and for depth of thought, rather than simply the quantity of posts. Also, one might create specific criteria, dimensions or scoring rubrics prior to grading. Another way to focus one's grading and commenting is to have students reference pages from their respective texts in their posts. And, if class size exceeds 25 or 30 students, ask for some departmental support in terms of grading.
10. Technology swiftly changes or is too slow. In addition, servers are inaccessible, computers crash and programs malfunction. Finally, software bugs or glitches can frustrate students who want to complete their work on time.	Keep your students informed about the latest technology agreements available within your organization or institution. Avoid trying more than a couple of new ideas each semester. Instead of using many tools at the cutting edge, use what works for all students and stay within a reasonable range of activities that have worked in the past.

Additional guidance undoubtedly will emerge from online pedagogical experiments. Bonk, Ehman, Hixon and Yamagata-Lynch (2002), for instance, explored variations in peer mentoring such as helping students form constructive or critical friend activities. The learners in that study had high praise for their critical friend activities. Along these same lines, corresponding with students

Copyright © 2004, Idea Group Inc. Copying or distributing in print or electronic forms without written permission of Idea Group Inc. is prohibited.

from other universities or with foreign peers who actually read and cite research is a useful tactic for helping students understand the importance of justifying their claims (Angeli et al., 2003; Dennen & Bonk, 2003). Exposing students to peers from other countries also can demonstrate a myriad of problem solving strategies as well as cultural differences in online collaborative behaviors. For instance, one recent study of preservice teacher online case discussions showed that American students were extremely pragmatic, Finnish students were more theoretical and Koreans tended be more social when transcripts were coded and compared (Kim & Bonk, 2002). In addition, the Finnish students backed up more of their claims with research references than the other groups.

Another e-learning problem — students being too nice to each other online — is the flip side to the benefit of minimal online disruptions, noted earlier. Assigning roles such as pessimist and idea squelcher to weekly reading discussions or online debates will definitely shake up the dialogue. Assigning student pairs as "critical friends" will also give license for students to both critique and support each other. Our incorporation of critical and constructive friend activities at Indiana University during the past couple of years indicates that this is a rather useful e-learning technique, since it simultaneously fosters community building and individualized assessment.

Perhaps the most difficult dilemma facing the online instructor is how to foster online learning communities. Part of the problem is that difficulty in pinpointing when an online learning community exists. Some may confuse an online portal, database, network, listserv or interest group for a learning community (Stuckey, Hedberg, & Lockyer, 2002). To often casual references to online communities do not match reality. True learning communities require membership, goals, stated purpose(s), sense of identity, shared knowledge, member participation or contributions and levels of trust that portals and online newsletters generally lack. They may be marked with moderators, mentors, team members and reviewers, instead of passive consumers or receivers of knowledge. Part of the problem also stems from different types of learning communities; some may be more focused on completing certain tasks (task-oriented), some on acquiring relevant expertise and knowledge (knowledge-oriented) and others on becoming part of the common practice or profession (practice-oriented). According to Riel and Polin (in press), these three forms of communities — task-based, knowledge-based and practice-based — have different task features, learning goals, participation structures and growth mechanisms. At the same time, they typically are goal directed, focus on helping novices become more like the experts in the community and have mechanisms for interpersonal interaction, knowledge construction, collaboration and knowledge sharing.

Research suggests that interaction among online participants is vital to the establishment and growth of online communities (Barab & Duffy, 2000; Cummings et al., 2002). Even in brief course experiences, there are many ways to build rich

Copyright © 2004, Idea Group Inc. Copying or distributing in print or electronic forms without written permission of Idea Group Inc. is prohibited.

communities of learners with a sense of purpose, shared histories and identity (Schwier, 1999). For instance, opening icebreaking activities and coffee house discussion threads allow students to tell their peers more personal types of stories. In addition, a weekly ritual, such as a guest speaker, can lend expert knowledge to the community, while also providing a common event to talk about. A shared history provides members with stories to tell new members as well as a sense of joint accomplishment. In effect, there are others in that community who experienced something in the same way or have had similar reactions. Such experiences provide some psychological safety and opportunities for informal conversation as well as inside jokes or humor. Other strategies, such as weekly classroom polls or competitive online games, might create a set of common events and shared knowledge that can be referred to later on. As expertise grows and the semester unfolds, those in an online learning community might create joint products or engage in team related article discussions, panel discussions or debates. During many of these activities, instructors might be more informal and conversational in their commenting, thereby creating a feeling of psychological safety on the part of students.

A final major e-learning issue relates to grading and assessment (Champagne & Wisher, 2000). It is always vital to know if the course has been a success. Of course, the instructor must have a sense of what to actually assess and provide feedback on. When one creates a highly interactive environment, it naturally is difficult to respond to all student online work. Having a peer act as a Web buddy or e-mail pal, who provides weekly or even monthly feedback, can limit the time requirements placed on the instructor and free him or her for more facilitative roles. Grading can also be simplified by asking departments for grading support, when classes exceed a certain level. It is also streamlined by finding ways to grade key items in a portfolio of student online work.

Assessment and grading, nevertheless, remains a fairly open and unresolved area of e-learning for instructors who want to embed constructivist and learner-centered activities into their online courses. It is also a ripe area for further research and tool development. Some of this research may address why many online instructors are satisfied with traditional examinations and proctored or controlled testing centers, while others are anxious about any Web-based testing and evaluation and still others want to explore more progressive or constructivist assessment techniques.

Final Remarks and Next Steps

In this chapter, we outlined some of the changes and forces taking place in collaborative online environments. Many of these should help administrators and policy makers in forming new distance learning policies and practices as well as training programs for students and instructors. As pointed out throughout this chapter, anyone moderating within the online learning world must know how to

Copyright © 2004, Idea Group Inc. Copying or distributing in print or electronic forms without written permission of Idea Group Inc. is prohibited.

create and support a learner-centered experience. Just how can online learning be more meaningful, authentic and engaging? At the same time, it is vital to know some of the benefits and implications as well as potential problems and solutions with online learning. Instructors who understand such issues will likely find e-learning success. Such instructors will quickly discover that a complex mix of social, technical, pedagogical and managerial skill is required in this strange new world of e-learning. At the same time, they will understand that extensive course planning and task structuring as well as timely student feedback may be the most important skills for the online instructor.

What is next in the world of the online instructor? Given the time required for extensive e-learning feedback and the many pressing deadlines typically confronting instructors and trainers, perhaps intelligent e-learning agents will be developed to provide questions or advice on certain tasks (Kearsley, 1993). Along these same lines, intelligent tutoring systems or modules might be inserted into existing online courseware or tools to provide advice or support for student learning (Ritter & Koedinger, 1996). Such systems or learning aids might interpret or identify what the student needs to know and suggest appropriate activities, information or advice. Online mentoring programs and freelance instructor portals might sprout up simultaneously to offer human support and scaffolding. Given the increase in distance education needs and the unfamiliarity of instructors within these environments, the development of intellectual support tools and features is certainly an area ripe for exploration. Whether such tools can moderate e-learning from a learner-centered framework is still unknown. Whether intelligent tools will lighten the e-learning roles required of instructors is also unknown. What is known, however, is that as additional e-learning research and development occurs, we will begin to better understand how to successfully moderate or facilitate student collaboration and interaction in e-learning environments. Whatever the direction of e-learning, it will be exciting.

REFERENCES

Alexander, P. & Murphy, P. K. (1994). *The research base for APA's learned-centered psychological principles.* Paper presented at the annual meeting of the American Educational Research Association, New Orleans, Louisiana, USA.

American Psychological Association. (1993). *Learner-Centered Psychological Principles: Guidelines for School Reform and Restructuring.* Washington, DC: American Psychological Association and the Mid-continent Regional Educational Laboratory.

Angeli, C., Valanides, N., & Bonk, C. J. (2003). Communication in a Web-based conferencing system: The quality of computer-mediated instruction. *British Journal of Educational Technology, 34*(1), 31-43.

Copyright © 2004, Idea Group Inc. Copying or distributing in print or electronic forms without written permission of Idea Group Inc. is prohibited.

Ashton, S., Roberts, T., & Teles, L. (1999). *Investigation the role of the instructor in collaborative online environments*. Poster session presented at the Computer-Supported Collaborative Learning 1999 Conference, Stanford University, California, USA.

Bailey, M. L. & Luetkehans, L. (1998). *Ten Great Tips for Facilitating Virtual Learning Teams* (Report No. IR018979). Paper presented in at the Distance Teaching and Learning Conference '98, Madison, WI. Proceedings of the annual conference on distance teaching and learning. (ERIC Document Reproduction Service No. ED 422 838).

Barab, S. A. & Duffy, T. (2000). From practice fields to communities of practice. In D. Jonassen, & S. M. Land. (Eds.), *Theoretical Foundations of Learning Environments* (pp. 25-56). Mahwah, NJ: Lawrence Erlbaum Associates.

Barab, S. A., MaKinster, J. G., & Scheckler, R. (in press). Designing systems dualities: Characterizing an online professional development community. In S. A. Barab, R. Kling, & J. Gray (Eds.), *Designing for Virtual Communities in the Service of Learning*. Cambridge, MA: Cambridge University Press.

Barbian, J. (2002). Blended works: here's proof! *Online Learning, 6*(6), 26-28, 30-31.

Berge, Z. L. (1995). Facilitating computer conferencing: Recommendations from the field. *Educational Technology, 35*(1), 22-30.

Besser, H., & Bonn, M. (1997). Interactive distance-independent education. *Journal of Education for Library and Information Science, 38*(1), 35-43.

Bonk, C. J. (2001). *Online teaching in an online world*. Retrieved Nov. 17, 2002, from the web site: http://PublicationShare.com.

Bonk, C. J. & Cummings, J. A. (1998). A dozen recommendations for placing the student at the centre of Web-based learning. *Educational Media International, 35*(2), 82-89.

Bonk, C. J. & Dennen, V. P. (1999). Teaching on the Web: With a little help from my pedagogical friends. *Journal of Computing in Higher Education, 11*(1), 3-28.

Bonk, C. J. & Kim, K. A. (1998). Extending sociocultural to adult learning. In M. C. Smith & T. Pourchot (Eds.), *Adult Learning and Development: Perspectives from Educational Psychology* (pp. 67-88). Mahwah, NJ: Lawrence Erlbaum Associates.

Bonk, C. J. & King, K. S. (eds.). (1998). *Electronic Collaborators: Learner-Centered Technologies for Literacy, Apprenticeship, and Discourse*. Mahwah, NJ: Lawrence Erlbaum.

Bonk, C. J. & Reynolds, T. H. (1997). Learner-centered Web instruction for higher-order thinking, teamwork, and apprenticeship. In B. H. Khan (Ed.),

Copyright © 2004, Idea Group Inc. Copying or distributing in print or electronic forms without written permission of Idea Group Inc. is prohibited.

Web-Based Instruction (pp. 167-178). Englewood Cliffs, NJ: Educational Technology Publications.

Bonk, C. J. & Wisher, R. A. (2000). *Applying collaborative and e-learning tools to military distance learning: A research framework.* (Tech. Rep. No. 1107). Retrieved Nov. 17, 2002, from the web site: http://courseshare.com/Reports.php.

Bonk, C. J., Angeli, C., Malikowski, S., & Supplee, L. (2001, August). *Holy COW: Scaffolding case-based "Conferencing on the Web" with preservice teachers.* Retrieved Nov. 17, 2002, from the web site: http://www.usdla.org/html/journal/AUG01_Issue/article01.html.

Bonk, C. J., Appelman, R., & Hay, K. E. (1996). Electronic conferencing tools for student apprenticeship and perspective taking. *Educational Technology, 36*(5), 8-18.

Bonk, C. J., Cummings, J. A., Hara, N., Fischler, R., & Lee, S. M. (2000). A ten level Web integration continuum for higher education. In B. Abbey (Ed.), *Instructional and Cognitive Impacts of Web-Based Education* (pp. 56-77). Hershey, PA: Idea Group Publishing.

Bonk, C. J., Ehman, L., Hixon, E., & Yamagata-Lynch, E. (2002). The pedagogical TICKIT: Teacher institute for curriculum knowledge about the integration of technology. *Journal of Technology and Teacher Education, 10*(2), 205-233.

Bonk, C. J., Hansen, E. J., Grabner-Hagen, M. M., Lazar, S., & Mirabelli, C. (1998). Time to "connect": Synchronous and asynchronous case-based dialogue among preservice teachers. In C. J. Bonk & K. S. King (Eds.), *Electronic Collaborators: Learner-Centered Technologies for Literacy, Apprenticeship, and Discourse* (pp. 289-314). Mahwah, NJ: Erlbaum.

Bonk, C. J., Hara, H., Dennen, V., Malikowski, S., & Supplee, L. (2000). We're in TITLE to dream: Envisioning a community of practice, "The Intraplanetary Teacher Learning Exchange." *CyberPsychology and Behavior, 3*(1), 25-39.

Bonk, C. J., Kirkley, J. R., Hara, N., & Dennen, N. (2001). Finding the instructor in post-secondary online learning: Pedagogical, social, managerial, and technological locations. In J. Stephenson (Ed.), *Teaching and Learning Online: Pedagogies for New Technologies* (pp. 76-97). London: Kogan Page.

Bonk, C. J., Malikowski, S., Angeli, C., & East, J. (1998). Web-based case conferencing for preservice teacher education: electronic discourse from the field. *Journal of Educational Computing Research, 19*(3), 267-304.

Bourne, J. R. (1998). Net-learning: strategies for on-campus and off-campus network-enabled learning. *Journal of Asynchronous Learning Networks, 2*(2), 70-88.

Copyright © 2004, Idea Group Inc. Copying or distributing in print or electronic forms without written permission of Idea Group Inc. is prohibited.

Bracewell, R., Breuleux, A., Laferrière, T., Benoit, J., & Abdous, M. (1998). *The Emerging Contribution of Online Resources and Tools to Classroom Learning and Teaching.* Burnaby, British Columbia, Canada: TeleLearning Network Inc.

Brescia, W. (2001). *Using a telementoring taxonomy in a World Wide Web instructional environment.* Unpublished doctoral dissertation, Indiana University, Bloomington, Indiana, USA.

Brown, J. S., Collins, A., & Duguid, P. (1989). Situated cognition and the culture of learning. *Educational Researcher, 18*(1), 32-41.

Carr, S. (2000, Feb. 11). As distance education comes of age, the challenge is keeping the students. *The Chronicle of Higher Education,* 1-8. Retrieved Nov. 17, 2002, from the web site: http://chronicle.com/free/v46/i23/23a00101.htm.

Champagne, M. & Wisher, R. (2000). Design considerations for distance learning evaluations. In K. Mantyla (Ed.), *The ASTD 2000 Distance Learning Yearbook: The Newest Trends and Technologies,* pp. 261-286. New York: McGraw-Hill.

Chong, S. M. (1998). Models of asynchronous computer conferencing for collaborative learning in large college classes. In C. J. Bonk & K. S. King (Eds.), *Electronic Collaborators: Learner-Centered Technologies for Literacy, Apprenticeship, and Discourse* (pp. 157-182). Mahwah, NJ: Erlbaum.

Chung, H., Rodes, P., & Knapczyk, D. (1998). *Using Web conferencing to promote ownership in distance education coursework* (Report No. IR019242). Orlando, FL: Presented at WebNet 98 World Conference of the WWW, Internet, and Intranet Proceedings. (ERIC Document Reproduction Service No. ED 427 691).

Collis, B. & De Boer, W. (1999). The TeleTOP method at the University of Twente. *International Journal of Educational Telecommunications, 5*(4), 331-359.

Cooney, D. H. (1998). Sharing aspects within Aspects: real-time collaboration within the high school English classroom. In C. J. Bonk & K. S. King (Eds.), *Electronic Collaborators: Learner-Centered Technologies for Literacy, Apprenticeship, and Discourse* (pp. 263-287). Mahwah, NJ: Erlbaum.

Cummings, J. A. (2000). *Debate in the virtual classroom.* Unpublished manuscript, Indiana University at Bloomington, USA.

Cummings, J. A., Bonk, C. J., & Jacobs, F. R. (2002). Twenty-first century college syllabi: Options for online communication and interactivity. *Internet and Higher Education, 5*(1), 1-19.

Dennen, V. & Bonk, C. J. (2003). *Cases, conferencing, and communities of practice: a qualitative study of online mentoring for preservice teachers.* Manuscript submitted for publication.

Copyright © 2004, Idea Group Inc. Copying or distributing in print or electronic forms without written permission of Idea Group Inc. is prohibited.

Dennen, V. P. (2001). *The design and facilitation of asynchronous discussion activities in Web-based courses.* Unpublished doctoral dissertation, Indiana University at Bloomington, USA.

Dillon, C. L. & Walsh, S. M. (1992). Faculty: the neglected resource in distance education. *The American Journal of Distance Education, 6*(3), 5-21.

Doherty, P. B. (1998). Learner control in asynchronous learning environments. *Asynchronous Learning Networks Magazine, 2*(2), 1-11.

Duffy, T. H., Dueber, W., & Hawley, C. L. (1998). Critical thinking in a distributed environment: a pedagogical base for the design of conferencing systems. In C. J. Bonk & K. S. King (Eds.), *Electronic Collaborators: Learner-Centered Technologies for Literacy, Apprenticeship, and Discourse* (pp 51-78). Mahwah, NJ: Erlbaum.

Firdyiwek, Y. (1999). Web-based courseware tools: Where is the pedagogy? *Educational Technology, 39*(1), 29-34.

Ganzel, R. (2001, May). Associated learning. *Online Learning, 5*(5), 36-38, 40-41.

Gaud, W. S. (1999). Assessing the impact of Web courses. *Syllabus, 13*(4), 49-50.

Halpern, D. (1999) Teaching for critical thinking: Helping college students develop the skills and dispositions of a critical thinker. *New Directions for Teaching and Learning, 80,* 69-74.

Hannafin, M. J. & Land, S. M. (1997). The foundations and assumptions of technology-enhanced student-centered learning environment. *Instructional Science, 25,* 167-202.

Hannafin, M. J., Hill, J. R., & Land, S. M. (1997). Student-centered learning and interactive multimedia: Status, issued, and implication. *Contemporary Education, 68*(2), 94-99.

Harasim, L. (1990). Online education: An environment for collaboration and intellectual amplification. In L. Harasim (Ed.), *Online Education: Perspectives on a New Environment* (pp. 39-64). New York: Praeger Publishers.

Harasim, L. M. (1993). Networlds: Networks as a social space. In L. M. Harasim (Ed.), *Global Networks: Computers and International Communication.* Cambridge, MA: MIT Press.

Harasim, L. (2003). *Online collaborative learning: a paradigm shift in educational models and practice.* Unpublished manuscript. Simon Fraser University, Burnaby, British Columbia, Canada.

Hoffman, J. (2001). Blended learning case study. *Learning Circuits.* Retrieved Nov. 17, 2002, from the web site: http://www.learningcircuits.org/2001/apr2001/hofmann.html.

Kearsley, G. (1993). Intelligent agents and instructional systems: Implications of a new paradigm. *Journal of Artificial Intelligence and Education, 4*(4), 295-304.

Copyright © 2004, Idea Group Inc. Copying or distributing in print or electronic forms without written permission of Idea Group Inc. is prohibited.

Kim, K. J. & Bonk, C. J. (2002). Cross-cultural comparisons of online collaboration among pre-service teachers in Finland, Korea, and the United States. *Journal of Computer-Mediated Communication, 8*(1). Retrieved Nov. 17, 2002, from the web site: http://www.ascusc.org/jcmc/vol8/issue1/kimandbonk.html.

Kulp, R. (1999). *Effective Collaboration in Corporate Distributed Learning: Ten Best Practices for Curriculum Owners, Developers and Instructors*. Chicago, IL: IBM Learning Services.

Laster, S. J. (2003, February). Creating a blended MBA program. *Syllabus, 16*(7), 33-35.

Lawrence, B. H. (1996-1997). Online course delivery: Issues of faculty development. *Journal of Educational Technology Systems, 25*(2), 127-131.

Learner-centered psychological principles revised. (1996). *Newsletter for Educational Psychologists, 19*(2), 10.

Levin, D., & Ben-Jacob, M. G. (1998). *Using collaboration in support of distance learning* (Report No. IR019267). Orlando, FL: Presented at WebNet 98 World Conference of the WWW, Internet, and Intranet Proceedings. (ERIC Document Reproduction Service No. ED 427 716.)

Levin, J. & Waugh, M. (1998). Teaching teleapprenticeships: Electronic network-based educational frameworks for improving teacher education. *Interactive Learning Environments, 6* (1/2), 39-58.

Lotus Institute. (1996). *Distributed learning: Approaches, technologies, and solutions*. White Paper. Cambridge, MA.

Mantyla, K. (2001). *Blended e-learning: The power is in the mix*. Alexandria, VA: American Society for Training & Development.

Mason, R. (1991). Moderating educational computer conferencing. *DEOSNEWS, 1*(19), 1-11.

Mason, R. (1998). Models of online courses. *Asynchronous Learning Networks Magazine, 2*(2), 1-11.

McIsaac, M. S., Blocher, J. M., Mahes, V., & Vrasidas, C. (1999). Student and teacher perceptions of interaction in online computer-mediated communication. *Educational Media International, 36*(2), 121-131.

Murray, B. (2000, April). Reinventing class discussion online. *Monitor on Psychology, 31*(4), 54-56.

National Center for Education Statistics (NCES). (1999). (Lewis, L., Snow, K., Farris, E., Levin, D., & Greene, B.) (1999). *Distance education at postsecondary education institutions: 1997-98* (NCES 2000-013). Washington, DC: U.S. Department of Education.

National Education Association. (2000). A survey of traditional and distance learning higher education members. Washington, DC: National Education Association. Retrieved Nov. 17, 2002, from the web sites: http://www.nea.org/he; http://www.nea.org/he/abouthe/dlstudy.pdf.

Copyright © 2004, Idea Group Inc. Copying or distributing in print or electronic forms without written permission of Idea Group Inc. is prohibited.

Oliver, R. (1999). Exploring strategies for on-line teaching and learning. *Distance Education, 20*(2), 240-254.

Oliver, R. (2001). Exploring the development of critical thinking skills through a Web-supported problem-based learning environment. In J. Stephenson (Ed.), *Teaching and Learning Online: Pedagogies for New Technologies* (pp. 98-111). London: Kogan Page.

Oliver, R. & McLoughlin C. (1999). Curriculum and learning-resources issues arising from the use of Web-based course support systems. *International Journal of Educational Telecommunications, 5*(4), 419-436.

Olsen, F. (2001, Dec. 21). Getting ready for a new generation of course management systems. *The Chronicle of Higher Education.* Retrieved April 2, 2003, from the web site: http://chronicle.com/weekly/v48/i17/17a02501.htm.

Orvis, K. L., Wisher, R. A., Bonk, C. J., & Olson, T. (2002). Communication patterns during synchronous Web-based military training in problem solving. *Computers in Human Behavior, 18*(6), 783-795.

Paul, R. (1995). *Critical Thinking: How to Prepare Students for a Rapidly Changing World.* Santa Rosa, CA: Foundation for Critical Thinking.

Paulsen, M. F. (1995). Moderating educational computer conferences. In Z. L. Berge & M. P. Collins (Eds.), *Computer-Mediated Communication and the On-Line Classroom in Distance Education,* pp. 31-57. Cresskill, NJ: Hampton Press.

Peffers, K. & Bloom, S. (1999). Internet-based innovations for teaching IS courses: The state of adoption, 1998-2000. *Journal of Information Technology Theory and Applications, 1*(1). Retrieved July 21, 1999, from the web site: http://clam.rutgers.edu/~ejournal/spring99/survey.htm.

Report of the University of Illinois Teaching at an Internet Distance Seminar, The. (1999). *Teaching at an Internet distance: the pedagogy of online teaching and learning,* pp. 1-59. Urbana-Champaign, IL: The University of Illinois. Retrieved Nov. 17, 2002, from the web site: http://www.vpaa.uillinois.edu/tid/report/.

Rice-Lively, M. L. (1994). Wired warp and woof: An ethnographic study of a networking class. *Internet Research, 4*(4), 20-35.

Riel, M. & Polin, L. (in press). Learning communities: Common ground and critical differences in designing technical environments. In S. A. Barab, R. Kling, & J. Gray (Eds.), *Designing for Virtual Communities in the Service of Learning.* Cambridge, MA: Cambridge University Press.

Ritter, S. & Koedinger, K.R. (1996). An architecture for plug-in tutor agents. *Journal of Artificial Intelligence in Education, 7*(3/4), 315-347.

Rogan, J. M. & Denton, C. (1996). *Online mentoring: reflections and suggestions.* Paper presented at TelEd and Multimedia 96, Tampa, FL, December 5-8, 1996.

Copyright © 2004, Idea Group Inc. Copying or distributing in print or electronic forms without written permission of Idea Group Inc. is prohibited.

Rogers, D. L. (2000, Spring/Summer). A paradigm shift: Technology integration for higher education in the new millennium. *Educational Technology Review, 13,* 19-26.

Ross, J. A. (1996). *Computer communication skills and participation in a computer-m course* (Report No. IR017877). New York. Paper presented at the Annual Conference of the American Educational Research Association. (ERIC Document Reproduction Service No. ED 395565).

Salmon, G. (2000). *E-Moderating: The Key to Teaching and Learning Online.* Sterling, VA: Stylus Publishing.

Salomon, G. (1998). Novel constructivist learning environments and novel technologies: Some issues to be concerned with. *Research Dialogue in Learning and Instruction, 1,* 3-12.

Schwier, R.A. (1999, June). Turning learning environments into learning communities: Expanding the notion of interaction in multimedia. *Proceedings of the World Conference on Educational Multimedia, Hypermedia and Telecommunications,* pp. 282-286.

Selinger, M. (1997). Open learning, electronic communications and beginning teachers. *European Journal of Teacher Education, 20*(1), 71-84.

Selinger, M. (1999, August). *The role of the teacher/moderator in virtual learning environments.* Paper presented at the European Research on Learning and Instruction Conference, Gothenburg, Sweden.

Stephenson, J. (2001). Learner-managed learning — An emerging pedagogy for online learning. In J. Stephenson (Ed.), *Teaching and Learning Online: Pedagogies for New Technologies* (pp. 219-224). London: Kogan Page.

Stuckey, B. Hedberg, J., & Lockyer, L. (2002). *The Case for Community: On-Line and Ongoing Professional Support for Communities of Practice.* New South Wales, Australia: University of Wollongong.

Thach, L. (1993). Exploring the role of the deliverer in distance education. *International Journal of Instructional Media, 20*(4), 289-307.

Tharp, R. & Gallimore, R. (1988). *Rousing Minds to Life: Teaching, Learning, and Schooling in a Social Context.* Cambridge, MA: Cambridge University Press.

Vygotsky, L. S. (1978). *Mind in Society: The Development of Higher Psychological Processes* (ed. by M. Cole, V. John-Steiner, S. Scribner, & E. Souberman). Cambridge, MA: Harvard University Press.

Wagner, E. D. & McCombs, B. L. (1995). Learner centered psychological principles in practice: Esigns for distance education. *Educational Technology, 35*(2), 32-35.

Wood, R. E. (1999). Beyond the electronic reserve shelf: Pedagogical possibilities and resources in Web-enhanced courses. *Syllabus, 13*(4), 54-56.

Copyright © 2004, Idea Group Inc. Copying or distributing in print or electronic forms without written permission of Idea Group Inc. is prohibited.

ENDNOTES

[1]   For the purposes of this chapter, the term e-learning refers to online instruction and distance learning made possible by the World Wide Web.

[2]   For additional online moderator resources, see the eModerators homepage at http://www.emoderators.com/moderators.shtml or http://www.emoderators.com/index.shtml.

[3]   The findings and recommendations listed in Tables 3 and 4 stem from our previous research on online learning (e.g., Bonk & King, 1998; Bonk & Wisher, 2000). These tables are intended to provide practical information and suggestions for online instructors as well as for administrative decision makers in higher education and corporate or military training environments.

Copyright © 2004, Idea Group Inc. Copying or distributing in print or electronic forms without written permission of Idea Group Inc. is prohibited.

Chapter IV

Supporting Distributed Problem-Based Learning: The Use of Feedback Mechanisms in Online Learning

Joerg Zumbach
University of Heidelberg, Germany

Annette Hillers
University of Heidelberg, Germany

Peter Reimann
University of Sydney, Australia

ABSTRACT

In this chapter we discuss possibilities and shortcomings of Internet usage for distributed problem-based learning. Several problems with the use of computer-mediated communication for collaborative learning online are identified. In our approaches we use data that is automatically tracked during computer-mediated communication and extract relevant information for feedback purposes. Partly automatically, partly manually prepared the feedback is a rich resource for learners to manage their own collaboration

Copyright © 2004, Idea Group Inc. Copying or distributing in print or electronic forms without written permission of Idea Group Inc. is prohibited.

process as well as subsequent problem-solving processes. In a synchronous and an asynchronous distributed problem-based learning environment, we show how we applied this methodology to support learners' motivation and problem solving. Analyses show encouraging benefits of our approach in overcoming common problems with computer-mediated communication.

INTRODUCTION

When James Cook started his last journey to find the Northwest Passage through North America, his wife was angry with him because he had promised her that he would never go on a long voyage again. During the whole trip he was supposed to be in an ill-tempered mood totally different from his normal style, badly collaborating with his crew and behaving harshly and unfairly to the native people he met. No wonder that he was killed on the islands of Hawaii in 1779. What he did not know was that his wife had already forgiven him, so some might say that if he had seen her smile, this would have changed the whole course of history. Is this true? Does such a form of emotional feedback have an impact on people's performance in a group situation? Did Cook die due to a lack of feedback?

Nowadays, most of the white spots on Earth have been explored and Internet technologies have made the world smaller. People communicate, collaborate and even learn together using the Internet. There is much ongoing research about how to use computer-mediated communication (CMC) for task oriented groups. Actually, little research is dedicated to the use of technology for feedback purposes during online collaboration, especially in distributed problem-based learning. There are also many studies exploring feedback mechanisms in individual computer-based learning, especially for knowledge acquisition purposes. Research concerning intelligent tutoring systems (ITS) has provided evidence for a meaningful use of individual feedback based on learner-program interaction (Wenger, 1987). Unfortunately, this tradition has yet not reached contemporary learning approaches using computer-supported collaborative learning (CSCL).

Besides the use of computer generated feedback on a task level, there is hardly any exploration of its effects on a group's interaction level. Although interacting and communicating is crucial to problem-based learning (PBL), most approaches transferring PBL into a network-based learning environment do not pursue approaches to give learner support on this level.

Some earlier research, for example Mandl, Fischer, Frey and Jeuck (1985), discusses some computer-based feedback mechanisms and functions, but does not specifically refer to a group context. So far, these investigations have not been carried further. Possible reasons might be a lack of underlying theoretical assumptions and derivations of specific hypotheses.

Copyright © 2004, Idea Group Inc. Copying or distributing in print or electronic forms without written permission of Idea Group Inc. is prohibited.

Our investigations so far let us assume that different kinds of feedback mechanisms can influence online learning groups in a positive manner. We examined the influence of providing groups with feedback about members' interactions as well as their problem-solving processes. These selected feedback mechanisms have a positive impact on an online collaborative learning group's motivation, interaction, problem-solving abilities and learning. If these findings can hold true in future replications, questions about how to use feedback approaches in the most appropriate form and quantity, as well as when and why to use them will be of great interest. For the beginning, however, we first need to find out more about feedback effects in the online group situation in general. In this chapter, we (1) provide a theoretical background to explain feedback effects within groups, (2) explore techniques of how to provide feedback in a CSCL environment, and (3) give two concrete examples of empirical studies (including our own), showing how to implement different kinds of feedback into online learning environments and investigate their effects on groups' performances.

BACKGROUND: PBL GOES INTERNET

Our hypotheses about feedback effects in CSCL are mainly derived from two research areas: PBL (e.g., Barrows, 1985; Thomas, 1997) and the time interaction and performance theory (TIP) by McGrath (1991). PBL is related to the CSCL paradigm with regard to its philosophy (Koschmann, 1996): Both approaches regard learning rather as a distributed process than a result. Knowledge acquisition happens in an implicit manner. When using PBL as a distributed learning approach over the Internet (dPBL) (e.g., Björck, 2001), both approaches merge together.

PBL

The basic principles of PBL can be summarized as follows (e.g., Barrows, 1985; Thomas, 1997): Learning in small groups is initiated through authentic and mostly ill-structured problems. Students discuss these problems in order to identify their state of knowledge and what they need to know. This leads them to the definition of learning objectives and the organization of each individual's tasks and learning steps. Afterwards, each student gathers problem-relevant information from literature, databases, experts, etc., in order to complete his or her objectives and to solve the problem. The individual results are collected and discussed in a follow-up meeting, which is also moderated by a tutor. Then a new problem is given.

The small group discussion among students and tutor is crucial to the PBL process (Viller, 1991). Small group discussions are important in identifying

Copyright © 2004, Idea Group Inc. Copying or distributing in print or electronic forms without written permission of Idea Group Inc. is prohibited.

learning issues resulting from the problem in the initial phase of a PBL session and the problem-solution phase. While students are discussing, they define what to learn, distribute tasks, apply previous and newly collected knowledge and discuss solutions to the problem (Dolmans, Schmidt, & Gijselaers, 1994). Small group discussions enhance knowledge acquisition and deepen students' understanding by means of social knowledge construction. Taking a look at a single PBL unit, that is students working on one problem taken out of a complete curriculum, we often find the following typical process (see Figure 1).

At the beginning of a PBL unit, there is a problem that should initiate discussion among learners about what they actually know about the problem, what caused the problem and how to solve it. Students have to identify learning objectives and to collect all the information they already have (Dolmans et al., 1994; Gijselaers, 1996). Providing a well-designed problem, the group members have to discuss (a) which problems should be addressed, (b) which possible learning objectives can be identified, (c) how a problem could be solved, (d) how to distribute single tasks among group members, and (e) where to locate possible resources for the collection of relevant information. As this collaborative task is a crucial phase in the whole process, it should be supported by a tutor supervising the learners' progress (e.g., Schmidt & Moust, 1995). After the initial discussion process, students have to seek and collect the necessary information to solve the problems and reach the objectives. This information can be found in textbooks, libraries or by asking experts from the faculty. Usually this phase of individual study lasts from one day to several weeks, depending on the organization of the curriculum.

A PBL unit ends with a final discussion of the problem, including recommendations for one or more possible solutions. At this point, the results should be

Figure 1: The Process of Working on a Single Problem During a PBL Course or Curriculum

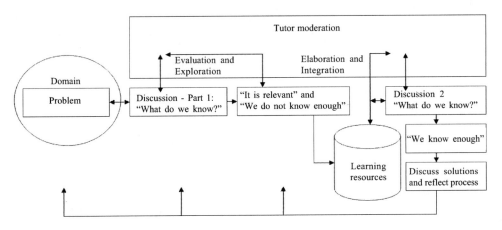

Copyright © 2004, Idea Group Inc. Copying or distributing in print or electronic forms without written permission of Idea Group Inc. is prohibited.

presented in a structured and organized way, combined with an argumentation resolving the results. Each student should present his or her own work concerning the learning objectives. Learners should also reflect critically on (a) their own and others' contributions, (b) the process, (c) experiences during the problem-solving process, (d) other possible solutions, and (e) what they have actually learned (Koschmann, Feltovich, Myers, & Barrows, 1995). The role of the tutor is crucial to the PBL process, because he or she is guiding students during the problem-solving process. While research provides no clear evidence whether a tutor should be an expert in the field of the problem or not, he has to guide small group discussion and to lead students in accomplishing their learning objectives.

In addition to the already mentioned PBL principles, we pursued an approach that combines PBL with a more constructionist approach: learning by design (LBD) (e.g., Kolodner, 1997). LBD implies that problem solving always demands creation of deliverables. This kind of learning requires students to externalize their knowledge, to discuss different possible solutions and to provide a design rationale. In our approaches, we combine LBD, PBL and CSCL by means of Internet technologies.

Bringing Together PBL and CSCL: dPBL

During the last two decades there have been some attempts to combine PBL with CSCL. In early approaches (e.g., Koschmann, Myers, Feltovich, & Barrows, 1994), local area networks have been used to foster a technology-based PBL. Nowadays, Internet technology allows us to export collaborative problem solving out of the classroom into the digital world. There are several reports about synchronous as well as asynchronous PBL courses accessible over the Internet. One example for dPBL is provided by Cameron, Barrows and Crooks (1999). In their study they reported a synchronous computer-mediated PBL scenario. Students and their facilitator communicated during small group problem discussions via conferencing software (they used Microsoft's NetMeeting). Their qualitative analysis showed advantages of CMC in regards to student participation: CMC led to an equal distribution of comments among all participants. That means, technology allows each group member to answer the facilitator's questions. During face-to-face sessions, only one student was able to provide an answer to a question. If this answer was correct and exhaustive, all other participants remained passive until another question came up. Furthermore, CMC provided an automatic storage of all students' as well as facilitator's contributions from the problem discussion. This is not always advantageous as Cameron et al. (1999) showed: especially navigation and scrolling, e.g., long chat protocols can influence students' concentration and/or their focus on discussions.

Although research on dPBL is growing, there are rarely studies with controlled experimental groups. Most authors remain on a qualitative level (e.g.,

Copyright © 2004, Idea Group Inc. Copying or distributing in print or electronic forms without written permission of Idea Group Inc. is prohibited.

Milter & Stinson, 1999a, b; Steinkuehler, Derry, Woods, & Hmelo-Silver, 2002). There are few studies comparing dPBL and PBL. Thomas (2000) reported higher drop-out rates in an MBA-program using a dPBL course (65%), compared to a face-to-face course (10%). He also mentioned several technical problems. Such difficulties are also reported by Björck (2001). Technological problems (e.g., getting connected or usability problems) are not the only obstacle in online learning. Dobson and McCracken (1997) mention problems resulting from insufficient group facilitation. What are the causes for these problems reported from many collaborative online courses? An answer can be found at the interface of CMC theory and technological restrictions.

A useful theoretical framework to explain determinants of successful and less successful (online learning) groups is the Time, Interaction and Performance Theory (McGrath, 1991). Besides many other propositions about the nature of groups, it states that groups always undertake three functions at the same time: One is working on the common task together (production function), another is maintaining the communication and interaction among group members (group well-being) and the last is helping the individual members where necessary (member support).

Performance and success of a group depend on how well the group can reconcile its functions and tasks with the help of its members' activities. Therefore, methods are needed to support group members in all three functions as well as possible, in order to use the group's potential in the best possible way and to obtain best results[1].

Another crucial element that has to be discussed in regard to the background of a group's functioning is communication. Communication among group members in face-to-face situations differs greatly from online learning groups. In many cases, the latter communicate only via text-based tools, such as an online platform or other text-based Internet technologies. Any form of non-verbal communication, like gestures and facial expressions, cannot be perceived by the other group members. Typing on a keyboard needs more time than talking to each other, therefore corresponding text-messages discussing well-being are less likely to be sent. Hence, online groups presumably have more difficulties with the maintenance of their member support and well-being functions (e.g., Kiesler & Sproull, 1987; Thomas, 2000).

Several studies support findings that the kind of media that is used for the group interaction has an impact on various dimensions of group performance and outcomes. Some studies show that groups that communicate via computer are less productive than face-to-face groups, though some task performances, like overall effectiveness, do not show differences (e.g., Straus & McGrath, 1994). The picture still remains unclear. Questions concerning methodologies are still not, or are only insufficiently, answered especially in regard to how best to provide cognitive, emotional and social support to online groups.

Copyright © 2004, Idea Group Inc. Copying or distributing in print or electronic forms without written permission of Idea Group Inc. is prohibited.

Supporting Online Learning Communities by Means of Feedback

Recent research is dedicated to finding support mechanisms for online collaborators. Many authors discuss possibilities of scaffolding by structuring CMC (e.g., Dobson & McCracken, 1997; Jonassen & Remides, 2002; Reiser, 2002). Common to all these approaches is the provision of a structure for discourse and/or problem solving. Instead of pre-structuring, we pursue a way to structure post-hoc interaction in online learning groups.

CMC itself provides the basis for this possibility. During CMC, all data can easily be stored and re-used for feedback purposes. In addition, software interfaces designed for CSCL allow the collection of individual quantitative data that can be used for further calculations in real time. Both data sources combined can easily be used to analyze individuals' as well as groups' behavioral processes automatically. In this way online learning groups provide the basis for feedback on their process by just collaborating.

So far, there has been only little research on this methodology. Barros and Verdejo (2000) describe an approach to provide feedback on group characteristics and individual behavior during computer-supported collaborative work, based on a set of attributes that are computed from data derived from learners' interactions. Their automatic feedback gives a qualitative description of a mediated group activity concerning three perspectives: a group's performance in reference to other groups, each member in reference to other members of the group and the group by itself. Their distance environment for group experiences (DEGREE) approach allows for extracting relevant information from online collaboration at different levels of abstraction. Although this approach seems to be very advantageous for enhancing online collaborators, Barros and Verdejo (2000) give no empirical evidence for the effectiveness of their asynchronous system. Jerman (2002) describes another possibility for providing feedback based on interaction data. He provides feedback on quantitative contribution behavior as well as learner interaction during a synchronous problem-solving task (controlling a traffic sign system). In an experiment, Jerman (2002) compared a group that received feedback about each individual learner's behavior. Another experimental group received feedback about the whole group's success. He showed that a detailed feedback containing each individual's data, enhanced learners' use of meta-cognitive strategies regarding problem solving as well as discourse.

Our research group follows this line of feedback research. We conducted two studies to examine feedback effects on online collaborators during CSCL. One purpose of these investigations is to provide post-hoc scaffolding for subsequent problem solving. Another purpose is to use CMC, extract data from discourses and provide abstracted views as a substitute for missing communication cues. In particular we investigated how the interaction in, and the perfor-

Copyright © 2004, Idea Group Inc. Copying or distributing in print or electronic forms without written permission of Idea Group Inc. is prohibited.

mance of, small problem-based learning groups that cooperate via Internet technologies in a highly self-organized fashion can be supported by means of interaction feedback as well as problem-solving feedback. Since the possibility of tracking and maintaining processes of participation and interaction is one of the advantages of online collaboration, ephemeral events can easily be turned into histories of potential use for the groups. We chose two ways to analyze how such group histories can be used for learning purposes. First, parameters of interaction like participation behavior, learners' motivation (self-ratings) and amount of contributions were recorded and fed back in a computationally aggregated manner as an additional information resource for the group. This data could thus be used to structure and plan group coordination and group well being. Second, we tracked group members' problem-solving behavior during design tasks and provided feedback by means of problem-solving protocols. These protocols can be used to enhance a group's problem-solving process for further tasks. Both studies testing our methodology in a synchronous and an asynchronous setting shall now be introduced more completely.

STUDY 1: AUTOMATIC FEEDBACK IN SYNCHRONOUS DPBL

Our first laboratory experiment (Zumbach, Mühlenbrock, Jansen, Reimann, & Hoppe, 2002) was designed as an exploratory study to test specific feedback techniques and their influence in an online collaboration learning environment.

For this purpose we designed a dPBL environment. In a sample of 18 students from the University of Heidelberg, we evaluated six groups of three members each. All students worked together synchronously via a computer network solving an information design problem. Each group collaborated for about two and a half hours (synchronously in one session). The task — strictly consistent for all groups and presented as a problem — was to design a hypertext course for a fictitious company. All necessary task materials were provided online. In addition, all learning resources related to online information design were accessible as hypertext.

As a communication platform, the software EasyDiscussing was specifically developed for this experiment in cooperation with the COLLIDE research group at Duisburg University, Germany. This Java-tool makes it possible to display a shared work space to the whole group that can be modified by each member simultaneously. It contains drag-and-drop functions, thematic annotation cards like "text" (for general comments or statements), "idea," "pro" and "con" to structure the discussion and offers a chat opportunity as well (see Figure 1). All parameters were recorded in so-called "action protocols" and analyzed either directly or after the study. This made it possible to check certain argumentative

Copyright © 2004, Idea Group Inc. Copying or distributing in print or electronic forms without written permission of Idea Group Inc. is prohibited.

structures that became obvious during the course work, and also opened up the possibility to provide feedback based on the data produced.

Feedback parameters were gained in the following way: every 20 minutes students were asked about their motivation and their emotional state on a five item ordinal scale (parameters relating to the well-being function: "How motivated are you to work on the problem?" and "How do you feel actually?"). These were displayed to the whole group by means of dynamic diagrams (see Figure 3), showing each group member's motivation and emotional state with the help of a line graph. As a quantitative parameter supporting the production function, the two diagrams showed each group member's absolute and relative amount of contribution.

In order to test feedback effects we divided the groups into experimental groups that received feedback and into control groups that did not receive any feedback. Both groups had to do a pre- and post-knowledge test, a test about attitudes towards cooperative learning (Neber, 1994), as well as some questions about their current motivation and emotional state. We assumed that the experimental groups would be more productive since they were given parameters that would enable them to fulfill their well-being and production functions more easily. They were assumed to contribute more ideas in an equally

Figure 2: The Design of the Communication Platform EasyDiscussing

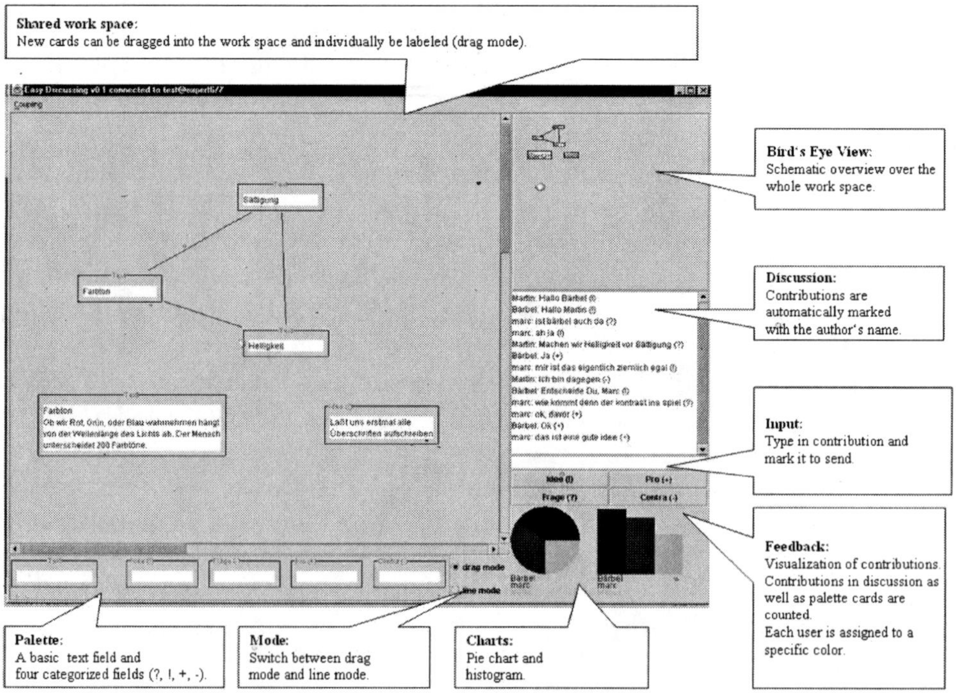

Copyright © 2004, Idea Group Inc. Copying or distributing in print or electronic forms without written permission of Idea Group Inc. is prohibited.

distributed manner, and show a greater amount of reflection, as far as interaction patterns were concerned, as opposed to the control groups.

The results of subjects' performance in the pre-test revealed no significant differences concerning domain knowledge. There were also no differences between both groups in post-test performance. Both groups mastered the post-test significantly better than the pre-test. There was no significant interaction between both tests and groups. We also found no significant differences regarding subjects' emotional data. The groups also showed no differences in pre- and post-tests regarding motivation except a significant interaction between groups and time of measurement. While subjects in the control condition without feedback did not show differences in motivation, experimental groups had an increase from pre-test to post-test. A closer view on interaction patterns in

Figure 3: Feedback on Emotion and Motivation

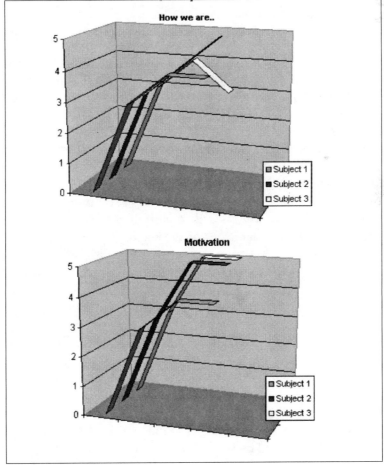

Copyright © 2004, Idea Group Inc. Copying or distributing in print or electronic forms without written permission of Idea Group Inc. is prohibited.

subjects' discussions also yielded a significant difference in the number of dyadic interactions in groups that received feedback on their contributions.

Overall, the effects of this study indicate that some processes in computer-supported collaboration can be influenced in a positive manner by means of a steady tracking of parameters outside the task itself and by immediate feedback of these to a group. Although intervention time in this experiment was short, we found positive influence of motivational feedback as well as feedback on contributions: communication patterns showed more interactive behavior for subjects of the experimental group. As a consequence of these effects, which indicate that our mechanisms have a positive influence on groups' production function as well as well being, we decided to examine these feedback strategies further. For that purpose we arranged a long-time intervention study containing the same kind of visual feedback.

STUDY 2: INVESTIGATING THE ROLE OF FEEDBACK MECHANISMS IN LONG-TIME ONLINE LEARNING

Our main target of this study was to test different treatment conditions concerning feedback with groups that collaborated solely through an asynchronous communication platform over a period of four months. In this study we examined groups from three to five members — 33 participants on the whole. These groups participated in a problem-based course about instructional design that was a mixture of PBL and learning-by-design. Learners were required to design several online courses for a fictitious company. These tasks were presented as problems within a cover story. Each problem had to be solved over periods of two weeks (i.e., an instructional design solution had to be presented for the problem). As in study one, all materials were accessible online and, additionally, tutors were available during the whole course to support the students if questions emerged. At the end of each task, the groups presented their results to other groups. The asynchronous communication facility was based on a Lotus Notes platform with merging tools that can manage documents with automatic display possibilities for interaction parameters and problem-solving protocols (see Figure 4).

All created documents as well as attachments were accessible over the collaboration platform. Provided meta-information showed when a document was created and who created it, so that interaction patterns became obvious and could be recorded. With the same technique of diagrams as in study one, motivational and quantitative production parameters could be fed back to the user, referred to as interaction histories. Students' problem-solving behavior, however, had to be analyzed by the tutors themselves and had to be provided as text documents (design histories) on the group's workspace. Invisible for the

Copyright © 2004, Idea Group Inc. Copying or distributing in print or electronic forms without written permission of Idea Group Inc. is prohibited.

Figure 4: Asynchronous Collaboration Platform with Feedback Mechanisms

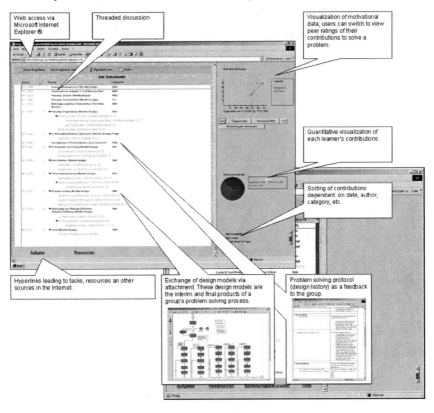

students, many detailed action protocols were recorded in the background and could later be used for exploratory or hypotheses testing analyses, depending on the research design.

In our study, the groups were randomly assigned to one of four treatment conditions: with interaction history only, with design history only, with both histories and without any feedback histories, i.e., a 2x2 design with the factors interaction history and design history. Several quantitative and qualitative measures to assess motivation, interaction, problem solving and learning effects were collected before, during and after the experimental phase on different scales, such as the student curriculum satisfaction inventory (Dods, 1997), or an adapted version of the critical thinking scale (Newman, Johnson, Webb, & Cochrane, 1997). We tried to answer the following question: What kind of influence does the administration of feedback in the form of design and interaction histories, as well as their different combinations, have on students' learning? Generally, we assumed that groups with any form of histories would perform better than those without, especially as far as the motivational and emotional aspects supporting the well-being function and the production aspects supporting the production function of a group are concerned.

Copyright © 2004, Idea Group Inc. Copying or distributing in print or electronic forms without written permission of Idea Group Inc. is prohibited.

The results show encouraging outcomes in favor of the application of feedback within the group process. Groups that were shown design histories on their work spaces presented significantly better results in knowledge tests, created qualitatively better products in the end, produced more contributions to the task and expressed a higher degree of reflection concerning their organization and coordination. At the same time, the presence of interaction histories influenced the group members' emotional attitude towards the curriculum and enhanced their motivation for the task. The interaction history's visualization regarding the number of contributions also slightly influenced the production function: Learners receiving this feedback produced more contributions than their counterparts without feedback. So far, it seems reasonable to conclude that different kinds of feedback influence different aspects of group behavior. Whereas feedback in the form of design histories seemed to influence a group's production function according to McGrath's (1991) conception of group functions, feedback in the form of interaction histories mainly effects a group's well-being function.

PROBLEMS AND FUTURE TRENDS

Since research on feedback effects in online environments is still in its infancy, our studies also struggled with some problems that need to be solved for future investigations. In particular, difficulties occurred with regard to the technical aspects of the software equipment, data organization, statistical analyses and the practical implementation of the learning environment. Besides the problem that the Lotus Notes platform could be unstable at times, some communication features could also be made more user-friendly as far. Moreover, the program created a large amount of informational data that took a long time to disentangle before it could be used further. An early filtering that already takes place during the information collection as well as further programs to structure the data pool are needed. For future research, it is desirable and necessary to carry on with analyses that take into account the sequential nature of the observations.

Given that the — just outlined — improvements can be put into practice, there are multiple perspectives for future research in the area of feedback effects. Questions can range from whether there are even more kinds of feedback supporting different aspects of group behavior, over which techniques can be used in an online learning environment, to the theoretical foundations of feedback effects in general. From our point of view, the most attractive question is whether there is an optimal combination of the two kinds of feedback we explored? Or should they just serve as separate measures? The aim must be to increase the benefits of feedback, while not overloading students with too much

Copyright © 2004, Idea Group Inc. Copying or distributing in print or electronic forms without written permission of Idea Group Inc. is prohibited.

superfluous information. This is what we tried to do by extracting data out of all available information and presenting these extractions as feedback.

CONCLUSION

Feedback in general has an impact on a group's performance, enhancing both qualitative and quantitative parameters of students' achievement. Due to the short history of research in the area of feedback in group-based computer-supported collaborative learning environments, the groundwork for more specific applications and the derivation of more precise hypotheses must be continued before it can reach more validated results on a larger scale.

In Cook's case, he would probably have liked to see that his wife had forgiven him. But whether a line diagram of his wife's positive emotional state towards him would have changed Cook's negative behavior will still remain a mystery.

REFERENCES

Barros, M. & Verdejo, M. (2000). Analysing student interaction processes in order to improve collaboration. The DEGREE approach. *International Journal of Artificial Intelligence in Education, 11,* 221-241.

Barrows, H. S. (1985). *How to Design a Problem-Based Curriculum for the Preclinical Years.* New York: Springer.

Björck, U. (2001, April). *Distributed problem-based learning in social economy — A study of the use of a structured method for education.* Paper presented at the Annual Meeting of the American Educational Research Association, Seattle, Washington, USA.

Cameron, T., Barrows, H. S., & Crooks, S. M. (1999). Distributed problem-based learning at Southern Illinois University School of Medicine. In C. Hoadley & J. Roschelle (Eds.), *Computer Support for Collaborative Learning. Designing New Media for a New Millenium: Collaborative Technology for Learning, Education, and Training* (pp. 86-94). Palo Alto, CA: Stanford University.

Dobson, M. & McCracken, J. (1997). Problem based learning: A means to evaluate multimedia courseware in science & technology in society. In T. Muldner & T. C. Reeves (Eds.), *Educational Multimedia & Hypermedia 1997.* Calgary, Canada: AACE.

Dods, R.F. (1997). An action research study of the effectiveness of problem-based learning in promoting the acquisition and retention of knowledge. *Journal of the Education of the Gifted, 20*(4), 423-437.

Copyright © 2004, Idea Group Inc. Copying or distributing in print or electronic forms without written permission of Idea Group Inc. is prohibited.

TOURO COLLEGE LIBRARY

Dolmans, D., Schmidt, H. G., & Gijselaers, W. H. (1994). The relationship between student-generated learning issues and self-study in problem-based learning. *Instructional Science, 22*(4), 251-267.

Gijselaers, W. H. (1996). Connecting problem-based practices with educational theory. In L. Wilkerson & W. H. Gijselaers (Eds.), *Bringing Problem-Based Learning to Higher Education: Theory and Practice* (pp. 13-21). San Francisco, CA: Jossey-Bass.

Jerman, P. (2002). Task and interaction regulation in controlling a traffic simulation. In G. Stahl (Ed.), *Computer Support for Collaborative Learning: Foundations for a CSCL Community* (pp. 601-602). Hillsdale, NJ: Erlbaum.

Jonassen, D. & Remides, H. (2002). Mapping alternative discourse structures onto computer conferences. In G. Stahl (Ed.), *Computer Support for Collaborative Learning: Foundations for a CSCL Community* (pp. 237-244). Hillsdale, NJ: Erlbaum.

Kiesler, S. & Sproull, L. S. (eds.). (1987). *Computing and Change on Campus.* New York: Cambridge University Press.

Kolodner, J. L. (1997). Educational implications of analogy. *American Psychologist, 52*(1), 57-66.

Koschmann, T. (Ed.) (1996). *CSCL. Theory and Practice of an Emerging Paradigm.* Mahwah, NJ: Lawrence Erlbaum.

Koschmann, T. D., Feltovich, P. J., Myers, A. C., & Barrows, H. S. (1995). *Implications of CSCL for problem-based learning.* Paper presented at the CSCL Conference in Bloomington, Indiana.

Koschmann, T. D., Myers, A. C., Feltovich, P. J., & Barrows, H. S. (1994). Using technology to assist in realizing effective learning and instruction: A principled approach to the use of computers in collaborative learning. *The Journal of the Learning Sciences, 3(3),* 227-264.

Mandl, H., Fischer, P. M., Frey, H.-D., & Jeuck, J. (1985). Wissensvermittlung durch ein computergestütztes Rückmeldungssystem [Teaching by means of a computer-assisted feedback system]. In H. Mandl & P.M. Fischer (Eds.), *Lernen im Dialog mit dem Computer* [Learning in dialogue with the computer] (pp. 179-190). München, Germany: Urban und Schwarzenberg.

McGrath, J. E. (1991). Time, interaction and performance (TIP). A theory of groups. *Small Group Research, 22,* 147-174.

Milter, R. G. & Stinson, J. E. (1999a). *Design and implementation of an electronic collaborative learning platform.* Retrieved on July 21, 2003 from the web site: http://www.ouwb.ohiou.edu/this_is_ouwb/papers/paper5.htm.

Milter, R. G. & Stinson, J. E. (1999b). *Using Lotus Notes to faciliate action learning.* Retrieved November 11, 2001, from the web site: http://mbawb.cob.ohiou.edu/paper1.html.

Copyright © 2004, Idea Group Inc. Copying or distributing in print or electronic forms without written permission of Idea Group Inc. is prohibited.

Neber, H. (1994). Entwicklung und Erprobung einer Skala für Präferenzen zum kooperativen und kompetitiven Lernen [Developing and testing a scale for cooperative and competitive learning]. *Psychologie in Erziehung und Unterricht, 41,* 282-290.

Newman, D. R., Johnson, C. Webb, B., & Cochrane, C. (1997). Evaluating the quality of learning in computer supported co-operative learning. *Journal of the American Society for Information Science, 48,* 484-495.

Reiser, B. (2002). Why scaffolding should sometimes make tasks more difficult for learners. In G. Stahl (Ed.), *Computer Support for Collaborative Learning: Foundations for a CSCL Community* (pp. 255-264). Hillsdale, NJ: Erlbaum.

Schmidt, H. G. & Moust, J. H. C. (1995). What makes a tutor effective? A structural-equations modeling approach to learning in problem-based curricula. *Academic Medicine, 70*(8), 708-714.

Steinkuehler, C. A., Derry, S. J., Woods, D. K., & Hmelo-Silver, C. E. (2002). The STEP environment for distributed problem-based learning on the World Wide Web. In G. Stahl (Ed.), *Computer Support for Collaborative Learning: Foundations for a CSCL Community* (pp. 227-226). Hillsdale, NJ: Erlbaum.

Straus, S. G. & McGrath, J. E. (1994). Does the medium matter? The interaction of task type and technology on group performance and member reactions. *Journal of Applied Psychology, 79*(1), 87-97.

Thomas, R. (2000). Evaluating the effectiveness of the Internet for the delivery of an MBA programme. *Innovations in Education and Training International, 37*(2), 97-102.

Thomas, R. E. (1997). Problem-based learning: Measurable outcomes. *Medical Education, 31*(5), 320-329.

Viller, S. (1991). The group facilitator: a CSCW perspective. In L. Bannon, M. Robinson & K. Schmidt (Eds.), *Proceedings of the Second European Conference on Computer-Supported Cooperative Work* (pp. 145-152). Amsterdam: Kluwer.

Wenger, E. (1987). *Artificial Intelligence and Tutoring Systems.* Los Altos, CA: Morgan Kaufmann.

Zumbach, J., Mühlenbrock, M., Jansen, M., Reimann, P., & Hoppe, H.-U. (2002). Multidimensional tracking in virtual learning teams. In G. Stahl (Ed.), *Computer Support for Collaborative Learning: Foundations for a CSCL Community* (pp. 650-651). Hillsdale, NJ: Erlbaum.

Copyright © 2004, Idea Group Inc. Copying or distributing in print or electronic forms without written permission of Idea Group Inc. is prohibited.

ENDNOTE

[1]   In this chapter we try to provide possible enhancements of the production function and the group well being by means of enriching CMC (we do not directly focus on the member support function here).

Copyright © 2004, Idea Group Inc. Copying or distributing in print or electronic forms without written permission of Idea Group Inc. is prohibited.

Chapter V

Online Collaborative Learning in Mathematics: Some Necessary Innovations

Rod Nason
Queensland University of Technology, Australia

Earl Woodruff
OISE - University of Toronto, Canada

ABSTRACT

This chapter discusses why computer supported collaborative learning (CSCL) environments have been unsuccessful in facilitating knowledge building in mathematics. It identifies two of the major reasons why this is so and suggests these issues could be overcome by the inclusion of model-eliciting mathematical problems and comprehension modeling tools within CSCL environments. Theoretical frameworks to inform the design of these two types of artifacts are presented. The authors argue that such innovations in the design of CSCL environments are necessary for students to achieve in mathematics the kind of sustained, progressive knowledge building that can now be found in other subject areas.

Copyright © 2004, Idea Group Inc. Copying or distributing in print or electronic forms without written permission of Idea Group Inc. is prohibited.

INTRODUCTION

One of the most promising pedagogical advances for online collaborative learning that has emerged in recent years is Scardamalia and Bereiter's (1996) notion of knowledge-building communities. In knowledge-building communities, students are engaged in the production of conceptual artifacts (e.g., ideas, models, principles, relationships, theories, interpretations, etc.) that can be discussed, tested, compared, hypothetically modified and so forth, and the students see their main job as producing and improving such artifacts, not simply the completion of tasks (Bereiter, 2002a).

Anecdotal evidence from teachers using computer supported collaborative learning (CSCL) environments, such as Knowledge Forum[1] and its predecessor CSILE, and from formal evaluation studies indicates that computer-mediated knowledge-building communities are excellent for nurturing collaborative learning and communities of practice in subject areas such as social studies, art, history, geography, language arts and science (Bereiter, 2002a; Scardamalia & Bereiter, 1996). However, establishing and maintaining knowledge-building communities of practice with Knowledge Forum (and other CSCL software environments such as CSILE) in the domain of mathematics has been found to be a rather intractable problem (Bereiter, 2002a; De Corte, Verschaffel, Lowyck, Dhert, & Vanderput, 1999; Nason, Brett, & Woodruff, 1996; Scardamalia & Bereiter, 1996).

In this chapter, we begin by identifying two major reasons why computer-supported knowledge-building communities in mathematics have been difficult to establish and maintain:

1. Inability of most "textbook" math problems to elicit ongoing discourse and other knowledge-building activity either during or after the process of problem solving.
2. Limitations inherent in most CSCL environments' math representational tools and their failure to promote constructive discourse or other mathematical knowledge-building activities.

Therefore, we argue that if mathematics education is to exploit the potentially powerful new ways of learning mathematics being provided by online knowledge-building communities. Then, the following innovations need to be designed and integrated into CSCL environments:

1. Authentic mathematical problems that involve students in the production of mathematical models that can be discussed, critiqued and improved, and
2. Comprehension modeling tools that: (a) enable students to adequately represent mathematical problems and to translate within and across representation modes during problem solving, and (b) facilitate online student-student and teacher-student hypermedia-mediated discourse.

Copyright © 2004, Idea Group Inc. Copying or distributing in print or electronic forms without written permission of Idea Group Inc. is prohibited.

Both of the above innovations are directed at promoting and sustaining mathematical discourse. The requirement that the mathematical problems be authentic ensures that the students will have the contextual understanding necessary to promote a discussion about the mathematical models. Comprehension modeling (Woodruff & Nason, 2003; Woodruff, in press) further promotes the discourse by making student understanding an additional object for discussion.

It should be noted that we are using modeling in two different senses. Mathematical modeling refers to the representation of an idea or concept in externalized mathematical language. Within this chapter, the mathematical models are often the mathematical formulae the students invent. Comprehension modeling, on the other hand, refers to external representations that allow us to "see" the internal representations that a student may have with regard to a concept or idea. In this chapter, comprehension modeling is apparent in the documented spreadsheets that accompanied students' mathematical formulae and the documented animations that the students produced using our constructivist hypermedia interactive learning environment (CHiLE).

The main point of this chapter is to argue that effective CSCL environments must promote discourse around both the internal and external representations of an idea. Below, we outline how authentic problems and reasonably simple comprehension modeling tools can accomplish this goal.

BACKGROUND

A good starting point for a discussion about mathematical knowledge-building communities is mathematics practitioners working in the living discipline of mathematics. A major pursuit of these mathematicians is the production and improvement of mathematical conceptual artifacts (e.g., mathematical ideas, principles, relationships, theories, interpretations, models, etc.). Mathematical conceptual artifacts are human constructions like other artifacts, except that they are immaterial and, instead of serving purposes such as cutting, lifting and inscribing, they serve purposes such as constructing, explaining and predicting (Bereiter, 2002a; Lesh & Doerr, in press). In order to produce and improve these mathematical conceptual artifacts, mathematicians often form research communities who invest their resources in the collective pursuit of understanding by engaging in knowledge-building discourse, where problems are formulated, posed and investigated (Halmos, 1980), conjectures are made and findings are shared and critiqued (Bruce & Easley, n.d.).

An essential characteristic of mathematical problems formulated, posed and investigated by communities of mathematicians is that they tend to be open ended and non-trivial in nature, and typically involve several "modeling cycles"

Copyright © 2004, Idea Group Inc. Copying or distributing in print or electronic forms without written permission of Idea Group Inc. is prohibited.

in which descriptions, explanations and predictions are gradually refined, revised or rejected — based on feedback from trial testing before closure is achieved (Lesh & Doerr, in press).

This contrasts with the sort of mathematical activity most students engage in when they are working on textbook math problems. In almost all textbook math problems, students are required to search for an appropriate tool (e.g., operation, strategy) to get from the givens to the goals, and the product that students are asked to produce is a definitive response to a question or a situation that has been interpreted by someone else (Lesh, 2000). Most textbook math problems thus require the students to produce "an answer" and not a complex conceptual artifact, such as those generally required by most authentic math problems found in the world outside of schools and higher education institutions. Most textbook math problems also do not require multiple cycles of designing, testing and refining that occurs during the production of complex conceptual artifacts. Most textbook math problems therefore do not elicit the collaboration between people, each with special abilities that most authentic math problems outside of the educational institutes elicit (Nason & Woodruff, in press). Another factor that limits the potential of most textbook math problems for eliciting ongoing discourse and other knowledge-building activities is the nature of the answer produced by these types of problems. Unlike complex conceptual artifacts that provide many stimuli for ongoing discourse and other knowledge-building activity, the answers generated from textbook math problems do not provide students with much worth discussing. Once they have produced an answer, most students feel it is time to move onto the next problem (Bereiter, 2002a).

Another factor that has prevented most school and higher education students from engaging in ongoing discourse and other mathematical knowledge-building activity within CSCL environments is the limitations inherent in their mathematical representational tools (De Corte et al., 1999; Nason et al., 1996).

Mathematical representations can be categorized into two classes: internal representations and external representations (Janvier, Girardon, & Morand, 1993; Porzio, 1994). Internal representations particularly concern mental images corresponding to internal formulations that we construct of reality. External representations refer to all external symbolic organizations (symbol, schema, diagrams, etc.) that have as their objective to represent externally a certain mathematical "reality" (Porzio, 1994). Janvier et al. (1993) noted that external representations, such as charts, tables, graphs, diagrams, models, computer graphics and formal symbol systems, act as stimuli on the senses and that they are often regarded as embodiments of ideas or concepts. Computer-based math representation tools fall under the rubric of external representations.

External mathematical representations have at least two crucial roles to play within the process of mathematical knowledge building. First, the process of solving authentic mathematical problems more often than not calls for making

Copyright © 2004, Idea Group Inc. Copying or distributing in print or electronic forms without written permission of Idea Group Inc. is prohibited.

connections between different types of mathematical representations (Moschkovich, Schoenfeld, & Arcavi, 1993; National Council of Teachers of Mathematics, 2000). According to Kaput (1992), "Complex ideas are seldom adequately represented using a single notation system. The ability to link different representations helps reveal the different facets of a complex idea explicitly and dynamically" (p. 542). Second, mathematics at all levels use multiple mathematical representations in order to appropriately communicate ideas and, more importantly, to transmit meaning, sense and understanding (Avilés-Garay, 2001; De Jong, Ainsworth, Dobson, van der Hulst, Levonen, Reimann, et al., 1998; Greeno & Hall, 1997). Therefore, if students within CSCL environments are to engage in math knowledge building, it is essential that they be provided with math representation tools that enable them to: (1) generate multiple representations of mathematical concepts, (2) link the different representations, and (3) communicate the mathematical ideas they have constructed and transmit meaning, sense and understanding.

Unfortunately, most of math representational tools that currently can be utilized within CSCL environments, such as Knowledge Forum and CSILE, are not able to carry out these functions. This has been noted by a number of different researchers, such as De Corte et al. (1999) and Nason et al. (1996). When De Corte et al. (1999) investigated the value of Knowledge Forum for facilitating learning how to solve and pose mathematical application problems and to communicate higher-order processes among upper primary school children, they found that the quality of mathematical thinking and the exchange of ideas both within and between the groups of students was limited by the fact that the Knowledge Forum environment did not enable the students to: (1) work with multiple forms of knowledge representation and (2) insert and manipulate tables and figures. In a similar vein, Nason et al. (1996) found that knowledge-building discourse within the CSILE environment was limited by CSILE's math representation tools. For example, they found that CSILE's math representation tools did not enable the students to transfer their dynamic concrete/pictorial representations, constructed during the face-to-face inquiry phase of a mathematical investigation, to the CSCL phase of the investigation. The students thus were not able to communicate to other participants in the CSCL community the process that led to their solution to the mathematical investigation.

Two clear implications can be derived from this review of the previous research conducted into the establishment of mathematical knowledge-building communities within CSCL environments. First is that different types of mathematical problems that have more in common with the authentic types of mathematical problems investigated by communities of mathematicians, than most existing types of textbook math problems, need to be designed and integrated into CSCL environments. And second, that new iconic mathematical representation tools that (1) enable students to adequately represent mathemati-

Copyright © 2004, Idea Group Inc. Copying or distributing in print or electronic forms without written permission of Idea Group Inc. is prohibited.

cal problems and to translate within and across representation modes during problem solving and (2) facilitate online student-student and teacher-student hypermedia-mediated discourse also need to be designed and integrated into CSCL environments. In order to differentiate these tools from previous iconic math representation tools, we have labeled our new generation of tools as comprehension modeling tools. Each of these two issues will be discussed in the next two sections of this chapter.

NEED FOR DIFFERENT TYPE OF MATHEMATICAL PROBLEM

Credence for the viewpoint that the integration of more authentic types of mathematical problems into CSCL environments may lead to conditions necessary for the establishment and maintenance of knowledge-building activity is provided by the findings from two recent research studies, conducted by the co-authors into model-eliciting problem solving. Although both of these studies were situated within elementary schools, it should be noted that the same math problems used in these research studies could also be used in online CSCL environments, to facilitate the development of mathematical subject-matter knowledge in pre-service teacher education students (see Brett, Nason, & Woodruff, 2002). Therefore, we believe that the findings from these two studies have much relevance for the establishment and maintenance of math knowledge-building communities not only in elementary schools, but also in higher education institutions, too.

In model-eliciting mathematical problems, the products that students produce include more than answers to questions; they involve producing models or other conceptual artifacts for constructing, describing, explaining, manipulating, predicting and controlling complex systems (Lesh & Doerr, in press; Lesh, Hoover, Hole, Kelly, & Post, 1999). The types of models that can be generated from model-eliciting problems can include a pattern, a procedure, a strategy, a method, a plan or a tool kit. Model-eliciting mathematical problems thus have much more in common with the authentic mathematical problems investigated by mathematics practitioners, than traditional textbook problems.

In a series of research studies, Nason and Woodruff in conjunction with Lesh (2002) have been investigating whether having students engage in model-eliciting mathematical problems with collective discourse mediated by Knowledge Forum would achieve the kind of authentic, sustained and progressive online knowledge-building activity that has been achieved in more content-rich discipline areas such as science. In this section, we focus on two of these research studies.

Copyright © 2004, Idea Group Inc. Copying or distributing in print or electronic forms without written permission of Idea Group Inc. is prohibited.

STUDY 1

In the first of the research studies (Nason & Woodruff, in press), a cohort of 21 students in grade six at a private urban Canadian school for girls were asked to devise an alternative model that could be used for ranking nations' performance at Olympic games, which de-emphasized the mind set of "gold or nothing."

Initially, the students were presented with a table that listed the top 25 nations (as ranked by gold medals) for the 2000 Sydney Olympic Games, and contained information about how many gold, silver and bronze medals each country had won, plus its population in millions. After looking at and discussing the contents of the table, the students were presented with an article entitled "The Post-Olympic Accounting" (Canadian Broadcasting Corporation, 2000) that questioned the validity of ranking countries' performance by number of gold medals won. A whole class discussion based around a set of four focus questions followed the reading of the article. The purpose of these questions was to help the students "read with a mathematical eye," while also familiarizing them with the context of the model-eliciting activity — so that their solutions would be based on extensions of the students "real life" knowledge and experiences (Lesh, Cramer, Doerr, Post, & Zawoiewski, in press). The warm-up activities took about 45 minutes.

After the warm-up activity, the students went through the phases of: (1) initial model building (one session of 45 minutes), (2) sharing of initial models (one session of 45 minutes) and (3) iterative online critiquing and revision of models within Knowledge Forum (four sessions of 45 minutes). The sharing of the initial models in phase 2 was done face to face within the classroom. The purpose of this phase was to ensure that the initial models addressed the problem being investigated and to provide the students with guidelines for productive commenting and questioning. After the face-to-face sharing of the initial models had been completed, each group attached their math model to a Knowledge Forum note, where it could be viewed and evaluated by other participants within the online CSCL community. During the online critiquing and revision of models in phase 3, Knowledge Forum provided the contexts and scaffolds for inter-group online discourse. It enabled the best ideas from the groups to surface, be explored and evaluated and then modified/improved[2]. Knowledge Forum also provided students with the opportunity to see other groups' varying degrees of success. This peer modeling promoted the thinking of all, provided examples of success and moved the class ahead — often overcoming impasses that stalled the efforts of groups working alone. Without the contexts and scaffolds provided by Knowledge Forum, it is highly unlikely that the models would have undergone as many of the extensive iterative revisions as they did[3].

Copyright © 2004, Idea Group Inc. Copying or distributing in print or electronic forms without written permission of Idea Group Inc. is prohibited.

Four important elements of knowledge-building activity were observed during the course of this study: (1) redefinition of problem, (2) inventive use of mathematical tools, (3) posing and exploration of conjectures, and (4) incremental improvement of the mathematical models.

Redefinition of the Problem

When engaged in mathematical investigations, mathematicians continually redefine the problems they are investigating (Lesh & Doerr, in press). They find that this often leads to the construction of new and interesting conceptual artifacts and/or to the improvement of existing conceptual artifacts.

During the course of this study, all the groups of students engaged in this type of behavior. This is well exemplified by the Ca group. At the beginning of the study, the Ca group defined the problem as one of generating a model that "proved" that Canada performed better than the U.S. at the Sydney Olympics. During their investigation of this problem, the Ca group first used the spreadsheet to generate the total number of medals won by each of the countries, and then to calculate the number of medals won per million of population. When the medals won per million ratios were rounded off to the second decimal place, the group found that its spreadsheet model indeed "proved" that Canada performed better than the U.S. at the Sydney Olympics (see Figure 1).

Figure 1: Ca's Group's Math Model — Mark 1

	G	S	B	Total Medals	Population (m)	Medals per Million
Australia	16	25	17	58	19	3.1
Cuba	11	11	7	29	11	2.6
Norway	4	3	3	10	4.5	2.2
Hungary	8	6	3	17	10	1.7
Belarus	3	3	11	17	10	1.7
Bulgaria	5	6	2	13	8	1.6
Netherlands	12	9	4	25	16	1.6
Sweden	4	5	3	12	9	1.3
Romania	11	6	9	26	22	1.2
Greece	4	6	3	13	11	1.2
Germany	14	17	26	57	82	0.7
France	13	14	11	38	59	0.6
Russia	32	28	28	88	146	0.6
S.Korea	8	9	11	28	47	0.6
Italy	13	8	13	34	58	0.6
Britain	11	10	7	28	59	0.5
Kazakhstan	3	4	0	7	15	0.5
Ukraine	3	10	10	23	50	0.5
Canada	3	3	8	14	31	0.5
Poland	6	5	3	14	39	0.4
USA	39	25	33	97	273	0.4
Spain	3	3	5	11	40	0.3
Japan	5	8	5	18	126	0.1
Ethiopia	4	1	3	8	60	0.1
China	28	16	15	59	1,251	0.0

Copyright © 2004, Idea Group Inc. Copying or distributing in print or electronic forms without written permission of Idea Group Inc. is prohibited.

However, when the Ca group used the spreadsheet's SORT function to rank the countries in terms of medals won per million, they found that their model ranked Canada 19th, well behind countries such as Australia and Cuba. The students therefore thought it would be interesting to see if they could modify their model, so that Canada could be ranked ahead of Australia. This redefinition of the problem led them to the development of many new and powerful mathematical conceptual artifacts, and ultimately to the generation of a rather sophisticated spreadsheet model for ranking different countries performances at Olympic games. Their first modification to the model was to generate weighted scores by awarding five points for each gold medal, four points for a silver medal and three points for a bronze medal (see Column H in Figure 2).

Despite experimenting with different weightings for each type of medal, the Ca group found that weighting of scores for different types of medals did not provide a solution to their problem. Ca then conjectured that if countries with populations of less than 32 million could be awarded bonus points, then maybe Canada's ranking could be further improved. After being shown how to enter If-Then condition formulae into the spreadsheet, the Ca group then produced a "Real Score" column into their model in which countries with populations less than 32 million were awarded 400 bonus points (see Column I in Figure 2). When they used the SORT function to rank the countries in their new model, they found that eight countries (including Australia) were still ranked ahead of Canada.

Figure 2: Ca's Group's Math Model — Mark 3

	A	G	S	B	Total Medals	Population (m)	Medals per Million	Score	Real Score
2	Australia	16	25	17	58	19	3.1	231	631
3	Cuba	11	11	7	29	11	2.6	120	520
4	Netherlands	12	9	4	25	16	1.6	108	508
5	Romania	11	6	9	26	22	1.2	106	506
6	Hungary	8	6	3	17	10	1.7	73	473
7	Belarus	3	3	11	17	10	1.7	60	460
8	Bulgaria	5	6	2	13	8	1.6	55	455
9	Greece	4	6	3	13	11	1.2	53	453
10	Canada	3	3	8	14	31	0.5	51	451
11	Sweden	4	5	3	12	9	1.3	49	449
12	Norway	4	3	3	10	4.5	2.2	41	441
13	Kazakhstan	3	4	0	7	15	0.5	31	431
14	USA	39	25	33	97	273	0.4	394	394
15	Russia	32	28	28	88	146	0.6	356	356
16	China	28	16	15	59	1,251	0.0	249	249
17	Germany	14	17	26	57	82	0.7	216	216
18	France	13	14	11	38	59	0.6	154	154
19	Italy	13	8	13	34	58	0.6	136	136
20	Britain	11	10	7	28	59	0.5	116	116
21	S.Korea	8	9	11	28	47	0.6	109	109
22	Ukraine	3	10	10	23	50	0.5	85	85
23	Japan	5	8	5	18	126	0.1	72	72
24	Poland	6	5	3	14	39	0.4	59	59
25	Spain	3	3	5	11	40	0.3	42	42
26	Ethiopia	4	1	3	8	60	0.1	33	33

Copyright © 2004, Idea Group Inc. Copying or distributing in print or electronic forms without written permission of Idea Group Inc. is prohibited.

The Ca group then looked very carefully at the data of each of the eight countries still ranked ahead of Canada on the spreadsheet model. They noted that all of these countries (like Canada) had populations of less than 32 million, but that (unlike Canada) their ratio of medals per million was greater than one (see Column G in Figure 2). This led the group to the development of a two condition If-Then formula, in which only countries with populations of less than 32 million and with a ratio of less than one medal per million were awarded the bonus points. The inclusion of this new mathematical artifact into the spreadsheet model resulted in a model that ranked Canada as being the best performing nation at the Sydney Olympics (see Figure 3).

Other groups also redefined the problem during the course of the study from one of "proving" that Canada performed better than the U.S. to one of "proving" Canada performed better than Australia, and finally to one of "proving" that Canada was the best performing nation at the Sydney Olympic Games. It was very interesting to note that most redefinition of the problem occurred after the groups perused other groups' models online via the means of Knowledge Forum. Similar to the Ca group, the other groups also experimented with weighted scores and If-Then formulae. Like the Ca group, the other groups also found that the redefinitions of the problem led them to many new, and for them exciting mathematical insights about weightings of scores, If-Then condition rules and

Figure 3: Ca's Group's Final Model

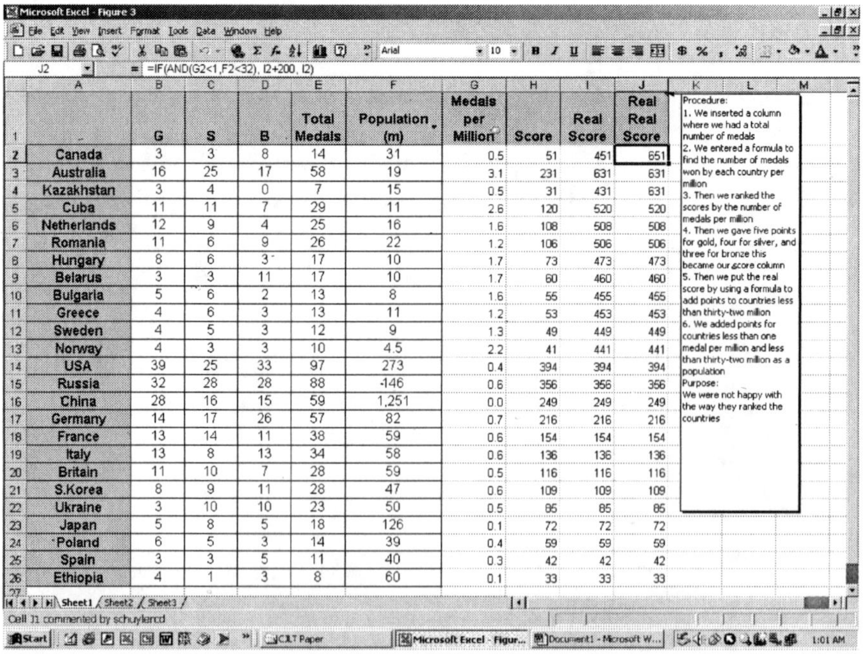

=IF(AND(G2<1,F2<32), I2+200, I2)

	G	S	B	Total Medals	Population (m)	Medals per Million	Score	Real Score	Real Real Score
Canada	3	3	8	14	31	0.5	51	451	651
Australia	16	25	17	58	19	3.1	231	631	631
Kazakhstan	3	4	0	7	15	0.5	31	431	631
Cuba	11	11	7	29	11	2.6	120	520	520
Netherlands	12	9	4	25	16	1.6	108	508	508
Romania	11	6	9	26	22	1.2	106	506	506
Hungary	8	6	3	17	10	1.7	73	473	473
Belarus	3	3	11	17	10	1.7	60	460	460
Bulgaria	5	6	2	13	8	1.6	55	455	455
Greece	4	6	3	13	11	1.2	53	453	453
Sweden	4	5	3	12	9	1.3	49	449	449
Norway	4	3	3	10	4.5	2.2	41	441	441
USA	39	25	33	97	273	0.4	394	394	394
Russia	32	28	28	88	146	0.6	356	356	356
China	28	16	15	59	1,251	0.0	249	249	249
Germany	14	17	26	57	82	0.7	216	216	216
France	13	14	11	38	59	0.6	154	154	154
Italy	13	8	13	34	58	0.6	136	136	136
Britain	11	10	7	28	59	0.5	116	116	116
S.Korea	8	9	11	28	47	0.6	109	109	109
Ukraine	3	10	10	23	50	0.5	85	85	85
Japan	5	8	5	18	126	0.1	72	72	72
Poland	6	5	3	14	39	0.4	59	59	59
Spain	3	3	5	11	40	0.3	42	42	42
Ethiopia	4	1	3	8	60	0.1	33	33	33

Procedure:
1. We inserted a column where we had a total number of medals
2. We entered a formula to find the number of medals won by each country per million
3. Then we ranked the scores by the number of medals per million
4. Then we gave five points for gold, four for silver, and three for bronze this became our score column
5. Then we put the real score by using a formula to add points to countries less than thirty-two million
6. We added points for countries less than one medal per million and less than thirty-two million as a population
Purpose:
We were not happy with the way they ranked the countries

Copyright © 2004, Idea Group Inc. Copying or distributing in print or electronic forms without written permission of Idea Group Inc. is prohibited.

most importantly about ranking tables. The new deeper insights the students had attained about ranking tables is exemplified by this comment made to the teacher/experimenter by Ca near the end of the study:

Professor N, you know you could show that any country performed best at the Sydney Olympic Games.

Inventive Uses of Mathematical Tools

As the students continually redefined the problem, they invented new ways (for them) of utilizing the power of the spreadsheet tools. For example, when the notion of taking cognizance of population when generating weighted scores was first proposed by Ca, the teacher/researcher showed the students in her group how to create If-Then formulae (e.g., If population is < 32 million, Then add 50 points to score) on Excel spreadsheets.

Soon after this, the seven groups of students, without any prompting from the teacher/researcher, rapidly began exploring how If-Then formulae could be extended/modified. The teacher/researcher's role when this occurred was limited to helping the students overcome Excel syntax problems[4]. As was noted in the previous section, the Ca group modified its If-Then formula to include a second condition for the awarding of bonus points, namely that a country not only had to have a population of less than 32 million, but also that its ratio of medals per million population had to be less than one (see Column J in Figure 3).

The R group modified the initial If-Then formula (i.e., If population is < 32 million, Then add 50 points to score) in a different way. Instead of adding a second condition, they instead subtracted 50 points off the scores of those countries whose population was not less than 32 million (see Column J of Figure 4). When this did not achieve the desired result, they further modified the If-Then formula so that 200 points were deducted from the scores of countries whose population was not less than 32 million (see Column K of Figure 4).

Kelly's group experimented with both the addition of a second condition to the If-Then formula, and with deducting 50 points from those countries that did not meet either of the two conditions. Its final model for ranking the countries' performances at the Sydney Olympic Games, thus included an If-Then formula that awarded 290 bonus points to a country, if its population was less than 32 million and whose ratio of medals per million population was less than 0.6. If a country did not meet both of these conditions, 50 points were deducted from their score.

The Cl group experimented with modifying the initial If-Then formula but soon reached an impasse. Instead of adding a second condition to the formula (like the Ca group) or deducting points if the population was not less than 32 million (like the R group), the Cl group went back to the original data and noted that Canada had won 14 medals. They then created a different If-Then formula

Copyright © 2004, Idea Group Inc. Copying or distributing in print or electronic forms without written permission of Idea Group Inc. is prohibited.

Figure 4: R's Group's Math Model — Mark 5

	# of gold medals	# of silver medals	# of bronze medals	Total # of Medals	Population (m)	Total Medals /million	Score	Real Score	Using the Population	Too many people, less points
Belarus	3	3	11	17	10	1.7	131	181	181	181
Canada	3	3	8	14	31	0.5	101	151	151	151
Kazakhstan	3	4	0	7	15	0.5	26	76	76	76
USA	39	25	33	97	273	0.4	533	533	483	333
Russia	32	28	28	88	146	0.6	484	484	434	284
Australia	16	25	17	58	19	3.1	327	377	377	377
Germany	14	17	26	57	82	0.7	373	373	323	173
China	28	16	15	59	1,251	0.0	286	286	236	86
France	13	14	11	38	59	0.6	206	206	156	6
Cuba	11	11	7	29	11	2.6	147	197	197	197
Italy	13	8	13	34	58	0.6	196	196	146	-4
Romania	11	6	9	26	22	1.2	142	192	192	192
S.Korea	8	9	11	28	47	0.6	171	171	121	-29
Netherlands	12	9	4	25	16	1.6	109	159	159	159
Ukraine	3	10	10	23	50	0.5	156	156	106	-44
Britain	11	10	7	28	59	0.5	142	142	92	-58
Hungary	8	6	3	17	10	1.7	76	126	126	126
Greece	4	6	3	13	11	1.2	68	118	118	118
Sweden	4	5	3	12	9	1.3	63	113	113	113
Bulgaria	5	6	2	13	8	1.6	60	110	110	110
Norway	4	3	3	10	4 5	2.2	53	103	103	103
Japan	5	8	5	18	126	0.1	100	100	50	-100
Spain	3	3	5	11	40	0.3	71	71	21	-129
Poland	6	5	3	14	39	0.4	67	67	17	133

that only awarded bonus points to countries who had won exactly 14 medals (i.e., If the medals add up to 14, you add 150 to the score. If the medals equal 15 or more, you take away 150 points).

Conjecturing

High levels of conjecturing were observed during the development of weighted scores and If-Then formulae. For example, the C and R groups first allocated 10 points for a gold medal, five points for a silver medal and one point for a bronze medal. When they found that this weighting lowered Canada's ranking with respect to the U.S., they conjectured that the difference in scores between Canada and the U.S. would be decreased if five points were awarded for a gold medal, four for a silver medal and three for a bronze medal. When they confirmed this conjecture, both groups tried to work out why this was so. They soon realized that this was because most of Canada's medals were bronze medals, whereas the U.S.'s were mainly gold or silver. This led the C group to conjecture that the difference in weighted scores could be further decreased by awarding the one point for each medal won. The R group conjectured that a weighted score even more favorable to Canada could be produced by awarding 10 for a bronze medal, five for a silver medal and one for a gold medal.

Copyright © 2004, Idea Group Inc. Copying or distributing in print or electronic forms without written permission of Idea Group Inc. is prohibited.

The conjecturing about If-Then formulae was more sophisticated. The Ca group was the first group to conjecture that some mechanism had to be included in their model to take cognizance of different populations. Ca hypothesized that if countries with less than a 32 million population had bonus points added to their weighted scores, then Canada's performance vis-à-vis U.S., China and Germany would be made to appear much better. The Ca group experimented with bonus points of 50, 100 and finally 400, and found that this could certainly make Canada appear to have performed much better than most countries. However, because Australia and Kazakhstan both also had populations of less than 32 million, Canada's performance vis-à-vis these two countries seemed to worsen. This led to Ca and four other groups conjecturing that a second condition that excluded countries whose medals per millions of population ratio was greater than Canada's from being awarded bonus points needed to be included in the If-Then formula.

Incremental Improvement of Models

During the course of the study, the models developed by the groups of students were incrementally improved and became mathematically more complex and sophisticated. In the initial stages of developing an alternative model for ranking countries' performances at the Olympic games, the students attempted to develop models which "proved" that Canada performed better than the U.S. by totalling the medals each country had won, and then dividing the total number of medals won by the population in millions. However, because this model did not rank Canada's performance above the U.S.'s, the students then developed models with weighted scores. Finally most groups of students used If-Then formulae to modify the weighted scores. Indeed, by the end of the study, most groups of students had developed models with If-Then formulae that included two or three conditions.

STUDY 2

In the second research study (Nason, Woodruff, & Lesh, 2002), a group of 22 students in another sixth grade class at the private urban Canadian school for girls, where the first research study was conducted, were presented with the following problem:

Ms. Markova has recently emigrated from Russia. Although she has been living in Toronto for about a year, she has not yet made up her mind about where she would like to live in Canada. In order to help her decide, she wants to create a table ranking Canadian cities in terms of quality of life. Your task is to create a model that will enable her to create this table.

Copyright © 2004, Idea Group Inc. Copying or distributing in print or electronic forms without written permission of Idea Group Inc. is prohibited.

The production and the revision of the models proceeded in a similar manner to that in the first study. That is, after the initial warm-up activity, in which the students were introduced to the problem, the students went through the phases of: (1) initial model building, (2) sharing of initial models, and (3) iterative online critiquing and revision of models within Knowledge Forum.

During this study, it was noted that the students engaged in the posing and exploration of conjectures and in the incremental improvement of the mathematical models just like the students who participated in Study 1. However, it was also noted that students in this study also engaged in the collective pursuit of a deeper understanding of key mathematical concepts, a behavior often observed within communities of mathematics practitioners as they engage in the process of generating and improving mathematical conceptual artifacts.

Each of the models generated by the groups of students in this study contained a list of categories for evaluating the cities of Canada (e.g., Culture, Quality of Life, Law Enforcement, Entertainment, Government, Attractions and Transportation). In order to generate a score for each city, a number of points were awarded to each city in each category. As the students engaged in the iterative revisions of their models, it was noted that each of the groups continuously delved deeper into the meaning of the scores their models generated for each category. This was reflected in the qualitative changes made to the explanations of how the models generated the scores for each of the categories.

During the earlier iterations of their models, each group of students usually just indicated the total number of points to be allocated for each category, and what factors they had considered when generating the scores for each city. For example, Ayn's group initially provided the following explanation of its model's scoring schema for "Quality of Life":

Quality of living is how good life is in the city: safety, education, multiculturism, leisure (recreation), etc. Score out of 10.

Like all of the other initial explanations provided by the groups, this explanation did not provide details about: (1) how the score for each city had been generated or (2) what a score such as 6/10 meant (e.g., is it a poor, average or quite a good score).

As they continuously received comments, propositions and questions from other groups of students and their teachers via Knowledge Forum during Phase 3, the students delved deeper into the meanings of their scores. As a result, their explanations were elaborated on and when necessary clarified, so that the readers were provided with more details about how the models generated the scores and what the scores meant. For example, by its final iteration, Ayn's group had modified the explanation of its model's scoring schema for "Quality of Life" to:

Copyright © 2004, Idea Group Inc. Copying or distributing in print or electronic forms without written permission of Idea Group Inc. is prohibited.

Quality of living is how good life is in the city: safety, education, multiculturism, leisure (recreation), etc.

How to Determine the Score: If the city was in the top six of the 24 cities for its crime rates, then we gave it 10 points. If the city was between seven and 12 for crime rates, we gave it seven and a half points. If the city was between 13 and 18 for crime rates we gave it a score of five. If it was between 19 and 24 we awarded it two and a half points.

We added on three points for good entertainment, two points for fairly good entertainment, and one point for poor entertainment. Next, we gave the city a score out of three for education based on the population. We divided the cities into categories based on the population: millions, hundred thousands, and ten thousands. Points were awarded, giving the cities with the highest number of number of secondary school graduates highest number of points in each of the categories. Three points were added for good multiculturalrism, two for fairly good, and one for poor.

The score is out of 19. (/19)

Another qualitative change in the explanations that reflected how students were delving deeper into the meanings of the scores by the end of the research study was that many of the groups utilized If-Then conditional statements in the later versions of their models, to indicate that a score generated by their model for any category would be based not only on objective information (e.g., average temperatures, etc.), but also on the personal preferences of the person using its system. A good example of this is provided by Mary's group, when the members explain how Ms. Markova could use their model to generate scores for "Environment":

Environment means the climate, biome, and landforms. The climate should meet what Ms. Markova likes. If she likes warm climates, maybe she could move to the prairies; if she likes cold climates, maybe she will like Iqaluit. The biome will depend on which part of the country you are. If Ms. Markova likes a temperate biome, Toronto would be a nice place...

DISCUSSION

Scardamalia (2002) has proposed 12 principled socio-cognitive and technological determinants of knowledge building. Consistent with these principles, five important elements of knowledge-building activity were observed during the

Copyright © 2004, Idea Group Inc. Copying or distributing in print or electronic forms without written permission of Idea Group Inc. is prohibited.

course of these two studies: (1) redefinition of the problem, which highlights the principles of improvable ideas and rising above, (2) inventive use of mathematical tools, which highlights the principle of improvable ideas, (3) the posing and exploration of conjectures, which highlights the principles of idea diversity and knowledge-building discourse, (4) the collective pursuit of understanding of key mathematical concepts — highlighting the principles of community knowledge and collective responsibility, and (5) the incremental improvement of mathematical models, which highlights the principle of improvable ideas. Therefore, there can be little doubt that the students in these studies engaged in authentic, sustained and progressive online knowledge-building activity. Indeed, it could be argued that the quality of their symbolizing, communicating, "mathematizing" and collective pursuit of understanding had much in common with that observed in many mathematical research communities.

Much of the success we had in establishing and maintaining the online mathematics knowledge-building communities in these two studies can be attributed to the rich context for mathematical knowledge-building discourse provided by the model-eliciting problems. In both of these problems, students were required to produce a mathematical model for issues that the students found meaningful and worthy of investing their time and effort in. Therefore, they were willing to proceed through multiple cycles of developing, evaluating and revising their models. This process of proceeding through multiple cycles encouraged much online discourse between the groups in each of the classes. The model-eliciting problems also had many different possible solutions. Because of this, there was much heterogeneity in the initial models, produced by the groups of students. In order to understand other groups' models and also to explain their own model to other groups, each group had to engage in much iterative online discourse with other groups. During this discourse, they had to ask good questions, propose how other groups' models could be improved and elaborate on and/or modify their explanations. Finally, the models themselves provided students with artifacts that could be discussed, evaluated, compared and improved (just like the artifacts built by mathematics practitioners). Unlike the answers produced in most textbook problems that tend to only enable discourse about correctness (or incorrectness), the models produced from the model-eliciting problems were artifacts that could be evaluated and discussed in terms of not only correct usage of mathematical concepts and processes but also in terms of subjective, non-mathematical factors.

COMPREHENSION MODELING TOOLS

Evidence to support the notion that the inclusion within CSCL learning environment of comprehension modeling tools that: (1) enable students to adequately represent mathematical problems and to translate within and across

Copyright © 2004, Idea Group Inc. Copying or distributing in print or electronic forms without written permission of Idea Group Inc. is prohibited.

representation modes during problem-solving, and (2) facilitate student-student, and teacher-student hypermedia-mediated discourse could do much to facilitate the establishment and maintenance of knowledge-building discourse has been provided by two separate research programs whose major focus has been on the learning of fraction concepts. First, there is the Tools for Interactive Mathematical Activity (TIMA) research program of Olive and colleagues at Vanderbilt University (Olive, 2000; Olive & Steffe, 1994). Second, there is the Constructivist Hypermedia interactive Learning Environment (CHiLE) program of Nason and colleagues at the Queensland University of Technology (Charles & Nason, 2000; Nason & Pham, in preparation). Although both of these research programs initially focused on the learning of fractions by young children, in recent times both programs have been extended to pre- and in-service teacher education programs[5]. Therefore, the findings from these two research programs have relevance not just for teaching and learning in elementary schools but also for teaching and learning in tertiary teacher education programs, too.

TIMA was designed to aid teachers in helping children in grades one through seven to construct knowledge of fractions. The tools do this by allowing teacher and students to create problem situations and to solve those problems by performing mathematical operations on iconic models created on the computer (Olive, 2000). Through simple mouse actions, students can make region models (see Figure 5), linear models (sticks) and set models (strings of toy triangles, squares, pentagons, hexagons and heptagons), and then perform operations on these three types of representations to investigate numerical relationships and develop strategies for finding sums and differences of fraction quantities, for building equivalent fractions and for finding fractions of fractions (Olive & Steffe, 1994). In addition, the tools were designed to provide children a medium in which they could enact the mathematical operations of unitizing, uniting, fragmenting, segmenting, partitioning, replicating, iterating and measuring.

Olive and his colleagues (Olive, 2000; Olive & Steffe, 1994) have found that the ease with which children can use TIMA to generate different types of dynamic iconic models, not only enables children to investigate important fraction concepts and processes in many different "real world" contexts, but also enables them to engage in deep-level synchronous knowledge-building discourse with other students and their teacher, as they engage in the process of constructing knowledge about fractions. Many children have great difficulty in communicating mathematical patterns and relationships they have discovered because of the limitations of their natural language and mathematical language vocabularies (Lemke, 2001). The dynamic iconic tools provided by TIMA, however, enable young children to communicate meaning via showing and telling rather than by merely telling. For example, when trying to explain a part/whole fraction relationship to other children or their teacher, a child can create a rectangular bar, move it around the screen, copy it or mark it both horizontally and vertically into

Copyright © 2004, Idea Group Inc. Copying or distributing in print or electronic forms without written permission of Idea Group Inc. is prohibited.

Figure 5: TIMA Bars Model (From Olive, 2000)

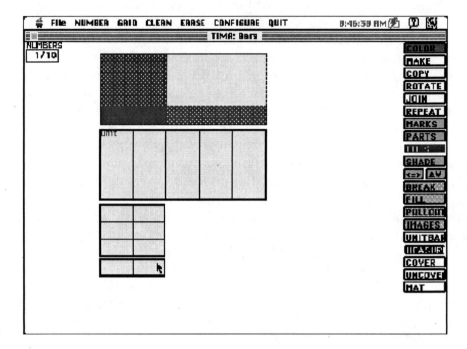

equal-sized parts. The child can then pull out parts of a bar to help compare between parts of a whole and the whole, while not destroying the whole. Other children or the teacher can also manipulate the model to provide a meaningful context for the questions and/or propositions being addressed in reply to the child who created the model.

CHiLE also was developed to facilitate the construction of knowledge about fractions (Charles & Nason, 2000). CHiLE has a constructivist approach to teaching and learning and builds on children's informal knowledge of partitioning. It aims to embody realistic contexts in which children construct their own knowledge, as a consequence of their experiences with the fraction tasks. CHiLE therefore situates the learning of fractions in the context of a restaurant in which the children play the role of a waiter, and are asked to partition and share out equally objects, such as pizza and apple pies, to customers sitting at the restaurant table (see Figure 6). The number of customers sitting at the table and the number of objects to be partitioned and shared can be varied. CHiLE provides the children with five different slicers that enable objects to be cut in halves, thirds, fifths, sevenths and ninths. With these slicers, the children can also create other fractions, such as quarters (by halving the halves) and sixths (by halving the thirds).

In a manner similar to that provided by TIMA, CHiLE enables children to generate multiple representations of fraction problems and provides the iconic

Copyright © 2004, Idea Group Inc. Copying or distributing in print or electronic forms without written permission of Idea Group Inc. is prohibited.

Figure 6: CHiLE Interface

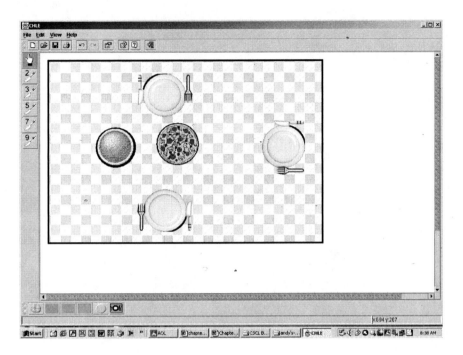

tools for facilitating synchronous hypermedia-mediated knowledge-building child-child and teacher-child discourse. CHiLE, however, has an added facility that enables teachers and children to also engage in online asynchronous knowledge-building discourse. With CHiLE, children are able to make a viewlet (a sequence of animation slides with accompanying notes and explanation text balloons) that not only enables them to communicate the solution to a fraction problem but also the strategy (or model) that was utilized to generate the solution. CHiLE thus uses hypermedia as a way to animate and promote mathematical discourse: the strategy (or model) is reified on the screen via the iconic representation; the animation shows the "story" and everything is recorded thus promoting reflection and revisitation. This is illustrated in Figure 2 by the sequence of five slides generated by two eight-year-old children who had been asked to share one pizza fairly between three people.

When students have produced a CHiLE viewlet, they can attach it to a Knowledge Forum note, where it can be viewed and evaluated by other participants within the online CSCL community. After they have viewed the CHiLE viewlet as many times as they need to, the other participants can use the commenting facilities provided by Knowledge Forum to provide online feedback in the form of praise, questions and propositions to the authors of the viewlet. The authors then, if they so choose, can use the feedback and make modifications/

Copyright © 2004, Idea Group Inc. Copying or distributing in print or electronic forms without written permission of Idea Group Inc. is prohibited.

Figure 7a: Slide 1

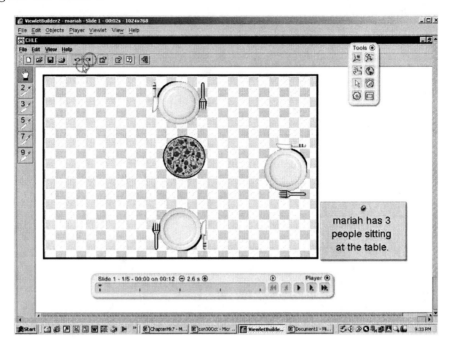

Figure 7b: Slide 2

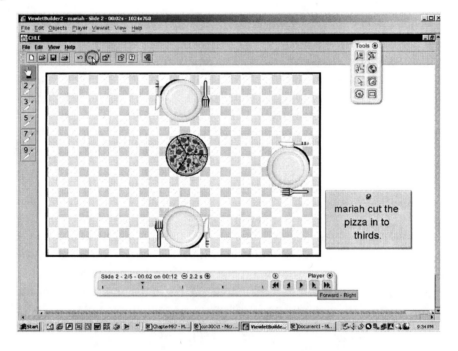

Copyright © 2004, Idea Group Inc. Copying or distributing in print or electronic forms without written permission of Idea Group Inc. is prohibited.

revisions to their viewlet or create an alternative viewlet. The revised and/or alternative viewlet is then reposted on the Knowledge Forum online database for further viewing and evaluation. CHiLE, in conjunction with the commenting and feedback facilities provided by Knowledge Forum, thus enables the students to engage in iterative revisions and modifications of their viewlets.

Nason and his colleagues (2003) have found that online knowledge-building discourse facilitated by CHiLE operates on two different levels. First, the discourse can occur at the global level and focus on the overall strategy (or model). For example, another group of students, when given the same problem as in Figure 7, decided to slice the pizza into sixths and give two sixths to each person. After looking at one and another's viewlets, the two groups of students engaged in robust online debate about which was the "better" strategy (and solution). During this debate, they were able to identify similarities and differences between the strategies, but more importantly build conceptual links between thirds and sixths. Second, the discourse can occur at the language level. For example, there can be discourse about the best language to insert in the notes and text balloons of each viewlet slide. This discourse often provides the contexts for the introduction of formal mathematical language as a more precise way of communicating meaning within mathematical contexts than natural language.

The hypermedia facilities provided by CHiLE enable children to engage in online knowledge-building discourse synchronously and asynchronously via the means iconic, natural language and/or mathematical language representations. CHiLE thus provides one of the most important technological dynamics that Scardamalia (2002) identified as being a technical determinant of knowledge building and knowledge advancement within online CSCL environments.

CHiLE also provides two other technological dynamics that Scardamalia (2002) indicated were technological determinants of knowledge building and knowledge advancement. First, there is her notion that computer technology should include facilities for bringing together different ideas in such a way that productive use can be made of diversity. The iconic tools provided by CHLE meet this criterion by enabling children to readily:

- Generate diverse solutions and solution processes to the same mathematics problem and
- Communicate both synchronously and asynchronously their diverse solutions and solution processes to others within the online learning community via the iconic models, natural and mathematical language, and mathematical symbols.

Scardamalia (2002) also indicated that the computer technology should provide children with the opportunity and the means to make revisions. Without this, she claimed that children will not be able to work continuously to improve the quality, coherence and the utility of their ideas. As was noted above, one of

Copyright © 2004, Idea Group Inc. Copying or distributing in print or electronic forms without written permission of Idea Group Inc. is prohibited.

the major qualities of CHiLE is the ease with which children can revisit and revise the sequences of slides and their accompanying notes and text balloons.

The comprehension modeling tools provided by CHiLE thus promote the notions of idea diversity, improvable ideas and knowledge-building discourse, which are three of the sociological and technological determinants of knowledge building identified in Scardamalia (2002).

FUTURE TRENDS

The research in progress reported in the previous two sections of this chapter indicates that the inclusion of model-eliciting problems and of comprehension modeling tools (such as CHiLE) into online collaborative learning environments have the potential to facilitate the establishment and maintenance of online collaborative mathematics knowledge-building communities in schools and higher education institutes. However, some important issues still need to be addressed before this potential can be realized. Two of the most pressing of these issues are the lack of adequate theoretical frameworks to inform the design of the mathematics problems and of the comprehension modeling tools.

The design of the model-eliciting problems utilized in studies 1 and 2 was informed by a set of six principles for model-eliciting activities developed by Lesh et al. (1999). However, this set of principles was not developed with online collaborative learning environments (that could be distributed across classrooms in different locations) in mind; instead, it was developed to inform the design of mathematics problems that would be utilized in a particular classroom or school with a particular cohort of students. While analyzing why the two problems used in studies 1 and 2 were so successful in providing contexts for knowledge building within the online CSCL community, we came to the conclusion that Lesh et al.'s (1999) six principles possibly needed to be modified to take cognizance of what we had observed, and also to take into account the unique set of characteristics operating in a distributed online collaborative learning environment. We, therefore, have generated the following set of modified principles to inform the design of math problems that provide the contexts necessary for the establishment and maintenance of math knowledge-building activity within online CSCL communities:

1. Collectively meaningful principle: Will members of the community be able to collectively make sense of the situation presented in the math problem?
2. The model construction principle: Does the math problem create the need for a model to be constructed or modified, extended or refined? Is attention focused on underlying patterns and regularities?
3. Negotiated collective-evaluation principle: Will all members of the online community be able to judge for themselves when the responses are good enough? For what purposes are the results needed? By whom? When?

Copyright © 2004, Idea Group Inc. Copying or distributing in print or electronic forms without written permission of Idea Group Inc. is prohibited.

4. The model documentation principle: Will the math problem require students to explicitly reveal how they are thinking about the situation? What kind of system (math objects, patterns, regularities) are they thinking about?

5. The simple prototype principle: Will the solution to the math problem provide a useful prototype (or metaphor) for interpreting a variety of other structurally similar situations?

6. The model generalization principle: Can the model generated be applied to a broader range of situations? Is the model reusable, sharable and modifiable?

In the near future, we intend to have students in an Australian school and the students at a Canadian school working on ranking list problems similar to those utilized in studies 1 and 2. Then via the means of Knowledge Forum, the Canadian and Australian students will comment on one another's models and iteratively revise their models based on these comments. This will provide us with opportunities to engage in further analysis of inter-group data (with a condition that looks at cross-country configurations) and also with opportunities to:

• Evaluate and verify/modify our set of principles for the design of model-eliciting math problems generated from the two studies; and

• Generate a unified conceptual framework (based on this set of modified principles) to inform the design of model-eliciting mathematical problems that provide contexts for establishing and maintaining knowledge-building discourse and activity within distributed, online collaborative learning environments, such as Knowledge Forum.

In this study, pre-service teacher education students from Australia and Canada will act as online mentors and co-problem solvers with the primary school students. This will enable us to investigate how online CSCL math knowledge-building communities can be used to facilitate, not only the development of math subject matter knowledge, but also the development of pedagogical content knowledge in pre-service teacher education students.

The findings that have emanated from the TIMA and CHiLE research programs clearly indicate that comprehension modeling tools (such as those found in TIMA and CHiLE) can facilitate the construction of mathematical knowledge by enabling students to adequately represent mathematical problems and to translate within and across representation modes during problem solving. The findings also clearly indicate that these tools also do much to facilitate synchronous face-to-face knowledge-building discourse between students. However, the tools provided by TIMA do not enable students to reify the strategy (or model) used to solve a math problem on the screen, to animate the "story" of the problem and to reflect on and revisit the problem on many occasions after it has been solved. All of these conditions that the research from the CHiLE

Copyright © 2004, Idea Group Inc. Copying or distributing in print or electronic forms without written permission of Idea Group Inc. is prohibited.

research program has found seem to be essential for asynchronous online knowledge-building discourse.

Although CHiLE represents a significant advance on math representation tools that hitherto have been used in CSCL environments, a number of issues related to the communication of ideas/models and the transmission of meaning, sense and understanding[6] need to be addressed, before it can become an optimal tool for facilitating knowledge-building discourse. Data from the studies conducted in 2002 clearly indicate that if these issues are to be resolved, then a new theoretical framework to inform the research and development of CSCL environment comprehension modeling tools needs to be developed. This new theoretical framework needs to include not just ideas from research into external mathematical representations (e.g., De Jong et al., 1998; Kaput, 1992; Olive, 2000), but also ideas from research conducted in other areas such as online collaboration (e.g., Suthers, Hundhausen, & Girardeau, 2002; Klopfer & Woodruff, 2002) and cognitive science and multimedia learning (e.g., Mayer, 2001; Moreno & Mayer, 2000; Sweller, 1999).

Therefore, in the near future, we intend to develop a theoretical framework that takes cognizance of the findings from research into external mathematical representations and the findings from research into online collaboration and cognitive science and multimedia learning. Then in a series of design experiments (Bereiter, 2002b), we intend to evaluate and revise the theoretical framework in order to generate a set of guidelines to inform the design of comprehension modeling tools that will enable students to engage in online hypermedia discourse that leads to the building of mathematical artifacts.

CONCLUSION

In this chapter, we addressed the question of whether the mathematics education community was ready to utilize online, collaborative knowledge-building communities of practice, one of the most promising manifestations of online learning. We identified two of the major reasons why mathematics educators have had much less success in establishing online knowledge-building communities than their peers in other discipline areas, such as social studies, art, history, geography, language arts and science. The reasons are:

1.   The inability of most textbook math problems to elicit ongoing discourse and other knowledge-building activity either during or after the process of problem solving, and

2.   The limitations inherent in most CSCL environments' math representational tools.

We then proposed two possible ways in which these two problems could be overcome, namely the inclusion within CSCL environments, such as Knowledge

Copyright © 2004, Idea Group Inc. Copying or distributing in print or electronic forms without written permission of Idea Group Inc. is prohibited.

Forum, of model-eliciting mathematical problems and comprehension modeling tools. However, we also argued that the development of model-eliciting problems suitable for use in online CSCL environments and of comprehension modeling tools is being restricted by the lack of adequate theoretical frameworks to inform the research and development of these two types of artifacts. Therefore, we have proposed that the development of adequate theoretical frameworks should be a major research priority in this field.

REFERENCES

Avilés-Garay, E. J. (2001). *Using multiple coordinated representations in a technology-intensive setting to teach linear functions at the college level.* Doctoral dissertation, University of Illinois at Urbana-Champaign, USA. [Web document] Retrieved Oct. 16, 2002, from the web site: http://ponce.inter.edu/cai/tesis/eaviles-index.htm.

Ball, D., Lubienski, S., & Mewborn, D. (2002). Research on teaching mathematics: The unsolved problem of teachers' mathematical knowledge. In V. Richardson (Ed.), *Handbook of Research on Teaching* (4th ed., pp. 433-456). Washington, DC: AERA.

Bereiter, C. (2002a). *Education and Mind in the Knowledge Age.* Mahwah, NJ: Erlbaum.

Bereiter, C. (2002b). Design research for sustained innovation. *Cognitive Studies, Bulletin of the Japanese Cognitive Science Society, 9*(3), 321-327.

Brett, C., Nason, R. A., & Woodruff, E. (2002). Communities of inquiry among pre-service teachers investigating mathematics. *THEMES in Education 3*(1), 39-62.

Bruce, B. C., & Easley, J. (n.d.). *Emerging communities of practice: collaboration and communication in action research.* Retrieved October 26, 2002, from the web site: http://www.mste.uiuc.edu/dime/collab_com.html.

Canadian Broadcasting Corporation (CBC). (2000). *The post-Olympic accounting.* Retrieved September 11, 2001, from the web site: http://www.cbc.ca/insidecbc/newsinreview/nov2000/sydney/post.htm.

Charles, K., & Nason, R. A. (2000). Towards the specification of a multimedia environment to facilitate the learning of fractions. *Themes in Education, 1*(3), 263-288.

De Corte, E., Verschaffel, L., Lowyck, J., Dhert, S., & Vanderput, L. (1999). Networking minds in a collaborative learning environment for mathematics problem solving and problem solving using "Knowledge Forum." In K. Cox, B. Gorayska, & J. Marsh (Eds.), *Networking Minds: Proceedings of the Third International Cognitive Technology Conference* (pp. 187-204).

Copyright © 2004, Idea Group Inc. Copying or distributing in print or electronic forms without written permission of Idea Group Inc. is prohibited.

East Lansing, MI: Media Interface & Network Design Lab, Michigan State University.

De Jong, T., Ainsworth, S., Dobson, M., van der Hulst, A., Levonen, J., Reimann, P., et al. (1998). Acquiring knowledge in science and mathematics: the use of multiple representations in technology-based learning environments. In M. W. Van Someren, P. Reimann, H. P. A. Boshuizen, & T. De Jong (Eds.), *Learning with Multiple Representations* (pp. 9-40). Oxford, UK: Pergamon.

Greeno, J. G., & Hall, R. P. (1997). Practicing representation: Learning with and about representational forms. *Phi Delta Kappan, 78*(5), 361-367.

Halmos, P. (1980). The heart of mathematics. *American Mathematical Monthly, 87,* 519-524.

Janvier, C., Girardon, C., & Morand, J. C. (1993). Mathematics symbols and representations. In P. S. Wilson (Ed.), *Research Ideas for the Classroom: High School Mathematics* (pp. 79-102). New York: Macmillan Publishing Company.

Kaput, J. J. (1992). Technology and mathematics education. In D. A. Grouws (Ed.), *Handbook of Research on Mathematics Teaching and Learning* (pp. 515-556). New York: Macmillan.

Klopfer, E., & Woodruff, E. (2002, January). The impact of distributed and ubiquitous computational devices on the collaborative learning environment. In G. Stahl (Ed.), *Proceedings from the Annual CSCL Conference,* p. 702. Boulder, CO: University of Colorado and CSCL2002.

Lemke, J. L. (2001). *Mathematics in the middle: Measure, picture, gesture, sign and word.* Retrieved November 22, 2002, from the web site: http://academic.brooklyn.cuny.edu/education/jlemke/papers/myrdene.htm.

Lesh, R. (2000). Beyond constructivism: Identifying mathematical abilities that are most needed for success beyond school in an age of information. *Mathematics Education Research Journal 12*(3), 177-95.

Lesh, R., & Doerr, H. (in press). Foundations of a models and modelling perspective on mathematics teaching, learning and problem solving. In H. Doerr & R. Lesh (Eds.), *Beyond Constructivism: A Models and Modelling Perspective on Mathematics Learning, Problem Solving and Teaching.* Mahwah, NJ: Erlbaum.

Lesh, R., Cramer, K., Doerr, H., Post, T., & Zawoiewski, J. (in press). Model development sequences. In H. Doerr & R. Lesh (Eds.), *Beyond Constructivism: A Models and Modelling Perspective on Mathematics Learning, Problem Solving and Teaching.* Mahwah, NJ: Erlbaum.

Lesh, R., Hoover, M., Hole, B., Kelly, A., & Post, T. (1999). Principles for developing thought-revealing activities for students and teachers. Retrieved September 4, 2001, from the web site: http://tango.mth.umassd.edu/ResearchDesign/Digests/HoleLesh.html.

Copyright © 2004, Idea Group Inc. Copying or distributing in print or electronic forms without written permission of Idea Group Inc. is prohibited.

Mayer, R. E. (2001). *Multimedia Learning.* New York: Cambridge University Press.

Moreno, R., & Mayer, R. E. (2000). A learner-centered approach to multimedia explanations: Deriving instructional design principles from cognitive theory. *Interactive Multimedia Electronic Journal of Computer-Enhanced Learning, 2*(2). Retrieved February 16, 2003, from the web site: http://imej.wfu.edu/articles/2000/2/05/index.asp.

Moschkovich, J., Schoenfeld, A. H., & Arcavi, A. (1993). Aspects of understanding: On multiple perspectives and representations of linear relations and connections among them. In T. A. Romberg, E. Fennema, &. T. P. Carpenter (Eds.), *Integrating Research on the Graphical Representation of Functions* (pp. 69-100). Hillsdale, NJ: Lawrence Erlbaum Associates Publishers.

Nason, R., & Pham, H. T. (2003). An evaluation of a constructivist hypermedia learning environment for teaching and learning of fractions. Manuscript in preparation.

Nason, R. A., & Woodruff, E. (in press). Promoting collective model-eliciting mathematics activity in a Grade 6 CSCL classroom. *Canadian Journal of Learning and Technology.*

Nason, R.A., Brett, C., & Woodruff, E. (1996). Creating and maintaining knowledge-building communities of practice during mathematical investigations. In P. Clarkson (Ed.), *Technology in Mathematics Education* (pp. 20-29). Melbourne, Australia: Mathematics Education Research Group of Australasia.

Nason, R. A., Woodruff, E., & Lesh, R. (2002, July). Fostering authentic, sustained and progressive mathematical knowledge-building activity in CSCL communities. In B. Barton, C. Irwin, M. Pfannkuch & M.O.J. Thomas (Eds.), *Mathematics Education in the South Pacific, Proceedings of the Annual Conference of the Mathematics Education Research Group of Australasia*, Auckland, pp. 504-511. Sydney: MERGA.

National Council of Teachers of Mathematics (2000). *Principles and Standards for School Mathematics.* Reston, VA: National Council of Teachers of Mathematics.

Olive, J. (2000). Computer tools for interactive mathematical activity in the elementary school. *International Journal of Computers for Mathematical Learning, 5*(3), 241-62.

Olive, J., & Steffe, L. (1994). *Tools for interactive mathematical activity. TIMA: BARS–A tool designed to help teachers help children construct their own knowledge of whole numbers and fractions.* (ERIC Document No. ED389510.), Columbus, OH: ERIC.

Porzio, D. T. (1994). The effects of differing technological approaches to calculus on students' use and understanding of multiple representations

Copyright © 2004, Idea Group Inc. Copying or distributing in print or electronic forms without written permission of Idea Group Inc. is prohibited.

when solving problems. Doctoral dissertation, University of Illinois, *Dissertation Abstracts International, 55*(10), 3128A.

Scardamalia, M. (2002). Collective cognitive responsibility for the advancement of knowledge. In B. Smith (Ed.), *Liberal Education in a Knowledge Society* (pp. 67-98). Chicago, IL: Open Court.

Scardamalia, M., & Bereiter, C. (1996). Adaption and understanding: A case for new cultures of schooling. In S. Vosniadou, E. De Corte, R. Glaser, & H. Mandel (Eds.), *International Perspectives on the Psychological Foundations of Technology-Based Learning Environments* (pp. 149-165). Mahwah, NJ: Lawrence Erlbaum Associates.

Suthers, D. D., Hundhausen, C. D., & Girardeau, L. (2002, December). Comparing the roles of representations in face to face and online collaborations. In Kinshuk, R. Lewis, K. Akahori, R. Kemp, T. Okamoto, L. Henderson, & C.-H. Lee (Eds.), *Proceedings of the International Conference for Computers in Education (ICCE2002)* (pp. 186-194). Auckland, New Zealand: Association for the Advancement of Computing in Education (AACE).

Sweller, J. (1999). *Instructional Design in Technical Areas.* Melbourne, Australia: ACER.

Woodruff, E. (in press). Comprehension modeling tools in computer supported discursive environments. *OISE/Papers in STSE Education.*

Woodruff, E., & Nason, R. (2003). Math tools for knowledge-building and comprehension modeling in CSCL. In B. Wasson, R. Baggetun, U. Hoppe, & S. Ludvigsen (Eds.), *CSCL2003 Community Events Communication and Interaction.* Bergen, Norway: University of Bergen, pp. 31-34.

ENDNOTES

[1]   Knowledge Forum is a single, communal multimedia database into which students may enter various kinds of text or graphic notes. Knowledge Forum activities do not stand apart from the regular school program the way most computer activities usually do. They are integral to the whole classroom process. When offline, the students are planning knowledge-building projects, seeking information from a variety of sources and engaging in small group and whole class discussions of questions, ideas and findings. When online, the students are entering and following the plans, entering new information through text and graphic notes and carrying on more pointed discourse on questions, ideas and findings. Constructive commenting on other students' notes is proactively encouraged and has been shown to be effective in facilitating the advancement of knowledge (Bereiter, 2002a; Scardamalia, 2002).

Copyright © 2004, Idea Group Inc. Copying or distributing in print or electronic forms without written permission of Idea Group Inc. is prohibited.

2   In face-to-face contexts, students often find it impossible to look at and evaluate all the other groups' math models. Therefore, some of the best ideas do not always surface within face-to-face contexts. Knowledge Forum provides students with the opportunity to look at and evaluate all of the other groups' models

3   Research on model-eliciting problem solving in face-to-face contexts conducted by Lesh and his colleagues (Lesh & Doerr, in press) indicates that most groups of students only engage in one to four iterative revisions of their models. In the two studies being reported in this chapter, each group of students engaged in five to eight iterative revisions.

4   This was conducted in a face-to-face mode.

5   This is due to the fact that most pre- and in-service teacher education students have been found to have impoverished repertoires of subject matter knowledge about fractions, ratio and proportion (Ball, Lubienski, & Mewborn, 2002).

6   Some of the issues with respect to communication of ideas/models and the transmission of meaning, sense and understanding that need to be addressed include: (1) the coordination of and linkages between different types of math representations, (2) links between math representation tools and Knowledge Forum, (3) the juxtaposition of text notes and the iconic representations within the animation slides, (4) the inclusion of narration, and (5) the elimination of excess information.

Copyright © 2004, Idea Group Inc. Copying or distributing in print or electronic forms without written permission of Idea Group Inc. is prohibited.

Chapter VI

Thinking Out of a Bowl of Spaghetti: Learning to Learn in Online Collaborative Groups

John M. Dirkx
Michigan State University, USA

Regina O. Smith
Michigan State University, USA

ABSTRACT

Online learning programs have been expanding at exponential rates. To help encourage the development of learning communities within these environments, practitioners and scholars are advocating more collaborative learning approaches. Yet, many students express reservations about learning in small groups, particularly online. In this chapter, we explore more deeply the nature of student ambivalence about online collaborative learning. Weaving the findings of case studies of online groups with research and theory in collaborative learning and group dynamics, we argue that students hold on to highly subjective and individualistic understandings of teaching and learning. These perspectives manifest themselves in their overall approach to group inquiry and decision making. To embrace a more

Copyright © 2004, Idea Group Inc. Copying or distributing in print or electronic forms without written permission of Idea Group Inc. is prohibited.

interdependent and intersubjective perspective requires a paradigm shift among members with regard to teaching and learning, and a working through of the powerful emotional dynamics associated with group development. We conclude with suggestions for designing and facilitating online environments that addresses these issues.

INTRODUCTION

At a regional educational conference several years ago, two participants were observed walking out during the introduction of a concurrent session. After introducing the topic, the presenter asked participants to form into small groups for further work. Obviously distraught over this methodological turn in the session, one turned to the other and said, "Don't they just lecture anymore? I get so sick of this group stuff."

This comment reveals the profound ambivalence that many learners feel towards collaborative learning methods in general and group work, in particular. While learners often express a desire to be more engaged and active in their learning, they are often less than enthusiastic about learning through small group work. Online technologies often exacerbate learners' ambivalence toward group work (Bernard, Beatriz, & St. Piere, 2000; Bullen, 1998).

This chapter focuses on the experiences of adults in online collaborative learning groups, and their struggles with learning to learn in these groups. Online learning is perhaps the most rapidly expanding dimension of higher education and professional development. The number of courses offered online was expected to nearly triple during the last decade. In 1999, 85% of higher education institutions were projected to offer online courses (Distance Learning May Soar, 1999). A variety of institutions are now providing extensive postsecondary programs online, increasing pressure on traditional colleges and universities to quickly and efficiently enhance their online distance education (Schrum, 1998; Sorg & McElhinney, 2000). Within our own institution, faculty are scrambling to meet the demand for courses and advising, created by unanticipated growth in an online masters program barely two years.

The emergence of collaborative learning in online environments is related to this rapid growth. Early efforts were largely characterized by a kind of electronic correspondence study, in which passive learners were exposed to large volumes of printed material and worked largely in solitude, with occasional interactions with the instructor (Boshier, Mohapi, & Boulton, 1997). As this form of delivery became increasingly popular, emerging problems of attrition and motivation among participants (Bullen, 1998; Haraism, Hiltz, Teles, & Turoff, 1995; McConnell, 2000) suggested more attention was needed in the overall design of the learning environment, the specific instructional methodologies being employed (Harasim, 1990; Gunarwardena, 1998; McConnell, 2000) and

Copyright © 2004, Idea Group Inc. Copying or distributing in print or electronic forms without written permission of Idea Group Inc. is prohibited.

experiences that participants were having in these programs (Burge, 1994; Sage, 2000). To address these issues, practitioners were encouraged to design learning environments that actively engaged participants (Gunarwardena, 1998; Harasim et al., 1995), focused on real-life problems (Barrows, 1994; Koschmann, 1996), included learning activities grounded in learner's life contexts and experiences (Jonassen, 1997; Koschmann, 1996) and fostered a sense of community (Palloff & Pratt, 1999).

Such characteristics, reflective of basic principles of adult learning (Eastmond, 1995; Merriam & Cafferrella, 1999), imply a paradigm shift in learners' beliefs about teaching and learning (Barr & Tagg, 1995). In the new paradigm, learners confront real-world practice problems or issues that have no clear solution. Working together in small consensus groups, they pursue the study of these problems through processes of inquiry and research. In the learning process, learners are expected to integrate their understanding of relevant research and theory and their own relevant experiences.

In theory, collaborative learning sounds like the answer to many of the emerging problems for online learning. From our own experiences as both teachers and learners in face-to-face settings, however, we have become aware of students' reluctance toward and even dissatisfaction with group work. These perceptions, as well as the fact that all of this would be attempted in an environment where most, if not all, interactions would occur virtually led us to wonder how students experience consensus group work in a formal online course.

To this end, we have been studying students' perceptions of and experiences in small, online collaborative groups. In this chapter, we argue that students demonstrate a profound ambivalence toward online collaborative learning, fueled in part by the emotional dynamics associated with the forces of individuation (Boyd, 1991) and group development (Smith & Berg, 1997). Our research suggests that online learning groups get stuck between opposing fears of loss of individual voice and identity, associated with belonging, and fears of isolation, alienation and estrangement from the group, associated with asserting one's individuality. As the group attempts to move forward, these fears contribute to a growing sense of ambivalence, by making it difficult for its members to successfully navigate the paradigmatic shift required of them by collaborative environments. Online relationships and communications, already made difficult by these emotional dynamics, are further complicated by the technologies that students use to interact. Our research suggests that students struggle with the development of a sense of interdependence and intersubjectivity within their online groups (Lushyn & Kennedy, 2000), but end up holding fast to subjective, individualistic conceptions of learning.

Our research is situated within the theoretical perspectives of collaborative learning (Bruffee, 1999) and group dynamics (Boyd, 1991; Smith & Berg, 1997;

Copyright © 2004, Idea Group Inc. Copying or distributing in print or electronic forms without written permission of Idea Group Inc. is prohibited.

Durkin, 1984). To help illuminate our argument, we weave a discussion of this literature with the voices of students from our case studies. Following this discussion, we explore the theoretical and practical implications of this argument, concluding with recommendations for designing and facilitating online groups to constructively work through these issues. First, however, we present a brief discussion of the context and methods of our case studies.

CASE STUDIES OF ONLINE COLLABORATIVE LEARNING

To learn more about students' experiences in online collaborative environments, we conducted case studies of collaborative learning groups in an online course within a graduate program in higher and adult education. Twenty-six students were purposively assigned by the instructor to groups of three to four per group, to maximize heterogeneity with each group. The groups were diverse in terms of academic status, age, ethnicity, professional experience, gender and race.

The course lasted for 16 weeks, spanning a traditional academic semester. The course was conducted entirely online. Individual groups, however, could decide to meet face to face, if they desired, although only one group chose to sporadically meet face to face. A two-week orientation was provided on the technology of learning online, problem-based learning and working collaboratively in online groups. In addition, each learner was afforded opportunities to become familiar with technical skills for online work, such as uploading and downloading a file, and participating in both the chat and discussion boards.

Following completion of the orientation activities, the groups began to work on the problems that constituted the core of the curriculum. Each group was assigned three real-life problems, which represent issues that students were likely to face as practitioners in higher and adult education. Using their own experiences of similar situations and research, and theory related to the scenario, the students were instructed to define the issues in the problem, what makes it a problem and how they would address the problem. Each group was expected to produce a written product that specified and further developed their definition of the problem, the proposed solution and its rationale. Time periods given to complete the three problems ranged from three to five weeks. The first problem was perceived to be somewhat less complex and required less time to address. The final problem was thought to be the most complex and groups were given the most time to complete this problem.

Following each problem, the groups were expected to debrief by discussing both the group and task processes. Individual debriefing papers were turned in to the instructor. While there was a small amount of individual work associated

Copyright © 2004, Idea Group Inc. Copying or distributing in print or electronic forms without written permission of Idea Group Inc. is prohibited.

with this process, the bulk of the learning experience was bound up within this problem-based structure.

The instructor for this class was a senior faculty member in the graduate program, with a strong background in group dynamics and experience-based learning. He monitored and occasionally participated in group discussion boards and chat rooms, held online office hours for students and facilitated class-wide asynchronous discussions.

Each student participated in one or more in depth interviews and completed a brief background survey to identify their demographic information and computer experience. They also allowed us to use their class journals, reflection papers and the archives of their discussion boards and chat rooms. The stories of their experiences presented in this chapter are derived from these sources of data. The interview data were used as the primary data source. These data were subjected to a constant comparative method of data analysis. Tentative findings emerging from this source were triangulated with data from the students' journals, reflection papers and the class archives. Based on these further analyses, tentative themes were modified or revised as appropriate.

We present accounts of the students' experiences within the context of our theoretical frameworks. This stylistic approach might create an impression that we are making broad claims of generalizability about our findings. Such claims are not our intention. Rather, we wish to suggest, based on our analysis of our findings and the literature, a series of tentative understandings that might lead to a deeper understanding of why so many students are not happy with group learning experiences. These claims about consensus group work will require additional studies in other contexts, with different instructional approaches.

COLLABORATIVE LEARNING AS A PARADIGM SHIFT

In these case studies, the majority of formal learning experiences took place within the context of small, collaborative groups. Like many educational ideas, collaborative learning means different things to different people. For example, cooperative leaning is an increasingly popular approach in higher education (Cohen, 1986; Johnson & Johnson, 1978; Sharan, Hertz-Lazarowitz, & Ackerman, 1980; Slavin, 1983, 1985), and is the focus of numerous faculty development workshops, designed to promote collaboration in the college classroom. Cooperative learning involves individual effort (Allen & Plax, 1999; Bruffee, 1999), but brings students together in small groups to work on specific, well-defined and well-structured problems and questions, for which there are clear and correct answers or solutions (Jonassen, 1997). For the most part, students work with well-defined rules and remain under the direction and control of the teacher

Copyright © 2004, Idea Group Inc. Copying or distributing in print or electronic forms without written permission of Idea Group Inc. is prohibited.

(Bruffee, 1999). Often, the process involves a kind of division of labor, as in the popular jigsaw, in which the students help one another master the appropriate body of knowledge that is designed and predetermined by the teacher (Flannery, 1994). Ultimately, learning is regarded as an individual effort that is facilitated by participation in the group.

Collaborative learning shares many of the characteristics of cooperative learning. It differs, however, primarily in the nature of the tasks assigned, where the overall control for the learning process resides, the nature of knowledge and how learning is conceptualized. In consensus collaborative learning, groups confront complex, real-life situations that are messy, ill-structured and have no clear resolution or right answer (Bruffee, 1999). The goal of group work is to shift the locus of control in the classroom from the teacher to the student peer groups (Abercrombie, 1960; Bruffee, 1999; Crook, 1994). Learners are entrusted with the ability to govern themselves, in order to help them acknowledge dissent and disagreement, and cope with difference (Bruffee, 1999; Gerlach, 1994; Flannery, 1994).

While collaborative learning groups also make heavy use of subject matter, they are more interested in using this information to help address the assigned problem, rather than just to facilitate mastery of it among individual learners. As students work in small, heterogeneous groups, they learn both the subject matter content, appropriate problem-solving and critical thinking skills, and skills necessary to work together collaboratively (Abercrombie, 1960; Bruffee, 1999; Flannery, 1994). Students are considered co-constructors of knowledge (Bruffee, 1999), rather than just consumers of it.

Consensus is critical to the process (Abercrombie, 1960; Crook, 1994), because it is only through consensus that the members of the group are required to listen, hear, understand and finally accept the view point of fellow group members. When students are forced, through dialogue and deliberation, to come to consensus, they must work harder to consider all viewpoints, in order to reach agreement (Gerlach, 1994; Flannery, 1994). In collaborative learning, students call into question, through self-reflection or self-critique, the assumptions, values, beliefs, symbols and rules of conduct that characterize their existing ways of meaning making.

Benefits and Limitations of Group Work

Thus, learning to learn collaboratively often involves a dramatic shift in one's views of teaching and learning. Central to this shift are changing perspectives on the nature of knowledge and the roles of the teacher and one's peers in the process of learning. As a student, one might easily reject methods that might render one passive recipients of information. Many adult learners want to be actively involved in the learning process and become impatient and frustrated with online methods that render them passive recipients of information

Copyright © 2004, Idea Group Inc. Copying or distributing in print or electronic forms without written permission of Idea Group Inc. is prohibited.

(Bernard et al., 2000; Bullen, 1998). Similar to other reports in the literature (Bullen, 1998; Eastmond, 1995; McConnell, 2000; McDonald & Gibson, 1998), our students express a desire to spend time working in small groups, and report that they enjoy interactions with other students and benefit from their diverse perspectives.

For example, Luther told us, "Working in small groups is like having a supportive network, a place where you can talk with peers to get suggestions, to get constructive criticism." Walden, too, appreciates the value of group work:

"I find group work to be incredibly challenging and exciting because it's vibrant. There is so much that happens there and as knowledge gets constructed and reconstructed constantly. And it's just amazing to stay on top of that and be engaged in that. And I love it."

Marcella believes that "working in groups is good for hearing diverse perspectives."

While course participants expressed support for the value of learning in groups, it was clear that they struggled with the shift in perspective demanded by consensus group work. Consistent with much of the face-to-face literature (Bruffee, 1999), most of our online students express dissatisfaction with group work, and they often find various ways to convert what is intended to be a collaborative activity into a collection of individual efforts (Kitchen & McDougall, 1999). In some contexts, students seem to view group work as an onerous component of their course expectations. As Marie suggests, collaborative learning is just another thing to be checked off:

I don't think we actually did what the professor was expecting. ...It seems that there is nothing really to talk about online with all of the class and in my group. I really do not see the point in having to make contact three times per week. It seems that I will put anything on the board just to get points.

Walden's reflections on his course experiences suggest a lack of energy and enthusiasm for group-related activities assigned by the instructor. He compares these activities with those of co-authoring an article:

There's a different energy level associated with it. The article has a more compelling energy to it because we were compelled by the experience to write the article. ...The class piece is not unlike this but the energy is different because it has more of a task like feel to it. ...the article has kind of a compelling life experience. This has a feel of fulfilling the task to meet the requirement.

Copyright © 2004, Idea Group Inc. Copying or distributing in print or electronic forms without written permission of Idea Group Inc. is prohibited.

Working with Others

Trying to get work done with other students is also a source of consternation for some students. India moaned, "For me it's like pulling teeth. It's like I have to sit here and I have to go through and respond to my ideas. I have to put the ideas there and then everybody puts their ideas there and somehow we come up with a group paper." Several students found it difficult to get fellow group members to pull their weight. Paul commented on the difficulty of dividing the work online: "It's frustrating when you feel like you're doing more work for something than other people are, which is maybe the nature of some group anyway. But in a classroom it's easier to divvy that up equally."

India felt that some took advantage of the policy that provided group-wide grades for group products:

If you are going to be graded as a team effort, those people will only take a backseat and the ones who are not comfortable step-out [then] you end up all getting the same grade. And there is a tremendous amount of resentment about that. I mean to me, it's just doing a good job. I don't want to be embarrassed.

Donald commented, "I think these are two areas why people don't like to work together. One they don't show up and two members of the group don't put up quality work."

Learning Collaboratively as an Individual

It seems clear that it is not so much working in groups that concerns our learners, as it is working together to accomplish group goals or producing a common product, such as writing a report together. India "Can you be an individual learner in a collaborative setting? That's the tension." In reflecting on his group experience, Walden describes his concerns about being held responsible for a common group product:

I find that when it becomes time to create a product that group work will frustrate me, because I have less patience for the product's creation than the time that it takes to produce the product to the group, than I have to do for the knowledge creation, which I think is the part of the group work that I really like.

At the end of problem one, Sophia wrote:

Tonight we chatted about putting the final project together. It seems like this is always the most difficult aspect of the work for me tying it all up. The ideas are fun, exciting, interesting, learning-oriented, stimulating. The

Copyright © 2004, Idea Group Inc. Copying or distributing in print or electronic forms without written permission of Idea Group Inc. is prohibited.

process is limiting, challenging, the project is always disappointing because it naturally leaves out some fun ideas.

Students' ambivalence toward group work is clearly evident in their longing to work on their own (Ragoonaden & Borledeau, 2000). Hoping to work independently, online learners are often resentful of the time required to work with a small group. Our observations suggest that in online learning environments, students seem to seek experiences in which they are able to individually share their perceptions and experiences, to be listened to and heard by others, but in which they are ultimately individually responsible and held accountable for their own learning.

Luther said that in other graduate courses, he was given the opportunity to work in small groups, but he states emphatically, "You could work by yourself." Autumn looked forward to the final capstone project for the course, where she saw the "chance to really try to do some writing on my own and not feel like I have to be the cheerleader and bring other people along for the ride." The relatively large amount of group work caught Scarlett by surprise:

I understood that there would be a lot of group interaction — however, I didn't realize how difficult this would be. It is very challenging to balance life, work, an always-changing schedule and taking classes. I had hoped that by taking a course on line, I would have more time to work on it at my own pace and my own schedule. Working with a group makes that virtually impossible — and that's not a bad thing, it's just not what I had expected when considering getting my degree online.

Autumn reflected similar concerns, "I started to realize that I'm not sure in some projects I want to invest the time in the team process to get to the product."

The Problem of Difference in Reaching Consensus

Differences among students generated high levels of frustration, which left them feeling overwhelmed and unsure of how to proceed. Students like Chris indicated that the differences seemed insurmountable at times:

OH MY GOSH! talk about frustrating...weren't on the same page. We didn't discuss how we would proceed and everyone just kind of threw their ideas out there. We all agreed on the problem, but did not agree on the components of the problem. ... I kept trying to get more of an explanation if I did not understand someone's rationale behind a component but ended up giving up when it wasn't portrayed effectively. Some components were too huge to tackle but I couldn't get that across to the others.

Copyright © 2004, Idea Group Inc. Copying or distributing in print or electronic forms without written permission of Idea Group Inc. is prohibited.

Ann explained the extent of their differences: "at one point we had four distinctly different perspectives from the same writing we were reflecting personal and professional place, life experiences, generational and situational biases." India found it difficult to think clearly when trying to work with other students:

This group process is thrusting it upon me. I can't think straight. It's like thinking out of a bowl of spaghetti. And that for me is I cannot think logically, as much as India, can ever think logically. I can't think straight. And that's my biggest problem. Whereas if you gave me the problem to do myself, asking me to go out-I could do it.

Most seem to think they could get the work done quicker and at a much higher level of quality, if they were left to do it themselves. For the group work on problem two, India explains:

When Matthew...did the first draft he pretty much lumped it all together and didn't do anything with it. ...it didn't make sense, because it wasn't copying and pasting, and putting ideas where they belonged; it was copied and pasted, period. And, then, the other team member wrote an introduction, because they didn't like Matthew's introduction and then to me it never read like an introduction at all. And then...I never really felt that it was a coherent paper because I always like an introduction and conclusion. I never felt it gelled, this whole paper. ...I find myself saying I could have had this paper done a week ago.

Often it appears that the only thing that kept groups working and creating a final product was the perception that the assignment was required. Janis commented:

If you didn't participate and if you're weren't really saying anything and raising questions or bringing up good, you know, making good ideas or observations about how to approach the problems at hand, then you know my grade would suffer, and I know that. So I just I felt pressure.

To openly challenge the group nature of the assignment would be to challenge the teacher's authority and risk punitive consequences in the form of a poorer grade, sadly a fear too often grounded in reality.

The participants' reflections on their experiences of collaborative learning reflect the struggle they are experiencing in shifting to an interdependent perspective of learning in small groups. Their perceptions reveal the persistence

Copyright © 2004, Idea Group Inc. Copying or distributing in print or electronic forms without written permission of Idea Group Inc. is prohibited.

of beliefs that the individual learner should be the primary focus of the process, and that others are helpful to one's learning so long as one is only accountable to one's self. Consensus group work insists on a paradigm shift that most seem unwilling or unable to make.

Making this shift to a more social and interdependent sense of learning, however, is made more problematic by the emotional demands placed on the learner by the evolving and developing nature of the group.

THE GROUP DYNAMICS OF COLLABORATIVE LEARNING

Collaborative group approaches often evoke strong affective issues among learners that influence their online experiences. In the words of Brookfield and Preskill (1999), they can become "emotional battlegrounds" (p. 40). These affective issues are often associated with the group's dynamics and processes of development. The students in our case study described powerful emotional responses to what was occurring within their small groups. Research and theory in group dynamics helps illuminate how this affect and emotion reflects paradoxi-cal, but evolving, tensions within the group (Smith & Berg, 1997). Little research, however, has focused on these issues in the online environment. For this reason, we draw largely on the literature of face-to-face groups.

Traditionally, teachers who direct the agenda and control the flow of information and activity within a learning setting largely retain authority in the class. Students look to the teacher for direction, guidance and structure, and even take refuge in the safety that this strong figure represents for them. They are largely emotionally dependent on the leadership provided by a strong, powerful teacher figure.

In consensus group work, learners are confronted almost immediately with a different authority structure. Teachers voluntarily de-authorize themselves and, over time, play less and less of a role as an expert or source of structure and direction. Group members are encouraged to assume responsibility for their own structure and direction. As the teacher role is de-authorized, a small group is born. Small groups demonstrate developmental movement, by creating their own goals, guidelines and rules (Wheelan, 1994). As they mature, they struggle with emotionally evocative paradoxes and recurring cycles of progressively interde-pendent behaviors that persistently call into question the relationship of the individual to the group (Smith & Berg, 1997).

Authority Issues

In consensus group work, members must confront and resolve their dependence on the instructor and texts for definitive answers to questions raised

Copyright © 2004, Idea Group Inc. Copying or distributing in print or electronic forms without written permission of Idea Group Inc. is prohibited.

in the learning experience (Bennis & Shepard, 1956). When the teacher makes clear that the small groups will be in charge of their own learning, he or she creates one of the first emotional crises for group members. In this first stage that Bennis and Shepard (1956) describe as dependence, individual members look to the teacher for direction and relationship. If they approach and interact with each other at all in these initial stages of the group, it is largely through the authority of the teacher. While they are often excited about being a member of the group, most members do not want to stand out, and they do little to bring attention to themselves. They look to the teacher to protect them from the tensions and anxieties that lurk just below the surface, usually masked by an aura of politeness and humor. It is a period marked by the paradoxes of belonging (Smith & Berg, 1997), when members begin to explore what it means to be a member of the group and the implications that such membership might have them as an individual.

In consensus group work, the teacher is voluntarily de-authorized. Not available to provide traditional classroom direction, the teacher's move often frustrates students' traditional expectations for direction, structure and relationship. At first, most group members find this somewhat unsettling. In our case studies, the impact of the teacher's nontraditional role was perceived and felt by most members. As learners worked together in small groups, they found themselves wanting from the instructor more guidance, more structure and more information about the task. Donald remarks:

If I could have more teacher-directed information, that would be helpful...if I had lecture notes in front of me and the teacher talking...about major points or major concepts that we want to go over and introduce that and then the problem...I'm pretty much old school...Lecture format, the teacher is talking.

Other group members were implicitly chosen to play the role of a teacher surrogate in their small groups. Chris describes how she and others came to rely on a group member perceived to be far more experienced and knowledgeable than they:

She'd been taking classes for longer. She's more involved in the adult learner type curriculum because she's an administrator. So she just has a lot more experience both book work and job related. And she is amazing. I mean you can ask her a question and she immediately knows and can explain it to you in layman's terms...even though we alternated facilitators, she was always the facilitator. She would say, 'oh, you guys are doing such a great job'...but she took the bull by the horns and just went with it and we totally appreciated that.

Copyright © 2004, Idea Group Inc. Copying or distributing in print or electronic forms without written permission of Idea Group Inc. is prohibited.

These surrogate teachers often resent the imposition of this new responsibility and blame the teacher for not doing his job more effectively. Nard commented, "I felt put upon. ...The faculty member needs to step in, and it didn't happen as well as I think it needed to happen in this course."

For the most part, however, the group's anger and resentment toward the teacher for abdicating the role of authority appears only later in the group's development. In the early stages of the group, members do not usually explicitly voice their displeasure with the teacher, out of deference to an authority that they still wish and hope for. Instead, they do what they must do, turning to one another. To move the work of the group forward, they must learn to authorize one another. With the teacher no longer available as a source of authority or to mediate relationships among the group members, they must turn to one another, eliciting yet another series of difficult emotional paradoxes around the problem of engaging (Smith & Berg, 1997). The group must authorize it members.

As they seek to authorize themselves as individuals in the group, learners run the risk of de-authorizing other group members. For example, Janis felt that her group members did not care about her as an individual. She felt her group's perspective was "if she meets with us fine, if she doesn't fine, we're going to go ahead and just do what we have to do. We're not going to depend on her." Clearly, Janis felt de-authorized by her fellow group members. As group members confront and struggle to work through this issue, they find themselves caught in a vicious, seemingly endless paradoxical cycle of back and forth movement between these two orientations to authority. The capacity, however, of authorizing fellow group members seems critical to the development of interdependency and an intersubective group identity.

Intimacy and Interdependency

In turning toward one another for authorship, group members enter perhaps the most difficult and prolonged series of issues they will face in their group work. From a relatively undifferentiated whole, small groups develop through the gradual individuation of its members from the whole (Boyd, 1991). Being able to turn to one another as sources of authority in the group requires the elaboration of difference and development of self-other relations. That is, realizing one's self as a group member requires the recognition and realization of the other. This is what Benjamin (1988) refers to as intersubjectivity. According to her:

The intersubjective view maintains that the individual grows in and through the relationship to other subjects. Most important, this perspective observes that the other whom the self meets is also a self, a subject in his or her own right. It assumes that we are able and need to recognize the other subject

Copyright © 2004, Idea Group Inc. Copying or distributing in print or electronic forms without written permission of Idea Group Inc. is prohibited.

as different and yet alike, as another who is capable of sharing similar mental experience. (Benjamin, 1988, p. 19)

That is, through the process of individuation within the group, a member begins to see himself or herself and other members as distinct but interrelated beings.

This level of individuation, however, is not a foregone conclusion and, indeed, fails to adequately develop in many groups. The gradual development of interdependence and intersubjectivity requires the cultivation of a culture of intimacy within the group. Intimacy involves an ability to open oneself up to another, as well as being receptive to the otherness and difference of group members. We saw in our case studies how difficult it was for group members to learn to work across difference. In the problem-based consensus groups with which we are working, students need to be able to bring their own issues to the group (subjectivity), but also be willing to allow these issues to change and be redefined as they work with others on broader group issues (intersubjectivity). It involves attending to the concerns and world views of others, to enter more fully into the lives of fellow group members, to be listened to and to actively listen.

As they continue to work, they begin to realize that, in order for the group to progress, they have to be willing to take risks, to disclose more. As one group member suggested, "The whole thing is about learning. I think you do need to learn how to work with other people." But they also realize that, if they do take more risks and begin to interact more authentically with others, they run the risk of not being liked or appreciated by their peers, or even rejected by the group as a whole. This perception is often reflected in the emergence of an impersonal stance among members, expressing reservations about getting too close to fellow group members. Janis comments, "I think...sometimes there can be a little too much interaction to where the focus is so much on you interacting with these people." Others expressed a desire to change groups so that they were not working with the same group throughout the course (requests that were not granted by the instructor). India notes, "Some of it is laborious and this particular part of this program has been laborious. Because we were not even been able to change teams."

Similar to working through issues of authority, students experience a back and forth, paradoxical movement around issues related to intimacy. On the one hand, they may be initially excited about working together with others in a small group. India remarked, "Some of the group stuff is fun. And it enhances learning." At some level, the group is valued by its members, as Ginger suggests:

I don't think I would have learned as much [on my own]... We start out very quietly and look at everything that possibly could be influencing the

Copyright © 2004, Idea Group Inc. Copying or distributing in print or electronic forms without written permission of Idea Group Inc. is prohibited.

problem and what could be an issue... [I] have learned a lot more from the things that we've looked at than actual solving the problem.

Faced with the need to rely on each other, they are forced to question how much they are willing to disclose as a group member, whether they can rely on others and how close they want to draw toward one another. Bennis and Shepard (1956) refer to this as the phase of interdependence and intimacy.

It is a critical and emotionally demanding period in the life of a developing group. To move forward and develop the interdependence needed for effective collaborative learning, they must let go of their own ego needs, and they may be seeking to have them met by the group. Paradoxically, it is only through allowing themselves to more fully and authentically enter into the group that they realize themselves as an individual member of the group (Smith & Berg, 1997). It is during this phase of a group's life, when the tension between the individual and the group seems to emerge into bold relief.

Group members in our case study clearly articulated this tension with the ambivalence surfacing in their work. Their concerns regarding the development of interdependence revolved around several issues: (a) interpersonal issues; (b) perceptions that not all members were working at equal levels or were equally committed to the process; (c) fear of loss of voice; and (d) difficulty with working across differences among group members. Technological concerns seem to compound their difficulties in addressing these issues.

Turning to one another to get the work done precipitates underlying interpersonal tensions and conflicts within the online group experience. David told us that two female members of his group were constantly disagreeing with one another, and he felt helpless to do anything about it. "I just sat there and watched the two of them disagree... I did not want to take sides in a three person group." Scarlett's observations further underscore reluctance among other group members to attend to these tensions, reflecting a fundamental lack of trust within the group: "I don't think people are willing to challenge points of view." These comments reflect tensions around unresolved interpersonal issues that persisted throughout the semester. Janis commented, "I found the communication online was still an issue. There's a problem today and there's a problem tomorrow. So I felt like an attitude was already built up." Sophia, one of Janis' group members, agrees: "I think they kind of felt like she was just kind of out of the loop a little bit or maybe we were out of her loop, you know. I think that was kind of there throughout the semester."

During the second week of problem one, as the group had begun to work together toward the development of their product, Sophia comments in her journal: "I don't know that this group thing is very comfortable for me. I am not sure that I appreciate this." During the last week of problem one, when they are trying to finish their report, she continues:

Copyright © 2004, Idea Group Inc. Copying or distributing in print or electronic forms without written permission of Idea Group Inc. is prohibited.

Group process: I am convinced that [member] is clueless. This forces me to couch everything in terms of her cluelessness... This week has been all about learning group process, nothing about adult learning... I've learned that I can get very frustrated with miscommunication. I am an adult who cares about learning, so when miscommunication happens, it frustrates me. This happens in life and in e-life.

Several students found it difficult to get fellow group members to pull their weight. Marie even found this to be true for fellow members she considered her friends: "[He] is not really around. I did not want to say anything, but I know that Anne has to be disappointed, because I am, but he is my friend and I do not understand his situation... [He] is such a slacker." India complained, "For me it's like pulling teeth. It's like I have to sit here, and I have to go through and respond to my ideas. I have to put the ideas there and, then, everybody puts their ideas there; and somehow we come up with a group paper." In reflecting on his group's work, Donald commented, "I think these are two areas why people don't like to work together. One they don't show up; and two members of the group don't put up quality work." India felt that some took advantage of the policy that provided group-wide grades for group products:

If you are going to be graded as a team effort, those people will only take a backseat and the ones who are not comfortable step-out [then] you end up all getting the same grade. And there is a tremendous amount of resentment about that. I mean to me, it's just doing a good job. I don't want to be embarrassed.

Students are also discouraged by individuals who dominate group discussions or don't appear to listen to all voices expressed in group meetings (Weisband, Schneider, & Connolly, 1995). The loss of their individual voices is at the center of this concern. Lisa told us, "We've got one particular person, and she just wanted to write the whole paper. And then get our input, like afterwards, and so after awhile, you just let her do it." Janis laments:

[I was] beginning to feel this like exclusion, or like my voice was not really all that important. It wasn't validated — my opinions, my thoughts, whatever. I didn't feel my participation was really all that necessary...we were not communicating effectively as a group. I felt left in the cold...non-existent.

As the group approached the deadline for one of the problems, Sophia wrote, "I think that most of my ideas on this one are being left out. ...I'm discovering that in the process, it's easy to then check out when you're ideas aren't central. This makes me wonder about our group."

Copyright © 2004, Idea Group Inc. Copying or distributing in print or electronic forms without written permission of Idea Group Inc. is prohibited.

Differences among individual members also represented a substantial challenge to developing interdependence within the groups. Differences in beliefs and opinions seem almost insurmountable at times, leaving students to feel that they were spinning their wheels and that group meetings were largely a waste of their time (Kitchen & McDougall, 1999). Students like Scarlet felt that group work was challenging because "Everyone works at their own pace and has different styles." Others like India, who prefer to start the writing project early, were frustrated waiting for students who left things go until the last minute. She remarked, "They [the group members] get in the way of my learning...if I have to wait for somebody to do their bit." Lisa noted the extreme challenge of working across difference. "It's hell," she asserted.

In reflecting on her group, Marcella observed, "Writing together is too hard...people have different writing styles, perspectives and commitments to assignments." During the middle of the problem-solving process, Sophia commented:

It's hard for us, as a group, to all see eye to eye on how this problem plays itself out. It's hard to see how things work together and don't work together, especially when we all have different agendas when we come to the table. How does a paper get written when each person disagrees?

HOW TECHNOLOGY MEDIATES GROUP AND INTERPERSONAL DYNAMICS

In developing the authority and interdependency necessary for effective collaboration online, learning groups face substantial emotional hurdles and difficulties. Added to the socio-emotional challenges associated with online group work are the technical challenges typically associated with online learning. Among these challenges are adjusting to the fact that the groups seem to always be meeting (McConnell, 2000), the unique nature of what it means to work in online groups and how the computer mediates students' frustration with the process and other group members.

Unlike face-to-face groups, students' experiences of online groups reflect the perception that 'they are meeting all the time. You are never not meeting with your group.' You turn on the computer and the group is there, in the form of e-mail messages or postings to the discussion board.

But the nature of participation is also quite different. It is all text-based, lacking the subtle nuance of nonverbal communications of face-to-face groups. The texts, and the ways in which they are portrayed and constructed, carry with

Copyright © 2004, Idea Group Inc. Copying or distributing in print or electronic forms without written permission of Idea Group Inc. is prohibited.

them their own nuances, which we are only just beginning to appreciate, let alone realize or understand. Substantial logistical and technical difficulties challenge learners in synchronous, or "chat" environments, to say nothing of the multiple and somewhat schizophrenic patterns of interaction that often characterize these conversations. In asynchronous discussions, there are often time lapses between contributions (Bullen, 1998; Eastmond, 1995; McConnell, 2000). No pressure exists to immediately or spontaneously respond, and group members often take time to carefully reflect on the postings of their group members and to construct their reactions.

As a result, participation in online groups proceeds on its own rhythm and timing that is quite different from face-to-face groups. Students, however, may bring to their involvement in the group perspectives and schemata of group participation acquired from face-to-face groups, only to find that they are not fully appropriate, or useful for this technologically-mediated environment. This notion is revealed in Donald's observations of some of the frustrations with trying to work together online:

Right now we're getting down to trying to finalize our final problem, and it's hard to get everybody's thoughts and feelings into this paper — just communicating over the computer. Where if we were in a group together, it would be a lot easier to exchange ideas and information, as opposed to over the computer, where you have to always type everything. It's hard to refer back to something else and see what's going on.

The constraints of the online group work show up in students' feelings about the experience. Donald said:

Like my group, I've never met them. I don't know who they are face to face, but I know them a little bit. And except for a couple of people that I met this summer down there [on campus], I don't know these people at all. And so there is no real connection there for me, I guess. I feel like I'm missing out on some things maybe. Because I probably zero in on my group and I want to get this project done; so I just zero in on my group and we do that.

Comparisons of the online group work with face-to-face settings are inevitable, and often reveal what students' perceive as missing for them in the online experience:

Like this summer, most people will sit in the same place every time, and they will get to know those people who are pretty close to them; or if you are working in a group, you get to know that group... Now [in this class] our groups are pretty much the same; and it's kind of nice, because you don't

Copyright © 2004, Idea Group Inc. Copying or distributing in print or electronic forms without written permission of Idea Group Inc. is prohibited.

have that awkward time there where [you're] getting to know each other time. We can kind of pretty much get in and get to work, but, at the same token, I don't necessarily [know] what these other people are thinking either.

The disconnect between that with which they are familiar and what they face in online collaborative learning may also be contributing to a sense of ambivalence and dissatisfaction.

Finally, technical issues, such as connection speeds, lack of articulation among various software programs and instability in telephone connections, contribute to students' ongoing frustrations with online collaborative learning (Bernard et al., 2000; Bullen, 1998; Clarebout & Elsen, 2001; Eastmond, 1995; McConnell, 2000). Unfortunately, these factors, as well as the computer itself (Reeves & Nass, 1996), often become scapegoats for the learner's frustrations, derived more from their experiences with some of the socio-emotional issues discussed earlier. As India told us, at one point in her group's discussion, she got so frustrated that she felt like putting her foot through the computer:

I was so disgusted with the last process…so the other thing was I wrote this big thing on issues. You know what are the issues? It was one of the questions. So by Tuesday, I wrote my issues. Two posts down [someone wrote], "India, could you post what your issues are?" I was about ready to put my foot through the computer. Haven't you read? …Needless to say I was ticked off.

In reflecting on his own ambivalence about the process, Donald revealed moments when he was yelling at the computer: "It's frustrating…even though I might be sitting there yelling at my computer and saying that this person isn't the brightest person in the world; but it's still a learning process, because we're going to have to deal with these types of people."

Thus, students' experience of the technology shapes and influences their perceptions of online collaborative learning. While there are aspects of this technology that clearly contribute to their own individual learning outcomes, the students see technological dimensions, as often inhibiting or detracting from their ability to connect and effectively interact with fellow group members.

Despite the theoretical claims of collaborative learning, which suggests that learning is inherently a social phenomenon (Dewey, 1963; Bruffee, 1999; Vygotsky, 1978), learners hold tightly to individualistic, subjective conceptions of learning and use these conceptions to inform their expectations for educational experiences online. Not being able to act on their own subjectivity in completing the assignment appears to be a major source of the dissatisfaction and unhappiness with group work.

Copyright © 2004, Idea Group Inc. Copying or distributing in print or electronic forms without written permission of Idea Group Inc. is prohibited.

THE STRUGGLE FOR INTERDEPENDENCE AND INTERSUBJECTIVITY

In this section, we want to explore the implications our observations might hold for a deeper understanding of the tension in collaborative learning, between the individual and the group, that is, between a view of learning grounded in a subjective view of the self and one informed by an intersubjective sense of self. Our observations suggest that students bring to their online learning environments a strong desire for individual voice and subjectivity. Online experiences that rely heavily on either "lecture" or problem-based consensus group work run the risk of minimizing, or even ignoring, individual identity or subjectivity, of not allowing individual learners to have a voice in the experience. As a result, students actively resist both kinds of learning experiences. The added stress of consensus group work, the associated emotional dynamics of group development, the concomitant logistical and technical challenges, lack of nonverbal communication cues and lack of spontaneity serve only to add to participants' ambivalence and uncertainty about its value in their learning (Ragoonaden & Bordeleau, 2000). Collaborative learning online seems haunted by a strong desire among learners to express their own identity within a group context and to be individually responsible for their own learning.

Yet, collaborative learning, as we have defined it here (Bruffee, 1999), revolves around a shift from independence to interdependence and from a subjective to an intersubjective sense of identity. We have demonstrated that students' experiences of online consensus groups encounters revolve around the core issues of authority and intimacy. These are two fundamental dimensions of collaborative learning (Bruffee, 1999) and of group life (Bennis & Shepard, 1956; Smith & Berg, 1997). Both tasks carry with them inherent risks that encourage learners to retreat into their own experiences of the group. Such moves, however, reduce the collaborative nature and effort of the work, and the energy and enthusiasm associated with the work. Not working through these tensions results in the creation of a host of additional strategies that may contribute to the completion of the product, but seem to significantly detract from both the process and the outcome of the learning experience.

When viewed through the lenses of collaborative learning and group dynamics, student ambivalence and dissatisfaction within online collaborative group work is indicative of normal anxieties surrounding transitional periods in group life. Central to this transition process is the need for group members to reconstruct a sense of identity that is grounded in the intersubjective realities of their group contexts, rather than holding on to individualistic, subjective senses of themselves as learners. Both issues of authority and intimacy, however, carry with them an implicit threat of either alienating the individual learner from others in the group or of obliterating a sense of who he or she is as a group member.

Copyright © 2004, Idea Group Inc. Copying or distributing in print or electronic forms without written permission of Idea Group Inc. is prohibited.

It is this sense of threat that seems to be the core challenge to the development and emergence of intersubjectivity within the online collaborative group.

Our case studies suggest that, at some level, group members sense the group's movement toward intersubjectivity and the reconstruction of individual identity. India suggests, "You do try and help your teammates. You do try to say to them well why don't you try this or why don't you do that." Sophia comments,

"I feel myself changing in group settings." However, as India alludes to, the process has its limits: "[I]t just seems that many instances, the group process doesn't work. ...This does not mean a team member should not be helped or that we should not find out what their barriers are. I am suggesting there should be a ceiling for tolerance."

It is this sense of change and transformation in one's identity within the group that may be resisted. We argue that it is the perception of this threatened loss and potential rebirth of one's identity as a group member that is the source of this profound sense of ambivalence toward group work.

Our work with collaborative learning groups has helped us understand more deeply the frustrations, anxieties and uncertainties that online group learning evokes among our learners. But we also have much to learn. In many respects, our research and theory in online collaborative learning seem in a period of infancy, with numerous questions remaining to be explored. Given what we have learned, however, and what we know from the collaborative learning and group dynamics literature, there are several ways in which we, as teachers, can begin to work with online groups to help them negotiate these transitions more effectively. In the following, concluding section, we address some of the ways in which online teachers can help their learners recognize and work through the tension between the individual and the group, their resistance to it and its related issues of authority and intimacy, so that they can move from a perspective of subjectivity to one of intersubjectivity.

HELPING STUDENTS LEARN TO LEARN IN ONLINE COLLABORATIVE LEARNING

In this section of the chapter, we will describe what we consider the implications of this perspective for structuring and facilitating collaborative learning online. Discussion of these implications is organized around three foci: (1) the instructor's overall orientation to collaborative learning; (2) providing for interventions in the group process; and (3) follow-up.

Copyright © 2004, Idea Group Inc. Copying or distributing in print or electronic forms without written permission of Idea Group Inc. is prohibited.

Instructor's Overall Orientation

Regardless of the specific teaching strategies used, many online instructors are oriented primarily to course content. In facilitating collaborative learning, however, and addressing the issues we have raised in this chapter, it is necessary for instructors to attend to process issues reflected in the group's work (McDonald & Gibson, 1998; Miller, Trimbur, & Wilkes, 1994; Gunarwardena, 1998), particularly as they relate to the broader tension between the individual and the group, and more specifically to issues of authority and intimacy.

As instructors attend more to the emotional and process dimensions of the group, they must also be increasingly aware of their own feelings and emotions relative to these issues, and to learn to not take what occurs within the group personally (Smith & Berg, 1997). It is important that instructors recognize these behaviors are normal, even necessary to group dynamics, and not to interpret these behaviors as some kind of personal attack.

In addition to orientating oneself to process issues within the group, the instructor must develop a capacity to identify and hold in consciousness apparent contradictory and paradoxical movements in the group (Smith & Berg, 1997). As we indicated earlier, it is not at all uncommon for a group of online learners to both express a desire to pursue their own specific objectives and interests and to want more structure and guidance from the instructor. These issues often become a focus of contention among group members. As these issues become evident in the group, it is important for the instructor not to "take sides," but to help the group name and further elaborate on all aspects of the apparent tensions and contradictions.

Finally, it is important for online instructors to realize that it is only through de-authorizing that they will further the self-directedness and self-authorship of the group and its members (Bruffee, 1999; Flannery, 1994). Because the institution, as well as the students, recognizes the instructor as a content expert, she or he must tread a very fine line. An instructor who constantly acts as a source of authority for the group will retard the development of this process.

Use Interventions Aimed at Naming Issues of Group Process

The instructor should make use of specific interventions that help the group become more aware of the underlying issues and how these issues may shape and influence the ways in which they work together. The term "intervention" is used purposefully here. That is, based on her or his observations of the group process, the instructor has identified some process issues that seem to be blocking the group's process. Unless the group addresses these issues, they may continue to struggle with moving forward with their work. The instructor's actions are designed specifically to help the group address these issues.

Copyright © 2004, Idea Group Inc. Copying or distributing in print or electronic forms without written permission of Idea Group Inc. is prohibited.

Much of the small group's interaction takes place away from the main or whole class discussion sites. Teachers need to carefully read and attend to the discussion boards and chat rooms maintained by each of the groups. The interactions that occur within these online locations are the major sources of information for the instructor to understand the underlying dynamics that may be surfacing within a group's work. While he or she may choose to not always intervene or participate (such actions should always be undertaken with care and thoughtfulness), reading and reflecting on these interactions becomes a critical dimension of facilitating the group's individuation processes.

To develop and make specific process interventions, the instructor should be cognizant of the need to name and give voice to dissatisfaction or resistance to the collaborative process that may be evident in the group's interactions. Instructor interventions aimed at group process are decidedly different than providing the group with additional resources about the problem it is addressing, clarifying aspects of the problem or research, and theory that may be relevant to the problem. The purpose of the intervention is to bring to the group's awareness a particular issue of which it may not be aware or, at least, is not explicitly recognizing (Smith & Berg, 1997). In doing so, however, the instructor needs to be careful not to pass judgment on the group's behavior, not to side with any particular group member or issue being discussed, or to suggest a way out of the apparent dilemma (Smith & Berg, 1997). Interventions should, whenever possible, also be directed to the group as a whole. Instructors should avoid providing interventions aimed at particular group members.

To help differentiate an instructor's interventions on group process from that of content, we recommend that a separate thread in the discussion board section of the online course for instructor interventions on group process. In this thread, the instructor would post his or her observations regarding a particular aspect of a group's interactions.

Provide Opportunities for Follow Up

Follow-up involves (a) receiving reaction from group members about particular interventions; (b) monitoring throughout the entire experience the extent to which instructor's and participants' actions reflect a collaborative orientation; and (c) working for broader programmatic and organizational consistency in the use of online collaborative learning. It is critical that educators design the online environment with opportunities to receive feedback from the group members (Sanchez & Gunawardena, 1998) in reaction to a given intervention. Monitoring group reactions to instructor process interventions are more easily accomplished if the instructor uses a separate thread or forum for process interventions, as suggested earlier.

The idea of collaborative learning needs constant reinforcement within the specific online experience. As much as possible, both the instructor's and the

Copyright © 2004, Idea Group Inc. Copying or distributing in print or electronic forms without written permission of Idea Group Inc. is prohibited.

participants' actions need to be continually and consistently informed, by a general understanding of collaborative learning as a paradigm of learning, as well as sets of specific techniques.

Implementation of collaborative learning, as we have discussed it here, will not be successful unless broader contextual and systemic issues are also attended to. There are distinct organizational implications for use of online collaborative learning. If the online collaborative learning experience is part of a broader online program, but is not sustained in other experiences within the program or interpreted in much different ways, it will be more difficult to sustain or effectively implement collaborative learning within a given course.

CONCLUSION

Learners' perceptions of and experiences with online problem-based consensus groups reflect a profound sense of ambivalence with learning in small groups. While many participants laud the opportunity to interact and work with fellow group members, they clearly find the consensus decision-making and the production of a common product much less satisfying. Difficulties with numerous interpersonal issues and getting group members to do their share seem to cloud the initial enthusiasm. In addition, limitations in the computer-mediated forms of communication and interaction only serve to exacerbate these concerns (Bernard et al., 2000; Bullen, 1998), with the computer and the technology becoming a potential scapegoat and outlet for frustrations (Reeves & Nass, 1996).

Clearly a number of factors potentially contribute to the overall nature and quality of students' experiences with online learning. It is possible that at least some of the students' dissatisfaction with collaborative learning might be addressed by some orientation and training in group process. Students in this course, however, received a two-week orientation in online problem-based collaborative learning prior to their work together, including explicit guidelines and ground rules for working in groups. Using the theoretical frameworks of collaborative learning and group dynamics, we suggest that these experiences in consensus group work are more indicative of a kind of psychological resistance to the need to move from a subjective to a more intersubjective form of identity.

Although intersubjectivity is requisite for mature group functioning, it is not a forgone conclusion that all, or even most, groups achieve this level of development. As is evident in the stories of the students reported here, this process is difficult and involves high levels of conflict and emotionality, with primary hurdles focused around issues of authority and intimacy. Both the teacher and the students are involved in working through these issues. Teachers need to be aware of their own emotional involvement around these issues, and how they might become unconsciously complicit in the students' resistance. Specific strategies can be employed that help the learners hold the tension of the

Copyright © 2004, Idea Group Inc. Copying or distributing in print or electronic forms without written permission of Idea Group Inc. is prohibited.

opposites and to work through the paradoxes and conflict reflected in this tension. These strategies are intended to help students move from a subjective sense of identity, in which they hold firmly to individualistic conceptions of learning, to intersubjective identity, in which they reconstruct their sense of self as a group member. It is in within this space that collaborative learning takes place.

Considerable research is needed to explore both the issues raised here, as well what group work means in these technologically mediated environments. Unless we acquire more knowledge about how to make these experiences more meaningful and satisfying for learners, we might as well be listening to learners leaving our online programs, saying, "Doesn't anybody just learn on their own anymore?"

REFERENCES

Abercrombie, M. L. J. (1960). *Anatomy of Judgement.* Harmondsworth, New York: Basic Books.

Allen, T. H., & Plax, T. G. (1999). Group communication in the formal educational context. In L. Frey, D.S. Gouran, & M. S. Poole (Eds.), *The Handbook of Group Communication Theory & Research* (pp. 493-519). Thousand Oaks, CA: Sage Publications.

Barr, R. B., & Tagg, J. (1995). From teaching to learning – a new paradigm for undergraduate education. *Change, 27*(5), 13-25.

Barrows, H. S. (1994). *Practice-Based Learning: Problem-Based Learning Applied to Medical Education.* Springfield, IL: Southern Illinois University of School of Medicine.

Benjamin, J. (1988). *Bonds of Love: Psychoanalysis, Feminism, and the Problem of Domination.* New York: Pantheon Books.

Bennis, W. G., & Shepard, H. A. (1956). A theory of group development. *Human Relations, 9,* 415-437.

Bernard, R. M., Beatriz, R. D. R., & St. Piere, D. (2000). Collaborative online distance learning: issues for future practice and research. *Distance Education, 21*(2), 260-277.

Boshier, R., Mohapi, M., & Boulton, G. (1997). Best and worst dressed Web courses: Strutting into the 21st century in comfort and style. *Distance Education, 18*(2), 327-349.

Boyd, R. D. (1991). The matrix model: A conceptual framework for small group analysis. In R. M. Boyd (Ed.), *Personal Transformations in Small Groups: A Jungian Perspective,* pp.14-40. Thousand Oaks, CA: Routledge.

Brookfield, S. D., & Preskill, S. (1999). *Discussion as a Way of Teaching: Tools and Techniques for Democratic Classrooms.* San Francisco, CA: Jossey-Bass.

Copyright © 2004, Idea Group Inc. Copying or distributing in print or electronic forms without written permission of Idea Group Inc. is prohibited.

Bruffee, K. A. (1999). *Collaborative Learning: Higher Education, Interdependence, and the Authority of Knowledge* (2nd ed.). Baltimore, MD: The John Hopkins University Press.

Bullen, M. (1998). Participation and critical thinking in online university distance education. *Journal of Distance Education, 13*(2), 1-32. Retrieved on October 14, 2001 from the web site: http://cade.athabascau.ca/vol13.2/bullen.html.

Burge, E. L. (1994). Learning in computer conferenced contexts: The learners perspective. *Journal of Distance Education, 9*(1), 19-43.

Clarebout, G., & Elsen, J. (2001). The ParlEuNet-project: Problems with the validation of socio-constructivist design principles in ecological settings. *Computers in Human Behavior, 17*(5-6), 453-464.

Cohen, E. (1986). *Designing Groupwork: Strategies for the Heterogeneous Classroom.* New York: Teachers College Press.

Crook, C. (1994). *Computers and the Collaborative Experience of Learning.* London: Routledge & Kegan Paul.

Dewey, J. (1963). *Democracy in Education.* New York: Collier.

Distance Education May Soar to 85% at Higher Education Schools by 2002. (1999, March). *Education Technology News, 16*(7), 54.

Durkin, H. (1964). *The Group in Depth.* New York: International Universities Press.

Eastmond, D. V. (1995). *Alone but Together: Adult Distance Study Through Computer Conferencing.* Cresskill, NJ: Hampton Press, Inc.

Flannery, J. L. (1994). Teacher as co-conspirator: Knowledge and authority in collaborative learning. In K. Bosworth & S. J. Hamilton (Eds.), *Collaborative Learning: Underlying Process and Effective Techniques* (Vol. 59), pp.15-23. San Francisco, CA: Jossey-Bass.

Gerlach, J. M. (1994). Is this collaboration? In K. Bosworth & S. J. Hamilton (Eds.), *Collaborative Learning: Underlying Processes and Effective Techniques* (Vol. 59, pp. 5-14). San Francisco, CA: Jossey-Bass.

Gunawardena, C. N. (1998). Designing collaborative learning environments mediated by computer conferencing: Issues and challenges in the Asian socio-cultural context. *Indian Journal of Open Learning 7*(1), 101-119.

Harasim, L. (1990). Online education: an environment for collaboration and intellectual amplification. In L. Haraism (Ed.), *Online Education: Perspectives on a New Environment* (pp. 39-64). New York: Praeger.

Harasim, L., Hiltz, S. R., Teles, L., & Turoff, M. (1995). *Learning Networks: A Field Guide to Teaching and Learning Online.* Cambridge, MA: MIT Press.

Johnson, R. W. & Johnson, R. T. (1978). Cooperative, competitive, and individualistic learning. *Journal of Research and Development in Education, 12*(1), 3-15.

Copyright © 2004, Idea Group Inc. Copying or distributing in print or electronic forms without written permission of Idea Group Inc. is prohibited.

Jonassen, D. (1997). Instructional design models for well-structured and ill-structured problem-solving learning outcomes. *Educational Technology: Research and Development 45*(1), 65-95.

Kitchen, D., & McDougall, D. (1999). Collaborative learning on the Internet. *Journal of Educational Technology Systems, 27*(3), 245-258.

Koschmann, T. (1996). Paradigm shifts and instructional technology: An introduction. In T. Koschmann (Ed.), *CSCL: Theory and Practice of an Emerging Paradigm* (pp. 1-23). Mahwah, NJ: Lawrence Erlbaum Associates.

Lushyn, P., & Kennedy, D. (2000). The pyschodynamics of community of inquiry and educational reform: A cross cultural perspective. *Thinking 15*(3), 9-16. Retrieved on November 13, 2002 from the web site: http://newfirstsearch.oclc.org.

McConnell, D. (2000). *Implementing Computer Supported Cooperative Learning* (2nd ed.). London: Kogan.

McDonald, J., & Gibson, C. C. (1998). Interpersonal dynamics and group development in computer conferencing. *The American Journal of Distance Education, 12*(1), 7-25.

Merriam, S., & Cafferella, R. (1999). *Learning in Adulthood: A Comprehensive Guide* (2nd ed.). San Francisco, CA: Jossey-Bass.

Miller, J. E., Trimbur, J., & Wilkes, J. M. (1994). Group dynamics: Understanding group success and failure in collaborative learning. In K. Bosworth & S. J. Hamilton (Eds.), *Collaborative Learning: Underlying Processes and Effective Techniques* (pp. 33-44). San Francisco, CA: Jossey-Bass.

Palloff, R. M., & Pratt, K. (1999). *Building Learning Communities in Cyberspace: Effective Strategies for the Online Classroom.* San Francisco, CA: Jossey-Bass.

Raggoonaden, K., & Bordeleau, P. (2000). Collaborative learning via the Internet. *Educational Technology & Society, 3*(3), 361-372.

Reeves, B., & Nass, C. (1996). *The Media Equation: How People Treat Computers, Television, and New Media Like Real People and Places.* Cambridge, MA: Cambridge University Press.

Sage, S. M. (2000, April). *The learning and teaching experiences in an online problem-based learning course.* Paper presented at the American Education Research Association, New Orleans, Louisiana, USA.

Sanchez, I., & Gunawardena, C. N. (1998). Understanding and supporting the culturally diverse distance learner. In C. C. Gibson (Ed.), *Distance Learners in Higher Education Institutional Responses for Quality Outcomes.* Madison, WI: Atwood Publishing.

Schrum, L. (1998, Summer). On-line education: A study of emerging pedagogy. *New Directions for Adult and Continuing Education, 78*, 53-62.

Copyright © 2004, Idea Group Inc. Copying or distributing in print or electronic forms without written permission of Idea Group Inc. is prohibited.

Sharan, S., Hertz-Lazarowitz, R., & Ackerman, Z. (1980). Academic achievement of elementary school children in small group vs. whole class interaction. *Journal of Experimental Education, 48,* 125-29.

Slavin, R. E. (1983). *Cooperative Learning.* New York: Longman.

Slavin, R. E. (1985). *Learning to Cooperate, Cooperating to Learn.* New York: Plenum.

Smith, K., & Berg, D. (1997). *Paradoxes of Group Life: Understanding Conflict, Paralysis and Movement in Group Dynamics.* San Francisco, CA: The Lexington Press.

Sorg, J., & McElhinney, J. H. (2000). *A case study describing student-experiences of learning in a context of synchronous computer-mediated communication in a distance education environment* (ERIC Document 447794).

Vygotsky, L.S. (1978). *Mind and Society: The Development of Higher Psychological Processes.* Cambridge MA: Harvard University Press.

Weisband, S. P., Schneider, S. K., & Connolly, T. (1995). Computer-mediated communication and social information: Statue salience and status difference. *Academy of Management Journal, 38*(4), 1124-1151.

Wheelan, S. A. (1994). *Group Processes: A Developmental Perspective.* Boston, MA: Allyn and Bacon.

Copyright © 2004, Idea Group Inc. Copying or distributing in print or electronic forms without written permission of Idea Group Inc. is prohibited.

Chapter VII

A New Taxonomy for Evaluation Studies of Online Collaborative Learning

Lesley Treleaven
University of Western Sydney, Australia

ABSTRACT

In this chapter, the literature of online collaborative learning (OCL) is extensively reviewed for contributions to evaluation. This review presents a new taxonomy for evaluation studies of OCL, identifying studies of students' experiences, studies of instructional methods and sociocultural studies. Studies that focus on evaluating students' experiences engage approaches from phenomenology and ethnography to explore students' perceptions of collaborative learning. Instructional method studies attend to evaluation of the tools, techniques and outcomes. Sociocultural studies emphasize the socially constructed nature of the teaching and learning processes and are concerned, therefore, with evaluation in its social context. The sociocultural studies fall broadly into three clusters: pedagogical studies, linguistic studies and cross-cultural studies. The analysis highlights the need for theory-driven empirical evaluation of OCL. Accordingly, three theoretical frameworks for OCL evaluation are discussed. Emphasis is placed on a Communicative Model of Collaborative Learning,

Copyright © 2004, Idea Group Inc. Copying or distributing in print or electronic forms without written permission of Idea Group Inc. is prohibited.

developed from Habermas' Theory of Communicative Action, for its contribution to evaluating what takes place within the social context of students' communicative practices that is productive of collaborative learning in an online environment.

INTRODUCTION

Collaborative learning, especially as it can now be supported by computer-mediated communication, is receiving significant attention by those concerned with developing higher education students' capabilities to meet the increasingly complex challenges of working in a postmodern world. Students indicate that they often enjoy and benefit from collaborative learning with and from their peers, when equity and group dynamics are appropriately addressed. Teachers are engaging new online communication tools and assessing different instructional design techniques to enable better collaborative learning and to improve student learning outcomes (Bonk & Dennen, 1999; Freeman, 1997). Higher education institutions are investing in Web-based learning systems and e-learning support units (Sheely, Veness & Rankine, 2001) often in the hope of saving costs associated with face-to-face delivery of instruction and in attempts to capitalize on globalized higher education markets.

But is collaborative learning actually happening in these new electronically-mediated spaces? What is the nature of that collaborative learning and, most importantly, how can we evaluate the quality of this collaborative learning? How do we know it is worth doing now, and continuing to improve? For whom is evaluation undertaken: students, teachers, educational developers, designers, e-learning specialists or those who stand beyond participation, yet hold the purse strings? What would we evaluate for such different audiences? And would such differently targeted evaluation be undertaken in the same way? Does a cautionary call need to be sounded against those in higher education whose agendas are shaped by assumptions that technologically advanced, flexible delivery, necessarily equates with learning, collaborative or otherwise? This chapter sets out to explore some of these questions, while raising others and, hopefully, provoking still more.

Whereas earlier chapters in this volume have defined and explored the nature of online collaborative learning (OCL), this chapter examines the evaluation of OCL. Evaluation has been defined by Gunawardena, Carabajal and Lowe (2001) as:

A systematic and purposive inquiry that includes the collection, analysis and reporting of data relating to the efficiency, appropriateness, effectiveness, and value of operational characteristics and outcomes of a procedure, program, process or product. (p. 3)

Copyright © 2004, Idea Group Inc. Copying or distributing in print or electronic forms without written permission of Idea Group Inc. is prohibited.

Such a definition needs to be applied to perhaps four questions: Why are we evaluating? For whom are we evaluating? What are we evaluating? How will we evaluate these aspects?

Evaluation of OCL requires attention not only to processes of collaborative learning, but also to the means through which they are achieved — computer-mediated communication. Furthermore, the goal of collaborative learning is understood here, as Ronteltap and Eurelings (2002) state, to "create a situation in which productive interactions between learners can be generated" (p. 14). This notion of productivity, what the learners produce together, necessarily involves evaluating the different contexts, processes and outcomes that facilitate and support such productivity. Evaluation in these new contexts challenge traditional approaches to evaluation and require new theoretical frameworks to guide analysis and interpretation.

Three components of collaborative learning have been identified by Brandon and Hollingshead (1999) as collaboration, communication and social context. While communicative processes have been examined in linguistic studies and the social contexts of these new online learning communities have been the subject of many sociological studies, the majority of the literature reports case studies that only evaluate collaborative learning implicitly, as they focus principally on its perceived benefits in achieving learning outcomes.

Much of our understanding as practitioners, who are deeply committed to the value of collaborative learning as we observe our students engage more fully when we incorporate it into our programs, and as researchers, who are attempting to study those transformative shifts facilitated by collaborative learning processes, rests powerfully on our tacit knowledge (Tsoukas, 2003) of what actually happens within these shared, interactive online spaces. What is therefore required is a theoretical framework that enables explicit and systematic investigation of what takes place within the social context of students' communicative practices that is productive of collaborative learning. In this way, the integration between the three components — collaboration, communication and social context — are investigated holistically, rather than reduced to their three constituent components.

Accordingly, this chapter argues that OCL may be effectively and usefully evaluated from within the students' online communicative practices. Three theoretical models that facilitate evaluation from such contextualized locations are presented: the collaborative learning model (Ronteltap & Eurelings, 2002), the interaction analysis model (Gunawardena, Lowe, & Anderson, 1997) and the communicative model of collaborative learning (Cecez-Kecmanovic & Webb, 2000a). The latter is advanced here as an appropriate theoretical framework for theory-driven empirical evaluation of OCL, based on its application in a number of empirical studies elsewhere (Treleaven & Cecez-Kecmanovic, 2001; Treleaven, 2003a; Treleaven, 2003b). This chapter is, therefore, structured into

Copyright © 2004, Idea Group Inc. Copying or distributing in print or electronic forms without written permission of Idea Group Inc. is prohibited.

three parts. First, in the major part, the literature of OCL is extensively reviewed for its contributions to evaluation. This wide-ranging review is presented within a new taxonomy for evaluation studies of OCL. Second, from this review, the relative absence of rigorous evaluation and appropriate theoretical models informing evaluation in the expanding body of OCL research is highlighted. Three theoretical frameworks, notably those of Ronteltap and Eurelings (2002), Gunawardena, Lowe and Anderson (1997) and Cecez-Kecmanovic and Webb (2000a) are elaborated. Particular attention is paid to the communicative model of collaborative learning (Cecez-Kecmanovic & Webb, 2000a) for its evaluation of OCL by examining students' linguistic acts as they are produced on electronic bulletin boards. Third, the conclusion points to the value of a theoretical model, such as the communicative model of collaborative learning, as a pedagogical tool for effectively evaluating not only students' collaborative learning but also for further improving and testing the design of OCL.

LITERATURE REVIEW OF OCL EVALUATION

This section reviews the nature and extent of the literature in the area of evaluating OCL (Mason, 1992; Alavi, 1994; Gunawardena, Carabajal, & Lowe, 2001). Clustering distinct approaches within the literature demonstrated clearly that no single study fits neatly into one mutually exclusive category. Nevertheless, it is useful to identify three trends in the literature concerned with evaluating OCL: studies of students' experiences, instructional method studies and socio-cultural studies. In turn, the focus of each domain is slightly different, respectively: students' perceptions, tools and techniques, and teaching and learning processes in a social context. This range of evaluative literature has extended significantly in the last decade, beyond the surveys (online and hard copy), case studies, empirical experiments and quantitative analyses (messages sent, logons, replies, threads), identified in Mason's 1992 review of methodologies for evaluating computer conferencing.

Studies of Students' Perceptions and Experiences

It is notable that in much of the literature on OCL, there is an implicit focus on evaluation. Often such implicit evaluations are descriptively orientated toward the students' experience of learning based on phenomenographic theories (Gosling, 2000). For these studies borrow implicitly from ethnographic methods as they focus on the general value of online learning in a wide range of settings, while they also borrow from phenomenology as they investigate the students' experiences and perceptions of their online learning (Sanders & Morrison-Shetlar, 2001; Sullivan, 2001; Gallini & Barron, 2002; Askov &

Copyright © 2004, Idea Group Inc. Copying or distributing in print or electronic forms without written permission of Idea Group Inc. is prohibited.

Simpson, 2001; Weiner, 2002). Fewer, however, are focused on the value of their collaborative learning.

Illustrative of phenomenological studies are Kitchen and McDougall's (1999) examination of graduate students' perceptions of the educational value of their collaborative learning in a course delivered via computer-mediated communication. Their research is based on interviews and analysis of students' communication practices, in order to determine the most important aspects associated with their collaborative experiences. Although students report enjoying the convenience and opportunity for collaboration, some also report dissatisfaction with the instructional strategy and the delivery medium. McAlpine (2000) examines the stimulus that students receive from the online learning approach in a Master's course and the value they perceive in learning from colleagues and lecturers in a collaborative way. McIsaac, Blocher and Mahes (1999) investigate student and teacher perceptions of interaction in online computer-mediated communication and suggest principles for distance educators to incorporate into online classes, such as providing immediate feedback, participating in the discussions, promoting interaction and social presence, and employing collaborative learning strategies. Salmon (2000), in her practical guide to e-moderating students' learning, draws on such evaluative approaches.

Instructional Method Studies: Tools, Techniques and Outcomes

Second, other more targeted investigations evaluate the effectiveness of different online learning tools and techniques for collaborative learning, and thereby student outcomes, in a wide range of settings (for example, Collings & Pearce 2002; Chen, Liu, Ou, & Lin, 2001; Chang, 2001; Nakhleh, Donovan, & Parrill, 2000; Chalk, 2000). Typifying this approach is Ravenscroft and Matheson's (2002) evaluation of two collaborative dialogue games, finding that they produce significant improvements in students' conceptual understanding. However, since these tools are differentially successful depending on the nature of the conceptual difficulties experienced by the learners, they conclude that developments in collaborative e-learning dialogue should be based on pedagogically sound principles of discourse. Bonamy, Charlier and Saunders (2001) focus on evaluation of products and how these can be useful "bridging tools." Nevertheless, they also see a role for evaluation beyond this specific focus on tools. In their project with a network of teachers, researchers and learners from different European institutions, Bonamy et al. (2001) adopt an approach to evaluation that is characterized by an evaluation distinguishing between individual experience and institutional contexts and an evaluation using monitoring data and qualitative validation. In the search for new knowledge in the area of changing practices in learning, their useful study points to the importance of attending to evaluation explicitly.

Copyright © 2004, Idea Group Inc. Copying or distributing in print or electronic forms without written permission of Idea Group Inc. is prohibited.

Relatedly, another cluster of studies analyze the link between online instructional techniques and different student outcomes (such as Grossman, 1999; Redding & Rotzien, 2001; Ellis & Cohen, 2001). Much of this work is evaluative and of interest for teachers wanting to improve course designs. For example, Alon and Cannon (2000) analyze an Internet-based learning forum that aims to link student teams in international collaborative learning projects. The purpose of the forum is to empower students to participate in setting learning goals and learning processes, and enabling instructors to be closer to the student in the learning process. The article reports on the experience of one college that used the forum and discusses likely outcomes that may emerge from using Internet-based experiential projects in the classroom. Nevertheless, it is not the concern of such research to focus on whether it is OCL, in particular, rather than some other features of the course design or implementation, that is contributing to student outcomes.

Sociocultural Studies: Socially Constructed Pedagogy Mediated by Language

The sociocultural studies fall broadly into three clusters: pedagogical studies, linguistic studies and cross-cultural studies. What they share is an understanding that learning occurs in a social context. As such, evaluation of learning needs to take into account the nature of the learning environment and social interaction processes, as well as the tools and techniques employed. What distinguishes the sociocultural studies from studies that give more emphasis to "instruction" via tools and techniques of "delivery" is recognition that meaning, and thus learning, is socially constructed. So the social context, especially, but not only, its cultural and cross-cultural demographics within which meaning is produced, becomes an integral part of the research.

Pedagogical Studies

Many pedagogical studies examine online learning communities and collaborative learning from a sociological orientation. They adopt the perspective that learning is a social process and cannot be seen independently of the social context (Tu & Corry, 2001; Kumpulainen, Salovaara, & Mutanen, 2001; Ronteltap & Eurelings, 2002). Tu and Corry (2001) emphasize the importance of the construction of online learning communities. Their study examines an online learning community drawing on Goffman's (1974) self-presentation and Short, William and Christie's (1976) social presence theory. They critique the limitations of research into online communities for the short-term period of study and analytic focus on products at the expense of the individual engaged. A further study by Tu (2002) examines the learner's perception of social presence in three computer-mediated communication systems. Using a social presence and pri-

Copyright © 2004, Idea Group Inc. Copying or distributing in print or electronic forms without written permission of Idea Group Inc. is prohibited.

vacy questionnaire, Tu identifies three dimensions of social presence as social context, online communication and interactivity.

Some very useful, systematic work has been undertaken by Ronteltap and Eurelings (2002), who analyze collaborative interactions for quantity (what types of learning issues generate most interactions?) and quality (what types of learning issues generate the highest level of information processing?), using a model that is discussed later in the chapter. Their highly structured experimental research examines the productivity of small group learning and the level of cognitive activity. Thus they classify documents according to whether they are low order cut and paste, summarizing or higher level original postings that require more processing of information with synthesis, interpretation, reflection and referencing to other contributions. They note that although tools and functionality are important, these do not necessarily produce interactions of a quality that lead to learning.

Other studies, such as Kumpulainen et al.'s (2001) examination of sociocognitive processes, evaluate multimedia learning while paying attention to the social interaction that takes place. Their investigation is facilitated in this regard by the use of a wide range of interactive media for their research (video and audio recordings, online observations, interviews, questionnaires and assessments of students' poster displays). Thus, they are able to summarize, in case-based analytic descriptions, the nature of students' navigation processes, social interactions and cognitive activities in the multimedia context. The authors conclude that more attention has to be paid to the design of instructional situations and pedagogical supports for multimedia-based learning.

Linguistic Studies

Research into dialogue and online discussions (Weasonforth, Biesenbach-Lucas, & Meloni 2002; Collot & Belmore, 1996; Yates, 1996), like much of the literature on OCL, has not given much attention to developing a theoretical model for the analysis of communicative practices in collaborative online learning (Gunawardena et al., 1997). Again, they focus on identifying features of the dialogue and discussions, examining the processes that take place online and sometimes comparing them with offline processes (Johnson & Johnson, 1996; Curtis & Lawson, 1999). Furthermore, as Jones (1998) argues, evaluation techniques, such as content analysis and single features of computer-mediated communication (Mason, 1992; Henri, 1992), do not include relevant data like casual chatting or ad hoc activity in student texts.

Nevertheless, many linguistic studies are located broadly within a theoretical framework that supports attention to the socially constructed and socially mediated processes of learning and meaning production. These studies draw on an ethnographic approach. For example, Jones (1998) explores online group work using ethnographic techniques, and argues that this approach stresses the

Copyright © 2004, Idea Group Inc. Copying or distributing in print or electronic forms without written permission of Idea Group Inc. is prohibited.

social context, refusing "a priori categories" of analysis, in order to concentrate specifically on the learning process.

This focus on the social processes mediating online communication has been researched by Tidwell and Walther (2002). They explore the exchange of personal communication and effects of communication channels on self-disclosure, question asking and uncertainty reduction between online partners.

A study by Hron, Hesse, Cress and Giovis (2000) raises significant questions for OCL and for evaluation, in particular. Their experiment tests the use of two different methods of dialogue structuring to keep the conversation coherent within virtual learning groups. Implicit structuring of collaborative exchanges elicited discussion on the subject matter and on key questions, arising from learning already undertaken together. In contrast, explicit structuring of dialogue by the designer provided additional rules for discussion, encouraging students to argue and participate equally. Both implicit and explicit structuring of discussion facilitate stronger orientation to subject matter and less "off-task talk," than in unstructured groups. Nevertheless, a post-test was not able to distinguish any differences in knowledge between the groups using the different dialogue approaches. Their finding points to the difficulty of such comparative evaluation, for it relies heavily on the effectiveness of the assessment of student learning.

The implication of such a statement is to question what we seek to evaluate and how we assess the kinds of knowledge that pedagogically oriented approaches may produce. In the context of knowledge (Tsoukas, 2003), can we indeed assess students' knowledge adequately and thus usefully evaluate the learning environments, behaviors and mechanisms that are employed in their online courses? It is for this reason that evaluating from within, where collaborative learning is enacted and productivity displayed, that the CMCL discussed below is so appealing.

Cross-Cultural Studies

As Web-based delivery of learning is employed for more diverse student populations, studies that evaluate OCL by taking into account demographic differences and cross-cultural factors are of increasing importance. With the range of flexible delivery of asynchronous learning programs set in global markets for higher education, the demographics of students are increasingly more diverse in age, culture, ethnicity, language, work experience and familiarity with technology (for example, Bates, 2001; Lauzon, 2000; Warschauer; 1998, Herring, 1996). Gunawardena, Nolla, Wilson, Lopez-Islas, Ramirez-Angel and Megchun-Alpizar (2001) conducted a cross-cultural study of group process and development in online conferences between participants in Mexico and the United States. In their survey, they identify significant differences in student perception of the norming and performing stages of group development. The

Copyright © 2004, Idea Group Inc. Copying or distributing in print or electronic forms without written permission of Idea Group Inc. is prohibited.

groups also differed in their perception of collectivism, low power distance, femininity and communication. Some of the challenges in cross-cultural studies, noted by Gunawardena et al. (2001) are finding equivalent samples for quantitative research and developing qualitative research that conceptualizes identity issues, so as to move past simplistic stereotyping and better understand how people define themselves.

Evaluating the impact of these cultural differences within and between groups becomes important in the context of OCL. For the dynamics of social interaction, and hence collaborative learning, are demonstrably affected by such differences. Evaluation studies in this specific context challenge pedagogical assumptions and highlight issues of generalizability across different cohorts and individual differences.

THEORETICAL FRAMEWORKS FOR EVALUATING OCL

Given the untheorized nature of much of the evaluation that is undertaken both implicitly and explicitly (Arbaugh, 2000), the findings of Alexander and McKenzie's (1998) investigation into innovation in information and communication technology (ICT) education in Australia are not surprising. They found that commonly used evaluation tools/forms at universities are inadequate for the purpose of improvement, and that ICT educators usually do not have the skills to implement educational designs that could improve their teaching. Following their recommendation to develop better ways of evaluating whether educational programs meet their intended aims, the Australian Universities Teaching Committee (AUTC) funded an action learning evaluation project conducted by the Computing Education Research Group at Monash University (Phillips, 2002). The learning-centered framework (for evaluating computer facilitated learning) adopted in this staff development intervention is based on work by Alexander and Hedberg (1994) and Bain (1999) and encompasses four stages — analysis and design, development, implementation and institutionalization. Arguably, the outcomes of such projects directed toward developing evaluation skills and wide-reaching change in practices need to be informed by, and may be enhanced by, empirical research into OCL evaluation, which is soundly conceptualized and theory-driven.

Toward addressing this gap in the empirical OCL research to date, three theoretical models from the literature of OCL are now discussed. Each of these models take into account the social interaction processes involved in OCL and have been developed by Ronteltap and Eurelings (2002), Gunawardena et al. (1997), and Cecez-Kecmanovic and Webb (2000a).

The first two frameworks are briefly presented before the latter is discussed as one approach that is proving useful in terms of theorizing, and then evaluating,

Copyright © 2004, Idea Group Inc. Copying or distributing in print or electronic forms without written permission of Idea Group Inc. is prohibited.

students' communicative practices and knowledge creation from within the collaborative learning spaces.

Collaborative Learning Model

A major contribution to identifying a framework for what requires evaluation in OCL has been developed by Ronteltap and Eurelings (2002). In their model, they distinguish the learning environment that in turn mediates the learning behavior engaging with a learning mechanism. These three dynamics and their inter-relationships are represented below in the schema (Figure 1) developed to illustrate their model. These elements, which can be employed generally for both design and analysis, are utilized to plan and evaluate their own study. The learning environment includes the curriculum and its learning materials, assessment processes and learning tools. The learning behavior refers to all aspects relevant to studying the interactions between learners, and thus includes learners (their learning styles, attitudes, motivation), activity prior to and during communication (writing, reading, reacting, information processing and knowledge management) and content. The learning mechanisms are generated by communicative activity and include explanation, justification, negotiation, reflection and reconstruction.

In Ronteltap and Eurelings' (2002) first application of the model to an experiment, their work points to how higher levels of information processing are achieved through issues related to practical learning. Their model is also helpful in articulating the transformative effects of asynchronous online collaboration as the opportunity for collaborative application of knowledge, reflection and restructuring of that knowledge by participants. The future directions of their work

Figure 1:   Collaborative Learning Model (Schema Based on Ronteltap & Eurelings, 2002)

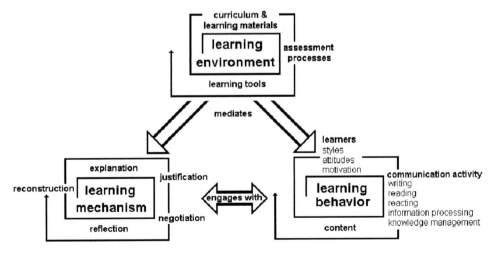

Copyright © 2004, Idea Group Inc. Copying or distributing in print or electronic forms without written permission of Idea Group Inc. is prohibited.

toward a theory of mediated action as a framework for analyzing the inter-related processes within the model holds potential for further theoretical developments applied to evaluating OCL.

Similar work, based on systems theory and earlier grounded theory, by Gunawardena and her colleagues (Gunawardena et al., 2001; Runawardena et al., 1997) parallels the systems, interactivity and outcomes of Ronteltap and Eurelings' (2002) framework. However, Gunawardena et al. (1997) applied their model for content analysis that dealt with only one part of this social interaction. In this later work they emphasize content, context, collaboration and control, and the interrelations between them. Like Alexander and Hedberg (1994), Housego and Freeman's (2000) conceptualization of Web-based learning operating at different levels adds the very important institutional dimension to a general evaluative framework.

Interaction Analysis Model

Recognizing that the development of theory on which to base collaborative learning in higher education is much needed, Gunawardena et al. (1997) developed an interaction analysis model for examining the social construction of knowledge in computer conferencing.

This model was designed to help answer two evaluation questions: namely, was knowledge constructed within the group by means of the exchanges among participants? and, second, did individual participants change their understanding or create new personal constructions of knowledge as a result of interaction within the group? (Gunwardena et al., 1997). Given that the professional development participants engaged online for only one week, the model and methodology itself is of more interest here than the substantive findings from its application.

Their model outlines five phases in the co-construction of new knowledge within which different types of cognitive activity (such as, questioning, clarifying, negotiating and synthesizing) takes place. The five phases are identified as sharing/comparing, dissonance, negotiation/co-construction, testing tentative constructions and statement/application of newly constructed knowledge.

Communicative analysis of the phases of knowledge co-creation pays attention not to the threads and the specificity of messages but to the broader evaluation of whether engagement in a collaborative forum successfully produces new knowledge. The researchers themselves have subsequently claimed that this model, focusing as content analysis tends to do on one aspect of the learning process itself, has not adequately engaged the issues of evaluation (Gunawardena et al., 2001). Nevertheless, their approach to investigating knowledge creation and sharing online may well be worth building on.

Copyright © 2004, Idea Group Inc. Copying or distributing in print or electronic forms without written permission of Idea Group Inc. is prohibited.

The Communicative Model of Collaborative Learning

The theoretical framework that shapes Cecez-Kecmanovic and Webb's (2000a) communicative model of collaborative learning is developed from Habermas' (1984) theory of communicative action. Despite critiques of Habermas' value for communication in teaching (see Heslep, 2001), other studies have productively drawn on his theory. For example, Gosling (2000) evaluates participants' perceptions of negotiated learning against the tutor's declared philosophy of "the ideal speech conditions." Ekstrom and Sigurdsson (2002) investigate international collaboration in nursing education through the lens of Habermas' theory, analyzing the influence that politics and economics have on active communication and the potential benefits of shared meaning and under-standing achieved by interaction and discourse.

The communicative model of collaborative learning (CMCL) is based on three assumptions, according to Cecez-Kecmanovic and Webb (2000a): first, that collaborative learning is enacted and mediated by language; second, that collaborative learning involves processes of social interaction and third, that acts of communication or language acts function as social interaction mechanisms through which collaborative learning and knowledge co-creation processes may be produced.

The CMCL (Table 1) identifies and classifies language acts as constituents of collaborative learning along two dimensions: the dominant orientation of learners and the domain of knowledge. First, the model identifies an orientation to learning (shown as a desire to know and to interact with others to increase mutual understanding and construct knowledge cooperatively), then an orienta-tion to achieving ends (shown in students' primary motivation to achieve a goal, such as passing the subject, getting a good mark or getting the best mark in the class) and an orientation to self-representation and promotion (shown in stu-dents' attempts to impress others by portraying a particular self-image).

Second, the model differentiates between language acts that refer to different domains of knowledge, such as those related to subject matter and any substantive issues (theory, application, problem solving, etc.); linguistic acts addressing norms and rules that regulate the conduct of interactions and interpersonal relations in the collaborative learning process; and linguistic acts addressing personal experiences, desires and feelings by which students express themselves and shape both their individual and collective sense of self and of their learning processes.

Using this 3x3 matrix, the CMCL enables classification of linguistic acts produced in specific learning situations. Communicative analysis based on this model takes into account both the knowledge domain (subject content, norms and rules, and personal experience) that a specific linguistic act refers to and, at the same time, its orientation (learning, achieving ends and self-representation) that

Copyright © 2004, Idea Group Inc. Copying or distributing in print or electronic forms without written permission of Idea Group Inc. is prohibited.

Table 1:   CMCL (Cecez-Kemanovic & Webb, 2000a, b)

Knowledge domains / Dominant orientation to	SUBJECT MATTER (1)	NORMS AND RULES (2)	PERSONAL EXPERIENCES, DESIRES AND FEELINGS (3)
LEARNING (A)	**A1** - Linguistic acts about subject matter raised in order to share views and beliefs, to provide arguments and counter-arguments leading to mutual understanding and knowledge creation	**A2** - Linguistic acts that establish norms and rules regarding interaction and collaboration; cooperative assessment of legitimacy, social acceptability and rightness of individual behaviour	**A3** - Linguistic acts expressing personal views and feelings about learning process and other learners aimed at sharing experiences and increasing mutual understanding
ACHIEVING ENDS (B)	**B1** - Linguistic acts that raise or dispute claims and provide arguments about subject matter, with an intent to frame attention, influence others and achieve goals	**B2** - Acts of changing or interpreting norms and rules about the interaction process so as to suit a particular student interest and goals (may be at the expense of others)	**B3** - Acts expressing personal experiences in a way that influences other learners and instructors so as to help achieve goals (e.g., emphasising personal success)
SELF-REPRESENTATION AND PROMOTION (C)	**C1** - Raising or disputing claims and arguments as a performance on a stage that serves personal promotion (often neglecting an ongoing argumentation process)	**C2** - Raising or disputing claims about norms/rules or their violation in order to attract attention and establish oneself as a distinguished student (e.g., a leader, an authority)	**C3** - Linguistic acts expressing personal experiences and feelings that project an impression of importance in a group or of a key role in a situation (e.g., domination)

shapes the productivity within the learning situation. Accordingly, the nature of the linguistic act and its productivity, and how it contributes and what it enables (in the flow of linguistic acts with and between postings) in the construction and maintenance of collaborative learning processes can be analyzed and differentiated. From such analysis, the type and extent of collaborative learning taking place can be identified.

Copyright © 2004, Idea Group Inc. Copying or distributing in print or electronic forms without written permission of Idea Group Inc. is prohibited.

To illustrate, the specific linguistic act may be of the same type, e.g., subject matter, however, what it actually produces depends on the student's orientation. A student oriented to learning may seek mutual understanding with other students on a topic, collaboratively creating new knowledge. Whereas, a student oriented to achieving a passing grade may attempt to fulfill course requirements instrumentally, without necessarily engaging in collaborative learning. A student oriented to self-representation may present their posting on a subject in such way as to try and make an impression on some members of their cohort, neglecting the ongoing processes of developing understanding that lead to knowledge sharing and creation. It is important to note, therefore, that interpretation of a linguistic act is always within the context of the learning situation itself and the flow of linguistic acts constituting that learning process.

While there is insufficient space in this chapter for more specific illustration, the CMCL has been applied, tested and developed as a theoretical framework in a collaborative action research study (Reason & Bradbury, 2001) of OCL in a Web-enhanced learning environment. The empirical investigation of students' communicative practices in an undergraduate management subject has been documented in a number of research papers, focusing on different aspects of the study (Treleaven & Cecez-Kecmanovic, 2001; Treleaven 2003). Central to this empirical investigation has been the deployment of the CMCL to analyze sets of student postings on an electronic bulletin board for the dominant modes of linguistic acts, and the flow between these postings as knowledge is created collaboratively. The first phase of the study traced the development and productivity of a collaborative learning space on an electronic bulletin board, by examining the numbers and types of postings made throughout the semester. Student demographics (gender and English as a second language) related to participation were also investigated. A number of methodological and pedagogical implications raised in this first action research cycle informed improvements in the Web-mediated learning design of the subject. The second phase examined the revised design, evaluating the extent and nature of the collaborative learning facilitated by more structured online discussion. Accordingly, the pedagogical implications for learners and for designers were the major outcomes of the second action research cycle. These two cycles are brought together elsewhere (Treleaven, in preparation) within the newly developed taxonomy here for examining the evaluation of OCL.

TOWARD MORE RIGOROUS EVALUATION

This chapter asked what we need to evaluate and how this has been done in the literature of OCL. The chapter detailed a new taxonomy of evaluation studies, identifying those which focus on student experiences; those concerned

Copyright © 2004, Idea Group Inc. Copying or distributing in print or electronic forms without written permission of Idea Group Inc. is prohibited.

with tools, techniques and outcomes; and those that emphasize the socially constructed nature of language. In particular, the chapter showed how we are in a better position now, than 10 years ago, to evaluate whether collaborative learning is taking place in these online learning environments.

Most importantly, the chapter addressed the issue of rigorous theoretical conceptualization that good teaching and learning practice deserves. It demonstrated how evaluation has been approached implicitly, without theory-driven empirical investigation, even in pedagogical studies. When the technological and pedagogical developments of the last decade are considered, there have been huge advances in opportunities for designing and delivering Web-mediated learning. It is arguably time for evaluation to make concomitant advances. Consideration was therefore given to three models with a sociocultural perspective that pays attention to the importance of the context of social interaction processes in which OCL takes place.

Application of one of these models, the CMCL developed by Cecez-Kecmanovic and Webb, has demonstrated in empirical studies that it is possible to evaluate OCL from within the social interaction space. The CMCL is a valuable pedagogical framework that enables useful and fine analytical distinctions to be made regarding students' orientation to collaborative learning online. Furthermore, the model enables the productivity of the OCL space to be evaluated by tracing how collaboration and knowledge co-creation is generated (and may be inhibited) within Web-mediated environments.

The CMCL model enables evaluation that is both descriptive as well as functional, and, significantly, can be applied indicatively to improve the design of Web-mediated collaborative learning environments. Thus, designers do not need to wait until student perceptions, tools and outcomes have been evaluated post-hoc. Each part of the design phase can be tested before its implementation.

Nevertheless, let us not assume that because evaluation can point to valued student experiences, effective instructional methods or even successful pedagogical outcomes, that all will be well for students and those who design, facilitate, monitor and evaluate for this innovative mode in higher education. Online learning and flexible delivery is becoming increasingly politicized. With the pressures currently on higher education, we are yet to see the emergence of evaluation research that demonstrates how courses can be delivered more efficiently via flexible delivery. Nonetheless, the interpolation of managerialism into our pedagogical research is not far off. Such assumptions concerning the instrumental efficiency of Web-mediated learning and its entrepreneurial potential are being widely voiced in the expansion of flexible delivery and online learning. It cannot be too long before we are required, or funding is made available, to research the economics of online delivery modes. Whether such research will be able to retain an emphasis on pedagogy remains to be seen. In looking to other areas of higher education from which to make inferences, there

Copyright © 2004, Idea Group Inc. Copying or distributing in print or electronic forms without written permission of Idea Group Inc. is prohibited.

is little reassurance available. It may well be those institutions that make, or can afford to make, substantial investment in and commitment to the provision of quality education will lead and inspire those that are less well endowed and less courageous in embracing and supporting change.

ACKNOWLEDGMENTS

The assistance of a University of Western Sydney Seed Grant is gratefully acknowledged.

REFERENCES

Alavi, M. (1994). Computer-mediated collaborative learning: an empirical evaluation. *MIS Quarterly, 18,* 159-174.

Alexander, S., & Hedberg, J. G. (1994). Evaluating technology-based learning: Which model? In K. Beattie, C. McNaught, & S. Wills (Eds.), *Interactive Multimedia in University Education: Designing for Change in Teaching and Learning, Vol. A59,* pp.233-244. Amsterdam: Elsevier B.V. (North Holland).

Alexander, S., & McKenzie, J. (1998). *An Evaluation of Information Technology Projects for University Learning.* Canberra, Australia: Committee for Committee for University Teaching and Staff Development and the Department of Education, Employment, Training and Youth Affairs.

Alon, I., & Cannon, N. (2000). Internet-based experiential learning in international marketing: The case Globalview.org. *Information Review, 24*(5), 349-356.

Arbaugh, J. B. (2000). How classroom environment and student engagement affect learning in Internet-based MBA courses. *Business Communication Quarterly, 63*(4), 9-26.

Askov, I., & Simpson, M. (2001). Researching distance education: Penn State's online adult education med degree on the World Campus [Electronic version]. Retrieved November 1, 2002 from http://www.avetra.org.au/PAPERS%202001/askov.pdf.

Bain, J. D. (1999). Introduction. *Higher Education Research and Development, 18*(2), 165-172.

Bates, T. (2001). International distance education: Cultural and ethical issues. *Distance Education, 22*(1), 122-136.

Bloom, B. (1956). *Taxonomy of Educational Objectives: The Classification of Educational Goals, by a Committee of College and University Examiners.* New York: Longmans, Green.

Copyright © 2004, Idea Group Inc. Copying or distributing in print or electronic forms without written permission of Idea Group Inc. is prohibited.

Bonamy, J., Charlier, B., & Saunders, M. (2001). "Bridging tools" for change: Evaluating a collaborative learning network. *Journal of Computer Assisted Learning, 17*(3), 295-305.

Bonk, C. J., & Dennen, V. (1999). Teaching on the Web: With a little help from my pedagogical friends. *Journal of Computing in Higher Education, 11*(1), 3-28.

Brandon, D. P., & Hollingshead, A. B. (1999). Collaborative learning and computer-supported groups. *Communication Education, 48*(2), 109-126.

Cecez-Kecmanovic, D., & Webb, C. (2000a). A critical inquiry into Web-mediated collaborative learning. In A. K. Aggarwal (Ed.), *Web-Based Learning: Opportunities and Challenges* (pp. 307-326). Hershey, PA: Idea Group Publishing.

Cecez-Kecmanovic, D., & Webb, C. (2000b). Towards a communicative model of collaborative Web-mediated learning. *Australian Journal of Educational Technology, 16*(1), 73-85.

Chalk, P. (2000). Webworlds-Web-based modelling environments for learning software engineering. *Computer Science Education, 10*(1), 39-56.

Chang, C. (2001). A study on the evaluation and effectiveness analysis of Web-based learning portfolio (WBLP). *British Journal of Educational Technology, 32*(4), 435-458.

Chen, D.-G., Liu, C.-C., Ou, K.-L., & Lin, M.-S. (2001). Web-learning portfolios: A tool for supporting performance awareness. *Innovations in Education and Training International, 38*(1), 19-32.

Collings, P., & Pearce, J. (2002). Sharing designer and user perspectives of Web site evaluation: A cross-campus collaborative learning experience. *British Journal of Educational Technology, 33*(3), 267-278.

Collot, M., & Belmore, N. (1996). Electronic language: A new variety. In S. C. Herring (Ed.), *Computer-Mediated Communication – Linguistic, Social and Cross-Cultural Perspectives* (pp. 13-28). Amsterdam: John Benjamins.

Curtis, D., & Lawson, M. (1999, July). *Collaborative online learning: An explanatory case study.* Paper presented at the HERDSA Annual International Conference, Melbourne, Australia.

Ekstrom, D. N., & Sigurdsson, H. O. (2002). An international collaboration in nursing education viewed through the lens of critical social theory. *Journal of Nursing Education, 41*(7), 289-295.

Ellis, T., & Cohen, M. (2001). Integrating multimedia into a distance learning environment: Is the game worth the candle? *British Journal of Educational Technology, 32*(4), 495-497.

Freeman, M. (1997). Flexibility in access, interaction and assessment: The case for Web-based teaching programs. *Australian Journal of Educational Technology, 13*(1), 23-39.

Copyright © 2004, Idea Group Inc. Copying or distributing in print or electronic forms without written permission of Idea Group Inc. is prohibited.

Gallini, J. K., & Barron, D. (2002). Participants' perceptions of Web-infused environments: A survey of teaching beliefs, learning approaches, and communication. *Journal of Research on Technology in Education, 34*(2), 139-156.

Goffmann, E. (1974). *Frame Analysis: An Essay on the Organization of Experience.* Cambridge, MA: Harvard University Press.

Gosling, D. (2000). Using Habermas to evaluate two approaches to negotiated assessment. *Assessment & Evaluation in Higher Education, 25*(3), 293-304.

Grossman, W. M. (1999). On-line U. *Scientific American, 28*(1), 41.

Gunawardena, C., Carabajal, K., & Lowe, C. A. (2001, April). *Critical analysis of models and methods used to evaluate online learning networks.* Paper presented at the Annual Meeting of the American Educational Research Association, Seattle, Washington, USA.

Gunawardena, C. N., Lowe, C. A., & Anderson, T. D. (1997). Analysis of a global online debate and the development of an interaction analysis model for examining social construction of knowledge in computer conferencing. *Journal of Educational Computing Research, 16*(4), 397-431.

Gunawardena, C. N., Nolla, A. C., Wilson, P. L., Lopez-Islas, J. R., Ramirez-Angel, N., & Megchun-Alpizar, R. M. (2001). A cross-cultural study of group process and development in online conferences. *Distance Education, 22*(1), 85-121.

Habermas, J. (1984). *The theory of communicative action – Reason and the rationalisation of society* (Vol. I). Boston, MA: Beacon Press.

Henri, F. (1992). Computer conferencing and content analysis. In A. R. Kaye (Ed.), *Collaborative Learning Through Computer Conferencing: The Najdeen Papers*, pp.117-136. Berlin: Springer-Verlag.

Herring, S. C. (ed.). (1996). *Computermediated Communication – Linguistic, Social and Cross-Cultural Perspectives.* Amsterdam: John Benjamins.

Heslep, R. D. (2001). Habermas on communication in teaching. *Educational Theory, 51*(2), 191ff.

Housego, S., & Freeman, M. (2000). Case studies: Integrating the use of Web-based learning systems into student learning. *Australian Journal of Educational Technology, 13*(3), 258-282.

Hron, A., Hesse, F. W., Cress, U., & Giovis, C. (2000). Implicit and explicit dialogue structuring in virtual learning groups. *British Journal of Educational Psychology, 70,* 53-64.

Johnson, D. W., & Johnson, R. T. (1996). Cooperation and the use of technology. In D. H. Jonassen (Ed.), *Handbook of Research for Educational Communications and Technology* (pp. 1017-1044). New York: Simmon and Schuster Macmillan.

Copyright © 2004, Idea Group Inc. Copying or distributing in print or electronic forms without written permission of Idea Group Inc. is prohibited.

Jones, C. (1998). Evaluating a collaborative online learning environment. *Active Learning, 9,* 31-35.

Kitchen, D., & McDougall, D. (1999). Collaborative learning on the Internet. *Journal of Educational Technology Systems, 27*(3), 245-258.

Kumpulainen, K., Salovaara, H., & Mutanen, M. (2001). The nature of students' sociocognitive activity in handing and processing multimedia-based science material in a small group learning task. *Instructional Science, 29*(6), 481-515.

Lauzon, A. C. (2000). Distance education and diversity are they compatible? *The American Journal of Distance Education, 14*(2), 61-70.

Mason, R. (1992). *Computer Conferencing: The Last Word.* Victoria, British Columbia, Canada: Beach Holme.

McAlpine, I. (2000). Collaborative learning online. *Distance Education, 21*(1), 66-80.

McIssac, M., Blocher, J. M., & Mahes, V. (1999). Student and teacher perceptions of interaction in online computer mediated communication. *Educational Media International, 36*(2), 121-131.

Nakleh, M. B., Donovan, W. J., & Parrill, A. L. (2000). Evaluation of interactive technologies for chemistry Websites: Educational Materials for Organic Chemistry Web site (EMOC). *The Journal of Computers in Mathematics and Science Teaching, 19*(4), 355-378.

Phillips, R. A. (2002). *Learning-centred evaluation of computer-facilitated learning projects in higher education: outcomes of a CUTSD Staff Development Grant, Staff Development in Evaluation of Technology-based Teaching Development Projects: An action inquiry approach.* Retrieved on April 20, 2003 from the web site: http://www.tlc.murdoch.edu.au/project/cutsd01.html.

Ravenscroft, A., & Matheson, M. P. (2002). Developing and evaluating dialogue games for collaborative e-learning. *Journal of Computer Assisted Learning, 18*(1), 93-102.

Reason, P., & Bradbury, H. (eds.). (2001). *Handbook of Action Research: Participative Inquiry and Practice.* London: Sage Publications.

Redding, T. R., & Rotzien, J. (2001). Comparative analysis of online learning versus classroom learning. *Journal of Interactive Instruction Development, 13*(4), 3-12.

Ronteltap, F., & Eurelings, A. (2002). Activity and interaction of students in an electronic learning environment for problem-based learning. *Distance Education, 23*(1), 11-22.

Salmon, G. (2000). *E-Moderating: The Key to Teaching and Learning Online.* London: Kogan Page.

Sanders, D. W., & Morrison-Shetlar, A. (2001). Student attitudes toward Web-enhanced instruction in an introductory biology course. *Journal of Research on Computing in Education, 33*(3), 251-262.

Copyright © 2004, Idea Group Inc. Copying or distributing in print or electronic forms without written permission of Idea Group Inc. is prohibited.

Sheely, S., Veness, D., & Rankine, L. (2001). Building the Web interactive study environment: mainstreaming online teaching and learning at the University of Western Sydney. *Australian Journal of Educational Technology, 17*(1), 80-95.

Short, J. A., Williams, E., & Christie, B. (1976). *The Social Psychology of Telecommunications.* London: John Wiley & Sons.

Sullivan, P. (2001). Gender differences and the online classroom: Male and female college students evaluate their experience. *Community College Journal and Practice, 25*(10), 805-818.

Tidwell, L. C., & Walther, J. B. (2002). Computer-mediated communication effects on disclosure, impressions, and interpersonal evaluations: Getting to know one another a bit at a time. *Human Communication Research, 28*(3), 317-348.

Treleaven, L. (2003). A tale of two evaluations: Better practice for learning collaboratively online. In C. Bond & P. Bright (Eds.), Learning for an Unknown Future, Research and Development in Higher Education, Vol. 26, pp. 547-556. Sydney: Higher Education Research and Development Society of Australasia.

Treleaven, L. (in preparation). Reframing the class as a "virtual organisation": A study of pedagogy, technology and innovation in management education.

Treleaven, L. (in press). Three approaches to evaluating online collaborative learning: A collaborative action research study.

Treleaven, L., & Cecez-Kecmanovic, D. (2001). Collaborative learning in a Web-mediated environment: A study of communicative practices. *Studies in Continuing Education, 23*(2), 169-183.

Tsoukas, H. (2003). Do we really understand tacit knowledge? In M. Easterby-Smith & M. A. Lyles (Eds.), *The Blackwell Handbook of Organizational Learning and Knowledge Management.* Blackwell, Oxford, pp. 410-427.

Tu, C. (2002). The measurement of social presence in an online learning environment. *International Journal on Elearning, 1*(2), 34-45.

Tu, C., & Corry, M. (2001). A paradigm shift for online community research. *Distance Education, 22*(2), 245-263.

Warschauer, M. (1998). Technology and indigenous language revitalization: Analyzing the experience of Hawaii. *The Canadian Modern Language Review, 55*(1), 139-159.

Weasonforth, D., Biesenbach-Lucas, S., & Meloni, C. (2002). Realizing constructivist objectives through collaborative technologies: Threaded discussions. *Language, Learning and Technology, 6*(3), 58ff.

Weiner, C. (2002). A new Alternative: adolescent students study in cyberspace. *Dissertation Abstracts International, 63*(1-A), 155.

Copyright © 2004, Idea Group Inc. Copying or distributing in print or electronic forms without written permission of Idea Group Inc. is prohibited.

Yates, S. C. (1996). Oral and written linguistic aspects of computer conferencing: A corpus based study. In S. C. Herring (Ed.), *Computer-Mediated Communication – Linguistic, Social and Cross-Cultural Perspectives* (pp. 29-46). Amsterdam: John Benjamins.

Copyright © 2004, Idea Group Inc. Copying or distributing in print or electronic forms without written permission of Idea Group Inc. is prohibited.

Chapter VIII

Computer-Mediated Learning Groups: Benefits and Challenges to Using Groupwork in Online Learning Environments

Charles R. Graham
Brigham Young University, USA

Melanie Misanchuk
Office of Open Learning, University of Guelph, Canada

ABSTRACT

With the increased availability of computers and Internet technologies, computer-mediated learning environments are on the rise in both higher education and corporate sectors of society. At the same time there has been an increased awareness among educators and researchers of the importance of human interaction in the learning process. Computer-mediated groupwork is an instructional strategy that combines online technologies with human interaction. This chapter defines computer-mediated learning groups and outlines critical differences between learning groups and work groups. The chapter further explores benefits and challenges associated with using

Copyright © 2004, Idea Group Inc. Copying or distributing in print or electronic forms without written permission of Idea Group Inc. is prohibited.

groupwork in online learning environments. Case examples and research related to (1) creating the groups, (2) structuring group activities, and (3) facilitating group interactions are provided.

INTRODUCTION

Advances in computer- and network-based technologies over the past decade have greatly expanded the possibilities for the development of online learning environments. Additionally, the demand for distance learning in public schools, higher education and especially the corporate sector is on the rise. The National Center for Educational Statistics in the United States reported the existence of over 50,000 distance education (DE) course offerings, with growth in the number of institutions of higher education offering DE courses increasing across all sizes and types, except two-year private institutions (Lewis, Snow, Farris, Levin, & B.G., 1999). Similarly, in the corporate sector, the American Society for Training & Development reported record levels of technology-mediated training (or e-learning), accompanied by slight decreases in face-to-face classroom training (Thompson, Koon, Woodwell, & Beauvais, 2002).

However, despite the benefits associated with increased access to distance learning opportunities, there is ample anecdotal evidence that much of the distance learning does not effectively take advantage of proven collaborative methodologies such as groupwork. Groupwork is a powerful instructional method that has been widely used in face-to-face learning environments, and the cooperative learning literature is full of research documenting the benefits of having learners work in groups (Cohen, 1994; Johnson & Johnson, 1999). Groupwork has also been an important feature of corporate innovation and productivity. While there is an increasing visibility of computer-mediated groupwork (often called "virtual teamwork") in the business and organizational sciences literature, there is very little research available in the educational literature. Those disciplines have recognized that there exists an increased need to coordinate work among individuals, across both organizational and geographical boundaries (Armstrong & Cole, 1995; Lipnack & Stamps, 2000; Townsend, DeMarie, & Hendrickson, 1998). Over the past decade, there has been a great deal of interest and research in collaborative and cooperative distance learning environments, as evidenced in the computer supported collaborative learning (CSCL) literature (Bonk & King, 1998; Harasim, 1990; Koschmann, 1996; Koschmann, Hall, & Naomi, 2002). Much of this research has focused on strategies for promoting collaboration and communication at a distance using various technologies but has not specifically focused on groupwork as an instructional strategy. While there has been much research done on groupwork in a face-to-face environment, there is little research in the field of education that has focused specifically on computer-mediated groups or groups whose mem-

Copyright © 2004, Idea Group Inc. Copying or distributing in print or electronic forms without written permission of Idea Group Inc. is prohibited.

bers are geographically dispersed and use technology as the primary means of communication.

The goal of this chapter is to raise the visibility of computer-mediated groupwork as an instructional strategy among those interested in CSCL environments. In order to do this, the chapter will address the following three questions:

- What are computer-mediated learning groups?
- What are some of the benefits to using computer-mediated learning groups in online environments?
- What challenges do computer-mediated learning groups face?

Understanding what computer-mediated learning groups are, how they can be beneficial and what challenges they face will help distance educators to feel more confident and prepared to use groupwork as an instructional strategy in their own online learning environments.

WHAT ARE COMPUTER-MEDIATED LEARNING GROUPS?

This section of the chapter defines what computer-mediated learning groups are by contrasting and elaborating on the three different concepts embedded in the term. First, the distinction between groupwork and other forms of collaboration is described. Secondly, important distinctions between learning groups and workgroups are outlined. Lastly, computer-mediated groups are contrasted with face-to-face groups and the use of the term "computer-mediated" group, instead of the term "virtual" group is discussed.

Groupwork vs. Other Forms of Collaboration

There are many different types of instructional strategies that involve interactions between individuals in a learning environment. Interactions can occur with instructors, peers or other individuals such as mentor experts (Bonk & King, 1998). Individuals who interact with each other will have differing levels of dependence on each other to accomplish the learning goals. Figure 1 shows a few of the possibilities across the spectrum. At the low end of the spectrum, the learners engage in minimal-to-no collaborative interactions and are not dependent on anyone but themselves and perhaps a grader with whom they have minimal contact. This is the model typical of independent or self-study programs. At the other end of the spectrum, the instructional activities are highly dependent on collaborative interactions. In collaborative groups, there is a high degree of interdependence among group members on learning tasks. Collaborative groups have a common purpose or goal and activities are structured in such a way that all group members contribute to all significant aspects of the group's work.

Copyright © 2004, Idea Group Inc. Copying or distributing in print or electronic forms without written permission of Idea Group Inc. is prohibited.

Figure 1:   Different Levels of Interdependence in Learning Environments

Additionally, grading or compensation for the work has a group component and is not completely individualistic, often including some form of peer evaluation.

Instructional strategies that involve intermediate levels of interdependence include discussion groups and cooperative groups as shown in Figure 1. While there is a range of interdependence possible in discussion groups, typically individuals are assessed based on their individual insights and contribution.

Cooperative groups differ from collaborative groups in that they tend to have a "divide and conquer" mentality, where the cooperative group divides the work into chunks that can be done independently, and then assigns the pieces to the individual group members, with greatest expertise to be able to complete the piece in question. Thus collaboration in cooperative groups tends to occur primarily in the administrative aspects of the group such as deciding how to divide and assign the work among group members.

Learning Groups vs. Work Groups

Much of the existing literature related to computer-mediated groupwork comes from the business and organizational development disciplines. While there is much to learn from that body of literature, it is important to understand that there are significant differences between work groups and learning groups. Some of these differences are outlined in Table 1.

First, work groups usually have a hierarchical leadership structure and clear role definitions. A work group might have a group manager and group members with specialized knowledge and skills. For example, an instructional design group might include a project manager, an instructional designer, a programmer, a

Copyright © 2004, Idea Group Inc. Copying or distributing in print or electronic forms without written permission of Idea Group Inc. is prohibited.

Table 1:   Differences Between Work and Learning Groups

Work Group Characteristics	**Learning Group** Characteristics
• Hierarchical leadership structure	• Flat leadership structure
• Clear role definitions	• No role definitions
• Collaboration is to maximize productivity	• Collaboration is to maximize learning
• Goals are product-oriented	• Goals are learning-oriented
• Group members take on tasks that reflect skills and strengths already acquired	• Group members may accept tasks to gain skills they have not already acquired in order to learn
• Focus is on the product or outcome	• Focus is on the process or learning

graphic artist, etc. The members of this group come together with a common purpose or goal which is completing the product within the cost and quality constraints. In these groups, collaboration occurs in defining how individual pieces of the design interface with each other, but work is specialized and done individually by those with particular expertise.

Learning groups, on the other hand, usually begin with no formal leadership structure. Often instructors will assume a consulting role with the group, but not participate as a member of the group. Members of a learning group are typically peers in a class with fairly equivalent levels of expertise and knowledge in the topic area. While learning groups are often project oriented (i.e., members are jointly producing a final product as their deliverable), the primary goal is individual learning and not just the quality of the final product. Thus, if a learning group used the same "divide and conquer" strategy as work groups do, the learners would focus on doing what they were already good at rather than working on the tasks that would result in learning new knowledge and skills. Obviously, the outcome requirements are also different for learning groups and work groups; in the latter case, the best possible product is imperative. For a learning group, instructors must emphasize the primacy of learning over production, so that group members can focus on the learning process, as opposed to primarily focusing on the product being created and delivered.

Computer-Mediated vs. Face-to-Face Groups

Groupwork in the traditional sense is carried out by individuals who are physically in the same location. Because the group members are co-located, they typically meet and interact in a face-to-face setting. The members of computer-mediated groups, on the other hand, use computer technology as their primary mode of interacting with each other. As computer technologies have improved and networking bandwidths have increased, computer-mediated groupwork has also become more prominent, especially in the global business environment. In

Copyright © 2004, Idea Group Inc. Copying or distributing in print or electronic forms without written permission of Idea Group Inc. is prohibited.

the business literature, these computer-mediated groups are commonly referred to as "virtual teams." The term virtual refers to the fact that the group meets in a "virtual," or online, space. The authors have chosen to use the phrase computer-meditated groups instead of virtual teams, because they feel that it more clearly and accurately communicates the nature of the term. For example, many individuals are familiar with the phrase "virtual reality," usually referring to something that is not reality or different from reality. If this same understanding is applied to the term "virtual team," it might be interpreted as a collective that is not a group or is different from a group. This problem is exacerbated when we talk about a group with a particular focus like a "virtual learning group." In this case the reader might think that the term "virtual" modifies the word learning, which might cause them to wonder what "virtual learning" is.

WHY USE COMPUTER-MEDIATED LEARNING GROUPS?

This section of the chapter will focus on two primary questions that should help in analyzing the tradeoffs for using computer-mediated learning groups as an instructional strategy for a given context. Vignettes shared as a part of this section will come from our work with an online master's degree program in instructional technology. The program was designed to be highly collaborative and was modeled after the university's on-campus program. Course work in the online program was largely project based and completed by small learning groups of three to four members each.

What are the Benefits Associated with Computer-Mediated Groupwork?

While there may be many documented benefits attributed to groupwork, this section of the chapter will address (1) benefits from a learning theory perspective, (2) benefits of cooperative learning over individualistic learning, and (3) benefits related to learner motivation.

Benefits from a Learning Theory Perspective

This section will discuss the theoretical implications of computer-mediated learning groups. Learning benefits found in the work on social interaction will be examined (Brown, Collins, & Duguid, 1989; Vygotsky, 1978). The importance of social interaction in learning has been characterized by social cognition theorists as necessary to the development of higher mental processes (Driscoll, 1994). In order for this interaction to be effective, collaboration is not simply a question of students talking to each other and sharing their individual knowledge. Indeed, collaboration focuses on the synergistic problem solving that often occurs when

Copyright © 2004, Idea Group Inc. Copying or distributing in print or electronic forms without written permission of Idea Group Inc. is prohibited.

work in a group is more than the sum of its parts (Brown et al., 1989). Cunningham (1992) argues that it is only through collaboration that students can challenge their own world views and begin to understand others' perspectives. Through defending their own ideas and challenging others', students learn to negotiate meaning. Johnson and Johnson (1996) call this type of cooperative learning "academic controversy" and note that it is "one of the most dynamic and involving, yet least-used, teaching strategies" (p. 1019). This challenge-and-explain cycle (Curtis & Lawson, 2001) occurs naturally in many types of group processes, but Johnson and Johnson suggest explicit techniques for engendering and supporting such controversy, the end result of which is that students with opposing views seek to reach a consensus on the topic. Johnson and Johnson (1992) found that such a process encourages re-conceptualization of prior knowledge, motivation to learn, curiosity, high quality decision making, insight into the problem, higher level reasoning and cognitive development. Explaining, elaborating and summarizing information and then teaching it to others results in a variety of group and individual gains. It increases the level of cognitive processing as well as the organization of information, of reasoning and of insights and the personal commitment to achievement. The other side of the challenge-and-explain issue is the active mutual influencing of reasoning and behaviors: if one group member has a more effective or efficient way to complete the work, other members will usually adopt it (Johnson & Johnson, 1996).

Benefits of Cooperative Learning Over Individualistic Learning

The next part of the chapter will examine research related to cooperative learning vs. individualistic learning, as addressed in the literature on face-to-face collaboration (Johnson & Johnson, 1996; Panitz, 1999a), and the new field of virtual collaboration (Black, 1995; Chin & Carroll, 2000; Hiltz & Benbunan-Fich, 1997; Yaverbaum & Ocker, 1998). In this chapter, the terms "collaborative" and "cooperative" will be used interchangeably to refer to work that groups undertake together. In general, authors use cooperative to describe work that is split up among group members and collaborative for work requiring more engagement and interdependence among members (Misanchuk & Anderson, 2000; Panitz, 1999a; Roschelle & Teasley, 1995). However, some authors have a more stringent definition of collaboration, and call "cooperative" what most educators would label collaborative. We are less concerned with the fine distinctions among these ways of working than we are with emphasizing the need for students to work together in small groups, in order to exchange ideas, challenge their own ways of thinking and create synergy to produce something that goes beyond what any of them could have done working separately.

With respect to general learning benefits accrued from cooperative learning, Johnson and Johnson (1996) assert that of more than 375 experimental studies on social interdependence and achievement, "cooperative learning

Copyright © 2004, Idea Group Inc. Copying or distributing in print or electronic forms without written permission of Idea Group Inc. is prohibited.

results in significantly higher achievement and retention than does competitive and individualistic learning" (p. 1022). They state that the more conceptual and complex a task is and the more it requires problem-solving and creative answers, then "the greater the superiority of cooperative learning over competitive and individualistic learning" (p. 1022). The reasons they give for the gains in a cooperative setting are that "competitive and individualistic structures, by isolating individuals from each other, tend to depress achievement" (p. 1023). They break down the benefits gained from cooperative learning into superiority in the following categories:

- Willingness to take on difficult tasks and persevere,
- Long-term retention,
- Critical thinking and meta-cognitive thought,
- Creative thinking,
- Learning transfer,
- Job/task satisfaction, and
- Time on task.

Panitz (1999a, b) lists some 67 benefits of cooperative learning, including improved critical thinking skills, improved classroom results, engagement of students in the learning process, use of problem-solving techniques, personalization of large lecture courses, increased motivation, social support system for students, development of learning communities, improvement of students' self-esteem and reduction of anxiety.

Much of the discussion in the new field of virtual collaboration centers on the relationship of technology to the collaborative process. In many instances, the tool-to-task relationship and the quality of available technology are very important in the potential success of the collaborative effort (Chin & Carroll, 2000; Hathorn & Ingram, 2002). Additionally, virtual collaboration offers some challenges to the collaborative procedure that are not present in groups working in a face-to-face environment: group members may not ever get to meet each other physically and communication among members is by definition mediated — and might be moderated. Although the "anonymity" of a computer-mediated communication (CMC) environment can attenuate certain characteristics, thereby allowing for more equal participation (Hiltz, 1998; Yaverbaum & Ocker, 1998), it can also remove the need for accountability and insert a barrier among members, including a lowering of inhibitions (Hathorn & Ingram, 2002). The literature on collaboration in a virtual setting is still in its infancy, but there is reason to believe that many of the learning and non-learning gains demonstrated in a face-to-face context will hold true in a virtual learning situation, with certain additional benefits being possible.

Copyright © 2004, Idea Group Inc. Copying or distributing in print or electronic forms without written permission of Idea Group Inc. is prohibited.

Benefits Related to Learner Motivation

The final part of this section will discuss motivational issues related to social learning. Johnson and Johnson (1996) describe the "long-term caring peer relationships" (p. 1019) born of what they call cooperative "base groups." These are groups designed to support students in their academic journey in a face-to-face context. The benefits of such base groups include improved attendance, personalization of students' work as well as the school experience and improved quality and quantity of learning. Even in shorter term cooperative groups, Johnson and Johnson (1996) found that members exchange work-related and personal advice as well as support, and that there is a significant positive correlation between achievement and helping behaviors (Hooper & Hannafin, 1991). Johnson and Johnson (1996) report that more than 100 studies comparing the impact of cooperative, competitive and individualistic efforts on social support have been conducted since the 1940s, and that cooperative experiences encouraged more task orientation and personal social support than the other two. Social support, which may be task related or on a more personal level, promotes achievement, productivity, physical and psychological health, and stress and adversity management.

Johnson and Johnson (1996) also found that students working in cooperative groups monitor each other's progress on both the work at hand as well as the process of groupwork, providing immediate feedback and assistance. They also report that cooperators "tend to like each other," both when they are in a homogenous group and when they differ in both abilities and demographic characteristics. Cooperators also value heterogeneity, which leads to varied perspective taking, feelings of acceptance and esteem, and psychological success (Johnson & Johnson, 1996). They find that the more positive the relationships among members of a group, the lower the absenteeism and drop-out rates; and the more likely members are to:

- Commit to academic goals,
- Feel personal responsibility for learning,
- Take on difficult tasks,
- Be motivated to learn,
- Persist in working towards goals,
- Have high morale,
- Be willing to endure frustration in order to learn,
- Listen to and be influenced by peers and instructors, and
- Commit to each other's learning/success.

Kitchen and McDougall (1999) and Hiltz (1994) noted that collaborative learning can decrease the tendency to procrastinate, even among motivated adults, in a computer-mediated learning environment.

Copyright © 2004, Idea Group Inc. Copying or distributing in print or electronic forms without written permission of Idea Group Inc. is prohibited.

Although groupwork is incontestably a strong pedagogical strategy from the point of view of the instructor, students often have mixed reactions to it. Some see it as a trial to work with others, fearing logistical challenges and worrying about "freeloaders." Nonetheless, some students report benefits ranging from "you learn what other people have to offer," "you help others as others help you," "things get done faster and better," "you get to meet people," "you get help interpreting the assignment," "you save time" and "you can spread the work around" (OERL, n.d.; Misanchuk, 2001).

What are the Challenges and Issues Associated with Computer-Mediated Groupwork?

The literature shows three general areas that are important for successfully facilitating and using groups in a computer-mediated environment (see Figure 2):
1. Creating the groups,
2. Structuring the learning activities, and
3. Facilitating group interactions (Graham, 2002a).

This section of the chapter will elaborate on the issues and challenges faced in doing each of these three things in a collaborative group-based online learning environment. Examples from actual computer-mediated groups will be used in describing each of the challenges.

Creating the Groups

This section will address two challenges related to creating successful computer-mediated learning groups:
- Choosing appropriate group size and
- Determining group composition.

Figure 2: Three Important Elements in Creating Effective Learning Groups

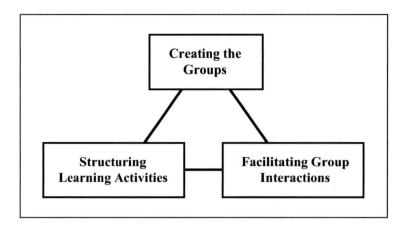

Copyright © 2004, Idea Group Inc. Copying or distributing in print or electronic forms without written permission of Idea Group Inc. is prohibited.

Choosing Appropriate Group Size.   Group size can range from two individuals upward. There is no magic number that would indicate the perfect group size, because appropriate group size is so dependent on the context in which the group is working. Prominent researchers in the area of cooperative learning have suggested a rule of thumb is that for learning effectiveness, "the smaller the better" (Johnson, Johnson, & Holubec, 1994). Larger groups have a greater possibility for diversity of ideas and input, at the cost of increased overhead coordinating the group members' efforts. This is a particularly important consideration in online learning groups, where communication already takes longer than in face-to-face environments (Bordia, 1997; Walther, 1996). A few factors that directly impact appropriate group size by impacting how easily communication can be coordinated in the online environment are:

- The different time zones of group members and
- The time availability (schedules) of the group members.

The constraints on the time of distance learners are often greater than the time constraints of face-to-face learners. Indeed, these constraints may be precisely the reason the learner is participating in a distance format, instead of a traditional learning format. Time zones and time availability are particularly critical to consider if the groups plan on doing any synchronous communication, which online groups often like to do.

The online groups in our distance master's degree program typically had only three to four group members; however, some groups experienced considerable difficulties coordinating their communication. One group developed a strategy of listing meeting times with all relevant time zones, like "10pm (Ind.)/ 10 (CDT)/11 (EDT)." Even then, in one instance, a meeting was scheduled for "noon" and half the group showed up to the meeting an hour late. One of the group members expressed the difficulty some groups had in coordinating schedules:

I enjoy working with the teams, but logistically it's just a nightmare sometimes...some of the people had plenty of time during the week, nothing on the weekend. I was the other way around, I've got a lot of time on the weekend, or can make time on the weekends, [but] don't have time during the week.

The time zones and schedules of group members should be considered when creating the learning groups, because, in a distance environment, these factors can have an enormous impact on the ability of a group to perform well. Many online groups plan to do at least some of their work synchronously, especially if they are on a tight timeframe and must make quick decisions. Having group

Copyright © 2004, Idea Group Inc. Copying or distributing in print or electronic forms without written permission of Idea Group Inc. is prohibited.

members living (or traveling) in distant time zones with conflicting schedules can be especially difficult if the group plans to engage in synchronous meetings.

Determining Group Composition. Another important consideration in forming computer-mediated learning groups is whether the groups will be homogeneous or heterogeneous. Heterogeneity in a group can come in the form of group members with widely different demographic backgrounds, skill sets, abilities and/or career and life experiences. While homogeneous groups tend to be more cohesive (Perrone & Sedlacek, 2000), heterogeneous groups have the advantage of bringing different perspectives to the group discussion and work, which can enrich the learning experience (Cohen, 1994). The practical trade off that this challenge often presents is one of efficiency vs. learning. The differences existing in heterogeneous groups are more likely to lead to controversies within the group, which increases the time required to come to consensus and complete the tasks. However, the dissonance created by controversies can be constructive and promote more effective group learning (Johnson & Johnson, 1997). A certain amount of conflict is necessary for group effectiveness (Forsyth, 1999). In particular, substantive conflict can help groups to increase creativity, make plans, solve problems and make decisions (McGrath, 1984). Conflict can also lead to more explicit goals and member roles (Borman, 1975; Thibaut & Coules, 1952). The authors are of the opinion that in educational learning environments, the advantages of having heterogeneous groups are generally greater than the advantages of using homogeneous groups. However, in order to avoid non-productive conflict, group members may need to be taught how to deal with conflict in a constructive way, as well as how to recognize and resolve conflict that has ceased to be productive.

The groups in the online program in this study were all assigned, rather than self-selected groups. The groups were mixed individuals with different career backgrounds and abilities. One dimension of heterogeneity that existed in online learning groups observed in our study was career background. Participants came from three general career backgrounds: the public school environment, service organizations in higher education and a corporate instructional design environment. We did not anticipate how different the practices in these environments were and how that would impact the relationships and work on the groups. The group members with a corporate background and those with a public school teaching background often conflicted with each other on issues such as skill level and the aggressiveness with which they approached a problem. One educator reflected on this after the course by saying:

I noticed a real difference between educators and the business people, and I noticed it in both groups. ...They're very, very direct people. They're saying "this is what I want done, let's get it done," you know...I think as

Copyright © 2004, Idea Group Inc. Copying or distributing in print or electronic forms without written permission of Idea Group Inc. is prohibited.

educators maybe [we] take a little more relaxed approach to it. They're not, you know, more accepting of things that are outside of [their] own personal expectations for a project.

Instructors who use learning groups have the option of assigning membership to the groups or letting the groups self-select. If left to their own devices, groups will almost always self-select into homogeneous groups. There are advantages and disadvantages to both options that should be considered, along with the goals of using groups as an instructional strategy. A logistical advantage of letting groups self-select is that the students can form groups with others who have compatible schedules. This moves the ownership of scheduling problems squarely onto the shoulders of the students as they form the groups. A disadvantage of letting groups self-select is that group members are likely to select group members who are similar to themselves, resulting in homogeneous groups, and in many cases, high-powered groups or groups in which the best students choose to work together.

Structuring the Learning Activities

There are two key challenges associated with structuring learning activities for computer-mediated groups that will be discussed:

- Establishing an appropriate level of interdependence and
- Creating learner accountability.

Establishing an Appropriate Level of Interdependence. One of the most difficult challenges with online learning groups is establishing an appropriate level of interdependence between group members. Interdependence is defined as the level of dependence that one group member has on other group members, in order to complete the learning tasks. A high level of interdependence might require students to work jointly on all aspects of a project or task (a more collaborative model). A lower level of interdependence might allow students to take a "divide and conquer" approach to the learning tasks (a more cooperative model). Figure 1 shows a range of levels of interdependence that are possible in an online learning environment.

The tension that makes determining an appropriate level of interdependence a challenge is between task time and learning. The higher the level of interdependence between group members, the greater the communication overhead required to complete the learning task. Conversely, individual learning can be compromised if there is limited interdependence in a learning group.

We observed this tension in many of the learning groups that participated in our distance master's degree program. The groups were assigned a project and each group was allowed to determine how they would work together to complete the project. In essence, the groups were allowed to decide the level of

Copyright © 2004, Idea Group Inc. Copying or distributing in print or electronic forms without written permission of Idea Group Inc. is prohibited.

interdependence with which they were comfortable. Understandably, there was a range of levels. Some groups chose to work closely on every aspect of the project, while other groups decided to divide up tasks in order to be more efficient in completing the project.

A disappointing outcome of this approach was that in several cases the groups chose an efficiency focus over a learning focus. These groups chose to use the divide and conquer approach to completing the project and individual tasks were assigned based on group member strengths, rather than on areas of skill and knowledge that individual group members wanted to develop. In this respect, these groups mimic the ideal work group (see Table 1), but do not reap all the benefits of a learning group.

Creating Learner Accountability. Closely linked to the issue of interdependence is the challenge of creating learner accountability in learning groups. Accountability should be addressed at both the group and individual level, and determining the appropriate balance between the two is the challenge. Over emphasizing group accountability can lead to problems such as social loafing or free-riding (Latane, Williams, & Harkins, 1979; Wagner, 1995), where certain individuals pull back from fully contributing to the group efforts. On the other hand, over emphasizing individual accountability can undermine the cohesiveness of the group. The structure of assessment in the learning environment will have a big impact on learner accountability.

In the learning groups that we observed, assessments of the product and of the process were used to establish a mix of group and individual accountability. Group accountability was established through product assessments in which the project deliverables were scored and everyone on the group received the same score, regardless of effort or level of contribution to the group effort. Individual accountability was established through assessments that focused more on the learning process. For example, periodically during the group projects, individuals were required to submit progress reports in which they individually reported on the group progress and the contributions of each group member to the group progress. They also had individual reflection papers due throughout the project in which they individually reflected on project-related issues. Finally, at the end of the project, each group member turned in a self-evaluation and a peer evaluation for each of the other group members in which the contribution and effort of each group member was assessed.

Facilitating Group Interactions

Facilitating group interactions is perhaps one of the most critical elements for having successful computer-mediated learning groups. This is particularly important because there are different skills and norms required to communicate effectively in an online environment. This section of the chapter will discuss a

Copyright © 2004, Idea Group Inc. Copying or distributing in print or electronic forms without written permission of Idea Group Inc. is prohibited.

few of the challenges associated with developing cooperative group skills and establishing group norms in computer-mediated learning groups.

Developing Cooperative Group Skills. Students who have developed cooperative group skills are more likely to gain from their collaborative learning experience than others (Johnson & Johnson, 1987; Johnson & Johnson, 1999). Some important skills talked about in the literature are: decision making, consensus building, dealing with conflict and basic communication skills (Graham, 2002a). One might expect adult learners to have already developed many of these skills, or at least that the skills might transfer directly from prior experiences with face-to-face groups. However, we observed groups that had some significant conflicts that could have been avoided if group members had had greater group skills.

One area that caused conflict in some groups was how to provide constructive feedback to other group members regarding their contributions to the group project. Some group members were brutally honest with their feedback, while other group members were more tactful and constructive in providing feedback. Yet others, when asked to read over a document, responded with "yeah, it's fine," and others felt that the climate of the group was such that saying anything remotely challenging was out of place. It is possible that in some cases the emotional distance afforded by an online environment coupled with the increased time required for communication encouraged an "efficiency" approach to the communication in which learners considered the message and not the impact of the message on the other group members.

Another issue that all groups had to deal with was making decisions and coming to group consensus. This was not always easy because, as mentioned previously, learning groups are not hierarchical in nature, so all major decisions require a level of negotiation and compromise. Online learning groups must decide what decisions need to be made by the group and what decisions can be made by individuals. One group we observed developed a rule that all decisions would be made through unanimous consensus by the three group members. This idea quickly became unrealistic when one group member disappeared for a weekend and did not respond to e-mail, during which time the other group members needed his input to proceed with their work.

Establishing Group Norms

Norms are shared expectations that drive and inhibit the actions of group members. There are many types of norms including value norms, leadership and decision-making norms, communication norms and logistical norms that are important for computer-mediated learning groups (Graham, 2002b). This section of the chapter will focus on communication norms. For many learners, online communication is a challenge because it is a new experience with many

Copyright © 2004, Idea Group Inc. Copying or distributing in print or electronic forms without written permission of Idea Group Inc. is prohibited.

differences from face-to-face communication. Three areas in which we observed challenges with communication that could have been addressed by establishing explicit group norms were:

- Choosing modes of communication,
- Communicating the unseen, and
- Acknowledging communication.

The following three examples highlight the above issues, and some of the group experiences we observed related to these issues.

Example 1: Choosing Modes of Communication

It is very likely that computer-mediated learning groups will have several different tools for communication at their disposal. These potential tools include: e-mail, telephone, asynchronous discussion boards, synchronous chat, instant messaging, etc. It is important for group members to establish a shared understanding of when and how different communication tools will be used. The groups that we observed very heavily used asynchronous discussion, e-mail and synchronous chat. We observed instances where misunderstandings regarding the mode of communication led to tension and frustrations among group members. In one case, the group members began a project with different expectations. Based on previous group experiences, one group member thought that all important communication was going to occur on the asynchronous discussion forum, while the other group members assumed that it would occur via e-mail. This led to a group member missing a meeting, because she was regularly checking the discussion forum for information, while the information was being sent to her via e-mail, which she didn't have easy access to at her work.

Example 2: Communicating the Unseen

Communicating the unseen can be a challenge in an online environment. The following learner articulated his challenge in this way:

The fact that in a normal group setting when you are face to face, you can still be engaged in the conversation without saying anything. The group will go on and as people are talking if you're nodding your head, smiling, agreeing, your body posture, all those non-verbals, will say a lot about how involved you are in the process. In the distance format, though, if you didn't say anything for awhile, your group would perceive you as being uninterested or not involved or, if you didn't say anything, they'd just assume that you agreed with what they said and they could continue to go on.

Copyright © 2004, Idea Group Inc. Copying or distributing in print or electronic forms without written permission of Idea Group Inc. is prohibited.

Figure 3:   Example of a Norm for Communicating the Unseen (Silence)

Karl – (side) Since it is hard to figure out if we are all typing or just waiting on each other, how about anyone who is just waiting on a response types something like SH (for still here) if two minutes goes by without an update?

Alison – Or *wait*

45 minutes later:

Ethan – *wait*

Ethan – That sounds rude… Maybe just "…"

Betsy – "…" could mean thinking:-)

Karl – or "…" for thinking and *wait* for waiting on the comments of others. Either way we can assume no rudeness intended.

Another group faced the challenge of communicating the unseen in the decision-making process. Not knowing how to interpret silence by certain individuals after ideas were presented to the group caused the group some anxiety. One group member proposed the following norm to alleviate the group's uncertainty about the unseen:

In a face-to-face meeting, it might work for people to communicate approval by silence. I don't think that works well in a chat. We all need to get in the habit of signifying yes, no or undecided pretty quickly (which should speed up our chats).

Figure 3 shows another example of a norm that a group developed to deal with the uncertainty of knowing how to interpret silence during a synchronous group meeting. In this case the group developed a plan for how they would communicate that the silence meant they were thinking, and not in the process of writing a message.

Example 3: Acknowledging Communication

When using asynchronous communication, such as a discussion board or e-mail, it is often difficult for the group members to know if the other group members have read or received their communications. The computer-mediated groups that were observed often developed a norm of acknowledging that communication had been received or read. The following comment from a student describes an incident that led to the development of a group rule to acknowledge e-mail communication within 24 hours.

Copyright © 2004, Idea Group Inc. Copying or distributing in print or electronic forms without written permission of Idea Group Inc. is prohibited.

Everybody pretty much e-mailed everybody and everybody had to respond, if you didn't respond to the e-mail within 24 hours, we figured you were probably dead and we sent another inquiry out. So, that was one of the things we were pretty strict on. If you had to acknowledge, at least acknowledge that you got e-mail within 24 hours. Mainly because Ethan had some problems with his e-mail; and we thought he was getting stuff and he really wasn't for two or three days. So, we started saying you had to respond, you had to at least reply and say, "I got it," within 24 hours, so we knew that you'd actually seen it.

Another example occurred with a group that was using an asynchronous discussion board to post drafts of a document. The group members were unable to tell from looking at the postings if another group member had accessed or read the latest draft of the work. So the group developed a strategy of posting a brief message within the asynchronous discussion form, indicating that they had been able to access the draft. The norm of acknowledging communication helped to reduce anxiety among group members and facilitate more efficient group interaction.

CONCLUSION

In this chapter, we have examined computer-mediated learning groups, distinguishing them from workgroups, from face-to-face groups and from other forms of collaboration. The benefits of implementing learning groups in a distance environment have been discussed; we are confident that the ample evidence of learning gains found in the literature on collaborative learning will hold true for computer-mediated learning groups. Three important challenges regarding the successful implementation of computer-mediated learning groups were addressed: (1) group creation (including group size and heterogeneity), including the question of self-selection versus groups built by the instructor; (2) the structure of learning activities in order to create an appropriate level of member interdependence, while simultaneously supporting accountability; and (3) facilitating group interactions by helping students develop cooperative work skills and encouraging them to negotiate appropriate group norms.

There is a need for much additional research to increase our understanding of how groupwork might be used more effectively in computer-mediated learning environments. While many of the research questions and issues may be similar to those proposed for virtual work teams (Furst, Blackburn, & Rosen, 1999), this chapter outlines clear differences between work teams and learning teams that would suggest a need for focused research related to effective computer-mediated learning teams.

Copyright © 2004, Idea Group Inc. Copying or distributing in print or electronic forms without written permission of Idea Group Inc. is prohibited.

REFERENCES

Armstrong, D. L., & Cole, P. (1995). Managing distances and differences in geographically distributed work groups. In S. Jackson & M. Ruderman (Eds.), *Diversity in Work Teams: Research Paradigms for a Changing Workplace* (pp. 187-215). Washington, DC: American Psychological Association.

Black, P. (1995). Successful electronic distance collaboration: The importance of social negotiation. *Canadian Journal of Educational Communication, 24*(2), 133-148.

Bonk, C. J., & King, K. S. (1998). *Electronic Collaborators: Learner-Centered Technologies for Literacy, Apprenticeship, and Discourse.* Mahwah, NJ: Erlbaum.

Bordia, P. (1997). Face-to-face versus computer-mediated-communication: A synthesis of the experimental literature. *The Journal of Business Communication, 34*(1), 99-120.

Borman, E. G. (1975). *Discussion and Group Methods: Theory and Practices* (2nd ed.). New York: Harper and Row.

Brown, J. S., Collins, A., & Duguid, S. (1989). Situated cognition and the culture of learning. *Educational Researcher, 18*(1), 32-42.

Chin, G. J., & Carroll, J. M. (2000). Articulating collaboration in a learning community. *Behaviour and Information Technology, 19*(4), 233-246.

Cohen, E. G. (1994). *Designing Groupwork: Strategies for the Heterogeneous Classroom* (2nd ed.). Teachers College, NY: Teachers College Press.

Cunningham, D. J. (1992). Beyond educational psychology: Steps toward an educational semiotic. *Educational Psychology Review, 4*(2), 165-194.

Curtis, D. D., & Lawson, M. J. (2001). Exploring collaborative online learning. *Journal of Asynchronous Learning Networks, 5*(1) 21-34.

Driscoll, M. P. (1994). *Psychology of Learning for Instruction.* Needham Heights, MA: Allyn & Bacon.

Forsyth, D. R. (1999). *Group Dynamics* (3rd ed.). Belmont, CA: Wadsworth Publishing.

Furst, S., Blackburn, R., & Rosen, B. (1999). Virtual team effectiveness: A proposed research agenda. *Information Systems Journal, 9*, 249-269.

Graham, C. R. (2002a). Factors for effective learning groups in face-to-face and virtual environments. *Quarterly Review of Distance Education, 3*(3), 307-319.

Graham, C. R. (2002b). *Understanding and facilitating computer-mediated teamwork: A study of how norms develop in online learning teams.* Unpublished doctoral dissertation, Indiana University, Bloomington, USA.

Copyright © 2004, Idea Group Inc. Copying or distributing in print or electronic forms without written permission of Idea Group Inc. is prohibited.

Harasim, L. (1990). Online education: An environment for collaboration and intellectual amplification. In L. Harasim (Ed.), *Online Education: Perspectives on a New Environment* (pp. 39-64). New York: Praeger Publishers.

Hathorn, L. G., & Ingram, A. L. (2002). Cooperation and collaboration using computer-mediated communication. *Journal of Educational Computing Research, 26*(3), 325-347.

Hiltz, S. R. (1994). *The Virtual Classroom.* Norwood, NJ: Ablex Publishing.

Hiltz, S. R. (1998). *Collaborative learning in asynchronous learning networks: Building learning communities* (ERIC Document Reproduction Service No.ED427705).

Hiltz, S. R., & Benbunan-Fich, R. (1997, April). *Supporting collaborative learning in asynchronous learning networks.* Paper presented at the UNESCO/Open University Symposium on Virtual Learning Environments and the Role of the Teacher, Milton Keynes, UK.

Hooper, S., & Hannafin, M. (1991). The effects of group composition on achievement, interaction, and learning efficiency during computer-based cooperative instruction. *Educational Technology Research & Development, 39*(3), 27-40.

Johnson, D. W., & Johnson, F. P. (1987). *Joining Together: Group Theory and Group Skills* (3rd ed.). Englewood Cliffs, NJ: Prentice-Hall.

Johnson, D. W., & Johnson, F. P. (1997). *Joining Together: Group Theory and Group Skills* (6th ed.). Needham Heights, MA: Allyn and Bacon.

Johnson, D. W., & Johnson, R. T. (1992). Implementing cooperative learning. *Contemporary Education, 63*(3), 173-180.

Johnson, D. W., & Johnson, R. T. (1996). Cooperation and the use of technology. In D. H. Jonassen (Ed.), *Handbook of Research for Educational Communications and Technology*, pp. 1017-1044. New York: Macmillan Library Reference.

Johnson, D. W., & Johnson, R. T. (1999). *Learning Together and Alone: Cooperative, Competitive, and Individualistic Learning* (5th ed.). Boston, MA: Allyn and Bacon.

Johnson, D. W., Johnson, R. T., & Holubec, E. J. (1994). *Cooperative Learning in the Classroom.* Alexandria, VA: Association for Supervision and Curriculum Development.

Kitchen, D., & McDougall, D. (1999). Collaborative learning on the internet. *Journal of Educational Technology Systems, 27*(3), 245-258.

Koschmann, T. D. (ed.). (1996). *CSCL: Theory and Practice of an Emerging Paradigm.* Mahwah, NJ: Lawrence Erlbaum Associates.

Koschmann, T. D., Hall, R., & Naomi, M. (eds.). (2002). *CSCL: Carrying Forward the Conversation.* Mahwah, NJ: Lawrence Erlbaum Associates.

Copyright © 2004, Idea Group Inc. Copying or distributing in print or electronic forms without written permission of Idea Group Inc. is prohibited.

Latane, B., Williams, K., & Harkins, S. (1979). Many hands make light the work: Causes and consequences of social loafing. *Journal of Personality and Social Psychology, 37*, 822-832.

Lewis, L., Snow, K., Farris, E., Levin, D., & B., G. (1999). *Distance education at postsecondary education institutions: 1997-1998* (NCES Report No. 2000-013). Washington, DC: National Center for Educational Statistics, U.S. Department of Education.

Lipnack, J., & Stamps, J. (2000). *Virtual Teams: People Working Across Boundaries with Technology* (2nd ed.). New York: John Wiley & Sons.

McGrath, J. E. (1984). *Groups: Interaction and Performance.* Englewoods Cliffs, NJ: Prentice Hall.

Misanchuk, M. (2001). *Evaluation Report for P540 Offered at a Distance – Summer 2001.* Bloomington, IN: Indiana University.

Misanchuk, M., & Anderson, T. (2000, October). *Strategies for creating and supporting a community of learners.* Paper presented at the Association for Educational Communications and Technology, Denver, Colorado, USA.

Online Evaluation Resource Library (OERL) (1997). *Outside evaluation report of Drexel University's enhanced bioscience education program 1996-1997 (EBE).* Retrieved on July 16, 2003 from the World Wide Web: http://oerl.sri.com/reports/od/report4/.

Panitz, T. (1999a). *Collaborative versus cooperative learning: A comparison of the two concepts which will help us understand the underlying nature of interactive learning.* ERIC Document Reproduction Service No.ED448443.

Panitz, T. (1999b). *The case for student centered instruction via collaborative learning paradigms.* ERIC Document Reproduction Service No.ED448444.

Perrone, K. M., & Sedlacek, W. E. (2000). A comparison of group cohesiveness and client satisfaction in homogeneous and heterogeneous groups. *Journal for Specialists in Group Work, 25*(3), 243-251.

Roschelle, J., & Teasley, S. (1995). The construction of shared knowledge in collaborative problem-solving. In C. E. O'Malley (Ed.), *Computer Supported Collaborative Learning* (pp. 69-97). Heidelberg, Germany: Springer-Verlag.

Thibaut, J. W., & Coules, J. (1952). The role of communication in the reduction of interpersonal hostility. *Journal of Abnormal and Social Psychology, 63*, 53-63.

Thompson, C., Koon, E., Woodwell, W. H. J., & Beauvais, J. (December, 2002). *Training for the next economy: An ASTD state of the industry report on trends in employer-provided training in the United States.* American Society for Training and Development. Retrieved March 19, 2003, from the web site: http://www.astd.org/virtual_community/research/pdf/SOIR2002_Training_summary.pdf.

Copyright © 2004, Idea Group Inc. Copying or distributing in print or electronic forms without written permission of Idea Group Inc. is prohibited.

Townsend, A. M., DeMarie, S. M., & Hendrickson, A. R. (1998). Virtual teams: Technology and the workplace of the future. *Academy of Management Executive, 12*, 17-29.

Vygotsky, L. S. (1978). *Mind in Society*. Cambridge, MA: Harvard University Press.

Wagner, J. A. (1995). Study of individualism-collectivism: Effects on cooperation in groups. *Academy of Management Journal, 38*, 152-172.

Walther, J. B. (1996). Computer-mediated communication: Impersonal, interpersonal, and hyperpersonal interaction. *Communication Research, 23*(1), 3-43.

Yaverbaum, G. J., & Ocker, R. J. (1998). *Problem-solving in the virtual classroom: A study of student perceptions related to collaborative learning techniques.* Paper presented at the WebNet 1998 World Conference of the WWW, Internet and Intranet, Orlando, Florida, USA.

Copyright © 2004, Idea Group Inc. Copying or distributing in print or electronic forms without written permission of Idea Group Inc. is prohibited.

Chapter IX

Collaborative or Cooperative Learning?

Joanne M. McInnerney
Central Queensland University, Australia

Tim S. Roberts
Central Queensland University, Australia

ABSTRACT

With many educational institutions now making use of the Internet for the delivery of courses, many educators are showing interest in non-standard methodologies for teaching and learning — methodologies such as the use of online group collaborative or cooperative work. It is clearly beneficial for educators keen to introduce group learning into a tertiary environment to first familiarize themselves with the existing literature. However, much of the literature conflates the two terms, hence implementation methods and research results are hard to assess. This chapter attempts to clearly distinguish the two terms "collaborative" and "cooperative" so that they can be used appropriately and unambiguously, briefly describes the advantages and shortcomings of each, and concludes with some remarks as to the application of such methods in an online environment.

Copyright © 2004, Idea Group Inc. Copying or distributing in print or electronic forms without written permission of Idea Group Inc. is prohibited.

INTRODUCTION

The increasingly rapid movement of undergraduate and postgraduate courses to online Web-based forms of delivery would seem to provide the ideal circumstances for non-traditional methods of teaching and learning to be re-examined.

Online collaborative or cooperative learning is not widely practiced in undergraduate tertiary education, despite many widely recognized advantages (see, for example, Panitz, 2000). An examination of the literature in this area suggests that researchers and practitioners writing about online collaborative learning are often writing about online cooperative learning, and vice versa. This conflation of terms has resulted in implementation methods and research results being hard to assess. It, therefore, seems important to attempt to ascertain the important similarities and differences between the two, so that theoretical and empirical research on these group learning methodologies in an online environment may be properly carried out and assessed.

TRADITIONAL LEARNING

Traditional learning (see Figure 1) comes in a variety of forms and, therefore, cannot be easily characterized. However, common to most forms of traditional learning is the idea of the sage on the stage, with information provided by the instructor during lectures and the provision of printed course materials. The modes of learner interaction are, therefore, primarily learner-instructor and learner-content, with almost no learning taking place between the students, at least as part of the formal learning process.

Figure 1: Traditional Classroom Learning

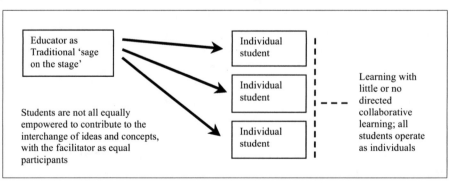

Copyright © 2004, Idea Group Inc. Copying or distributing in print or electronic forms without written permission of Idea Group Inc. is prohibited.

Figure 2: Collaborative Learning

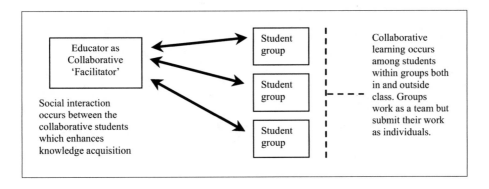

COLLABORATIVE LEARNING

Collaborative is an adjective that implies working in a group of two or more to achieve a common goal, while respecting each individual's contribution to the whole.

Collaborative learning (see Figure 2) is a learning method that uses social interaction as a means of knowledge building (Paz Dennen, 2000).

Bruffee (1999) states that "(educators must) trust students to perform in ways that the teacher has not necessarily determined ahead of time" (p.295) and further contends that "collaborative learning therefore implies that (educators) must rethink what they have to do to get ready to teach and what they are doing when they are actually teaching" (p.72).

COOPERATIVE LEARNING

The term cooperative is often used interchangeably with collaborative, but they have different meanings. Cooperative is an adjective meaning to work or act together as one to achieve a common goal, while tending to de-emphasize the input of particular individuals.

Millis (1996) states that cooperative learning (see Figure 3) is a "generic term used to describe a situation where students work together in small groups to help themselves and others to learn"; while Johnson and Johnson (2001) state that it "is the instructional use of small groups so that students work together to maximize their own and each other's learning."

Copyright © 2004, Idea Group Inc. Copying or distributing in print or electronic forms without written permission of Idea Group Inc. is prohibited.

Figure 3: Cooperative learning

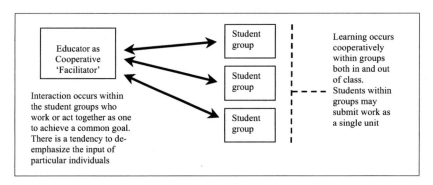

COLLABORATIVE OR COOPERATIVE?

Those seeking to make use of the literature will be aware of the confusion that can arise between the terms cooperative and collaborative. Often the title of a paper may use the word cooperative, while the body of the paper discusses collaborative learning, or vice versa.

When trying to distinguish between the two terms, it is instructive to examine the viewpoints of some distinguished researchers and practitioners in the field. Ted Panitz, a long-time advocate for all forms of collaborative and cooperative learning, clearly distinguishes between the terms collaborative and cooperative in this manner:

"Collaboration is a philosophy of interaction and personal lifestyle where individuals are responsible for their actions, including learning and respect the abilities and contributions of their peers... In the collaborative model groups assume almost total responsibility...[whereas] cooperation is a structure of interaction designed to facilitate the accomplishment of a specific end product or goal through people working together in groups...in the cooperative model the teacher maintains complete control" (Panitz, 1996).

Dillenbourg, Baker, Blaye and O'Malley (1996) distinguish collaborative learning from cooperative learning by saying that "collaboration involves the mutual engagement of participants in a co-ordinated effort to solve the problem" (p.190). While cooperative learning "is accomplished by the division of labour among the participants" (pg.190), where each student is responsible for a part of the information required to solve the problem (Dillenbourg et al., 1996). More recently he has suggested that "in collaboration, partners do the work 'together,'" whereas "in cooperation, partners split the work, solve sub-tasks individually and then assemble the partial results into the final output" (Dillenbourg, 1999, p.11).

Copyright © 2004, Idea Group Inc. Copying or distributing in print or electronic forms without written permission of Idea Group Inc. is prohibited.

Lally and McConnell (2002, p.71), from the University of Sheffield, say that collaborative learning occurs where "course participants work in small learning sets to define a problem....which is amenable to collaborative group work," whereas cooperative learning occurs where:

"individuals within a learning set define an agenda for carrying out a course assignment...this assignment is designed around a real problem or issue...which is amenable to being carried out by action research...this form of learning is based on principles of self-managed learning."

Other researchers, such as Johnson and Johnson (2001) and Hiltz (1998), appear to see little benefit in trying to tease out differences in meaning between the two words. However, if case studies are to be reported and empirical results are to be assessed, it would seem to be important that the two terms are not conflated.

The current authors, therefore, contend that the term collaborative should be used for those learning techniques that emphasize student-to-student interaction in the learning process, while the term cooperative should be used where students are required to work in small groups, usually under the guidance of the instructor.

CHARACTERISTICS OF COLLABORATIVE LEARNING

Academics cannot always know exactly how students will perform in a collaborative environment, but if they prepare and perform successfully as mediators and facilitators, both they and their students will benefit from the collaborative experience. Tinzmann, Jones, Fennimore, Bakker, Fine and Pierce (1990), writing from a k-12 perspective, suggest that there are four typical characteristics of collaboration.

- Shared knowledge between teachers and students: Shared knowledge is in many ways a characteristic of the traditional classroom, where the teacher is the information giver, but it also incorporates some student input, where the students share experiences or knowledge.
- Shared authority between teachers and students: Here the teacher shares the setting of goals within a topic with the students, thereby allowing the students to approach the completion of an assignment in a manner of their choosing.
- Teachers as mediators: In this area the teachers encourage the students to learn how to learn — this being one of the most important aspects of collaborative learning.

Copyright © 2004, Idea Group Inc. Copying or distributing in print or electronic forms without written permission of Idea Group Inc. is prohibited.

- Heterogeneous groupings of students: This characteristic teaches all students to respect and appreciate the contributions made by all members of the class, no matter the content.

These four characteristics appear to apply equally as well as in the university setting, where the traditional classroom model of the teacher giving information to the student, who will then go away and perhaps process and understand it, still applies (the sage on the stage syndrome). Bruffee (1999) has called this the foundational concept of teaching.

In many lecture rooms, the layout of the furniture is reminiscent of school; the teachers are at the front of the room and the students sit at desks or tables facing them. Clearly, this is inappropriate for a collaborative learning environment; everyone should be equally empowered to contribute to the interchange of ideas and concepts, with the instructor as facilitator or mediator and students as equal participants. Tinzmann et al. (1990) point out that a simple rearrangement of furniture allows students to take roles that are more prominent in the classroom as active participants.

A decrease in the size of tutorials and workshops to accommodate collaborative learning is likely to have an economic impact on the tertiary institution. As the size of classes decreases, the number of classes required increases. This means more staff, and greater expense (Hiltz, 1998). However, successful collaborative learning techniques will often enable students to learn at a faster rate and to gain more confidence in their ability to grasp concepts (Bruffee, 1999; Hiltz, 1998). The students teach each other to learn and understand with the active participation of the academic.

Students approximate what they will subsequently encounter in "the real world." Such a hard-line approach may also lead many to discover that they can often arrive at solutions to problems without the help of an instructor. This is what happens when students begin the process of learning to learn, rather than simply listening (Bruffee, 1999; Felder, 1995; Tinzmann et al., 1990). The imparting of knowledge is transferred from the "sage on the stage," or one-way transfer, to the "guide on the side" scenario, where the academic is the facilitator in the students' "construction of their own knowledge" (Hiltz, 1998).

Collaborative learning can only succeed when students share their doubts, comments and questions with other students who share the same or common educational goals (Olguin, Delgardo, & Ricarte, 2000). Dillenbourg and Schneider (1995) state that "when two people collaborate, they often have to justify their action to each other," and this will often lead to a great understanding of the information being shared.

Although Panitz (1997) is primarily writing about schoolteachers, many of his comments regarding the reasons for the widespread reluctance to explore new learning paradigms apply equally well to the university sphere.

Copyright © 2004, Idea Group Inc. Copying or distributing in print or electronic forms without written permission of Idea Group Inc. is prohibited.

- Teachers' egos: This comment is perhaps best described by quoting Panitz (1997), "Many teachers are wrapped up in their own self importance and enjoy being the center of attention. Lecturers do not trust students to learn. The egotistical side of teaching must be overcome in order for teachers to involve their students actively in the learning process." This egotism is particularly difficult to sustain in the online arena.

- Fear of loss of control in the classroom: Although many academics would maintain that by the time their students reach them they are adults, they still have a tendency to respond as if those students were still at "school," and the prospect of giving away any control in their classrooms is pedagogically abhorrent.

- Large class sizes and inappropriate classroom setup: Collaborative learning is best carried out in smaller settings, where students have greater access to the academic. All of the problems of class size and layout become irrelevant in the online collaborative "classroom," but a tighter control is needed in discussion groups.

- Lack of self-confidence by teachers: Academics are generally given no training in how to be an academic besides what they may "pick up" from their lecturers while students themselves. This is particularly true of relatively young academics, who may be faced with a class composed of students who are not much younger than themselves.

- Students' resistance to collaborative learning techniques: With this comment, Panitz (1997) agrees with Felder (1995) that students do not always take kindly to collaborative learning. It then becomes the academic's duty to change the students' attitudes.

The difficult aspect for some students, whether school leavers or mature age, is that collaboration may often have been encouraged in their school or workplace, but it is not always encouraged at the tertiary level (Brodsky, 1998). In fact, at the tertiary level, collaboration between students is often seen as an open invitation for cheating.

Despite this, students are occasionally actively encouraged to be collaborative in their learning processes. This will lead them to discussion, reflection and, one hopes, an understanding of the material being taught (Brown & Thompson, 1997). The conundrum is that in practice students are often warned against working in groups because of the fear of plagiarism, so the concept of collaboration is often very difficult to pursue. Again, a dichotomy arises between what is asked of the student and what is practiced. This dichotomy occurs because educational institutions often do not recognize collaboration as a pedagogically valid learning strategy, but rather as a means for the promotion of plagiarism (Bruffee, 1999).

Copyright © 2004, Idea Group Inc. Copying or distributing in print or electronic forms without written permission of Idea Group Inc. is prohibited.

The above comments are indicative of the fact that moving from traditional to collaborative learning methods is fraught with difficulties. While many of these difficulties are physical or logistical, perhaps the majority and certainly those that are hardest to overcome are those that appear in the minds of the educators.

CHARACTERISTICS OF COOPERATIVE LEARNING

Millis (1996) outlines five characteristics typical of cooperative learning:

- Students work together in small groups containing two to five members;
- Students work together on common tasks or learning activities that are best handled through groupwork;
- Students use cooperative, pro-social behavior to accomplish their common tasks or learning activities;
- Students are positively interdependent and activities are structured so that students need each other to accomplish their common tasks or learning activities; and
- Students are individually accountable or responsible for their work or learning.

Such characteristics would seem to be common across most cooperative learning environments. Slight variations might occur such as when slightly larger groups are allowed.

Ngeow (2000) provides five clear benefits of cooperative learning:

- Positive interdependence: Reliance upon one another to achieve the team goal — all for one and one for all — so if one member fails to participate in the team then all suffer.
- Face-to-face promotive interaction: Some work within the group is done individually, but the group does most work interactively.
- Individual and group accountability: The group as a whole is accountable for achieving the group's goal and the individual within the group is accountable for contributing to the group goal.
- Interpersonal and small group skills: Teaching students the skills to engage in taskwork and teamwork, simultaneously.
- Group processing: The group assesses its goals and how well it is progressing.

Johnson and Johnson (2001) point out that cooperative learning is preferably done face to face. Like Millis (1996), they point out the benefits of this process, but primarily from a k-12 perspective.

Copyright © 2004, Idea Group Inc. Copying or distributing in print or electronic forms without written permission of Idea Group Inc. is prohibited.

Felder and Brent (1994) maintain that students involved in the cooperative learning process exhibit a higher learning rate, excel academically and achieve more in the post graduate workplace. Panitz (1996), agreeing with Felder and Brent (1994), Millis (1996) and Johnson and Johnson (2001), maintains that the process of cooperative learning enhances a student's self-esteem and reduces classroom anxiety. Felder and Brent (1994) also point out an added benefit in the decreased number of assessment items that will need to be marked by the academic involved in the cooperative exercise.

Do students need to work together for the betterment of the group to be able to learn properly? While desirable, we contend that this is not necessary in every case. That is, individuals may still learn even if the group dynamics are not ideal.

However, one clear benefit of cooperative learning can be the high-quality learning atmosphere created when students feel included within a group. This feeling of inclusion is often missing for students learning in a more conventional way, particularly if they return to tertiary study from the workforce or are studying alone at a distance.

ONLINE COLLABORATIVE AND COOPERATIVE LEARNING

While there is already a vast literature about the theory and practice of online learning, there is less information about online collaborative and cooperative learning. Further, most of the current literature on collaborative and cooperative learning is written from a face-to-face, k-12 perspective.

In online collaborative learning, students learn primarily by communicating among themselves via the Internet. In online cooperative learning, students are allocated to, and learn in, small groups and communicate within those groups via the Internet.

The relative novelty of online education has tempted many educators to rush in without sufficient consideration of the many long-term consequences of the change from traditional modes of delivery to those online. Proper planning, expertise and resources are all required if a transformation from face-to-face to online delivery is to be successful.

Felder (1995) advises that the educator who implements online collaboration will often encounter strong opposition from the students taking such a course for the first time. This opposition is because the majority of the students are used to having their teachers tell them *everything they need to know*. Felder and Brent (2001) emphasize that the academic and, therefore, the tertiary institution is not there to make students happy, but rather to prepare them to solve problems in a real-world environment. Collaborative and cooperative learning do this by showing students the benefits of groupwork and initiating them into the real-world dynamics of being a team player.

Copyright © 2004, Idea Group Inc. Copying or distributing in print or electronic forms without written permission of Idea Group Inc. is prohibited.

Olguin et al. (2000) emphasize that for online collaborative learning to succeed there needs to be two factors implemented: group definition and the establishment of communication sessions (either synchronous or asynchronous). The task of assigning students to groups is also of paramount importance when the collaborative process goes online. The same researchers suggest that it becomes immeasurably easier if the groups are composed of students with uniform interests.

Hiltz (1998) makes the valid point that "one of the potential negative effects of online courses is a loss of social relationships," and goes further to state boldly that "collaborative learning strategies are necessary in order for Web-based courses to be effective."

Although there may be resistance to online collaborative learning, the concepts of collaboration can make the transition to the online environment more acceptable. Curry (2000) reaffirms Hiltz (1998) and says that "a thoughtful instructor, capable of balancing guidance with freedom is one critical factor" in the successful operation of an online collaborative course.

It is clear that there are many obstacles that must be overcome. Perhaps demand from external students will lead the way. McMurray and Dunlop (1999) point out that the value of online collaborative study is more obvious to the traditional distance education student than the "normal" on campus student:

"...because of the sense of isolation inherent in distance education, interactivity held a greater meaning and importance for the participants in this online study than might be the case for students encountering traditional face to face teaching."

The advantages of online collaborative learning techniques for distance education students are many, but so are the disadvantages. Neither should be underestimated.

SUMMARY

This chapter has attempted to explain some of the differences between the terms collaborative and cooperative as they are applied to learning and to briefly describe the important characteristics of each. The benefits of some form of collaborative education are well documented within the k-12 arena. It is hoped that over the next few years, educators and academics working in higher education will be courageous enough to experiment more widely with such techniques. However, it is also clear that there is still much room for further research, particularly with regard to the most appropriate forms of implementation of collaborative learning in an online environment.

Copyright © 2004, Idea Group Inc. Copying or distributing in print or electronic forms without written permission of Idea Group Inc. is prohibited.

REFERENCES

Brodsky, N. H. (1998). Learning from learners, Internet style. *Educom Review, 33*(2). Retrieved on November 15, 2002.

Brown, A., & Thompson, H. (1997). Course design for the WWW keeping online students onside. Presented to the *Australian Society for Computers in Learning in Tertiary Education (ASCILITE) conference,* December 7-10, 1997. Retrieved on July 23, 2003 from http://www.ascilite.org.au/conferences/perth97/papers/Brown/Brown.html.

Bruffee, K. A. (1999). *Collaborative Learning, Higher Education, Interdependence, and the Authority of Knowledge.* Baltimore, MD: John Hopkins University Press.

Curry, D. B. (2000). *Collaborative, connected, and experiential learning: Reflections of an online learner.* Retrieved on November 15, 2002 from the web site: http://www.mtsu.edu/~itconf/proceed01/2.html.

Dillenbourg, P. (1999). Introduction: What do you mean by "collaborative learning"? In P. Dillenbourg (Ed.), *Collaborative Learning: Cognitive and Computational Approaches*, pp. 1-19. Oxford, UK: Elsevier.

Dillenbourg, P., & Schneider, D. (1995, February). *Collaborative learning and the Internet.* Paper presented at the International Conference on Computer Assisted Instruction (ICCAI), Singapore.

Dillenbourg, P., Baker, M., Blaye, A., & O'Malley, C. (1996). The evolution of research on collaborative learning. In E. Spada & P. Reiman (Eds.), *Learning in Humans & Machines: Towards an Interdisciplinary Learning Science* (pp. 189-211). Oxford, UK: Elsevier.

Felder, R. T. (1995). We never said it would be easy. *Chemical Engineering Education 29*(1), 32-33.

Felder, R. T., & Brent, R. (1994). *Cooperative learning in technical courses, procedures, pitfall, and payoffs.* Retrieved on February 25, 2002 from the web site: http://www2.ncsu.edu/unity/lockers/users/f/felder/public/Papers/Coopreport.html.

Felder, R. T., & Brent, R. (2001). Effective strategies for cooperative learning. *Journal of Cooperation & Collaboration in College Teaching, 10*(2), 69-75.

Hiltz, R. S. (1998). *Collaborative learning in asynchronous learning networks, building learning communities.* Retrieved on February 25, 2002 from the web site: http://eies.njit.edu/~hiltz/collaborative_learning_in_asynch.htm.

Johnson, D., & Johnson, J. (2001). *Cooperative learning.* Retrieved on November 15, 2002 from the web site: http://www.clcrc.com/pages/cl.html.

Lally, V., & McConnell, D. (2002). Designing a virtual professional development centre for higher education staff. In S. Banks, V. Lally, & D. McConnell

Copyright © 2004, Idea Group Inc. Copying or distributing in print or electronic forms without written permission of Idea Group Inc. is prohibited.

(Eds.), *Collaborative E-Learning in Higher Education*, pp. 65-86. Sheffield, England: University of Sheffield.

McMurray, D. W., & Dunlop, M. E. (1999). The collaborative aspects of online learning: A pilot study. Retrieved on July 23, 2003 from http://ultibase.rmit.edu.au/Articles/online/mcmurry1.htm.

Millis, B. (1996, May). *Cooperative learning.* Paper presented at The University of Tennessee at Chattanooga Instructional Excellence Retreat, USA. Retrieved on February 25, 2002 from the web site: http://www.utc.edu/Teaching-Resource-Center/CoopLear.html.

Ngeow, K. Y.-H. (2000). *Enhancing student thinking through collaborative learning.* Retrieved on February 25, 2002 from the web site: http://www.uni-leipzig.de/~theolweb/sander/uebung/praxis.html.

Olguin, C. J. M., Delgardo, A. L. N., & Ricarte, I. L. M. R. (2000). An agent infrastructure to set collaborative environments. *Educational Technology & Society 3*(3), 65-73.

Panitz, T. (1996). *Collaborative versus cooperative learning – A comparison of the two concepts which will help us understand the underlying nature of interactive learning.* Retrieved on June 23, 2003 from the web site: http://home.capecod.net/~tpanitz/tedsarticles/coopdefinition.htm.

Panitz, T. (1997). *Why more teachers do not use collaborative learning techniques.* Retrieved on May 13, 2003 from the web site: http://home.capecod.net/~tpanitz/tedsarticles/whyfewclusers.htm.

Panitz, T. (2000). *The case for student centered instruction via collaborative learning paradigms.* Retrieved on May 11, 2003 from the web site: http://home.capecod.net/~tpanitz/tedsarticles/coopbenefits.htm.

Paz Dennen, V. (2000). Task structuring for online problem based learning: A case study. *Educational Technology & Society 3*(3), 329-336.

Tinzmann, M. B., Jones, B. F., Fennimore, T. F., Bakker, J., Fine, C., & Pierce, J. (1990). *What is the collaborative classroom?* Retrieved on July 24, 2003 from the North Central Regional Educational Laboratory web site: http://www.ncrel.org/sdrs/areas/rpl_esys/collab.htm.

Copyright © 2004, Idea Group Inc. Copying or distributing in print or electronic forms without written permission of Idea Group Inc. is prohibited.

Chapter X

Methods for Analyzing Collaboration in Online Communications

Albert L. Ingram
Kent State University, USA

Lesley G. Hathorn
Kent State University, USA

ABSTRACT

This chapter discusses the problems of defining collaboration in online discussions and measuring the extent to which true collaboration occurs. Drawing on a variety of previous studies, the authors present ways of dealing with both the computer-generated data and the discussions themselves to determine whether a discussion meets three basic criteria for collaboration. These criteria include roughly equal participation, genuine interaction among the participants, and the synthesis of work into a unified whole. The chapter develops coding procedures for content analysis that can be used to analyze discussions and compare different discussions to the extent to which they show that group members collaborated. It ends with a discussion of using these procedures in research on online collaboration to find out, for example, the factors that affect collaboration in small online discussion groups.

Copyright © 2004, Idea Group Inc. Copying or distributing in print or electronic forms without written permission of Idea Group Inc. is prohibited.

INTRODUCTION

Over the past several years, instructors, instructional designers and researchers have increased their reliance on collaborative and cooperative instructional strategies. As online learning becomes more prevalent, we see such strategies being implemented more and more, using both synchronous and asynchronous computer-mediated communications. By now, collaboration and cooperation are firmly established as teaching methods in face-to-face classes (e.g., Johnson, Johnson, & Smith, 1998). These methods are rapidly becoming widespread in online environments as part of both traditional and distance courses (e.g., Weigel, 2002).

Cooperative and collaborative teaching and learning are likely to be most effective if the methods are based on concepts and research that is firmly grounded in how people actually work together, rather than how we wish they would work together. One of the first steps is to try to define exactly what we mean by such terms. In this chapter, we make a distinction between cooperation and collaboration. Cooperation is defined as the style of working, sometimes called "divide-and-conquer," in which students split an assignment into roughly equal pieces to be completed by the individuals, and then stitched together to finish the assignment.

In contrast, we define collaboration as a more complex working together. Students discuss all parts of the assignment, adding and changing things in conjunction with one another as they come to understand more about the topic. At the end, the final product is truly a group product in which it is difficult or impossible to identify individual contributions. There appear to be differences between cooperation and collaboration in both the complexity of the interactions and the effectiveness for instruction and education. In this chapter, we concentrate on this definition of collaboration and measuring the extent to which online groups meet it.

Collaboration is a complicated concept, and it can be difficult to know when it is occurring, how effective it is, how to encourage it, or what is preventing it. Online collaboration can be easier to manage, track and understand because the communications are all written, and a record can be kept of everything that occurs during the online sessions. We define collaboration as consisting of three crucial elements: participation, interaction and synthesis. Participation is important, because collaboration cannot occur within a group unless there is roughly equal participation among its participants. If some participants do the bulk of the work while others barely contribute at all, then the group is not truly collaborating. Interaction requires that group members actively respond to one another. It is possible for group members, whether face-to-face or online, to talk past one another, never really reacting and changing as the discussion progresses. Such a discussion cannot be considered collaborative. Finally, the product that the group creates must represent a synthesis of ideas and input from all members of

Copyright © 2004, Idea Group Inc. Copying or distributing in print or electronic forms without written permission of Idea Group Inc. is prohibited.

the group. Without these three key characteristics, group interaction may be many things, but it cannot be called collaboration.

In order to study collaboration, as it is defined by these three factors, it is necessary to look closely at the actual patterns of communication that take place within groups. As noted, this can be easier to do with text-based online groups than with face-to-face ones, because there can be a permanent record of all interactions and there are fewer variables in a text-based online discussion, which does not include such things as intonations, facial expressions, and body language. Still, it is necessary to examine the transcripts of the discussions carefully to see beyond superficial aspects and to concentrate on underlying patterns of participation, interaction, and synthesis.

In this chapter, we propose ways to code and describe transcripts of online discussions that reveal the amount and patterns of collaboration that actually take place in the conversation. The method includes both a detailed coding of the statements that comprise the discussion and a graphical representation of discussion threads. Our objectives for this chapter include:

- To explain and support the definition of collaboration offered here;
- To describe the coding scheme in enough detail to allow it to be used by other instructors and researchers;
- To demonstrate the use of a graphical description of the flow of discussion;
- To point to some uses for these methods in research and teaching and to describe pitfalls using the methods and our suggestions for avoiding them.

METHODS FOR ANALYZING COLLABORATION IN ONLINE COMMUNICATIONS

The swift rise of computers and networks has introduced new modes of communication for education and training. Computer-mediated communications (CMC) take many forms, but asynchronous threaded discussions, in particular, give learners the time to think about a problem and the opportunity to discuss possible solutions in a group. In these online settings, students can read each other's responses and add to them over time, thereby actively participating in the construction of knowledge. Such discussion groups allow students to discuss ideas and solve problems, thus extending the classroom time.

During the same period collaboration has become an increasingly important instructional strategy for instructors in both education and training. Frequently, however, instructors place students into groups in the expectation that they will collaborate without a clear idea of what collaboration is or how to recognize and encourage it. Clearly, some groups collaborate more successfully than others. The research on collaboration, and especially online collaboration, is just

Copyright © 2004, Idea Group Inc. Copying or distributing in print or electronic forms without written permission of Idea Group Inc. is prohibited.

beginning to examine how such groups operate, as well as what works and what does not.

One problem facing researchers interested in studying online collaboration is the variety of ways to define the concept and analyze its characteristics. To develop a clear line of research that builds over time, we need to define collaboration operationally and measure the characteristics of collaborative groups. This chapter proposes analysis methods that are clear, consistent and capable of forming the basis for an understanding of the inner workings of collaborative groups online. They are based on both the research literature and on our own work.

So far, studies of computer-mediated discussion groups have generally analyzed the usage data available from Web server logs to establish that CMC is an effective means of extending learning beyond the classroom (Mason, 1992). Researchers have gathered such technical information as the number of logons, length of messages and other details that track the use of CMC (Ingram, 1999-2000). There has been relatively little research on the actual content of messages. Although usage statistics are useful for assessing participation in a conversation, they do not tell us about the educational content of the discussion: sharing ideas, constructing knowledge, solving problems and so forth. Research on these topics is sparse, in part, because analyzing and measuring the educational quality of such discussions is a complex procedure (Mason, 1992).

DEFINING COLLABORATION

Some writers (e.g., Dillenbourg, Baker, Blaye, & O'Malley, 1996) distinguish between cooperation and collaboration in learning groups. Cooperation is defined as individuals working in a group with each one solving a portion of the problem by dividing up the work. Collaboration is the interdependence of the individuals as they share ideas and reach a conclusion or produce a product. If a group of students were given a story to write, they could cooperate by assigning each member a portion of the story to write and then stitching the parts together. In contrast, to collaborate the students would discuss each part of the story, contributing ideas and discussing them until they reached consensus, writing the story together.

Cooperative and collaborative groups may also differ from each other in how competitive they are. Individuals in cooperative groups may compete as they strive to outdo each other to produce the best portion of the project. Individuals in collaborative groups cannot compete against one another, because they are accountable for the product as a group. Individuals in a cooperative group may all contribute and share a goal, but collaborative groups share ideas and then develop these into new products.

Copyright © 2004, Idea Group Inc. Copying or distributing in print or electronic forms without written permission of Idea Group Inc. is prohibited.

In deciding whether collaboration has occurred in a group, one must assess the amount and nature of the interaction among participants. Interaction may be defined, in part, by what it is not. It is not a set of independent statements, personal comments or questions and answers (Mason, 1992). Interaction occurs when group members refer explicitly or implicitly to prior messages in a discussion, while staying on topic. This is distinct from participation, which is measured by the total number and length of all the messages sent and received by all members of the group. Thus, all responses constitute participation in the discussion, but only on-task continuous discussion threads count as interaction.

CMC

CMC can be divided into synchronous and asynchronous modes. In synchronous communications all participants are online at the same time, while asynchronous communications occurs without time constraints. Synchronous discussion involves the use of programs, such as chat rooms, instant messengers or audio and video programs, in which all participants exchange messages in real time. Messages appear on the screen almost immediately after they are typed, and many threads can occur simultaneously. Those who have experienced these rapid exchanges of information, ideas, and opinions know that even extraordinary typing skill and quick response times do not guarantee that one can keep up with the constantly changing discussion. Hence, synchronous discussion may be best suited for brainstorming and quickly sharing ideas.

In asynchronous discussions students can participate at any time and from any location, without regard to what other discussants are doing. Asynchronous CMC allows participants to contribute to the discussion more equally because none of the customary limitations imposed by an instructor or class schedule apply. Full and free expression of ideas is possible. Although these communications are text-based, they have little in common with traditional printed information. Experienced users use a style that is characterized by abbreviated writing and emoticons (e.g., smileys). Asynchronous discussions, which can occur over e-mail or threaded Web discussion, allow more time for considered opinions (Kaye, 1992) and are more effective for deeper discussion of ideas (Smith, 1994).

We have applied the methods of analysis discussed here specifically to asynchronous CMC, using a threaded Web discussion board. In this method of communication, messages are arranged under defined topics, enabling students to add depth and complexity to the discussion by adding a new message to a series, or "thread." The chronological order in which contributions are written is less significant than in spoken language or synchronous communications. Messages can be added to a thread at any time. All participants can contribute significantly to the discussion, and the timing of their contributions is less

Copyright © 2004, Idea Group Inc. Copying or distributing in print or electronic forms without written permission of Idea Group Inc. is prohibited.

important. No one is necessarily the leader or expert, and participants must assess the value of each contribution on their own.

Messages usually remain on a threaded Web discussion for the duration of the discussion, so participants can re-read prior messages and add new ideas. This challenges them to think carefully before they write and to substantiate their arguments. The messages are structured hierarchically; if discussants are careful about where they place their replies, then threads are easy to follow. Software also usually allows contributors to insert hyperlinks to extend the two dimensional limitations of conventional text and thus enhance interactivity.

A threaded Web board is probably most useful for a focused discussion in which a concept is being developed or a problem solved. It works well if the group is required to reach a conclusion. It is less effective for generating ideas, for quick information exchanges, and for less goal-oriented discussions. By keeping discussion groups small (three to five participants) and limiting access to the discussion boards of others, students will be required to generate their own ideas, and social loafing is reduced (Olaniran, Savage, & Sorenson, 1996).

Web-based discussion programs enable instructors to use problem-solving strategies in which students solve complex scenarios based on real world situations. When the groups are successful, learning takes place as students acquire new knowledge and the ability to apply it to the project. Communication and collaboration are essential to solving these problems. The use of text-based messages enables reflection and rethinking of prior knowledge as students ask questions and discuss ideas with others in a group. In productive discussions, students reflect on ideas, while they develop their reasoning abilities through discussion, reading and analysis (Pugh, 1993). Thus text-based CMC acts as a cognitive amplifier (Warschauer, 1997). Learning is enhanced through reflection and interaction. Not only do participants read what others write, but also they influence the development of the answers by interacting with the one another.

OPERATIONALIZING COLLABORATION

Various authors have identified three critical attributes of a collaborative group: interdependence (Johnson et al., 1998), synthesis of information (Kaye, 1992) and independence (Laffey, Tupper, Musser, & Wedman, 1998). Here, we use these three factors to operationalize the definition of collaborative discussions in CMC.

The interaction in a group provides some insight into how individuals learn through discussion as they share information and test ideas (Henri, 1992). The key element here is the interdependence of the individuals in the group as they work towards the common goal (Kaye, 1992). This interdependence influences both individual behavior and outcomes of the group. Positive interdependence leads to individuals in the group promoting learning in others, rather than

Copyright © 2004, Idea Group Inc. Copying or distributing in print or electronic forms without written permission of Idea Group Inc. is prohibited.

obstructing (as in a competitive group) or ignoring (as in a group of individuals) the learning of others (Johnson et al., 1998). The individual's goal cannot be achieved unless the group goal is accomplished (Johnson et al., 1998; Kaye, 1992). Each group member is responsible for contributing to both other members' knowledge bases and the group project. This process is a complex one of offering, challenging, and defending information and experience and of concession and compromise. Interaction requires participation by all group members but is more than that. Group members have to respond and react to one another during the course of the discussion; that is, they have to interact.

The second characteristic of collaboration requires that the group generate a product that is distinct from the individual contributions of the group members. Collaboration is more than the exchange of information and ideas. It is the creation of new insights in the individuals of the group during the discussion (Kaye, 1992; Henri, 1992). For collaboration to occur, the group should have a shared goal. The individual resources combine to make the result that is more than the sum of the parts. Thus, it is the synthesis of shared information and ideas that creates a product different from any that the individuals could have produced alone.

Finally, the third requirement of a collaborative group in education is that the group should be independent of the instructor. This is often difficult for students who are accustomed to referring all questions and problems to the teacher, rather than collaborating with each other or seeking alternative sources to find a solution (Laffey et al., 1998). They may try to reproduce the classroom situation in which the teacher is believed to be the person with all the correct answers, instead of developing problem-solving skills with peers (Kaye, 1992). Unless they overcome this tendency, they cannot be a truly collaborative group.

ANALYZING DATA FOR COLLABORATIVE CMC

If collaboration in educational settings consists primarily of these three elements — interdependence, synthesis and independence — then how can we measure the amount of collaboration in a group? It is not possible to create a single decision rule that allows us to categorize groups definitively as collaborative or non-collaborative ones. Instead, there is a continuum for groups from highly collaborative to barely collaborative, and we need ways to measure the relative amounts of interdependence, synthesis, and independence. These measurements will then allow us to compare groups for the amount of collaboration they exhibit. In turn, this will allow us to try out various means of increasing collaboration, for example, and measure the results.

Copyright © 2004, Idea Group Inc. Copying or distributing in print or electronic forms without written permission of Idea Group Inc. is prohibited.

Computer Generated Data

Most World Wide Web servers automatically record logs of their activities, and, in turn, many Web-based discussion board programs automatically track usage statistics for those who sign on (Ingram, 1999-2000). The analysis of these logs is the usual way in which online participation is evaluated (Mason, 1992). Among the relevant data are the dates and times that the participants logged on and off, the order in which the messages are posted, and the threads in which the messages are placed. Individual student participation can be evaluated by determining the number and length of accesses and messages. These data can be used to diagram the threads of the messages, which may reveal the structure of the conversation. This technique is discussed and illustrated below. These data are incomplete, however, because participation does not necessarily indicate collaboration. This step does form the basis for a more detailed content analysis of the written comments.

In addition, analyzing the thread of messages as entered by the students and generated by the logs may be inaccurate and actually misleading. Students do not necessarily place messages and responses in the correct sequence. That is, a message that responds to the ideas in a previous message may be placed in a completely different thread, leaving the readers to make the connections on their own. In discussions we have analyzed, the transcripts showed that the number and length of messages, and the apparent links between messages, bore little resemblance to the actual structure of the interaction and were not necessarily an accurate indication of collaboration. Although the participants were communicating, and some of the communication was interactive, very little actual collaboration took place. Many statements simply repeated or reworded previously expressed ideas or information given in the scenario. Some new information was added, but participants made few attempts to challenge responses or even reply to comments. The software allowed each student to create new discussion threads or to place messages under any specific thread; but the participants used this facility poorly, so the messages were placed seemingly randomly.

Content Analysis of Online Asynchronous Discussions
Rationale

Researchers can easily collect transcripts of messages from a threaded Web discussion and use content analysis to determine the extent of collaboration in the discussion (Mason, 1992; Henri, 1992). Content analysis is an accepted method of studying text documents in communication (Silverman, 1993). It involves identifying categories and counting the number of items in the text that appear in the categories. The specific analysis schemes used for text such as newspaper articles, letters, or written statements may be inappropriate for CMC, even though it is also text-based communication (Henri, 1992). Communication

Copyright © 2004, Idea Group Inc. Copying or distributing in print or electronic forms without written permission of Idea Group Inc. is prohibited.

patterns are different in CMC, lying somewhere between spoken conversation and written discourse, because the discussion follows neither a logical nor predictable pattern (Mason, 1992). CMC does not have the planned structure of most written text; the discussion evolves in a style determined by the interaction of the group. Therefore, new coding schemes specific to online collaborative discussions are needed. By counting types of statements, rather than merely referring to specific examples of the discussion to justify an argument (as in a purely qualitative study), all the data are analyzed as a whole. The result is that a more credible analysis can be made, because there is less reliance on the researchers' subjective impressions (Silverman, 1993). Using categories established a priori enables the researcher to concentrate on specific aspects of CMC (Henri, 1992; Miles & Huberman, 1987). The categories presented here focus on the collaboration process. They were selected from the prior literature and were made uniform and consistent (Silverman, 1993).

Rourke, Anderson, Garrison and Archer (2001) discussed the methodological issues in using content analysis for CMC. A key step is to find or develop a protocol or coding scheme designed to examine the variables of interest. Researchers interested in collaboration must use a scheme specific to that construct. We identify three potential drawbacks of many current coding schemes. The first point may appear self-evident but is often overlooked. That is, a coding scheme may not be designed to measure collaboration but some other construct. For example, Qing (2001/2002), measured interactivity, not collaboration, among young school children. Other research in CMC has analyzed very specific aspects of the discussion, such as problem-solving techniques among engineering students, and the perception and satisfaction of the participants in the process (Jonassen & Kwon, 2001).

The second issue is that the measurement model may be based on questionnaires that measure perceived degree of communication or interactivity (Gallini & Barron, 2001-2002). This method allows for quick and easy data collection; however, it does not measure the discussion directly. It only measures opinions and attitudes to the quality of the discussion and the outcomes. Using less subjective categories avoids the self-presentation biases that occur with coding schemes that rely on self-report measures, as in Jonassen and Kwon (2001).

The third aspect of current models that limits their usefulness is that they may be based on face-to-face (F2F) collaboration rather than on online collaboration. Models that compare F2F and CMC (for example, Bennett & Dunne, 1991; Jonassen & Kwon, 2001; Hawkes & Romiszowski, 2001) have shortcomings in analyzing collaboration in CMC, because the coding schemes are created for F2F collaboration. Thus online collaboration is measured in terms of the qualities of F2F interaction it possesses or lacks, and not as a distinct process in its own right.

Copyright © 2004, Idea Group Inc. Copying or distributing in print or electronic forms without written permission of Idea Group Inc. is prohibited.

Bennett and Dunne (1991) developed a model to study F2F interaction in groups. The categories they proposed for direct discussion of a topic applied to F2F collaborative learning and were not entirely appropriate for CMC. Models for F2F interaction emphasize the social and nonverbal aspects of communication and its interpretation. For example, F2F conversation is often in fragments with incomplete sentences and with one idea being completed by different people (Wild & Braid, 1997). This rarely, if ever, occurs in asynchronous CMC. Models of interaction that are used to code F2F situations place a heavy emphasis on the coding of social or off-task behavior into a number of categories. As it happens, this is unnecessary in asynchronous CMC because such behavior forms an insignificant percentage of the interactions. CMC may eliminate or change some of the social aspect of interaction and all of the nonverbal communication. The lack of nonverbal communication makes coding such conversations less vulnerable to the vagaries of interpretation. Verbal social communication can be coded separately outside the issue of collaboration (e.g., Polhemus & Swan, 2002).

Henri (1992) proposed a model for studying collaborative learning in a CMC environment, but this model was of limited use to us because she emphasized measuring learning, rather than collaboration. She did identify the importance of the social aspect of CMC but did not clearly distinguish between statements that formed part of the on-task social or management discussion and the off-task social discussion. This model distinguished between explicit and implicit interaction. In this model explicit interaction is in the form of either a direct response or a direct comment, in which the participant referred to a question or comment by mentioning it, and implicit interaction is in the form of either an indirect response or an indirect comment, in which the question or comment was not specifically mentioned. Because threaded discussion software usually allows students to place responses to messages where they think appropriate, such transitional phrases as "in response to message…" are largely meaningless. There is an implied direct response by message placement.

We adapted the definition of independent statements to mean the presentation of information without leading to further discussion. We added categories that identified the difference between a statement that simply agrees with a prior statement and one that adds information so that not all responses are given equal weight. Thus, there is a meaningful distinction made between interaction that is an attempt to take the discussion further and responses that indicate little more than participation. This distinction becomes very important in the explanation of why groups that appear to be discussing topics in a highly interactive manner are actually producing few new ideas.

The following method of coding is appropriate for asynchronous CMC because all the communications between members of the group are in text form. The analysis of text is more objective than the analysis of F2F communication, where facial expressions and other forms of nonverbal communication are open

Copyright © 2004, Idea Group Inc. Copying or distributing in print or electronic forms without written permission of Idea Group Inc. is prohibited.

to interpretation by the other participants and the researcher, all of whom may interpret the same expressions differently. Measuring CMC comments depends less on the researcher's understanding of the context and is, therefore, more straightforward.

Coding Procedure

All discussion on the threaded Web discussion must be transcribed and coded. Messages should be arranged chronologically by date and time and then each message divided into statements. A statement is a complete sentence or a complete idea within a sentence. Complex sentences can contain more than one statement. It is important to divide messages into statements, because, in CMC discussion, one message can reply to one or many messages, as well as discuss various other topics that may or may not be related. The goal of the coding is to identify all of the ideas discussed as well as the true structure of the discussion threads.

Next, statements are coded according to the specific characteristics that determine collaboration. As noted, the three characteristics of collaboration are:

- Interdependence as the pattern of participation and interaction in the group (Johnson et al., 1998);
- Synthesis as the creation of something new as a result of discussion (Kaye, 1992); and
- Independence as autonomous actions of students who do not refer questions and problems to the teacher (Laffey et al., 1998).

Interdependence requires that each member actively contribute to the group discussion. At a superficial level, it requires simple participation by each member. This is measured by counting the number of messages and statements submitted by each discussant. Roughly equal participation at this level is a necessary but not a sufficient condition for interdependence. Once roughly equal participation has been established, however, we must dig deeper to see whether the discussants are genuinely interacting. How much the individuals contributed to solving the problem is indicated by the interaction in the group on the content of the problem. To a lesser extent, interdependence is also indicated by positive and negative comments about the scenario, and by off-task comments that create the social context in which the group interacts.

Synthesis requires that new information be created. There are two ways in which this can be measured. The first is by the interaction pattern of the discussion that occurs when a participant contributes a statement, another student then extends the idea and a subsequent message synthesizes the information. Thus, a synthesizing thread in a discussion requires at least three messages from a minimum of two group members. To evaluate this we have to look closely at the individual threads in a discussion. We also assess synthesis by

Copyright © 2004, Idea Group Inc. Copying or distributing in print or electronic forms without written permission of Idea Group Inc. is prohibited.

Table 1:   Characteristics of Collaboration

Characteristics of Collaboration	*Categories Used to Evaluate Characteristics*
Interdependence	Participation and Interaction
Synthesis	Interaction and Final Project
Independence	Participation and Interaction

examining the relationship between the original comments and the final product. Does the final product meld the contributions of the individual group members; does it consist primarily of the work of one discussant or can we identify individual work within the group product?

Independence is the ability of the group to work without the instructor. It is measured by analyzing the extent of instructor's influence in both participation and interaction. A discussion in which few or no threads occur without instructor input is not independent, and hence not truly collaborative. A summary of the three characteristics of collaboration and the categories used to evaluate these are shown in Table 1.

Tables 2 and 3 show a detailed schematic of the coding categories that we developed for our research. They are adapted from Bennett and Dunne (1991), Henri (1992) and Mason (1992). Each statement is coded three times to measure three characteristics of collaboration: participation, interaction and patterns of discussion. The pattern of statements is analogous to a pyramid. At the base of the pyramid is the first layer in which participation is coded. At the next layer, coding of interactions is more refined, and the top is where the actual patterns of discussion are coded. Table 2 provides a systematic look at the coding. First, the participation was coded and then the interaction. For further coding, we selected the features of the interaction sentences that we were most interested in, namely, on-task direct discussion of the scenario. The top portion of Table 2 shows participation and the middle portion shows interaction. Then, Table 3 shows the patterns of discussion that we coded. We have found these categories to be both exhaustive — giving a place to every type of statement likely to be found in asynchronous discussions — and useful in studying online collaboration.

Participation

Measuring participation is important in the analysis of both interdependence and independence. Participation forms the skeleton that supports interaction. It is measured by counting the number of messages and statements made by individuals and the group to the other participants and the instructor. Both groups and individuals within groups can be compared in their levels of participation.

Copyright © 2004, Idea Group Inc. Copying or distributing in print or electronic forms without written permission of Idea Group Inc. is prohibited.

Table 2:   Categories Reflecting Characteristics of Collaboration

Categories	*Details of Categories*			
Participation	Individual	Number of statements	Number of messages	To instructor
	Group			
Interaction	Off task	Negative and positive comments unrelated to the discussion, e.g., community building (introductions)		
	On task	Social and management of the group	Comments about the discussion that promote or inhibit it. Procedural tasks and technology problems and advice. Thanks for input or compliments.	
		Direct discussion of the scenario	Comments further coded into patterns of discussion (Table 3)	

Without further information, however, measures of participation are not suffi-cient to show collaboration.

Interaction

The analysis of interaction forms the foundation of all the characteristics of collaboration. Statements are classified first into the broad categories of off-task or on-task behavior. Off-task statements may include community building statements that are important in creating an environment that supports collabo-ration, such as introductions, references to status or experience or similar statements. Off-task comments may also be totally unrelated to the assignment, such as discussing the weather. Off-task discussion may be a distraction but may also serve as an icebreaker or means of leading into or closing a discussion.

Table 3:   Patterns of Discussion

Independent Statements	*Independent Statement (Neither an answer nor a commentary and does not lead to further discussion.)*		
Interaction	Length of the thread a-b-c-a		
	To whom		To educator
			To student
	Connections to previous messages	Direct response	Simple agreement, repeating a statement or answering a direct question.
		Direct comment	Adding information or comments to the interaction.
		Indirect comment	New idea or comment added to the interaction but connection to prior interaction is not clear.
	Quality of interaction	Simple agreement	Repeating information, simple agreement or disagreement.
		Adding information	Adding to the statement, disagreeing or adding new information.
		Synthesis of information	Synthesizing the information. Creating a new idea.

Copyright © 2004, Idea Group Inc. Copying or distributing in print or electronic forms without written permission of Idea Group Inc. is prohibited.

On-task statements are divided into the categories of (1) social and group management and (2) direct discussion of the scenario. Group management statements include discussion about the assignment and do not contribute directly to solving the problem. They do, however, set the environment for the discussion. Management may also include allocating tasks and deciding on the procedure for the discussion. Social aspects include community building comments that refer to the assignment, such as positive supportive statements (for example, congratulating each other on a job well done), complaints about the task or negative comments that inhibit the discussion. The management aspect of discussion about the scenario includes allocating tasks and deciding on the procedure for the discussion.

Comments that are classified as direct discussion of the scenario include all those statements that contribute directly to the actual topic of the discussion. In an active and collaborative discussion, one expects that these will form the bulk of the statements coded. These statements may be further coded into patterns of discussion.

Patterns of Discussion

Once the statements have been categorized into functional groups, they are coded to determine the patterns of interaction that occur in the discussion. Stand-alone comments are independent statements. They do not lead to further discussion, and they neither respond to a comment nor generate a response. A large number of independent statements might characterize a cooperative group but not a collaborative group. Collaboration requires more than just the exchange of information that occurs in a series of independent statements. Independent statements may contribute to the task, since they enable others to add information and learn from the group, but they are not true interaction and thus are not part of the collaborative effort.

Interaction requires at least a comment and a response to the comment, thus it is partly determined by the length of the dialogue. The response must refer to a previous statement, either implicitly or explicitly. In order for the interaction to be collaborative, there needs to be a third step to this process, so that there is a comment on the content, a response and a final answer that is a synthesis of all the responses (Kaye, 1992). The pattern of a thread is depicted by the number of responses and who made them. Thus an a-b-c-a thread would describe a thread in which three participants commented and then the first participant added a second comment. Discussion that involves the instructor is coded separately, to help assess independence.

Comments or answers to questions that require little insight are direct responses. Participants may agree with statements without giving reasons; they may repeat another's ideas by rewording their statements or they may answer a direct question. Direct comments occur when participants attempt to take the interaction further. These comments add new information or insights to the

Copyright © 2004, Idea Group Inc. Copying or distributing in print or electronic forms without written permission of Idea Group Inc. is prohibited.

interaction and are based on the prior discussion. Indirect comments are comments that are on topic, but the connection to prior interaction on the subject is not clear.

The final sections of Table 3 show a more subjective coding of the quality of the interactions in the discussion. Simple agreement refers to statements that add little new to the discussion; they just repeat information or opinions already expressed and state agreement (or disagreement). The second category of statements here includes those that add information in some way to preceding statements. Finally, the most complex statements here are those that present a synthesis of previously stated information, possibly with the addition of new information as well. These statements create new ideas and represent a key characteristic of real collaboration.

Discussion Diagrams

Diagramming the discussions can show how messages and statements are related to one another. We diagram each discussion in two ways. The first diagram presents the order of messages, exactly in the pattern the students place their messages on the discussion board. Students are free to add topics to the discussion whenever they want or to continue the discussion under an existing topic. Meaningful threads of messages can start at any point. Long threads show that students place new messages under the previous ones. In our experience, students place new messages with little regard for the content of the discussion. In addition, some messages reply to several previous messages, while others generate many replies.

The second diagram type reflects the discussion's actual content. Some messages may contain information and opinions that are related to more than one topic. These diagrams reflect the various topics expressed in each message. Messages that generate replies are connected to the replies with arrows. Each arrow points to a message that contains statements that reply to the original message. Thus, the connections among messages that are responses to many others or among messages that generate many different responses can be diagrammed. (See Figures 1-5, which are discussed in detail later in this chapter.)

In the first diagram type, threads may appear to be very long, but closer examination shows that this happens when a student submits many short messages (instead of one long one) and places all of the messages one after the other without attending to the different topics. When these messages are diagrammed again, using the second type, these long threads may disappear.

USING THE ANALYSES

The detailed coding shown here can describe a discussion more objectively than a more perfunctory analysis can. It presents the characteristics of the group

Copyright © 2004, Idea Group Inc. Copying or distributing in print or electronic forms without written permission of Idea Group Inc. is prohibited.

Table 4:   Messages and Statements: Most Collaborative Group

Parti-cipants	Number of messages				Number of statements			
	To Ins	To individuals in group		To entire group	Total	To Ins	To individuals in group		To entire group	Total
S4	0	1		15	**16**	0	11		123	**134**
		1	0				11	0		
S5	0	2		5	**7**	0	13		145	**158**
		2	0				13	0		
S6	0	2		5	**7**	2	14		90	**106**
		0	2				0	14		
Total	**0**	**5**		**25**	**30**	**2**	**38**		**358**	**398**
Mean	0	1.67		8	10	0.67	12.33		119.33	132.33
Ins		0		1	1		0		8	8
Total with Ins	0	5		25	31	2	38		366	406

Note. S4 = student 4; S5 = student 5; S6 = student 6 and Ins = instructor.

without being biased by fleeting impressions that single comments may cause. Conclusions can be checked against evidence, creating more objective, rather than intuitive, interpretations. Here we present examples of coding taken from a recent study of online collaboration (Hathorn & Ingram, 2002b). We discuss the detailed coding and analysis of two groups from that study, with a view toward describing how the analysis was done and the data used. We do not discuss the research questions of that study. The groups presented are the most and the least collaborative from that research.

Measures of Interdependence

Participation

Tables 4 and 5 show the analysis of participation in the two groups. In the most collaborative group, students sent 30 messages during the 11 days of the study, an average of 2.73 a day. In contrast, the participants in the least collaborative group sent 33 messages over the 11 days of the study, an average of three messages a day. The importance of breaking down messages into statements is seen by the fact that members of the most collaborative group made 398 separate statements, while members of the least collaborative group made 201. Statements appear to be a more interesting measure of participation, because messages can vary so widely in size and intellectual content.

Levels of participation can be analyzed statistically. As noted, it is our contention that groups can be collaborative if, and only if, the discussants

Copyright © 2004, Idea Group Inc. Copying or distributing in print or electronic forms without written permission of Idea Group Inc. is prohibited.

Table 5:   Messages and Statements: Least Collaborative Group

Partic-ipants	Number of messages				Number of statements			
	To Ins	To individuals in group	To entire group	Total	To Ins	To individuals in group	To entire group	Total
S10	1	0	7	**8**	4	0	45	**49**
S11	7	1	10	**18**	22	9	32	**63**
		1 | 0				9 | 0		
S12	2	1	4	**7**	23	14	52	**89**
		0 | 1				0 | 14		
Total	**10**	**2**	**21**	**33**	49	23	129	201
Mean	3.33	0.67	7	11	16.33	7.67	43	67
Ins		11	1	12		62	8	70
		8 | 2 | 1				31 | 30 | 1		
Total with Ins	10	13	22	45	49	85	137	271

Note. S10 = student 10; S11 = student 11; S12 = student 12 and Ins = instructor.

participate at least roughly equally. Therefore, we ran chi-square analyses of the proportion of statements contributed by each member of the group. Chi-square is a nonparametric test of significance used to compare observed and expected frequencies (Gay, 1996). It is used here to test the uniformity of participation in the groups. The hypotheses tested in these comparisons were

- H_0: The group was collaborative to the extent that each member contributed equally (i.e., the distribution is uniform);
- H_1: The group was not collaborative in that one member contributed significantly more or less than the others (i.e., the distribution is not uniform).

In a three person group, each participant should submit approximately one third of the statements or 33.33%. In order to be confident that the null hypothesis is rejected only for groups that did not exhibit equal participation among participants, the significance level, α, was set at 0.01. The tabulated value of χ^2 for two degrees of freedom and $\alpha \leq 0.01$ is 9.210. In our study, both the most collaborative group ($\chi^2 = 2.79$, p > 0.05) and the least collaborative group ($\chi^2 = 4.67$, p > 0.05) showed roughly equal participation and the null hypothesis was not rejected for them. It was rejected for another group, however ($\chi^2 = 20.56$, p < 0.001).

Interaction

Once the text had been coded into statements, the pattern of the discussion could be mapped using the procedure discussed above. Figures 1-4 are scaled-down versions of the mapped diagrams. Although detail is not discernable, the

Copyright © 2004, Idea Group Inc. Copying or distributing in print or electronic forms without written permission of Idea Group Inc. is prohibited.

Figure 1: Most Collaborative Group: Apparent Discussion

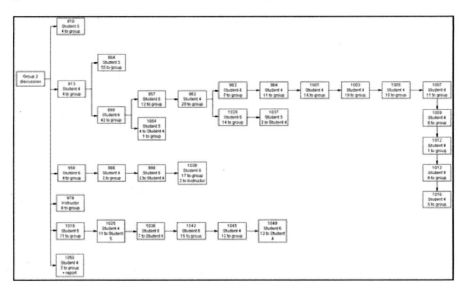

Figure 2: Most Collaborative Group: Mapped Discussion

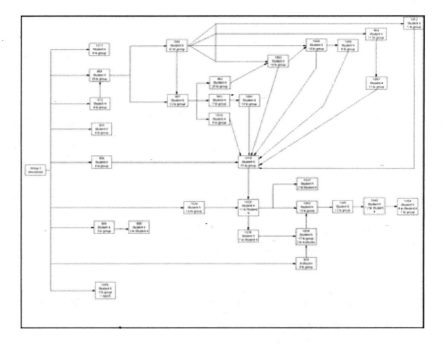

Copyright © 2004, Idea Group Inc. Copying or distributing in print or electronic forms without written permission of Idea Group Inc. is prohibited.

Figure 3: Least Collaborative Group: Apparent Discussion

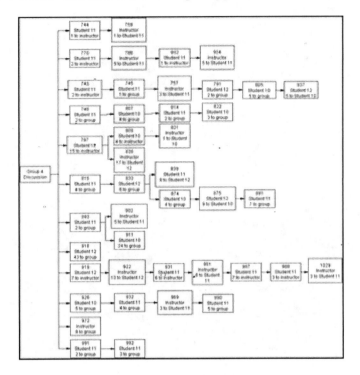

patterns of discussion can be seen. Figure 5 shows a small section of Figure 4 enlarged to full-size to demonstrate the information included in the mapped diagrams. Figure 1 is a diagram of the discussion of the most collaborative group, showing the order with which the participants placed the messages under topics in the threaded discussion. The actual structure of this discussion is very different (Figure 2). The six topics, up to six messages deep, that appear in the surface structure are actually eight topics initiated by the students and one by the instructor. These topics were up to 12 messages deep. One message even encompassed replies to eight other messages.

Figure 3 is a diagram of the messages from the least collaborative group, in the order in which the participants placed the messages in the threaded discussion. This discussion appears poorly organized; apparently the discussion had 12 different topics, up to six messages deep. The mapping of the underlying structure shown in Figure 4 shows that there were in fact 15 different topics in the discussion, up to 12 messages deep; 12 of these topics were initiated by the same person, and the instructor was involved in 12 of the 15 threads.

As Table 4 shows, one student seemed to dominate the group, as she was responsible for more messages than the other two students combined. When we examine the statements, however, the situation changes. This individual contrib-

Copyright © 2004, Idea Group Inc. Copying or distributing in print or electronic forms without written permission of Idea Group Inc. is prohibited.

Figure 4: Least Collaborative Group: Mapped Discussion

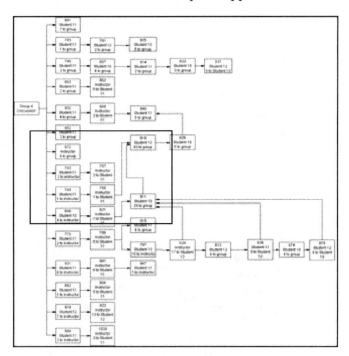

uted only 33.67% (134) of the total of 398 statements made by the students in the group. The other two participants contributed 39.7% (158) and 26.63% (106) statements to the discussion. Ninety percent of the messages from this group were addressed to the whole group. Table 4 also shows the goal-oriented nature of the discussion in which participants responded to one another's messages and involved the instructor minimally.

Table 6 shows the coding of messages and statements for the most collaborative group. Of the 396 statements that did not involve the instructor, more than two-thirds of the statements (68.18%, or 270) made in the group were interaction statements to and from other students in the group. One hundred, twenty-six statements (31.82%) were independent statements that either did not invite discussion or were ignored by the group.

In the most collaborative discussion there were six threads that did not involve the instructor in the discussion on the social aspect and management of the scenario (Table 7). Four of these were simple statement and response interactions expressing agreement, but the other two threads were more complex. The interaction was characterized by prolific contributions by individual participants. Not only did they contribute, but also they organized their messages under topics and followed threads in which all three participants

Copyright © 2004, Idea Group Inc. Copying or distributing in print or electronic forms without written permission of Idea Group Inc. is prohibited.

Figure 5: Enlarged Section of Least Collaborative Group: Mapped Discussion

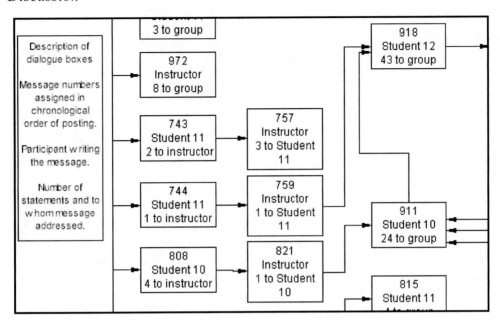

Table 6:   Interaction Statements: Most Collaborative Group

Task	Messages addressed	All statements	Independent statements	Statements in interaction							
				Total	Initial statements	Complexity			Refer to prior messages		
						SA	Add	Syn	DR	IC	DC
Off task:	To/from Instructor	2	2	0							
	To Individuals	7	7	0							
	To Group	10	10	0							
	Total	**19**	**19**	**0**	0	0	0	0	0	0	0
On task: about the scenario	To/from Instructor	8	0	8	6		2				2
	To Individuals	31	0	31	3	12	16	0	17	0	11
	To Group	76	33	43	17	3	23	0	7	10	9
	Total	**115**	**33**	**82**	**26**	**15**	**41**	**0**	**24**	**10**	**22**
Discussion of the topic	To/from Instructor	0	0	0	0	0	0	0	0	0	0
	To Individuals	1	1	0	0	0	0	0	0	0	0
	To Group	271	75	196	29	70	97	0	76	52	39
	Total	**272**	**76**	**196**	**29**	**70**	**97**	**0**	**76**	**52**	**39**
Total	Students Only	**396**	**126**	**270**	49	85	136	0	100	62	59
Total	Students and Instructor	**406**	**128**	**278**	55	85	138	0	100	62	61

Note. SA = simple agreement; Add = adding information; Syn = synthesis; DR = direct response; IC = indirect comment and DC = direct comment.

Copyright © 2004, Idea Group Inc. Copying or distributing in print or electronic forms without written permission of Idea Group Inc. is prohibited.

Table 7:   Discussion Threads: Most Collaborative Group

Task	Messages addressed	Statements in discussion	# of threads		Length of thread
Off task:	Total	0			
On task: about the scenario	To/from Instructor	8	1	1	a-b
	To Students	74	6	4	*a-b*
				1	*a-b-c-b-a*
				1	*a-b-c-b-c-a*
Discussion of the topic	To/from Instructor	0	0		
	To Students	196	7	6	*a-b-c-a*
				1	*a-b-c-a-b*

expressed opinions. The four threads that were short a-b threads indicated a question or a comment and a response. There were seven threads on the scenario itself. Although these threads all involved collaborative interaction in that there were statements, responses, and further responses, they were characterized by individuals ignoring each other's comments completely, or simply repeating them.

Table 8:   Interaction Statements: Least Collaborative Group

Task	Messages addressed	All statements	Independent statements	Statements in interaction							
				Total	Initial statements	Complexity			Refer to prior messages		
						SA	Add	Syn	DR	IC	DC
Off task:	To/from Instructor	4	4	0							
	To Individuals	5	5	0							
	To Group	10	10	0							
	Total	**19**	**19**	**0**	0	0	0	0	0	0	0
On task: about the scenario	To/from Instructor	25	10	15	3	0	12	0	4	0	8
	To Individuals	3	0	3	0	3	0	0	3	0	0
	To Group	34	10	24	8	0	16	0	9	0	7
	Total	**62**	**20**	**42**	**11**	**3**	**28**	**0**	**16**	**0**	**15**
Discussion of the topic	To/from Instructor	90	0	90	33	0	57	0	57	0	0
	To Individuals	15	0	15	1	7	7	0	7	0	7
	To Group	85	32	53	4	27	22	0	29	3	17
	Total	**190**	**32**	**158**	**38**	**34**	**86**	**0**	**93**	**3**	**24**
Total	Students Only	**152**	**57**	**95**	**13**	**37**	**45**	**0**	**48**	**3**	**31**
Total	Students and Instructor	**271**	**71**	**200**	**49**	**37**	**114**	**0**	**109**	**3**	**39**

Note. SA = simple agreement; add = adding information; syn = synthesis; DR = direct response; IC = indirect comment and DC = direct comment.

Copyright © 2004, Idea Group Inc. Copying or distributing in print or electronic forms without written permission of Idea Group Inc. is prohibited.

Table 9:   Discussion Threads: Least Collaborative Group

Task	Messages addressed	Statements in discussion	# of threads		Length of thread
Off task:	Total	0			
On task: about the scenario	To/from Instructor	15	4	2	a-b
				2	a-b-a
	To Students	*27*	*2*	*1*	*a-b-c*
				1	*a-b-a-b-c*
Discussion of the topic	To/from Instructor	90	15	11	a-b
				1	a-b-a
				1	a-b-c
				1	a-b-c-a
				1	a-b-c-a-b-c-a-d-c-d
	To Students	*68*	*3*	*2*	*a-b-c*
				1	*a-b-c-a*

Of the total of 152 statements that did not involve the instructor in the least collaborative discussion, over half were interaction statements (95 statements, or 62.5%) made to other students in the group (Table 8). Fifty-seven statements (37.5%) were independent statements that either did not invite discussion or were ignored by the rest of the group.

The pattern of interaction threads in the least collaborative group shows the importance of the instructor in the discussion (Table 9). Of a total of 24 threads, only 5 threads did not involve the instructor. (Two of these threads were on the management of the discussion, and three were on the actual scenario.

Synthesis of Information

Interaction

In the most collaborative discussion, out of 406 statements made by students and instructor, 5.68% (19) were off task, 28.33% (115) were on the social aspect and management of the discussion (mainly discussion of procedures) and 66.7% (272) were direct discussion of the scenario (Table 6). In the least collaborative group, there was a total of 271 statements. Nineteen (7.01%) were off task, 62 (22.88%) were on the social aspect and management of the discussion (mainly discussion of procedures) and 190 (70.11%) directly discussed the scenario (Table 8).

Of the seven threads on the scenario in the most collaborative group, six were of the form a-b-c-a and the seventh was longer (Table 7). There were 270 interaction statements made to others, excluding the instructor within the group (Table 6). One hundred thirty-six of these statements provided new information or comments, but 62 of them were not directly connected to the same topic. Eighty-five interaction statements just repeated or agreed with prior statements.

Copyright © 2004, Idea Group Inc. Copying or distributing in print or electronic forms without written permission of Idea Group Inc. is prohibited.

Only 59 statements (21.85% of interaction statements) were direct comments that added to the discussion. Most of the statements (100) were direct responses to a question or repeating of statements. In the least collaborative group, there were only five threads that did not involve the instructor and of these only two that showed any attempt to develop an idea beyond an a-b-c pattern in which each participant contributes a statement (Table 9).

Independence

One of the characteristics of the most collaborative group was the very low incidence of interaction with the instructor (Table 4). The group worked almost entirely independently. The only interaction with the instructor was a short reply to an instruction on chat procedures. There was no instructor involvement in the actual discussion of the scenario.

In contrast, the instructor was a significant contributor to the total number of messages in the least collaborative group, contributing the second most messages in the group (Table 5). Although instructor messages were short (5.83 statements per message), the instructor nevertheless contributed the second highest number of statements in that group. Of the total number of statements made in the group, 43.91% (119) were to or from the instructor. Of 24 threads in the discussion, 19 involved the instructor (Table 9).

FUTURE TRENDS

Online collaboration is likely to increase in educational settings in the future, as the trends toward group learning and online course activities and materials continue to merge. Some writers (e.g., Weigel, 2002) argue that combining more traditional courses with online collaborations represents a significant step forward in college teaching. Certainly it appears that this can be a very productive marriage of instructional strategy with technology.

Other questions remain. For example, how do we make online collaboration work, given the knowledge we have now? A number of writers have addressed that question, including some represented in this volume. Hathorn and Ingram (2002a) suggest that the effectiveness of online collaborations depends on such factors as the task, the technology available to the group, the group composition and size, the skills of the moderator and grading requirements, including individual accountability. To increase effective collaboration, they suggest using such strategies as giving the group a meaningful goal, instructing them to collaborate, providing a process for performing the task (as in a WebQuest), holding the group and individuals accountable for the result, fostering the interdependence that is so important in collaboration, and giving individuals and groups plenty of practice in collaboration.

Copyright © 2004, Idea Group Inc. Copying or distributing in print or electronic forms without written permission of Idea Group Inc. is prohibited.

At the same time there are many questions that remain to be researched, including which of these strategies are truly effective. The current chapter provides a route toward answering those questions. Although further work may refine the coding scheme presented here, using a common approach to analyzing online discussions for their collaborative features across several studies provides an opportunity to have research that actually builds toward solid conclusions. Issues that can be addressed include which factors can be manipulated to produce greater collaboration, and whether greater online collaboration actually results in better problem solving or increased learning.

CONCLUSION

When the results from this study (Hathorn & Ingram, 2002b) were compiled, there were clear differences among the various groups in the degree of collaboration they exhibited. The "most collaborative" group showed roughly equal participation, as well as the highest degree of interdependence, synthesis and independence. In contrast, the "least collaborative" group was lowest on most of these measures, even though superficially it showed roughly equal participation among group members. (Another group did not even show this.) As we continue to use these analysis methods, one question that arises concerns the correlations among interdependence, synthesis and independence. Conceptually, they are different, but it will be interesting to see whether actual groups tend to either show all of them or none of them.

Our goal in this chapter has been to describe and discuss a method for coding and analyzing online discussions. In particular, we have concentrated on asynchronous, text-based discussions in which one the key questions includes whether the discussion was collaborative and to what extent. Using this coding scheme allowed us to examine the effects on collaboration of such variables as whether the groups were instructed to collaborate and whether they interacted outside of the online discussion board (Hathorn & Ingram, 2002a). A variety of other questions come to mind:

- Do collaborative groups lead to more learning, as many educators think?
- What are the optimal group sizes for producing collaboration?
- How can we structure tasks and groups for optimal collaboration?

By using uniform analyses of group interactions such as those shown here, we can begin to answer these questions. Other analysis methods are possible, of course, but this one has proven to be useful in this situation. Wider use of this method could lead to a growing understanding of the processes of online collaboration.

In this chapter, the authors have concentrated on collaboration in asynchronous threaded discussions. There is no reason why the methods outlined here

Copyright © 2004, Idea Group Inc. Copying or distributing in print or electronic forms without written permission of Idea Group Inc. is prohibited.

could not be applied to other sorts of online discussions, especially synchronous ones. Before we decide that, however, we need to test them on this type of discussion. This suggests another line of future research.

REFERENCES

Bennett, N., & Dunne, E. (1991). The nature and quality of talk in co-operative classroom groups. *Learning and Instruction, 1*(1), 103-118

Dillenbourg, P., Baker, M., Blaye, A., & O'Malley, C. (1996). The evolution of research on collaborative learning. In P. Reinman & H. Spada (Eds.), *Learning in Humans and Machines: Towards an Interdisciplinary Learning Science* (pp. 189-211). New York: Pergamon.

Gallini, J., & Barron, D. (2001/2002). Participants' perceptions of Web-infused environments: A survey of teaching beliefs, learning approaches, and communication. *Journal of Research on Technology in Education, 34*(2), 139-156.

Gay, L. R. (1996). *Educational Research.* Upper Saddle River, NJ: Prentice-Hall.

Hathorn, L. G., & Ingram, A. L. (2002a, January-February). Online collaboration: Making it work. *Educational Technology, 42*(1), 33-40.

Hathorn, L. G., & Ingram, A. L. (2002b). Cooperation and collaboration using computer-mediated communications. *Journal of Educational Computing Research, 26*(3), 325-347.

Hawkes, M., & Romiszowski, A. (2001). Examining the reflective outcomes of asynchronous computer-mediated communication on inservice teacher development. *Journal of Technology and Teacher Education, 9*(2), 285-308.

Henri, F. (1992). Computer conferencing and content analysis. In A. R. Kaye (Ed.), *Collaborative Learning Through Computer Conferencing* (pp. 117-136). Berlin, Germany: Springer-Verlag.

Ingram, A. L. (1999/2000). Using Web server logs in evaluating instructional Web sites. *Journal of Educational Technology Systems, 28*(2), 137-157.

Johnson, D. W., Johnson, R. T., & Smith, K. A. (1998). Cooperative learning returns to college. *Change, 30*(4), 26-35.

Jonassen, D. H., & Kwon, H. G. (2001). Communication patterns in computer mediated versus face-to-face group problem solving. *Educational Technology Research and Development, 49*(1), 35-51.

Kaye, A. (1992). Learning together apart. In A. R. Kaye (Ed.), *Collaborative Learning Through Computer Conferencing* (pp. 117-136). Berlin, Germany: Springer-Verlag.

Copyright © 2004, Idea Group Inc. Copying or distributing in print or electronic forms without written permission of Idea Group Inc. is prohibited.

Laffey, J., Tupper, T., Musser, D., & Wedman, J. (1998). A computer-mediated support system for project-based learning. *Educational Technology Research and Development, 46*(1), 73-86.

Mason, R. (1992). Evaluation methodologies for computer conferencing applications. In A. R. Kaye (Ed.), *Collaborative Learning Through Computer Conferencing* (pp. 105-116). Berlin, Germany: Springer-Verlag.

Miles, M. B., & Huberman, A. M. (1987). *Qualitative Data Analysis.* London: Sage.

Olaniran, B. A., Savage, G. T., & Sorenson, R. L. (1996). Experimental and experiential approaches to teaching face-to-face and computer-mediated group discussion. *Communication Education, 45*(7), 244-259.

Polhemus, L., & Swan, K. (2002). Student roles in online learning communities: Navigating threaded discussions. In P. Barker & S. Rebelsky (Eds.), *Proceedings of ED-MEDIA 2002.* Norfolk, VA: Association for the Advancement of Computing in Education, pp.1589-1592.

Pugh, S. L. (1993). Using case studies and collaborative computer-assisted communication to support conceptual learning in a teacher-education course on critical reading. *Educational Technology, 33*(11), 30-38.

Qing, L. (2001/2002). Development of the collaborative learning measure in CMC. *Journal of Educational Technology Systems, 30*(1), 19-41.

Rourke, L., Anderson, T., Garrison, D. R., & Archer, W. (2001). Methodological issues in the content analysis of computer conference transcripts. *International Journal of Artificial Intelligence in Education, 12*(1), 8-22. Retrieved on July 21, 2003 from the web site: http://www.atl.ualberta.ca/cmc/2Rourke_et_al_Content_Anakysis.pdf

Silverman, D. (1993). *Interpreting Qualitative Data.* Thousand Oaks, CA: Sage Publications.

Smith, W. (1994). Computer-mediated communication: An experimental study. *Journalism Educator, 48*(2), 27-33.

Warschauer, M. (1997). Computer-mediated collaborative learning: Theory and practice. *Modern Language Journal, 81*(2), 470-481.

Weigel, V. B. (2002). *Deep Learning for a Digital Age: Technology's Untapped Potential to Enrich Higher Education.* San Francisco, CA: Jossey-Bass.

Wild, M., & Braid, P. (1997). A model for measuring children's interactions in small groups using computers. *Journal of Computing in Childhood Education, 8*(2/3), 215-225.

Copyright © 2004, Idea Group Inc. Copying or distributing in print or electronic forms without written permission of Idea Group Inc. is prohibited.

Chapter XI

Reflection and Intellectual Amplification in Online Communities of Collaborative Learning

Elsebeth Korsgaard Sorensen
Aalborg University, Denmark

ABSTRACT

An alternative theoretical framework for analyzing and designing computer-supported collaborative learning environments is introduced. Bateson's theory (1973) is used as a starting point for considering in what sense the specific dialogical conditions and qualities of virtual environments may support learning. We need more stringent analytical approaches of research that relate communicative qualities of virtual contexts to qualities of the collaborative knowledge-building process. This approach suggests that new didactic and instructional methods, addressing the learner's communicative awareness at a meta-level, need to be developed in order to fully utilize the interactive and reflective potential of online collaborative learning. A deeper understanding of the reflective nature of the online environment and its potential for enhancing intellectual amplification will give rise to the birth of new and more innovative designs of online collaborative learning.

Copyright © 2004, Idea Group Inc. Copying or distributing in print or electronic forms without written permission of Idea Group Inc. is prohibited.

INTRODUCTION

Flexible computer-supported learning is rapidly emerging as the educational method of choice in modern society. Although most applications of computer-supported learning are primarily interactions of the learner with software, the envisioned educational expectation within distributed computer-supported collaborative learning (CSCL)[1] is design and delivery of flexible learning environments with deeper collaborative and interactive learning qualities (Kaye, 1994). This expectation has so far not been realized (Collis, 1996; Fjuk, 1998; Sorensen, 1997b, 1998; Collins, Mulholland, & Watt, 2001), primarily because achieving peer interaction remains a complex challenge.

Several studies based on practical applications identify shortcomings in the technology as the main reason for the lack of collaborative learning. They conclude that learning situations unfolding face to face are more conducive to good quality learning than online CSCL situations. In contrast, within CSCL research, the problem of achieving online peer interaction is identified as a shortcoming of not being able to integrate pedagogy, organization and technology (Bates, 1995; Fjuk & Sorensen, 1997) in appropriate ways. CSCL researchers do not interpret online CSCL as lower level quality learning compared to face-to-face learning; instead there is a growing awareness that a more generalized understanding of human interaction and communication is the key to unlocking the interactive learning potential of CSCL (Dillenbourg, Baker, Blaye, & O'Malley, 1995). New insights are needed into the interactive learning conditions of virtual environments.

The general principles of collaborative learning theory are assumed to be at the core of CSCL (Harasim, 1990; Sorensen, 1996, 1997b). However, these principles are only vaguely defined in the continuum between theory and practice and are not focused enough to analyze learning qualities in the virtual environment. We need more stringent analytical approaches that relate communicative potential and qualities of the virtual communicative context to qualities of the learning process. Such insights are expected to inspire new, alternative instructional designs and didactic methods (Koschmann, 1996; Pea, 1994).

This chapter presents an alternative theoretical framework for analyzing and designing CSCL environments, and argues that online collaborative learning environments are conducive to intellectual amplification. It addresses the learning potential of distributed CSCL and the need for and role of meta-instruction. I will assert that the inability to stimulate online interaction may be traced to a lack of understanding among designers and instructors of the characteristics of dialogue in virtual environments. On this basis, I will attempt to explain how specific dialogical conditions and qualities of virtual environments may enhance interaction and intellectual amplification in asynchronous distributed CSCL. Based on the theoretical perspective of Gregory Bateson (1973) and basic "ontological" principles of online learning environments, I suggest potential

Copyright © 2004, Idea Group Inc. Copying or distributing in print or electronic forms without written permission of Idea Group Inc. is prohibited.

reasons for the mixed successes in previous attempts to achieve collaborative learning online. I assume that key impediments to success relate to interconnections between meta-communication and scaffolding (Bruner, Olver, Greenfield, et al., 1966). Empirical examples will be given to illustrate the hypothesis that successful online learning environments that are rich in opportunities for reflection require careful design of meta-communicative scaffolding and instruction.

"Premises of Collaborative Online Dialogue" describes "ontological" premises and conditions for inter-human interaction in asynchronous online learning environments that are significant from the perspective of designing for collaborative learning online. This is followed with a section that presents the core elements in Gregory Bateson's (1973) learning theory on which my theoretical approach and insights for reflective amplification in online collaborative learning are built. In Section 4, I introduce three reflective principles, which I assert contribute to making an online collaborative learning paradigm an amplified intellectual endeavor. Next, the chapter outlines some empirical findings illustrating the amplified reflective collaborative learning process of the online environment, enhanced through the implementation of meta-communicative instruction and scaffolding. The chapter then discusses my conclusions on collaborative learning environments as ideally promoting intellectual amplification, and concludes with a section that suggests areas of future research.

PREMISES OF COLLABORATIVE ONLINE DIALOGUE

Inter-human communication is the basic medium for collaboration and collaborative knowledge building in learning, so communication must be considered at a basic level before designing any structure that involves linguistic collaboration between learners.

The Missing Link: A New Dialogical Paradigm

Stimulating peer interaction is essential when designing distributed collaborative learning processes (Harasim, 1989; Sorensen, 1993). This applies to asynchronous virtual environments (be they client-server facilities or Web-based) as well as face-to-face environments. It is customary, however, to assume that conditions of face-to-face dialogues, and the way they are stimulated, are the basis for creating support for distributed interaction in virtual environments (Sorensen, 1997b). In other words, we have assumed that in design and management asynchronous distributed CSCL processes of online dialogues are the same as for face-to-face dialogues.

Copyright © 2004, Idea Group Inc. Copying or distributing in print or electronic forms without written permission of Idea Group Inc. is prohibited.

However, the thinking behind the design and management of distributed CSCL, before even considering learning processes, must have a deeper understanding of asynchronous online dialogue. We need to understand what happens to inter-human online dialogues that are no longer routed and embedded in a physical time and context. Such research must be central, when considering dialogue and interaction in online CSCL (Harasim, 1989; Sorensen, 1997a).

Characteristics of Online Dialogues

The assumptions of face-to-face interaction influence the way we understand and apply the role and tasks of the online instructor (Sorensen, 1999). Only a few research studies (Eklundh, 1986; Sorensen, 1993) have attempted to clarify the specific conditions and premises of online dialogue. Sorensen (1993) analyzed large quantities of electronic dialogues from a linguistic perspective and reported four basic characteristics of online dialogues.

The Elasticity of Time and Context

One feature of online dialogues is the dynamic relationship between the level of "interactivity" and the linguistic character of the interaction. Although the significance of social and organizational factors, like roles (e.g., moderator of conference, teacher of a course, etc.) and levels of formality, or "loyalty," toward the traditional style of writing in electronic dialogues should not be underestimated, there seems to be a dynamic relationship between frequency of interactive moves and the level of context dependency of the linguistic character of the moves.

Consider the example of a language game (Eklundh, 1986), which has an opening, perhaps one or more intermediate "moves" and a closing comment. Language games work toward termination. A context that is established and shared mentally stimulates a frequent exchange of moves (Sorensen, 1993). If too much time elapses between the exchanges, the context has to be rebuilt. In this case the speed of the information exchange is reduced. In other words, higher "interactivity" elevates the level of mentally shared context and background knowledge between interlocutors. Thus, higher "interactivity" moves toward "synchrony" in the interaction (i.e., toward the situation of face-to-face meetings), which leads to a more shared "presence" in the style of linguistic moves between interlocutors. Furthermore, the frequency of message exchange determines to what level the character and features of the linguistic interaction resemble the prototypical spoken interaction and language. When the exchange of messages occurs at longer intervals in time, the character of the interaction and use of language will resemble the prototypical written interaction.

Although this appears as a general dynamic principle of the electronic interaction, there seem to be certain properties of the electronic interaction that

Copyright © 2004, Idea Group Inc. Copying or distributing in print or electronic forms without written permission of Idea Group Inc. is prohibited.

distinguish it from spoken interaction. Even at a high level of interactivity, electronically mediated dialogue will never be as transient as spoken dialogue. The possibility for retrieval classifies electronic interaction more like written dialogue, even under high frequency of message exchange. Another invariant feature is the single communication pathway. Regardless of the level of interactivity, this will always be (at this point in time) a condition of the electronic interaction. A third constant feature, which the electronic dialogue seems to have taken over from written interaction, is the lack of tendency to practice "gear change" (i.e., a mechanism of slowing down the speed of the interaction in order to make explicit an implied presupposition made by the other interlocutor). The gear-shift mechanism is an important dialogic feature that is very valuable in various types of spoken interaction. In particular, in pedagogical design situations, it may be important to realize that high gear utterances, which often have highly embedded structures with many latent presuppositions, put much more strain on a listener than a low gear variant with a low level of embedding.

Compensational Behavior

An experience shared by many learners is that electronic interaction seems more similar to spoken dialogue than to written interaction. Nevertheless, the interaction is not a face-to-face interaction and does not share the same conditions as that of spoken dialogue. The only semiotic sign through which the interaction of an electronic dialogue can manifest itself is the written word.

Several elements, normally contained in nonverbal communication, are pertinent to the interpretation of spoken linguistic communication, and nonverbal communication is fundamental to us, in the sense that we cannot avoid nonverbal communication. Pragmatically, nonverbal behavior seems to entail not only the expression of social identity, personal traits and psychological states, but also sends a signal in parallel with the verbal component that stimulates the communication partner to react. In addition, it is fairly well established that the course of a conversation is strongly influenced by the participants' inferences and attributions as to the social identity, personality disposition and respective psychological states of their partners (Van Dijk, 1985).

Inability to communicate feelings, states of mind and attitudes to a communication partner is an obstacle in the electronic interaction. Because electronic interaction in conferencing systems is mainly monosemiotic (takes place mainly through writing), the most widely used method for communicating these elements, and, thereby, stimulating a stronger social connection between participants, is creation of a visual image by use of those written symbols offered by the computer keyboard (e.g., {{8-) — indicating a happy face with glasses). Compensational behavior clearly demonstrates a need for communication methods other than those offered by the written language. There seems to be a need to invest "presence" and personal aspects into the interaction. This need that

Copyright © 2004, Idea Group Inc. Copying or distributing in print or electronic forms without written permission of Idea Group Inc. is prohibited.

may be caused by a physical separation (where chances for "in between face-to-face encounters" are limited) and limitations imposed on the interaction as a consequence of the monosemiotic condition.

In principle, compensational behavior can be translated into traditional written descriptions. However, doing so would create a general delay and inertia in the communication process, which would be frustrating and would remove all the spontaneity of the interaction (and, after all, it is the social, interactive aspect of conferencing systems that stimulates communication). Compensating iconographical/indexical behavior can be viewed as a new and innovative element in writing, which has appeared concurrently with the increased importance of communication based on pictures or combinations of pictures and text. Iconic/indexical signs are easy to interpret because they do not require translation in the same sense as a written description, but are understood more directly through the impression they make on the senses. They may be superior to verbal communication for expressing feelings, states of minds, attitudes, etc.

The Continuing Dialogue

An ongoing electronic dialogue tends to be kept alive and to be experienced by learners as a never-ending discussion. If we adapt the perspective of language games (Wittgenstein, 1974; Sorensen & Takle, 2002), the interaction may be seen as parallel and/or as continuously progressing sequences of language games. The amount of closure in electronic language games (i.e., a condition where no language game is open and no expectations with respect to a continuation of the game are unfulfilled) is low in comparison to spoken dialogues.

This may be part of the reason for the rather common experience of conferencing systems users that response means success (at some level), while silence definitely indicates failure. If all expectations in a language game apparently are satisfied, there is a tendency to avoid closure and to provide instead "extra" information in order to create a sufficient and "legitimate" basis for keeping the dialogue alive. Typically, the language game will continue, for example, by one of the interlocutors responding to some extra information in the closing move, and in this way introducing a partly new frame.

Although the problem of termination of electronic dialogues is rather complex due to the many-to-many interaction (e.g., it is never too late to respond), the gradual displacement of linguistic frame/context to keep the language game going seems to be a general pattern. A large proportion of electronic language games has a phatic function by which social contact and interaction between the communicating parties is established and maintained. The frequency of attempts in electronic dialogues to avoid closure and promote continuing interaction clearly indicates the importance of the social/phatic aspects of the interaction. It seems to be vitally important to keep the interaction

Copyright © 2004, Idea Group Inc. Copying or distributing in print or electronic forms without written permission of Idea Group Inc. is prohibited.

going, so much so that it is conceivable that the "true" intention of many language games is not to achieve fulfillment of expectations, but rather to maintain social relations — even if the games, structurally, would be classified differently.

Newer learning environments, like, e.g., GCPortfolio (Takle, Sorensen, & Herzmann, 2003) and Knowledge Forum (Scardamalia, 2002), use descriptive categories as a way of supporting progression in online CSCL. Successful knowledge building is assumed to be characterized by reflective thinking skills and deep embedding of ideas in larger conceptual structures, as well as in the practices of the knowledge building community. While the GC Portfolio uses the category of "synthesis," Knowledge Forum uses the category "rise above" for promoting closure in the dialogue. This may be a fruitful way of managing the needed synthesis and convergence of ideas in knowledge building discourse. Yet to be determined is the extent to which such promising designs may handle the significantly enlarged social needs of a truly distributed group of learners.

The Independence of Time and Space

An electronic interaction appears like a complex mixture of distance and closeness. The feeling of distance may be related not so much to the "real" geographical distance between interlocutors, as to the impossibility of overcoming the asynchronous condition. Although the feeling of distance may vary quantitatively, an element of distance will always be present (of course, also reinforced by the lack of nonverbal behavior). It is conceivable that this condition reduces obligation, or a least urgency, to respond.

Similar behavior is common in face-to-face dialogues, but it is not considered a problem because it gets regulated through repair games/sub-games, which are easily and smoothly introduced. The feeling of closeness may derive partly from the fact that the interlocutor always has opportunity to "be close" or participate, if he wishes, by responding to or initiating a language game. The metaphor of a shared room for the interaction may engender a feeling of closeness.

A final consequence to be pointed out here, which is related to the independence of the interaction from time and space, is an issue mostly affecting the receiving situation of the interlocutor. As production and comprehension of messages occur at different times and independently of each other, a move is never topical viewed in relation to the mind of the author. Passing time separates author from subject. The importance of time intervals and the dynamic establishment of context/frame for the interaction can create interpretative problems, as the responding interlocutor cannot predict the time that will elapse before his answer gets read.

The above-mentioned characteristics of online dialogues inevitably will influence instructional and scaffolding decisions made as part of any online learning design (Sorensen, 1997a).

Copyright © 2004, Idea Group Inc. Copying or distributing in print or electronic forms without written permission of Idea Group Inc. is prohibited.

Presence Online

Social presence online, the fundamental element for creation of a collaborative knowledge-building (KB) process through what Wenger calls "negotiation of meaning" (Wenger, 1998, p. 87), is threatened by lack of both participation (interaction) and engagement (Gunawardena, 1995; Rourke, Anderson, Garrison, & Archer, 1999). Creation of an online presence in net-based distributed collaborative learning processes based on participation and mutual engagement in order to ensure the negotiation of meaning is a pedagogical challenge that is tied into the symbolic nature of the online environment.

Online presence is established through the process of submitting comments. A comment, therefore, has two communicative functions: to communicate its content and to communicate presence. (Co)existence in the virtual environment is established through interactive production of contributions. In other words, (co)existence and (inter)action takes place via communication (Feenberg, 1989; Sorensen, 1999; Bygholm, 2002). Far too many designs of online collaborative learning implicitly assume that self understanding, interaction and communicative actions in a virtual, asynchronous written universe are operationalized by the same mechanisms valid in a traditional, synchronous spoken face-to-face setting (Sorensen, 2000).

As pointed out earlier, virtual asynchronous communication rests on fundamentally different principles for communicative unfolding than face-to-face communication. We understand ourselves and our social behavior as phenomena closely related to the contexts of time and space. But we have failed to recognize and exploit the special communicative conditions for actions and interactions provided by a virtual, asynchronous written context. Our traditional social (co)existence in terms of social interaction is inextricably tied into a synchronous reality of time and space. In a virtual environment (co)existence is freed from these constraints.

A pedagogical model of design and virtual instruction for distributed CSCL, therefore, must take into account the interplay between collaborative principles of learning and the communicative conditions of virtual (co)existence and (inter)action. Basically, we need different analytical approaches that look not only at online dialogues themselves but that relate the communicative potential and qualities of the virtual environment to qualities of the learning process. Such an approach may be inspired by some general principles of the learning theory studies of Gregory Bateson (1973).

THEORETICAL PERSPECTIVE

In this section I outline the core elements in Gregory Bateson's learning theory (1973) that inspired my theoretical perspective on reflective amplification in online collaborative learning.

Copyright © 2004, Idea Group Inc. Copying or distributing in print or electronic forms without written permission of Idea Group Inc. is prohibited.

Communication and Learning in the Light of Bateson (1973)

Although Bateson is not a linguist, he works from the basic assumption known from the field of semiotics of communication as a multi-semiotic phenomenon (Sorensen, 1997b), viewing all signs in a communication (verbal and nonverbal) as communicators that play a role in creating and forming the communicative message. In his understanding, the meta-communicative context is essential in learning, as it is active in forming the communicative message. He considers all types of learning to be communication phenomena and that learning must, in some basic way, be subject to the same rules that apply to communication (Bateson, 1973). A very central idea in Bateson's theory is that incidents of learning — being basically communicative in their nature — unfold as meta-communicative movements in different levels of reflection[2] or communicative contexts[3], in a continuum bounded by "no reflection" on the one end and "several levels of reflection" on the other.

Bateson views meta-reflection as a necessary precondition, as well as a result of learning. His understanding of the learning phenomenon as processes of reflection and meta-communication may be visualized by Hermansen's model (see Figure 1, Hermansen, 1996).

Bateson conceptualizes learning as transcendence of levels of reflection taking place on hierarchical layers of context (meta-communication). In learning level 0 + 1, there is a direct relationship between the learner/subject (S) and

Figure 1: Learning as Transcendence of Levels of Reflection

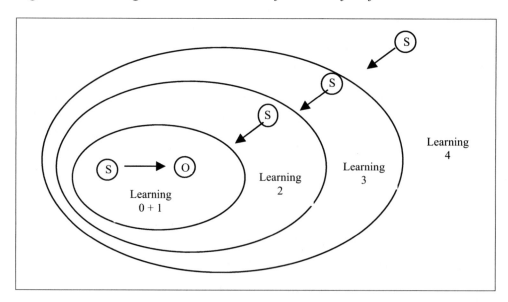

Copyright © 2004, Idea Group Inc. Copying or distributing in print or electronic forms without written permission of Idea Group Inc. is prohibited.

object (O), which has to be learned. At this point in learning, there is no reflection on the learning process, but the foundation for reflection is developed. We could say that there is a more or less random testing of possibilities.

Learning level 2 is characterized by an indirect relationship between the learner and the object, as the learner uses reflection as one of the means in his/her learning process. At this level there is a systematic reflection on how to solve a problem, and the learner is conscious about the fact that he/she is learning. He/she is consciously tied to the situated conditions (in a wide sense) and actively using what he/she has learned at other (lower) levels.

At learning level 3 there is a relationship of reflection, in relation to reflection, in learning. At this level the learner has a reflective attitude to how he/she approaches learning. This level of learning usually happens outside concretely related contexts.

Level 4 is difficult to conceptualize. Much interpretation of Bateson sees learning at this level as the momentary "aha!" experience in which we may sense faintly the whole connection of something. Other interpretations hold that this is the level of learning or insight, which may also bring a conscious opposition in the learner, and is a consequence of having achieved the problem-penetrating insight into a problem.

In summary, we could say that the general learning principle in the Bateson model is that "you should always relate yourself to yourself, while you relate to something," and that the level of learning achieved changes all the time because the frame (or context) within which it happens changes.

PRINCIPLES OF DISTRIBUTED CSCL: FROM REALITY TO VIRTUALITY

Engeström (1987) points out that reflection over the learning process is essential if learning is to develop and expand in depth and in width. Contrary to the physical world, in which some philosophers view the existential state of "involvement" to precede the state of "reflection" (Heidegger, 1986), the virtual universe provides a context and an "ontology" in which reflection may be viewed as preceding involvement (Sorensen, 2003). The move from physical reality to virtual reality creates a change in context, a change of principles and premises of being and, acting through insertion of a meta-level of symbols and representations, creates a reflective distance to the learner. With regard to "ontological" conditions for action and interaction, three basic "ontological" principles emerge in the move to the distributed, virtual symbolic world:

Copyright © 2004, Idea Group Inc. Copying or distributing in print or electronic forms without written permission of Idea Group Inc. is prohibited.

From Appearance (Being) to Representativity (Signs of Being)

It is only through signs and symbols produced by a learner that the learner is "present" in the shared virtual environment. In other words, presence in a discussion is confirmed through the action of making a comment. Thus, a comment communicates presence and content.

By extension, any action (communicative or non-communicative) taken by the learner is carried out not directly, but symbolically through manipulation of symbols and representations (Foucault, 1970; Sorensen, 1997b). Moreover, it is not only the learner's actions and interactions that take place through representative signs (e.g., the written sign). The signs and communication from the learner's context(s) — a concept of great complexity for the distributed learner (Sorensen, 1997b) — must, through processes of reflection, be transformed into verbal language and communicated with the language games of the interaction with other people. The only parts of the learning context, which are shared, are the virtual environment, as well as the context of the language games constructed socially through the interaction with other learners and with the teacher.

The view that "context" is an important factor in communication is not new. The linguist, Roman Jakobsen, in his model of communication talks about "the referential function to the context" (Ricouer, 1978, p. 222), and the American philosopher, Peirce, from the perspective of semiotics, focuses on the indexical relationship of any sign to the embedding world (Suchman, 1987). Also, the HCI-researcher Lucy Suchman is concerned with the role of context and states that the significance of a linguistic expression on some actual location lies in its relationship to circumstances (Suchman, 1987). Finally, Bateson uses the term "context" to describe the (not materialistic) situational conditions — that are communicatively effective in creating meaning — in which a message, incident or behavior occurs (Bateson, 1973).

From Primarily Being Involved in Interaction to Primarily Reflecting on Interaction

In the virtual environment the learner cannot interact (make a comment) without being prompted to reflect at a meta-level about the content of his/her comment. There is no level of (inter)action without a process of reflection (Sorensen, 2003).

The move of learning processes to a distributed virtual symbolic environment introduces a meta-communicative level in all of the learner's actions and interactions. This creates "distance" between the acting subject (the learner) and the object (the intended action or interaction).

Copyright © 2004, Idea Group Inc. Copying or distributing in print or electronic forms without written permission of Idea Group Inc. is prohibited.

Processes of reflection not only imply distance, they are preconditioned by distance. Consequently, we may conclude that the virtual universe — contrary to the physical world in which involvement may be viewed as preceding reflection (Heidegger, 1986) — provides a context and an "ontology" in which reflection precedes involvement. The fact that reflective processes (implying distance) precede involvement in distributed virtual environments may also explain the frequent instructional experience that transferring collaborative learning processes to virtual environments usually uncovers and makes visible (to a much higher extent than face-to-face processes) design features and the learners' communicative acts. The reflective character of our actions in the virtual space implies the distance, which causes us to acknowledge them.

At a practical level, the learner experiences an enlarged need for reflection in the virtual environment, when he/she makes the simple communicative act of composing a message. Before submitting the message, the learner is asked to reflect on the content of his/her message and, through reflective engagement at a meta-communicative level, to decide on a descriptive title in relation to the content of the message.

Summing up, we may conclude that the virtual environment enhances processes of reflection (Figure 2). More specifically, if we acknowledge that reflection is involved even at the first level of learner actions in virtual environments, then we may generally conclude that learning processes unfolding in virtual environments are initiated at a higher reflective level (level 2) of learning (Figure 2), than physical learning processes that unfold in relation to the learning content.

Figure 2: Virtual Learning Processes Initiated at a Higher Reflective Level

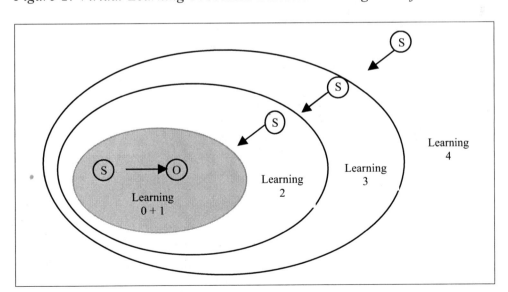

Copyright © 2004, Idea Group Inc. Copying or distributing in print or electronic forms without written permission of Idea Group Inc. is prohibited.

From Involved Speech to Reflective Writing

The move from dialogically composed speech to monologically composed writing is an environmental change that defines the basic reflective conditions for learning processes in distributed virtual environments.

From the theoretical view of Bateson (1973), insertion of a symbolic level through the use of the written sign in learning actions and interactions also has a clear learning value (Sorensen, 1999). Not only does it promote increased reflection and thinking at the shared collaborative and interactive level, it also represents a kind of "tool" for individual intellectual amplification. The process of writing something down creates a distance between the thought and the thinker. Much research and literature acknowledges this view on writing. For example, Johansen (1998) states that linguistic forms are the forms of thought and that writing is the technology of thinking. In the same way, writing is said to be thinking made tangible, and that the road to clearer understanding of one's thoughts is traveled on paper. It is often through the search for words to express ideas that we discover what we think. The need for explicitness that is implied in writing promotes learning processes when viewed, as in the case of Bateson, as transcendence of reflective levels in the continuum between no reflection and reflections on reflections on reflections.

The principles presented above and the requirement for enhanced meta-communicative awareness have significant implications for didactic and instructional design. They indicate a need for an enhanced focus and awareness at the meta-communicative level of instruction and scaffolding in communities of online collaborative learning.

EMPIRICAL EXPERIENCES

To illustrate the amplified reflective collaborative learning process of the online environment, I describe a study in which enhanced meta-communicative instruction and scaffolding was implemented.

A pedagogical design for encouraging reflection and meta-communication has been implemented in a course on global environmental change at Iowa State University (Takle et al., 2003). Global Change (GC)[4] is a conventional science course for senior undergraduates or beginning graduate students at a U.S. university. It gradually has been migrated to a Web base over the last nine years, with new features being added as ancillary software has become available. Learner-centred activities in place of or supplemental to conventional lectures have been introduced. The course consists of a sequence of learning modules on different global-change topics, each having evolved from a conventional university class. Each unit has a set of objectives, summary information on the topic, student-submitted collaborative (two-three students) summary of class time

Copyright © 2004, Idea Group Inc. Copying or distributing in print or electronic forms without written permission of Idea Group Inc. is prohibited.

discussion, "problems to ponder" as discussion starters for the electronic dialogue and extensive lists of Web and other information on the learning module topic. Each unit has its own electronic dialogue for student discussion among themselves and with outside experts or representatives of selected groups. Electronic dialogue on individual learning unit topics is graded. The course is viewed, by the designers, as a laboratory for experimenting with a variety of pedagogical techniques and initiatives (Taber et al., 1997).

Students are asked to employ reflection in their online dialogue on global change topics by declaring, as a label on their posting, the particular knowledge-building skill (KBS) they are using. At the end of each of three successive five-week periods, students are asked, by means of an online self-assessment, to reflect on their use of these skills, and how use of these skills has contributed to the knowledge base for each topic. The instructor evaluates (online) the self-assessments on the basis of students' understanding of KBS and its use in building a knowledge base. In the second and third assessment cycles, the student and instructor together (through online self assessment and evaluation in light of current and preceding assessment cycles) reflect on the progress the student is making toward effective use of KBS in the global change context. Meta-communication in the latter cycles, therefore, is at a higher level and examines fundamentals of the learning process (how specific KBS achieve specific goals of learning), in addition to building a global change knowledge base (primary focus of first assessment cycle).

Implementing categories of collaborative KBS requires a corresponding meta-functional pedagogy or instruction that facilitates and motivates a collaborative dialogue. Thus, students were given a set of meta-categories (i.e., a set of KBS) with examples of how each could be implemented. These categories were (Stahl, 1999):

- Brainstorming is the introduction of new ideas that relate to the topic or task and offer a perspective not previously considered;
- Articulating includes explaining complex or difficult concepts;
- Reacting provides an alternative or amplified perspective on a concept previously introduced by a student;
- Organizing refers to assembling existing thoughts or perspectives in such a way that a new perspective emerges;
- Analysis includes comparing or contrasting previously articulated views or puts new understanding on existing data; and
- Generalization takes comments or data already presented and extracts new information or knowledge that applies to a broader set of conditions.

An analysis of this course (Sorensen & Takle, 2002) reported on the role and nature of the instructions in the requirements given to students to stimulate

Copyright © 2004, Idea Group Inc. Copying or distributing in print or electronic forms without written permission of Idea Group Inc. is prohibited.

interaction. Characteristics of student dialogue and its relationship to course requirements were evaluated by assembling 10 comments from 1995, 10 from 1997, and 10 from 2000. The analysis assessed whether meta-communication in terms of providing meta-awareness of "the function of a comment" in the KB process would improve the quality of the KB dialogue and, thus, enhance intellectual amplification (Sorensen & Takle, 2002).

A subjective measure of quality (0-10) of online comments was applied to dialogue from (a) 1995 when no requirements were placed on the number of comments and KBS were not required; (b) 1997 when requirements were put on the minimum number of postings made by each student; and (c) 2000 when the KBS were described and required. Evaluation of a random sample of comments from these three implementations revealed that the quality value went from 4.4 (1995) to 3.2 (1997) to 5.3 (2000). We ascribe the drop in quality from 1995 to 1997 to the demand for more postings, which generated more but shallower comments. We attribute the rise in quality from 1995/1997 to 2000 to reflection, meta-communication and self-assessment surrounding the use of KBS. Average word counts of the comments in these three years went from 88 to 93 to more than 300, suggesting deeper engagement in the topic of the posting when KBS were required.

CONCLUSION

In this chapter, I have addressed the reflective nature of the online environment and its potential for enhancing intellectual amplification. From a Batesonian perspective, I have attempted to establish principles describing to what extent and in what sense virtual learning processes possess learning qualities hitherto unknown in face-to-face learning situations. On the basis of this initial theoretical exploration, I conclude that intellectual amplification — in as far as processes of reflection are viewed to be central aspects of learning — inherently receive special support in online learning environments.

Through the insertion of a meta-communicative layer of context, virtual environments seem to promote processes of increased reflection in learning. Thus, when learning processes move up the reflection ladder, we need to provide meta-communicative weaving techniques and to support meta-communicative structures of scaffolding. The fact that distributed collaborative learning processes unfold on the basis of a dialogical paradigm different from familiar face-to-face processes indicates that we need to review existing instructional techniques and to incorporate new and innovative methodological initiatives. The very different learning conditions provided through the new dialogical paradigm may be part of the reason for the general lack of success of learning design in terms of stimulating online interaction. The new dialogical conditions create a need for didactic change related to design of collaborative learning processes

Copyright © 2004, Idea Group Inc. Copying or distributing in print or electronic forms without written permission of Idea Group Inc. is prohibited.

and to teaching methods within collaborative learning. In this process, some central instructional CSCL concepts and ideas may have to be reviewed, broadened or redefined.

Viewed from the processes of meta-communication and meta-reflection as these appear through the glasses of Bateson, scaffolding should not primarily be related to the decomposition of learning content or tasks. Rather, as transcendence of learning levels appears to be the key in learning, scaffolding should be directed toward supporting the learners' navigation through meta-communicative levels. Promoting this thinking, however, is a challenge that is likely to affect, not only instruction, scaffolding, and didactic elements of distributed learning processes, but also the actual development and construction of virtual environments for distributed collaborative learning online.

FUTURE PERSPECTIVES

The emphasis on reflective processes in learning, however, should not lead us to overlook the important dimension of practice. Virtual spaces and virtual learning environments provide rich opportunities for future research aimed at finding ways to implement these concepts in the virtual universe of learning. New collaborative tools (e.g., white boards, shared documents, etc.) and new and innovative use of existing tools provide environments for conducting controlled, hypothesis-driven statistically-based research that will clarify which design structures most effectively exploit the virtual environment to enhance learning. This paper has addressed asynchronous distributed collaborative learning from the theoretical perspective, but the challenge ahead may be to investigate empirically, and more thoroughly, to what extent the reflective principles described are manifested in practice.

ACKNOWLEDGMENTS

Valuable and insightful comments on both the content and language of this chapter have been provided by Professor Eugene S. Takle, Department of Agronomy and Department of Geological and Atmospheric Sciences, Iowa State University, USA.

REFERENCES

Bates, A. W. (1995). *Technology, Open Learning and Distance Education.* London: Routledge.

Bateson, G. (1973). *Steps to an Ecology of Mind.* London: Granada Publishing Limited.

Copyright © 2004, Idea Group Inc. Copying or distributing in print or electronic forms without written permission of Idea Group Inc. is prohibited.

Bruner, J. S., Oliver, R. R., & Greenfield, P. M. (1966). *Studies in Cognitive Growth*. New York: John Wiley & Sons.

Bygholm, A. (2002). Kommunikation og samarbejde i netbaserede læringsmiljøer. In Ministry of Education (Ed.), *Uddannelse, læring og IT* (pp.87-96). Copenhagen: Undervisningsministeriets Forlag.

Collins, T., Mulholland, P., & Watt, S. (2001). Using genre to support active participation in learning communities. *Proceedings of the First European Conference on Computer Supported Collaborative Learning (Euro CSCL 2001)*, pp. 156-164.

Collis, B. (1996). *Tele-Learning in a Digital World*. London: International Thomson Computer Press.

Dillenbourg, P., Baker, M., Blaye, A., & O'Malley, C. (1995). The evolution of research on collaborative learning. In P. Reimann & H. Spada (Eds.), *Learning in Human and Machines: Towards an Interdisciplinary Learning Science* (pp. 189-211). London: Pergamon.

Eklundh, K. S. (1986). *Dialogue Processes in Computer-Mediated Communication: A Study of Letters in the COM System*. Malmö, Sweden: Liber Förlag AB.

Engeström, Y. (1987). *Learning by Expanding: An Activity-Theoretical Approach to Developmental Research*. Helsinki, Finland: Orienta-Konsultit.

Feenberg, A. (1989). The written world. In R. Mason & A. R. Kaye (Eds.), *Mindweave: Communication, Computers, and Distance Education* (pp. 22-40). Oxford, UK: Pergamon Press.

Fjuk, A. (1998). *Computer support for distributed collaborative learning: Exploring a complex problem area*. Unpublished doctoral dissertation, University of Oslo, Norway.

Foucault, M. (1970). *The Order of Things: An Archaeology of the Human Sciences*. London: Routledge.

Gunawardena, C. N. (1995). Social presence theory and implications for interaction and collaborative learning in computer conferences. *International Journal of Educational Telecommunications, 1*(2/3), 147-166.

Harasim, L. M. (1989). Online education. A new domain. R. Mason & A. R. Kaye (Eds.), *Mindweave: Communication, Computers, and Distance Education* (pp. 50-62). Oxford, UK: Pergamon Press.

Harasim, L. M. (ed.). (1990). Online education: An environment for collaboration and intellectual amplification. In L. M. Harasim (Ed.), *Online Education: Perspectives on a New Environment* (pp. 39-64). New York: Praeger Publishers.

Heidegger, M. (1986). *Sein und Zeit*. Tübingen, Germany: Max Niemeyer Verlag.

Hermansen, M. (1996). *Laeringens Univers*. Aarhus, Denmark: Forlaget Klim.

Copyright © 2004, Idea Group Inc. Copying or distributing in print or electronic forms without written permission of Idea Group Inc. is prohibited.

Johansen, A. (1998, Sept.). At tænke sig om skriftlig – og med stil. *Retorica Scandinavia,* 7(7), pp.20-33.

Kaye, A. R. (ed.). (1992). Learning together apart. In A. R. Kaye (Ed.), *Collaborative Learning Through Computer Conferencing* (pp. 1-24). Berlin Heidelberg, Germany: Springer-Verlag.

Koschmann, T. D. (ed.). (1996). Paradigm shifts and instructional technology. *CSCL: Theory and Practice of an Emerging Paradigm* (pp. 1-23). Mahwah, NJ: Lawrence Erlbaum Associates.

Pea, R. D. (1994). Seeing what we build together: Distributed multimedia learning environments for transformative communications. *Journal of the Learning Sciences, 3*(3), 285-299.

Ricoeur, P. (1978). *The Rule of Metaphor.* London: Routledge & Kegan Paul.

Rourke, L., Anderson, T., Garrison, D. R., & Archer, W. (1999). Assessing social presence in asynchronous text-based computer conferencing. *Journal of Distance Education, 14*(3), 51-70.

Scardamalia, M. (2002). Collective cognitive responsibility for the advancement of knowledge. In B. Smith (Ed.), *Liberal Education in a Knowledge Society* (pp. 67-98). Chicago, IL: Open Court.

Sorensen, E. K. (1993). Dialogues in networks. In P. B. Andersen, B. Holmqvist, & J. F. Jensen (Eds.), *The Computer as Medium* (pp. 389-421). Cambridge, UK: Cambridge University Press.

Sorensen, E. K. (1996). Learning online through linguistic interaction. *Innovation in Teaching and Learning: An International Journal for the Critical Practitioner, 2*(2), 12-17.

Sorensen, E. K. (1997a). På vej mod et virtuelt laeringsparadigme. In J. C. Jacobsen (Ed.), *Refleksive laereprocesser* (pp. 78-109). Copenhagen, Denmark: Politisk Revy.

Sorensen, E. K. (1997b). *Learning in Virtual Contexts: Navigation, Interaction, and Collaboration.* Unpublished doctoral dissertation, Aalborg University, Denmark.

Sorensen, E. K. (1998). Design of TeleLearning: A collaborative activity in search of time and context. In T. Chan, A. Collins, & J. Lin (Eds.), *Proceedings of ICCE'98: International Conference on Computers in Education: Global Education On the Net, 2* (pp. 438-442).

Sorensen, E. K. (1999). Collaborative learning in virtual contexts: Representation, reflection and didactic change. *Proceedings from The Sixteenth International Conference on Technology and Education, ICTE99* (pp. 454-456).

Sorensen, E. K. (2000). Interaktion og laering i virtuelle rum. In S. B. Heilesen (Ed.), *Universiteter i udvikling* (pp. 235-255). Copenhagen, Denmark: Forlaget Samfundslitteratur.

Copyright © 2004, Idea Group Inc. Copying or distributing in print or electronic forms without written permission of Idea Group Inc. is prohibited.

Sorensen, E. K. (2003). Designing for online dialogue and discussion in collaborative knowledge building networks (SOFF Rep. No. 1, pp. 21-34). Tromsoe, Norway: SOFF – Centralorganet for fleksibel laering i Hoegre utdanning.

Sorensen, E. K. & Fjuk, A. (1997). Drama as a metaphor for the design of situated, collaborative, distributed learning. *European Journal of Open and Distance Learning (EURODL),* http://www.eurodlen.org/eurodlen/index.html.

Sorensen, E. K., & Takle, E. S. (2002). Collaborative knowledge building in Web-based learning: Assessing the quality of dialogue. *International Journal on E-Learning (IJEL), 1*(1), 28-32.

Stahl, G. (1999). Reflection on WebGuide: Seven issues for the next generation of collaborative knowledge-building environments. In C. M. Hoadley & J. Roschelle (Eds.), *Proceedings of the Computer Support for Collaborative Learning (CSCL) 1999* (pp. 600-610). Mahwah, NJ: Lawrence Erlbaum Associates.

Suchman, L. (1987). *Plans and Situated Actions: The Problem of Human-Machine Communication.* Cambridge, MA: Cambridge University Press.

Taber, M. R., Takle, E. S. & Fils, D. (1997). Use of the Internet for student self-managed learning. Preprints, *Sixth Symposium on Education.* American Meteorological Society, February 2-7, Long Beach, CA.

Takle, E. S., Sorensen, E. K., & Herzmann, D. (2003). *Online dialog: What if you build it and they don't come?* Paper presented at the 12th Symposium on Education. American Meteorological Society, Long Beach, California, USA.

van Dijk, T. A. (ed.). (1985). *Handbook of Discourse Analysis, Vol. 2: Dimensions of Discourse.* London: Academic Press.

Wenger, E. (1998). *Communities of Practice: Learning, Meaning, and Identity.* Cambridge, UK: Cambridge University Press.

Wittgenstein, L. (1974). *Philosophical Investigations.* Oxford, UK: Basil Blackwell.

ENDNOTES

[1] The term "distributed CSCL" denotes computer-supported collaborative learning designs in which most of the educational dialogue in the learning process takes place asynchronously and collaboratively between people over the Web (Sorensen & Fjuk, 1997).

[2] Mads Hermansen has in his book "From the Horizon of Learning" introduced the interpretation of the various learning levels of Bateson, as corresponding to levels and meta-levels of reflection in learning (Hermansen, 1996).

Copyright © 2004, Idea Group Inc. Copying or distributing in print or electronic forms without written permission of Idea Group Inc. is prohibited.

3   Bateson uses the term "context" to describe the (not materialistic) situational conditions that are communicatively effective in creating meaning and in which a message, an incident or a behavior occur (Bateson, 1973).

4   The public access to the Global Change course is at the web site: http://www.meteor.iastate.edu/gccourse/.

Copyright © 2004, Idea Group Inc. Copying or distributing in print or electronic forms without written permission of Idea Group Inc. is prohibited.

Chapter XII

Do Online Collaborative Groups Need Leaders?

Agnes Kukulska-Hulme
The Open University, UK

ABSTRACT

This chapter explores the value and strategies of online group leadership through a review of published research literature. We examine the philosophies that underpin online groupwork, the tasks that learners engage in and the skills of online instructors and students. Concepts of self-direction and depth of learning are central to the discussion. Leadership styles, social roles, relationships and norms, and the effects of tools and media are all considered, in the context of a range of factors that impact on group dynamics. The chapter concludes with a summary of findings concerning the leadership value of online instructors and students, which is intended to further the understanding and professional development of all online educators.

Copyright © 2004, Idea Group Inc. Copying or distributing in print or electronic forms without written permission of Idea Group Inc. is prohibited.

INTRODUCTION

In her influential book, Laurillard (2002) analyzes what students need from learning technologies. There must be "a continuing iterative dialogue between teacher and student, which reveals the participants' conceptions, and the variations between them" (Laurillard, 2002, p. 71), and these in turn will determine the focus for further dialogue. This essential dialogue or conversation can be conducted in the online medium. In a sense, we might say that a learner collaborates with a teacher. However, it is more usual for collaborative learning to be understood as referring to a group of learners. A teacher may act as the guide or leader, or as a member of the group and a co-learner.

Online collaboration emphasizes student activity and signals changes in perceptions of who is responsible for leading groups of learners. It raises questions about the roles of teachers and students as leaders. This chapter aims to examine the proposition that the success or failure of online collaboration depends on the role and skills of a teacher or group leader. The backdrop for this proposition is the enterprise of designing collaborative learning with appropriate learner support.

There is reason to believe that online groups do need guidance. The key question seems to be the extent to which teachers make students conscious of their roles, and the degree to which the instructors are tangibly present in an online environment. There is also some evidence that learners may prefer to collaborate without input from a teacher, but questions of who leads the group, and how, remain important. A related issue is the skill set of the leader, variously known as the online moderator, facilitator, coordinator and so on, depending on his or her role. Field (2002) reports that leaders in general are seen as having vision, providing inspiration, giving people purpose, pushing the boundaries, creating change and innovating through others by coaching and building relationships. These are ways of operating that one might also observe in an inspirational and enterprising online teacher. A common underlying assumption is that there is one leader, but in fact there may be different ways in which group participants contribute to leadership, and numerous ways in which teams of teachers share responsibility for leading online groups.

Group leadership should always be considered in the context of a range of factors that impact group dynamics. Therefore, in this chapter, we begin by reminding ourselves of the different philosophies that underpin online discussion and groupworking, the tasks that learners engage in and the skills that online instructors already have or need to develop. Self-direction is a pivotal concept that moves us into a consideration of emergent leadership in online groups, and specifically, in relation to group composition. We review empirical work concerning leadership styles, social roles, relationships and norms, as well as work on tools and media that may play a role in how collaboration is experienced by

Copyright © 2004, Idea Group Inc. Copying or distributing in print or electronic forms without written permission of Idea Group Inc. is prohibited.

learners. This leads to a summing up of the leadership value of an online tutor, in relation to student leadership.

CONCEPTIONS OF COLLABORATION

Although much has been written on the subject of collaborative learning, it is not always clear what types of learning are understood to be taking place during, or as a result of, collaboration. A brief examination of terminology gives some insights. Panitz (1996) considers the distinction between collaboration and cooperation. Collaboration is a personal "philosophy of interaction"; it suggests ways of dealing with people that respect their abilities and contributions. There is an underlying premise of consensus building. On the other hand cooperation, or cooperative learning, is a "set of processes" geared to the accomplishment of specific goals or to developing an end product. The key to cooperative learning is that it is teacher-centered, directed and controlled.

Panitz (1996) goes on to say that cooperative learning has largely American roots, going back to John Dewey's writings on the social nature of learning. This tradition tends to focus on achievement or products of learning. Collaborative learning has British roots, based on the work of teachers encouraging students to take a more active role in their learning, and ties into the social constructivist movement. There is little point in polarizing these approaches, but an appreciation of differences is useful. We might add that one should be aware that in the research literature the term "collaborative learning" may be used to describe something that would more accurately be named "cooperative." An example of this can be found in Gokhale (1995, p. 22), who describes collaborative learning as "an instruction method in which students work together…in small groups toward a common goal." This is in accord with a view put forward by Dillenbourg and Schneider (1995): "under the label 'collaborative learning,' most research actually focuses on 'learning through collaborative problem solving.'"

Research and practice at the United Kingdom Open University has tended to focus on the consensus-building tradition, and claims for the efficacy of collaboration have been examined. As Laurillard (2002) points out, the claims made for the educational value of computer-mediated communication (CMC) "rest on the assumption that students learn effectively through discussion and collaboration… However, this is not a well-tested assumption as far as the research literature is concerned" (p. 147). She goes on to give some examples of studies that have shown benefits of CMC to students who have been part of thriving online communities. In addition to a "sense of community," these have brought opportunities for mutual support, for alternative perspectives and explanations, and the chance to learn from the mistakes and insights of other students. But there are limitations. Although "argument between students about a topic can be an extremely effective way of enabling students to find out what

Copyright © 2004, Idea Group Inc. Copying or distributing in print or electronic forms without written permission of Idea Group Inc. is prohibited.

they know, and indeed what they do not know ... it does not necessarily lead them to what they are supposed to know" (Laurillard, 2002, p. 158). Laurillard (2002) concludes that discussion between students is an excellent partial method of learning, but that students need to be able to consult a tutor.

TASKS AND THE NATURE OF ONLINE LEARNING

There are indications that a teacher's role in a collaborative online setting depends not only on the premise on which collaboration is established but also on the nature of the collaborative task. There are suggestions that a group of learners can only go so far on its own, and that at some point there will be a need for a teacher's intervention. It could then be a matter of judgment as to when that intervention should happen and what form it should take. To gain a better understanding of a teacher's online role, we can consider research that looks at the relationship between tasks and tutoring, and some of the claims made for the quality of online collaborative learning.

In his review of collaboration and task design in higher education, Rodriguez Illera (2001), from the University of Barcelona, Spain, focuses on exploring tasks that have genuinely interdependent components. He concludes that we should make use of the "many strategies of co-operative learning not mediated by computers" (Rodriguez Illera, 2001, p. 492) in rethinking ways of organizing online groups, the division of tasks and the role of the teacher. He describes the interdependence of university students who organize themselves into teams and produce a multimedia product. A complex activity of this kind requires negotiation of meanings among students, which can take place in an online environment. The author suggests that activities that involve interdependence among those who carry out various sub-tasks raise the question of whether there is such a thing as a "group zone of proximal development (ZPD)." A group ZPD might be thought of as "the gap between what the group can realize on its own in relation to a specific task and what it can learn through the help of a tutor from outside the group" (Rodriguez Illera, 2001, p. 491). In his opinion, "if the interdependent task is far from the group zone, the benefits of collaboration are zero" (Rodriguez Illera, 2001, p. 491).

Dillenbourg and Schneider (1995) have reviewed empirical work concerning conditions under which collaborative learning is efficient, and the mechanisms that have been proposed to explain the cognitive effects of collaboration. They stress that the findings apply to situations where individuals have to solve a problem together — i.e., they have a common goal and need to maintain agreement or understanding. The conditions for effective collaboration are examined under three headings: group composition, task features and communication media. It turns out that the conditions interact with each other, so the

Copyright © 2004, Idea Group Inc. Copying or distributing in print or electronic forms without written permission of Idea Group Inc. is prohibited.

picture is complex: "The distance tutor cannot set up conditions which guarantee efficient collaborative learning" (Dillenbourg & Schneider, 1995). According to the authors, the only way to achieve partial control of learning effects is monitoring interactions closely, and checking whether they offer a potential for at least some of the mechanisms that they have presented (for example, alternative proposal, self-explanation, etc.).

The effects of collaboration may vary according to the task. Dillenbourg and Schneider (1995) claim that some tasks are "inherently distributed," which means that group members work independently from each other, without sharing the process of reasoning. Other tasks are so straightforward that they do not leave any opportunity for conflict or disagreement, or they rely on processes that are not open to introspection. A task can be modified to make it more suitable for collaboration, e.g., by providing group members with partial data.

The nature and outcomes of online interactions have been examined at Queen's University Belfast, Ireland, by Newman, Johnson, Webb and Cochrane (1997), who evaluated CMC in a group learning context as a means of promoting deep learning and critical thinking. The researchers believe that critical thinking is a key skill that is required in deep learning. Their aim was to find out whether CMC could promote critical thinking in addition to "surface information transfer." Having compared face-to-face seminars with asynchronous computer conferencing in the same information management class, in general they found evidence for critical thinking in both situations. However the detail is important: According to the researchers, the seminars produced more spontaneous interaction, and stimulated more new ideas and greater participation. The computer conferencing, on the other hand, encouraged a "worthier," more considered style of interaction, with more important statements and linking of ideas (Newman et al., 1997).

In a similar vein, Armitt, Slack, Green and Beer (2002) make a case for deep learning in a pilot course that made use of synchronous communication for case studies in occupational therapy. Although in the research literature it is asynchronous communication that is more usually associated with deep, reflective learning, the authors claim that students who are used to working in groups, such as health care students undertaking problem-based learning, are used to taking advantage of opportunities for reflection in the process of interaction. Interestingly, they say their study confirms that students who have never met each other do not spontaneously collaborate in a peer group — instructors need to ensure at an early stage that learners understand their expectations regarding when and how to collaborate.

Depth or quality of learning may therefore depend on how online collaboration is managed. Setting expectations is an important skill of teaching, which may be magnified in online settings, and is particularly important in relation to group leadership. It is worth considering this skill in the context of other skills and abilities of the online tutor.

Copyright © 2004, Idea Group Inc. Copying or distributing in print or electronic forms without written permission of Idea Group Inc. is prohibited.

THE SKILL SET OF THE
ONLINE INSTRUCTOR

Alongside typical teaching tasks, such as looking for gaps in knowledge or understanding, asking questions, designating key actions and so on, teachers can use an array of skills and strategies that are more specific to the online medium. At the UK Open University, Salmon (1997) has summarized techniques for CMC, based on evidence from experienced CMC moderators. Examples include using e-mail until a conference is established; providing daily news flashes; setting up sub-conferences, if small interest groups emerge, archiving and threading. Instructors can also appoint students as moderators.

In her book published three years later, Salmon (2000) devotes a chapter to e-moderating qualities and roles. The desirable characteristics of online instructors are that they should be confident, constructive, developmental, facilitating, knowledge sharing and creative. These qualities can be apparent on several levels, for example, confidence can manifest itself in the way a teacher handles the online process, copes with technical issues, communicates online or shows content expertise. An online instructor also needs to be aware of a number of key issues that she or he will face: for example, deciding what is the right number of participants in an online conference, dealing with the confusion that some students may experience online, handling expectations in terms of teacher availability and time.

Cox, Clark, Heath and Plumpton (2000) have made the point that through conferencing, the technology to allow higher-level discussion between students is available, but the facilitation skills to encourage and stimulate such discussion are less well known. The authors considered the experience of more than 700 students who were part of the pilot presentation of the UK Open University course, T171: You, Your Computer and the Net. They say, "The role of the online tutor-facilitator is unique. In an environment where technological change is daily and understanding of student learning online is in its infancy, sometimes the expectations are paramount to herding cats through Piccadilly Circus" (Cox et al., 2000, p. 10). An online instructor should "be interactive," and should exhibit skills in weaving, summarizing, knowledge building and managing off topic contributions. The authors go on to give some recommendations for good practice in building online group processes. In particular, the online group should be developed "as a dynamic learning community," supported by activities that are intrinsically linked and build toward knowledge and concept learning. The authors also make a firm distinction between a facilitator and a moderator: "The main perception of moderator is control and power whereas the key perception of facilitator is fellow learner with a unique role to co-ordinate the interaction" (Cox et al., 2000, p. 14).

From a practical angle, Bailey and Luetkehans (2001) have distilled their experience into a set of guidelines for facilitating team activities in online training.

Copyright © 2004, Idea Group Inc. Copying or distributing in print or electronic forms without written permission of Idea Group Inc. is prohibited.

A first step is matching communication tools to specific training activities, which the authors classify under four categories: knowledge construction, skill development, problem solving, and motivation and attitude development. So for example, a threaded discussion tool might aid knowledge construction; hypertext could be used to develop skills such as creating Web resources; chat forums and whiteboards might be used for brainstorming; e-mail might be suitable for ice breakers or debriefing and so on.

Then, for each of the four categories of activity, the authors recommend a set of facilitation guidelines. As an example, to facilitate knowledge construction in a threaded discussion, a facilitator should provide scaffolding for the discussion, encourage learners to interact with one another and to build off each response, reward thoughtful contributions and summarize key concepts for reinforcement. What is particularly valuable in this approach is the systematic consideration of activity - tool - facilitator's actions. The authors also emphasize that the facilitator's focus should be on "removing obstacles to team learning" (Bailey & Luetkehans, 2001, p. 242), by intervening when conflicts arise, discouraging personal criticism and highlighting areas of common ground among team members.

Other researchers concur with the view that faculty members may know little about how to assist students online, and students may be ill-prepared for the new demands put on them. Schrum and Hong (2002) at the University of Georgia have sought to identify "dimensions of successful online learners" (e.g., technology experience, learning preferences, study habits and skills, etc.). Experienced online educators have been asked to review the dimensions and to provide strategies that they use to ensure student success. The resulting recommended online teaching strategies include: encouraging students to post an autobiography, frequent interaction with students, getting students to work collaboratively on their assignments and to benefit from feedback, establishing minimum levels of participation in a discussion and promoting "ongoing contributions to reciprocal knowledge building" (p. 65).

For those who need help in putting such recommended strategies into practice, online environments offer new opportunities for collaborative teaching that can help them develop as online instructors. Strohschen and Heaney (2001) from the Department of Adult and Continuing Education, National-Louis University, U.S., recount their experiences of team teaching online. Perhaps most important of all was the feeling that their collaboration gave them a certain freedom to try new methods, and to risk failure, as they could rely on the other person to help out. The authors adopted an "interactive team" approach, in which team members shared all responsibility and were present together in all online classes (other possible approaches are the "star team," where one teacher calls on other colleagues for specific topics, and the "planning team," where a collaborative plan is carried out by individual team members). They became "co-

Copyright © 2004, Idea Group Inc. Copying or distributing in print or electronic forms without written permission of Idea Group Inc. is prohibited.

discussants and co-learners" with their students and felt that they were modeling a new form of communication that involved the social construction of knowledge. Both teachers provided feedback to students on their writing. The differences in their evaluation of students' work shifted the emphasis from "seeking professorial approval and an acceptable grade" to understanding why the instructors had different opinions. Strohschen and Heaney (2001) conclude that situations like these create positive outcomes: "Students are encouraged to value their own contributions to discourse as they observe the varied perspectives and respectful disagreements among faculty. Over time this can result in a lessening of professorial authority, consistent with the practice of adult education."

STUDENT ROLES AND SELF-DIRECTED LEARNING

Having considered online instructors, we turn to learners in groups. The issues of online group collaboration and leadership benefit from being examined in relation to self-directed learning. We have to ask: Are learners prepared to learn by themselves, and to determine their own path of learning, perhaps helped along by other group members? Or are they dependent on their teacher? Deanie French has been interested in this issue for many years. "I began researching self-directed learning as the focus of my doctoral dissertation in the early 1970s," she writes. "At that time *self-directed learning* was contrasted with *teacher-directed learning*. My professors predicted that self-directed learning would be a reality in the '80s" (French, 1999, p. 12). She goes on to say that this has not happened. In her experience, the majority of students are reluctant to switch to new roles and to adopt new styles of learning. However, she also notes that we have reached a point where "both the teacher and learner are simultaneously 'guides' and 'sages,' as all of us become continual learners and peer teachers adapting rapidly to changing information" (French, 1999, p. 13). In order to facilitate the transition, French has taken to making definitions of self-directed learning explicit to her students at the beginning of a course of study. The students are asked to think about the skills of self-directed learning, for example: self-reward, tolerating ambiguity and helping peers learn (learning to value teaching others as an effective way of learning). French claims that students can change their manner of learning. "What's important is a desire to change," (1999, p. 18) she concludes, but adds that the mastery of specific skills can be very helpful.

Rourke and Anderson (2002) from the universities of Alberta and Athabasca, Canada, have tried to find out whether peer teams could fulfill all the "teaching presence" responsibilities of an effective online discussion leader. They inves-

Copyright © 2004, Idea Group Inc. Copying or distributing in print or electronic forms without written permission of Idea Group Inc. is prohibited.

tigated a graduate-level online course delivered asynchronously, in which groups of four students were used to lead online discussions. The research indicates that the peer teams fulfilled each of the three roles that the authors had identified as needing to be addressed, if online discussion were to be of value to students' learning. They were instructional design and organization; discourse facilitation and direct instruction. Crucially, the researchers report that "students preferred the peer teams to the instructor as discussion leaders" (p. 1). Students found discussions to be helpful in achieving higher order learning objectives but were of the opinion that they could have been more challenging and critical. As the authors point out, their findings have to be qualified by at least two considerations: the fact that in the study, peer teams did not discuss the same content as teams led by instructors; and the fact that the instructor continued to participate to some extent in discussions in which peer teams acted as leaders. Interestingly, they also add that as the peer teams worked in groups of four, they had "sufficient resources to fulfill all of the teaching presence responsibilities" (p. 17). This sharing of responsibilities could even be seen as an advantage over what an individual teacher is able to offer.

Collis and Meeuwsen (1999) at the University of Twente in The Netherlands advocate using the "jigsaw method" in which all students in a group have specific roles or responsibilities for specific tasks. In their online learning environment, which they claim has been used very successfully for a number of years, students work in groups with a structured schedule of tasks, and, much of the time, "students arrange their own work, and no instructor is present" (Collis & Meeuwsen, 1999, p. 37). Students are encouraged to ask one another for help, before turning to their instructor. Instructors set up, structure and monitor students' learning, but they do not have a highly visible role. This suggests that the instructors are directing learning, but in ways that students may not necessarily associate with the action of directing.

Researchers Veerman, Andriessen and Kanselaar (2000), also in The Netherlands, have focused on peer coaching between students of educational science. The students were learning through synchronous electronic discussion, using NetMeeting. In the project, "best students" were selected to become peer coaches, who would offer advice to other students in one of two ways: reflective (checking and linking arguments) and structural (considering opposite points of view). Overall, students in their study worked in three different conditions: reflective peer coaching, structure peer coaching and a control group with no coaching. The researchers state that the coaching instruction did not fulfill their expectations. Students seemed to need support to focus on meaning, rather than argumentation. Students also needed support to hold an overview, keep track of their discussion and to organize their interface.

Copyright © 2004, Idea Group Inc. Copying or distributing in print or electronic forms without written permission of Idea Group Inc. is prohibited.

EMERGENT LEADERSHIP
AND GROUP COMPOSITION

Self-directed learning is perhaps easiest to observe when students sponta-neously emerge as leaders from within the group. Yamaguchi, Bos and Olson (2002) at the University of Michigan have examined emergent leadership in small groups using CMC to play an online social dilemma game. They looked at groups working with different communication channels (face-to-face, videoconference, audio conference or Internet chat room) and analyzed how these communication channels affected emergent leadership styles. The researchers quote a number of sources supporting the claim that small groups are more effective when they experience emergent leadership, which can be either dominant (task-focused) or more democratic (relationship-focused). The most important finding of their own research is that narrower computer-mediated channels, such as text chat, seem to inhibit relationship-focused leadership. They go on to suggest that specific interventions could be used to help virtual teams develop relationship-focused self-management techniques, e.g., through team building exercises, by using richer channels such as videoconferencing, or simply by setting aside more time for socialization.

The above contrast between task leadership and relationship-focused leadership is a common way of defining leadership styles. Task leaders are generally concerned with completion of tasks, accomplishment of goals and group effectiveness. Relationship-focused, or socio-emotional, leaders are more supportive and concerned with group satisfaction, building trust and maintenance of high quality relationships. Most leaders tend to exhibit behaviors from both styles. In other words, they are combination leaders, but with a preference for one style over the other. Scholl (2003) summarizes this by stating that a combination leader "works to accomplish group goals by making you effective and recognizing your value. To improve the group's performance, she or he is likely to involve you in the improvement process and involve you in self-diagnosis of your own contribution."

Dominant versus social interaction styles are also the focus of an analysis offered by Oren, Mioduser, and Nachmias (2002). The researchers have summarized a series of studies carried out at Tel Aviv University's School of Education that examined the development of social climate in virtual discussion groups, including the role of the online teacher, with a view to drawing out practical implications. The authors recognize that teachers find it hard to change their dominant role to that of moderators and facilitators of learning. As a result, "students neither have enough opportunities to interact with each other, nor are they directed to develop self initiative and make active contributions to the collaborative learning process". The authors recommend that online tutors

Copyright © 2004, Idea Group Inc. Copying or distributing in print or electronic forms without written permission of Idea Group Inc. is prohibited.

should moderate the group's work in a way that enables student-to-student interactions. They should encourage a friendly and a relaxed atmosphere. Other recommendations relate to offering a legitimate platform for messages that have social, rather than solely content significance, and using supportive and peer feedback.

This basic distinction between orientations towards tasks and relationships is also applied to the analysis of online group interactions. As noted by Maloney-Krichmar and Preece (2002), who have studied an online health community, even informal groups need to achieve tasks (for example, information exchange) and to maintain relationships between members. The findings of Cho, Stefanone and Gay (2002) of Cornell University, who analyzed community-based activities in a computer-supported collaborative learning (CSCL) setting, show that social influences strongly affected the likelihood and the extent to which information was shared by peers in this learning community. In particular, the study analyzed how structural positions, e.g., central and peripheral actors, and relations emerged in a CSCL class, and how these structural properties mediated learners' perceptions and behaviors related to community-based information sharing. The results indicate that participants in a social network are more inclined to follow the lead of the network's central actors.

Online communities should be aware of the effects of vocal groups, however, and the pressures they can create for members that do not wish to conform. Palloff and Pratt (1999) have remarked that if this is happening in an online classroom, students who are uncomfortable may stop contributing, and even drop the course. The teacher then has to intervene, to make sure that quieter members have their say. Students with dissenting opinions may need special support.

Glazer (2002) at the University of Texas at Austin notes that early work on the emotional content of CMC used coding schemes that treated task-related and socio-emotional content as being separate. Today it is being acknowledged that cognition and emotion are inextricably linked; a person may convey task-related information and emotional content using the same words or symbols. Her research shows that students express individual emotions, emotions for the sake of peers and also maintain the balance among group members through the expression of gratitude, apology and praise.

The quality of collaborative learning may also depend partly on group composition. Yamaguchi et al. (2002) examined group gender composition as part of their research on emergent leadership in CMC. They found that in their experimental task, female-only groups had lower levels of leadership, and female-majority groups also had lower levels of relationship-focused leadership. The latter finding was unexpected. The authors speculate that this might have been due to a combination of the distancing media, which may inhibit the formation of strong group relationships, and the competitive task. They add that

Copyright © 2004, Idea Group Inc. Copying or distributing in print or electronic forms without written permission of Idea Group Inc. is prohibited.

it is also possible that the data on leadership strategies, which was self-reported, may reflect women's tendency to under-rate themselves in leadership.

Blum (1999) has investigated gender differences in asynchronous learning in higher education, in terms of learning styles, participation barriers and communication patterns. Asynchronous CMC-based distance education was examined to determine if the environment is equitable for male and female students. The research suggests that in the anonymized distance education institution that the author studied, males control the online environment, and there are clear gender differences in the tone, style and purpose of communication. In this research, females showed a preference for connected learning, by asking questions, asking for help and seemingly wanting to learn from other students. The author concludes that a learning environment is needed that "promotes and encourages collaborative learning for the female connected learner, but yet allows the male separate learner the freedom of learning in an abstract, autonomous manner. It also means that the professor in the CMC distance education environment must act as a facilitator who constantly looks for ways for the students to build a sense of community" (Blum, 1999, p. 58).

A sense of community may be partly achieved through the adoption and evolution of norms of communication and online behavior. Much has been written about rules of behavior and the affective side of being part of a group, which we turn to next.

NORMS OF BEHAVIOR IN GROUPS

Sullivan (2002) advises to think of Netiquette as "rules of good behavior adapted for electronic communications via e-mail, instant messaging, chat rooms and discussion forums" (p. 48). He claims that Netiquette has become a "universally understood behavioral standard that transcends cultures, businesses and geographical boundaries" (p. 48). In a similar vein, other authors offer advice on building interpersonal relationships through electronic networking. According to Crystal (2001), such guidance is subjective, expressing personal taste or institutional views.

Netiquette can also be considered at the level of rules adopted in a particular course, online community or group. As Underwood, Underwood and Wood (2000) have stated in a slightly different context (children working together on computer-based problem solving), if participants can "establish a group etiquette that allows for suggestions to be made and evaluated" (p. 461), then there is a chance that their task performance will be more effective. At the University of Saskatchewan, Canada, Porterfield (2001) puts an emphasis on the creation of the right atmosphere: "Learning communities, like terrestrial communities, call for guidelines to promote positive interactions among community members. Such guidelines may be in the form of a code of conduct explicitly stated within the

Copyright © 2004, Idea Group Inc. Copying or distributing in print or electronic forms without written permission of Idea Group Inc. is prohibited.

intent of the VLC (virtual learning community). The code of conduct will reflect the type of atmosphere or tone that the community wishes to create."

Hammond (2000), at the University of Warwick, United Kingdom, has reflected on communication within online forums used by small groups of learners. He makes the point that there is a steep threshold for learners to cross before they can establish online discussions. "They may more easily see the online forum as an environment for introductions and the occasional exchange of personal news, course information and essays rather than one that affords sustained communicative debate" (Hammond, 2000, p. 260). He notes that there are strategic learners with little desire to engage in theoretical discussion, while those who are academically inclined may become frustrated by chat or a lack of academic rigor and focus. Instructors therefore need to explain to students what they are being asked to do and why, and students need to be encouraged to "take the risk of going public on their learning" (Hammond, 2000, p. 260).

At the UK Open University, Kear (2001) has analyzed the conference messages of students on the undergraduate course Digital Communications in 2000, in which conferencing was optional. Kear (2001) looked carefully at affective aspects of the student interactions, and concludes: "one characteristic which stands out is the supportiveness that students show for each other" (p. 8). The specific ways in which students created a supportive and friendly community were: using the phrase "hope this helps" after an explanation; using deprecatory phrases, such as "sorry about spelling mistakes" at the end of messages and writing messages that emphasized that students were "all in the same boat" in relation to course-related problems. The author is unsure whether these practices were intentional or were "picked up subconsciously from the messages of other students and staff" (p. 9). In either case, she concludes, "there certainly seemed to be supportive 'norms' established within the community" (Kear, 2001, p. 9).

It seems that online communities and courses have to adopt some basic rules and attempt to strike a balance between formal and informal language. Informal conversations are regarded as an important aspect of group learning. "My students tend to use the chat room as one method for 'bonding' as a team. They laugh and share lighthearted information, as well as serious class-related information" (French et al., 1999, p. 66).

TOOLS AND MEDIA IN ONLINE COLLABORATION

Does the choice of communication media, or even specific tools, affect learning and group dynamics, and have an impact on the role of the instructor? Students often use synchronous media in a spontaneous way, without their teacher's involvement, as well as more structured ways.

Copyright © 2004, Idea Group Inc. Copying or distributing in print or electronic forms without written permission of Idea Group Inc. is prohibited.

One focus of investigation is on whether synchronous media facilitate student reflection. Armitt et al. (2002) from the universities of Liverpool and Sheffield Hallam, UK, have investigated synchronous collaboration in a 10-week online course, the Occupational Therapy Internet School (OTIS). The students in this course worked in groups to solve problems in patient case studies. Transcripts of communication sessions showed that in-depth discussions were taking place. The authors are convinced that students who are used to working on problem-solving tasks in groups, such as health care students, are capable of taking advantage of both synchronous and asynchronous media. Synchronous discussions allow "immediate clarification and development of thoughts" (Armitt et al., 2002, p. 157). However, they also point out that deep learning in synchronous groups does not happen spontaneously throughout the course. It is promoted by online discussion of the course content, and what is more, instructors have an important role to play in setting out expectations. Social interaction and bonding between students are equally important. Many in-depth online discussions among students were peer-to-peer in the absence of the tutor, at later stages in the course, which the authors attribute to the students becoming more autonomous as learners within their subject areas. The authors conclude that "a synchronous peer-to-peer element can be beneficial in promoting active reflection. We propose that the most cost-effective and educationally advantageous way to deploy synchronous communications is for peer-to-peer meetings later in the course, within courses primarily tutored asynchronously" (Armitt et al., 2002, p. 158).

Both synchronous and asynchronous means of communication have been examined by Curtis and Lawson (2001) at Flinders University of South Australia. The authors studied the communication patterns of mature education students undertaking collaborative online learning in a course entitled Internet and Education. Students used a Blackboard Classroom Web-based forum, but they were also able to contact each other by personal e-mail, fax, telephone and face to face. The researchers found that these additional media were used when a student disagreed with the contribution of another student. Rather than express disagreement publicly through the forum, critical comments were offered privately. In fact this approach had been advocated in guidelines issued to the students. Students also organized synchronous chat sessions. Those who contributed more online were likely to have been natural leaders within their groups. In one of the online groups, two forms of leadership were in evidence: one form was organizing group work and initiating activities, while the other was giving help and feedback.

Ng (2001) reports on a case study in which an e-mail system was used as a tool to foster collaboration among a group of students enrolled in an educational management course offered by the Open University of Hong Kong. The use of e-mail as a tool to foster collaboration was not very successful. Possible reasons

Copyright © 2004, Idea Group Inc. Copying or distributing in print or electronic forms without written permission of Idea Group Inc. is prohibited.

for its unsuccessful implementation were lack of provision of computer and online facilities and training to students; the fact that instructor's involvement in online activities was not a requirement and placing too much reliance on student initiative without integrating this mode of communication into their coursework.

E-mail puts teachers in more direct contact with learners than is the case in group conferencing environments. This may give online instructors the feeling that they are better able to influence processes and relationships through this communication medium. Woods and Keeler (2001) from Yellowstone Baptist College, Montana, and Regent University, Virginia, conducted a preliminary study into the effect of instructors' use of audio e-mail messages on student participation in and perceptions of online learning. The doctoral level students at Regent University were studying organizational leadership, using TopClass software for asynchronous discussion. Audio e-mail was used as a supplement to text-based interaction in their online course, and was chosen as a way of addressing the need for more meaningful student/faculty interactions, to combat feelings of isolation and dissatisfaction previously experienced by students. The short audio messages were sent to students at regular intervals. They paralleled or reinforced what was already communicated through textual messages, with a mixture of information and encouragement. The investigation did not confirm the researchers' assumptions that use of audio messages would result in greater and better quality of student participation in discussion, as well as more favorable perceptions and level of satisfaction. However, the research was only a preliminary study and the authors say that many factors could have influenced the outcome. Also, individual comments from students give some support to the idea that audio messages make students feel closer to their instructor and that some students appreciate them.

A key point that should not be lost in this discussion is that a commonly recognized mark of leadership is the ability to make rapid decisions about the best communication tools and media to suit specific circumstances or problems. If necessary, a leader will circumvent existing practices and find ways to overcome apparently insurmountable technical constraints to achieve whatever she or he set out to do. Students and teachers who assume leading roles may also be early adopters of new technologies and set an example of how to use both old and new technologies to best effect.

CONCLUSION

Online learning environments offer unprecedented opportunities to observe group dynamics and leadership behavior in unobtrusive ways. From lasting records of online dialogue, researchers know more about how teachers and learners operate, and can track some of the effects of what they say and do. The research reviewed in this chapter points to a multiplicity of roles available to

Copyright © 2004, Idea Group Inc. Copying or distributing in print or electronic forms without written permission of Idea Group Inc. is prohibited.

online teachers and learners, and to a wide range of skills that they should exercise and acquire.

A picture emerges of an online instructor who is principally a facilitator, with a strong sense of what it means to help learners develop dynamic communities in which they can experience the best kind of learning. There is an onus on the online instructor to develop a less tangible presence, allowing group members to emerge as leaders and to take on aspects of the teaching presence. However this should be backed up by a heightened awareness of the structure of tasks, mechanisms of collaboration and sensitivity to online group composition and dynamics, so that all participants are able to contribute. She or he must remove obstacles to collaboration and intervene when conflicts arise or when the most vocal students dominate. A teacher may also need to modify planned tasks in order to make them more suitable for collaboration, and to structure the learning environment.

In some reports, there is emphasis on interaction with students, but much of that interaction is concerned with setting up activities, setting expectations, providing overviews and monitoring the social and affective aspects of group dynamics. The online tutor is also cast as a fellow learner, but one who serves as a model of good ways of communicating, and who must surely be ahead of the game and able to lead others toward what they are supposed to know.

As there are usually more of them, students can share leadership roles and responsibilities with a teacher, or among members of a group. Student group leaders may well be found among successful online learners, those who are self-directed or have become autonomous in their learning. Students can be appointed as moderators and best students can be used to coach other students, but small groups may be more effective when they experience emergent leadership. There should be recognition that in any group, students have different goals, and some are strategic learners, while others are more academic.

As we have seen, student leadership can take the form of task-oriented initiating and organizing of activities, or relationship-focused help and feedback. Research has shown that alongside individual emotions, learners express emotions for the sake of peers and to maintain balance among group members. As preparation for these roles, informal bonding could be important. Just like instructors, students should acquire new skills in order to function well in online environments; for example, in collaborative activities, students need to become skilled in negotiation. One very useful leading role that students can play is to help group members extend their learning without relying on the instructor, but also to recognize when the group has gone as far as it can on its own, and needs input from the tutor.

When online activities are well designed and expectations have been set, students can have some good collaborative learning experiences without a teacher. However online collaborative groups still need leaders, and we already know a good deal about what qualities they should have.

Copyright © 2004, Idea Group Inc. Copying or distributing in print or electronic forms without written permission of Idea Group Inc. is prohibited.

REFERENCES

Armitt, G., Slack, F., Green, S., & Beer, M. (2002). The development of deep learning during a synchronous collaborative on-line course. In G. Stahl (Ed.), *Computer Support for Collaborative Learning: Foundations for a CSCL Community. Proceedings of CSCL 2002* (pp. 151-159). Hillsdale, NJ: Lawrence Erlbaum Associates.

Bailey, M., & Luetkehans, L. (2001). Practical guidelines for facilitating team activities in Web-based training. In B. Khan (Ed.), *Web-Based Training.* NJ: Educational Technology, pp. 235-244.

Blum, K. D. (1999). Gender differences in asynchronous learning in higher education: Learning styles, participation barriers and communication patterns. *Journal of Asynchronous Learning Networks, 3*(1), 46-66.

Cho, H., Stefanone, M., & Gay, G. (2002). Social information sharing in a CSCL community. In G. Stahl (Ed.), *Computer Support for Collaborative Learning: Foundations for a CSCL Community. Proceedings of CSCL 2002* (pp. 43-50). Hillsdale, NJ: Lawrence Erlbaum Associates.

Collis, B., & Meeuwsen, E. (1999). Learning to learn in a WWW-based environment. In D. French, C. Hale, C. Johnson, & G. Farr (Eds.), *Internet Based Learning: An Introduction and Framework for Higher Education and Business.* London: Kogan Page, pp. 25-46.

Cox, S., Clark W., Heath, H., & Plumpton, B. (2000). *Herding cats through Piccadilly Circus: The critical role of the tutor in the student's online conferencing experience.* Knowledge Network Internal Document KN257. Milton Keynes: The Open University. Available online at http://iet.open.ac.uk/pp/r.goodfellow/Lessons/cats/catsAUG00.htm.

Crystal, D. (2001). *Language and the Internet.* Cambridge, UK: Cambridge University Press.

Curtis, D. D., & Lawson, M. J. (2001). Exploring collaborative online learning. *Journal of Asynchronous Learning Networks, 5*(1), 21-34.

Dillenbourg, P., & Schneider, D. (1995). *Collaborative learning and the Internet.* Paper presented at the International Conference on Computer Assisted Instruction '95. Retrieved March 12, 2003, from the web site: http://tecfa.unige.ch/tecfa/research/CMC/colla/iccai95_1.html.

Field, R. H. G. (2002). *Leadership defined: Web images reveal the differences between leadership and management.* Submitted to the Administrative Sciences Association of Canada 2002 annual meeting in Winnipeg, Manitoba, January 9, 2002. Available online at: http://www.bus.ualberta.ca/rfield/papers/LeadershipDefined.htm.

French, D. (1999). Preparing for Internet-based learning. In D. French, C. Hale, C. Johnson, & G. Farr (Eds.), *Internet Based Learning: An Introduction and Framework for Higher Education and Business.* London: Kogan pp. 9-24.

Copyright © 2004, Idea Group Inc. Copying or distributing in print or electronic forms without written permission of Idea Group Inc. is prohibited.

Glazer, C. S. (2002). *Playing nice with others: The communication of emotion in an online classroom.* DEC 2002: 9th Annual International Distance Education Conference, Texas A&M University (January 22-25, 2002). Available online at: http://ww.cdlr.tamu.edu/dec_2002/Proceedings/Contents.pdf.

Gokhale, A. A. (1995). Collaborative learning enhances critical thinking. *Journal of Technology Education, 7*(1), 22-30. Retrieved March 12, 2003, from the web site: http://scholar.lib.vt.edu/ejournals/JTE/jte-v7n1/gokhale.jte-v7n1.html.

Hammond, M. (2000). Communication within on-line forums: The opportunities, the constraints and the value of a communicative approach. *Computers and Education, 35,* 251-262.

Kear, K. (2001). *Hope this helps: Peer learning via CMC.* Knowledge Network Internal Document KN876. Milton Keynes: The Open University. Available as a Telematics Technical Report at the Open University at: http://telematics.open.ac.uk/pub/reports/4.doc.

Laurillard, D. (2002). *Rethinking University Teaching: A Conversational Framework for the Effective Use of Learning Technologies* (2nd ed.). London: Routledge.

Maloney-Krichmar, D., & Preece, J. (2002). The meaning of an online health community in the lives of its members: Roles, relationships and group dynamics. *Social Implications of Information and Communication Technology. International Symposium on Technology and Society ISTAS'02* (pp. 20-27). Available online at: http://www.ifsm.umbc.edu/~preece/paper/17%20The%20meaning%20of%20an%20online%20health%20communityfinalv.pdf.

Newman, D. R., Johnson, C., Webb, B., & Cochrane, C. (1997, June). Evaluating the quality of learning in computer supported co-operative learning [Electronic version]. *Journal of the American Society for Information Science, 48*(6), 484-495.

Ng, K. C. (2001). Using e-mail to foster collaboration in distance education. *Open Learning, 16*(2), 191-200.

Oren, A., Mioduser, D., & Nachmias, R. (2002, April). The development of social climate in virtual learning discussion groups. *International Review of Research in Open and Distance Learning, 3*(1). Retrieved March 12, 2003, from the web site: http://www.irrodl.org/content/v3.1/mioduser.html.

Palloff, R. M., & Pratt, K. (1999). *Building Learning Communities in Cyberspace: Effective Strategies for the Online Classroom.* San Francisco, CA: Jossey-Bass Publishers.

Panitz, T. (1996). *A definition of collaborative versus cooperative learning.* Retrieved March 12, 2003, from the web site: http://www.lgu.ac.uk/deliberations/collab.learning/panitz2.html.

Copyright © 2004, Idea Group Inc. Copying or distributing in print or electronic forms without written permission of Idea Group Inc. is prohibited.

Porterfield, S. (2001). *Towards the development of successful virtual learning communities.* Retrieved March 12, 2003, from the web site: http://www.usask.ca/education/coursework/802papers/porterfield/porterfield.htm.

Rodriguez Illera, J. L. (2001). Collaborative environments and task design in the university. *Computers in Human Behaviour, 17,* 481-493.

Rourke, L., & Anderson, T. (2002). Using peer teams to lead online discussions. *Journal of Interactive Media in Education,* (1). Retrieved March 12, 2003, from the web site: http://www-jime.open.ac.uk/2002/1.

Salmon, G. (1997). *Techniques for CMC.* Knowledge Network Internal Document KN1244. Milton Keynes: The Open University. Available online at: http://www.atimod.com/presentations/ and also available at: http://www.atimod.com/presentations/download/cmctech.doc.

Salmon, G. (2000). *E-Moderating: The Key to Teaching and Learning Online.* London: Kogan Page.

Scholl, R. W. (2003). Leadership style: Class notes. Retrieved March 12, 2003, from the University of Rhode Island web site: http://www.cba.uri.edu/Scholl/Notes/Leadership_Approaches.html.

Schrum, L., & Hong, S. (2002). Dimensions and strategies for online success: Voices from experienced educators. *Journal of Asynchronous Learning Networks, 6*(1), 57-67.

Strohschen, G., & Heaney, T. (2001). *This isn't Kansas anymore, Toto: Team teaching online.* Retrieved March 12, 2003, from the web site: http://www2.nl.edu/facsenate/KansasFeb271.htm.

Sullivan, B. (2002, March). Netiquette. *Computerworld, 36*(10), 48.

Underwood, J., Underwood, G., & Wood, D. (2000). When does gender matter? Interactions during computer-based problem solving. *Learning and Instruction, 10,* 447-462.

Veerman, A. L., Andriessen J. E. B., & Kanselaar, G. (2000). Learning through synchronous electronic discussion. *Computers and Education, 34,* 269-290.

Woods, R., & Keeler, J. (2001). The effect of instructor's use of audio e-mail messages on student participation in and perceptions of online learning: A preliminary case study. *Open Learning, 16*(3), 263-278.

Yamaguchi, R., Bos, N., & Olson, J. (2002). Emergent leadership in small groups using computer-mediated communication. In G. Stahl (Ed.), *Computer Support for Collaborative Learning: Foundations for a CSCL Community. Proceedings of CSCL 2002* (pp. 138-143). Hillsdale, NJ: Lawrence Erlbaum Associates.

Copyright © 2004, Idea Group Inc. Copying or distributing in print or electronic forms without written permission of Idea Group Inc. is prohibited.

Chapter XIII

Drawing on Design to Improve Evaluation of Computer Supported Collaborative Learning: Two Complementary Views

John B. Nash
Stanford University, USA

Christoph Richter
University of Hannover, Germany

Heidrun Allert
University of Hannover, Germany

ABSTRACT

This chapter addresses theoretical frameworks for the evaluation of computer-supported learning environments. It outlines the characteristics and obstacles this evaluation must face with regard to projects that design learning experiences, stressing the notion that human-computer interaction is imbedded in social context that is complex and dynamic. The authors examine how scenario-based design and program theory can contribute to

Copyright © 2004, Idea Group Inc. Copying or distributing in print or electronic forms without written permission of Idea Group Inc. is prohibited.

the design and evaluation of computer-supported collaborative learning (CSCL) and present a case study in which both approaches are applied. Based on the revealed complementary frameworks, a compelling approach is drafted that combines both of them. Our goal is to make CSCL designers more aware of the benefits of evaluative thinking in their work and to introduce two tangible approaches to evaluation that, when implemented as a design step, can strengthen CSCL initiatives.

PROGRAM EVALUATION IN CONTEXT OF COMPUTER-SUPPORTED COLLABORATIVE LEARNING

This chapter addresses theoretical frameworks of evaluating computer-supported learning environments. We describe two approaches that facilitate the design for evaluation of computer-supported collaborative learning (CSCL) and then proffer ways in which the two approaches can be used together. Our perspectives on these matters are based, in part, on experiences as directors of evaluation in laboratories in the United States and Germany within the Wallenberg Global Learning Network (WGLN). Our collective experience includes work on technology and teaching reform in higher education, program evaluation theory, evaluation of CSCL and learning design.

It is increasingly common for the academic community at large (and grant-giving organizations, in particular) to call for some kind of program evaluation as an integral part of proposals for the development of computer-supported learning environments. Within this call, we see a growing need for formative evaluation approaches that address the specific requirements and characteristics of computer-supported learning environments (Keil-Slawik, 1999). Keil-Slawik (1999) points out that one of the main problems with evaluating computer-supported learning environments is that some goals and opportunities just arise in the course of the development process and cannot be specified in advance. Therefore an evaluation that aims to test if the specified goals were met is not helpful. We believe that this is due to the fact that design in this context addresses ill-structured and situated problems. Therefore it requires evolutionary and cyclic processes. As Weiss (1998) notes, "much evaluation is done by investigating outcomes without much attention to the paths by which they were produced" (p. 55). We argue that the evaluation processes in CSCL projects must draw out "the reality of the program rather than its illusion" (Weiss, 1998, p. 49).

For investigators designing and carrying out projects at the intersection of information and communication technology (ICT) and the learning sciences, evaluation is difficult. Evaluation efforts are often subverted by a myriad of

Copyright © 2004, Idea Group Inc. Copying or distributing in print or electronic forms without written permission of Idea Group Inc. is prohibited.

confounding variables, leading to a garbage in, garbage out effect; the evaluation cannot be better than the parameters that were built in the project from the start (Nash et al., 2001). Leaving key parameters of evaluative thinking out of CSCL projects is exacerbated by the fact that many investigators lack the tools and expertise necessary to cope with the complexity they face in addressing this field of learning.

According to Mertens (1998), evaluation is the systematic investigation of the merit or worth of an object (for our purposes, a CSCL project) for the purposes of reducing uncertainty in decision making. We stress that evaluation can facilitate decision making and reveal information that can be used to improve not only the project, but also outcomes within the project's target population.

In this chapter we point out how tenets of evaluation can efficiently facilitate design processes within CSCL projects. We focus on evaluation approaches, which support reflection and decision making within the design process. Project teams that prefer to adopt and use such utilization-focussed evaluation approaches will find that they can better support their own design process, rather than exclusively drawing on accountability models of evaluation that look only toward questions posed by funding stakeholders.

In the remainder of the chapter, we explain how evaluation contributes to design, and, in doing so, we outline two concrete evaluation approaches: scenario-based design and program-theory evaluation. In order to draw a more vivid picture, we present a case study in which both approaches are applied. After a brief comparison of these two approaches, we sketch ways in which the two approaches can be used in combination to form a compelling approach to improving design and evaluation of CSCL experiences.

EVALUATION CONTRIBUTING TO DESIGN

This section addresses the interrelation between evaluation and design. First we outline some general requirements for design and evaluation of CSCL experiences.

Imbeddedness in Social Contexts

It is crucial for the development of learning technologies and CSCL environments to consider the overall context in which software will be used and operated. This is the universe of discourse (Leite, Hadad, Doorn, & Kaplan, 2000). There is growing recognition that the development of new e-learning systems should be intertwined with the development or reorganization of the learning situation in which the new system is to be used (e.g., Janneck, 2002). Baumgartner (1997) states that pedagogical and educational evaluation must not be restricted to the software but also has to focus on the social situation where

Copyright © 2004, Idea Group Inc. Copying or distributing in print or electronic forms without written permission of Idea Group Inc. is prohibited.

the software will be used. Similarly Pfister and Wessner (2000) stress that CSCL systems should be analyzed from a pedagogical, technical, organizational and cultural perspective. Therefore, the primacy of the learning environment should reign over the technical artifact being created. However, reductionism often creeps into projects, focus on the development of a technical system. Sole reliance on the development of a technical system is not appropriate because, as Carroll (2000) notes, computers "unavoidably restructure human activities, creating new possibilities as well as new difficulties" (p. 46). By considering the universe of discourse, developers must think clearly about the educational outcomes enhanced by a computer-supported solution and not just the usability of the computer support.

Solving Situated Problems

Due to being imbedded in a social context, every computer-supported learning environment is confounded with complexity, dynamic changes and intransparency (c.f., Dörner, 1993). Therefore the design of computer-supported learning environments can be seen as a process of solving situated problems (e.g., Carroll, 2000; Jonassen, 1997). According to Carroll (2000), one must cope with the following six characteristics, which constitute the difficult properties of design:

- Incomplete description of the problem to be addressed;
- Lack of guidance on possible design moves;
- The design goal or solution state cannot be known in advance;
- Trade offs among many interdependent elements;
- Reliance on a diversity of knowledge and skills; and
- Wide-ranging and ongoing impacts on human activity.

In solving situated problems, it is not possible to plan the entire program in advance. Problems spaces are dynamic, which means that the problem space itself can change during the project life cycle (even without explicit intervention by the project). The availability of technical options can enable completely new and unforeseen ways of developing a system, and lead to new requirements. Furthermore, socio-cultural changes in the target setting might slow down or degrade support for the use of technical options. The evolutionary aspects of software have already been highlighted by Lehman (1980) who states: "we must be concerned with the fact that performance, capability, quality in general, cannot at present be designed and built into a program *ab initio*. Rather they are gradually achieved by evolutionary change and refinement" (p. 1061). According to Lehman (1980), software does not only solve given problems, but is as a part of the real world. It is a source of change itself.

Copyright © 2004, Idea Group Inc. Copying or distributing in print or electronic forms without written permission of Idea Group Inc. is prohibited.

The Role of Evaluation in Solving Situated Problems

Given the notion that computer-supported learning environments are meant to solve situated problems, the role of evaluation becomes ever more important, and CSCL designers must think beyond using only goal-oriented evaluation approaches, if they use any approach at all. The social environment surrounding CSCL development efforts involves different stakeholders, who have diverse, if not incompatible, opinions about the causes leading to the problem and useful strategies to deal with the problem.

In situated problems, evaluation should not be restricted to testing, if all specified goals were met. It also has to contribute to answering the following questions:

- What is the problem we want to address? Is there shared evidence that this problem really exists?
- What are the causes that led to this problem? What are the conditions that perpetuate the problem?
- Is our idea of solving the problem an appropriate one? Are there other imaginable ways to solve the problem?
- What will happen if we solve that problem? Which new problems might arise from solving the given one?

To address these questions evaluation also has to comprise context and input evaluation. Context and input evaluation (e.g., Stufflebeam, 2000) can be seen as decision-oriented evaluation.

Evaluation Supporting Project Management

How can a project team benefit from evaluation? Evaluation approaches must take into account the needs of multidisciplinary teams. In the design process, multidisciplinary teams require approaches that facilitate communication across disciplinary boundaries.

- Project teams need a shared understanding of how the project will work and what the program will look like in the end, in order to coordinate the efforts of all contributors. Therefore project members need approaches that allow communication of the ideas of all contributors, independent of individual backgrounds.
- Underlying assumptions held by the project team have to be discovered in order to rethink and revise them as necessary. The identification of assumptions becomes crucial especially if the consequences of decisions are far reaching or irrevocable.
- Project teams need methods that help to depict the intended outcome as well as the process to get there.

Copyright © 2004, Idea Group Inc. Copying or distributing in print or electronic forms without written permission of Idea Group Inc. is prohibited.

- Coping with the myriad of variables that interfere with computer-supported learning environments is one of the most challenging tasks within design and evaluation. On one hand it is important to disentangle the supposed interrelations within the universe of discourse. But, on the other hand, project teams need to have a holistic representation that reflects the irreducible complexity and dynamics within the universe of discourse.
- No single discipline or theory can explain such a complex phenomenon like a computer-supported learning environment sufficiently. Therefore the core working representations should not reflect a certain domain specific theory, but be the result of the contributions of all stakeholders.

The design of a computer-supported learning environment requires divergent as well as convergent strategies. Convergent strategies help to structure and coordinate a project, while divergent strategies help to reveal alternative solutions and divergent perspectives, as well as anticipate likely outcomes.

TWO DIFFERENT DESIGN AND EVALUATION APPROACHES

Here we begin our discussion of two approaches to evaluation that we believe are useful tools for CSCL designers. The perspectives discussed here are scenario-based design and program theory evaluation. We feel that both approaches draw explicitly on the notion that designers must develop a rationale for, and logical picture of, the change they hope to have happen as a result of people engaging their system. The evaluation approaches we describe borrow language from computer science, design engineering and quality literature. The approaches assume that the ultimate goal of a project should be at the center of the design and evaluation discussion, ensuring a project is not about only developing a usable tool or system, but is also about developing a useful tool or system that improves outcomes for the user.

Scenario-Based Design

Scenario-based approaches are widely used in the fields of software engineering, requirements engineering, human computer interaction and information systems (Rolland, Achour, Cauvet, Ralyté, Sutcliffe, Maiden, et al., 1996). Scenarios have also been used for purposes of strategic planning in fields such as business, economics and politics (e.g., Kahane, 2000).

Scenarios are a method to model the universe of discourse of an application, that is, the environment in which the system will be deployed (Breitman & Leite, 2001). A scenario can be an important resource for eliciting requirements for an application's design and evaluation. But the use of scenarios is not limited to

Copyright © 2004, Idea Group Inc. Copying or distributing in print or electronic forms without written permission of Idea Group Inc. is prohibited.

describing the artifact and its use. They are also useful to describe any system or interpersonal process that is situated in a complex environment (see Benner, Feather, Johnson, & Zorman, 1993).

For the purposes of this chapter, we refer to a scenario as a concrete story about use of an innovative tool, software, etc. (Carroll, 2000). Scenarios include protagonists with individual goals or objectives and reflect exemplary sequences of actions and events.

Rosson and Carroll (2002) list the following characteristic elements of user interaction scenarios:

- *Setting.* Situational details, that motivate or explain goals, actions, and reactions of the actor(s);
- *Actors.* Human(s) interacting with the computer or other setting elements; personal characteristics relevant to scenario;
- *Task goals.* Effects on the situation that motivate actions carried out by actor(s);
- *Plans.* Mental activity directed at converting a goal into a behavior;
- *Evaluation.* mental activity directed at interpreting features of the situation;
- *Behavior.* Observable behavior; and
- *Events.* External actions or reactions produced by the computer or other features of the setting; some of these may be hidden to the actor(s) but important to scenario.

The following scenario shows how some of these characteristic elements might interact in an imagined situation. While a scenario can contain all of the characteristics listed above, not all of them are expressed explicitly in the following example.

Tom is a computer science student at the University of Hannover, Germany. He is attending an introductory lecture about artificial intelligence. The lecturer asks the students to use a work space in order to share their homework. Tom has a first look at it that night. He explores some of the functionalities: one can upload documents and anyone participating in the course can annotate these documents and write comments. "Ugh," he thinks to himself, "that means fellow students, as well as the lecturer can write comments that are visible to all? Does that mean I have to share my mistakes and imperfect work?" He is displeased with the system because he felt the atmosphere in this course was quite competitive and not at all collaborative.

As the story about Tom demonstrates, scenarios focus on specific situations and only enlighten a few important aspects, rather than drawing a complete

Copyright © 2004, Idea Group Inc. Copying or distributing in print or electronic forms without written permission of Idea Group Inc. is prohibited.

picture of the universe of discourse (e.g., Benner et al., 1993). At the same time scenarios include characteristics that refer to different layers of socio-technical systems. This feature is of great importance when a team is involved in designing a computer-supported learning environment. A learning environment is inevitably embedded in a social system that is shaped by instructional ideas as well as organizational requirements. Therefore scenarios are not restricted to human-computer interaction but might include the whole range of social processes the learner is involved in. Figure 1 shows a diagram reflecting different layers that have an impact on socio-technical systems.

There are several ways to develop scenarios. Scenarios can be elicited via ethnographic field study, participatory design, re-use of prior analyses, scenario typologies, theory-based scenarios, technology-based scenarios, and brain-storming techniques (Carroll, 2000).

To date there is no systematic adaptation of the scenario-based approach to the field of design and evaluation of computer-supported learning environments. Below we begin to rectify this by showing the role of scenarios in the design and evaluation of computer-supported learning environments.

Scenarios Provide a Common Level of Communication Among the Different Stakeholders of the Project

Scenarios, in the form of narrative stories, are easy to produce and understand. Describing the universe of discourse at the level of concrete user activity allows every stakeholder to communicate her or his ideas about an educational environment, instructional ideas and technical constraints, without being an educationalist or a software engineer, relying on one's own theories and jargon.

It is crucial for any project team to model the universe of discourse and to get a common understanding of the "thing" that's being designed. Scenarios are

Figure 1: Layers of Socio-Technical Systems (Based on a Diagram by Koch, Reiterer, & Tjoa, 1991)

Culture / Subculture	Social Systems	
Clusters of Settings		
Settings		
Interactions		
Tools	Software-Applications	
User-Interface		
Middleware	Technical Infrastructure	
Hardware / OS		

Primary direction for design process

Copyright © 2004, Idea Group Inc. Copying or distributing in print or electronic forms without written permission of Idea Group Inc. is prohibited.

useful for designing and evaluating innovative learning environments that are supported by technology. As noted in the introduction, the description of context is crucial within the design of any socio-technical system such as learning environments.

According to Koch et al. (1991), the design of computer-supported systems, like the scenarios describing them, should start at the social and organizational level. Later, as a project progresses, scenarios should also address the technology that supports learning and teaching. Scenarios help to make assumptions explicit. In the scenario presented above, the competitive atmosphere may be changed and transformed to a more collaborative one. But it is also imaginable that the developers could change the technology by reducing the number of collaborative features or at least allow users to make comments in a private fashion.

Scenarios, in the Form of Narrative Stories, Can be Used to Describe Learning Situations on Every Level of Granularity

Granularity can range from describing the organizational setting of a course to specific computer-supported tasks a student might accomplish within a course. Scenarios provide examples of what could occur in a learning environment, rather than complete pictures of all aspects of the learning environment. Because of being selective, it is important to identify a set of diverse scenarios that highlight specific aspects of the learning situation. Existing scenarios can also be a starting point to find new scenarios. To obtain a more systematic impression of the universe of discourse, Bødker and Christiansen (1997) suggest the use of checklists with questions as a way to help clarify and complete the scenarios. For example, in their 14 item work-oriented checklist, one item deals with materials and outcomes. Items include a short definition and clarifying questions, such as (in the case of the materials and outcomes item) "What kinds of materials (documents, pictures, drawings, etc.) are involved in the production of which kinds of products?" (Bødker, Christiansen, & Thüring, 1995). The checklists enable the stakeholders "to find out relevant constrains and key-concerns" (Bødker et al., 1995, p.269).

The checklist of Bødker et al. (1995) is work oriented and technical; a checklist applicable for learning situations might be of great use and is yet to be developed in the field. Checklists that cover technical, educational and organizational aspects of proposed computer-supported learning environments would help to link the planned learning environment to its contextual setting.

Inevitably, scenarios have to be described at increasingly finer levels of granularity. Technical aspects at one end of the granularity scale relate to questions of the overall technical infrastructure. At the other end of the granularity scale, they relate to input-output devices. Organizational aspects at one end of the granularity scale relate to possible changes in a whole institution that might be activated by the introduction of new learning scenarios. At the other

Copyright © 2004, Idea Group Inc. Copying or distributing in print or electronic forms without written permission of Idea Group Inc. is prohibited.

end of the granularity scale, they relate to efforts to be accomplished by a single person in order to manage different tasks in which one is involved.

Scenarios Help to Identify and Make Explicit Underlying Assumptions of the Stakeholders

Stakeholder assumptions might include those related to instructional theories, the learner, the environmental context and its impact on learning or technical requirements. Underlying assumptions such as these are typically hidden from view of others but easily developed and held strong within individuals developing CSCL environments. Tacitly held, these assumptions can remain untested or, worse yet, plausible but unfounded. Underlying assumptions that underpin rationales in computer-supported learning environments can be drastically oversimplified by designers if the assumptions are not exposed in a scenario. It is easy to convince one's self to accept an underlying development assumption such as "if knowledge is organized systematically learning will be much easier." But without having considerable knowledge of the cognitive science and educational research literature, the process of developing a computer-supported learning environment to systematically organize knowledge could end up reflecting the presuppositions of a computer scientist or engineer striving for usability. Scenarios help reveal the thinking of designers so that others can participate in the design process.

Other common examples of assumptions we've seen in our work include:
- The learner has to be reinforced externally in order to motivate him or her;
- The learning context is of importance in the design process;
- Every learner has access to the Internet free of charge; and
- The use of meta-data facilitates searching and finding learning objects on the World Wide Web.

If these assumptions, hypothesis and expectations are not expressed explicitly nor defined operationally, they might influence the design process in an unpredictable way, or might provoke misunderstandings between the stakeholders.

Scenarios Can Also Be Used to Identify the Pros and Cons of a Certain Decision Within the Design Process

Many decisions are made during the design process of a computer-supported learning environment, some of which can be tested and revised. Other decisions once reached cannot be undone because of limited resources or other constraints. In these cases it is critical to discuss the possible implications of a specific choice in advance, especially as they relate to usability. These are questions related to prospective or anticipatory evaluation (c.f., Wottawa & Thierau, 1998).

Copyright © 2004, Idea Group Inc. Copying or distributing in print or electronic forms without written permission of Idea Group Inc. is prohibited.

A assuming that "the use of metadata facilitates search and find of learning objects on the World Wide Web" may lead to the decision that one should develop a system that annotates learning objects with meta-data. But it is also possible that meta-data distracts the students from other relevant material, which is not annotated. Only explicit decisions can be tested to see if they lead to the intended effect. Knowing the underlying assumptions of a certain decision helps to develop a hypothesis as to why the decision leads to the intended effect or not. For this purpose Carroll (2000) suggests employing "claim analysis." Claims are the positive or negative, desirable and undesirable consequences related to a certain characteristic of a scenario.

Scenarios Go Beyond a System Perspective and Observable Behavior

Scenarios as descriptions of concrete human activity help keep in mind the users for whom the educational setting is be designed. Without considering human needs and requirements, the design of software that is meant to support learning processes is often seen as only developing a system. In practice, questions like "How should we design the system architecture?" can easily dominate the discourse. According to Nygaard (1986), a designer who adopts such a perspective may interpret the universe of discourse as consisting of data flows, transactions, record, relations, objects, etc. As a consequence, he might be prone to ignoring the fact that human activity is part of complex social processes, and that a user is a self-organized subject, who steadily constructs and re-constructs his view on the world by communicating with other human beings and tries to accomplish personal goals. Similarly the concept of "use-cases" just focuses on the observable behavior occurring in the user system interaction, while cognitive processes, prior experience and organizational constrains stay implicit (c.p., Carroll, 2000). While the system perspective in general, and use-cases, in particular, are very important for the design of useful software artifacts, they are insufficient to describe educational settings and learning processes.

We now turn our discussion to the second perspective we wish to address, program theory evaluation.

Program Theory Evaluation

Program theory evaluation assumes that underlying any initiative or project is an explicit or latent theory (or theories) about how the initiative or project is meant to change outcomes (Granger, 1998). An evaluator should bring those theories to the surface and lay them out in as fine detail as possible, identifying all the assumptions and sub-assumptions built into the program (Weiss, 1995). This approach has been promoted as useful in evaluating CSCL projects (Strömdahl & Langerth-Zetterman, 2000; Nash, Plugge, & Eurlings, 2001), where investigators across disciplines find it appealing. For instance, for designers (in mechanical engineering or computer science) program theory

Copyright © 2004, Idea Group Inc. Copying or distributing in print or electronic forms without written permission of Idea Group Inc. is prohibited.

evaluation reminds them of their own use of the design rationale. Among the economists, program theory evaluation reminds them of total quality management (TQM). In the program theory approach (Weiss, 1995, 1998; Chen & Rossi, 1989), one constructs a project's theory of change or program logic by asking the various stakeholders: "What is the project designed to accomplish, and how are its components intended to get it there?" Also known as a theory-based evaluation strategy, the process helps the project stakeholders and the evaluation team to identify and come to consensus on the project's theory of change. By identifying and describing the activities, outcomes and goals of the program, along with their interrelationships, the stakeholders are then in position to identify quantifiable measures to portray the veracity of the model.

Theory-based evaluation identifies and tests the relationships between a project's inputs or activities and its outcomes via intermediate outcomes. The key advantages to using theory-based evaluation include (Connell & Kubisch, 1998; Weiss, 1995):

- It asks project practitioners to make their assumptions explicit and to reach consensus with their colleagues about what they are trying to do and why.
- It articulates a theory of change at the outset on which all stakeholders can agree, reducing problems associated with causal attribution of impact.
- It concentrates evaluation attention and resources on key aspects of the project.
- It facilitates aggregation of evaluation results into a broader context based of theoretical program knowledge.
- The theory of change model identified will facilitate the research design, measurement, data collection and analysis elements of the evaluation.

Program logic maps are used to develop and communicate program theory. The program logic map provides a graphical description of the initiative or project, the intended outputs and the intended outcomes as defined by the intervention's theory of change. Program logic maps show temporal sequences, building left to right and portraying relationships with arrows. Program logic mapping forces project teams to make an explicit statement about the relationship between project activities (inputs) and project goals (outputs). The map (and the mapping process itself) is then used to plan an evaluation, develop indicators, choose instrumentation and decide when indicators should be measured.

A program logic map is comprised of four basic shapes: clouds describing the project context, rectangles describing inputs, rounded rectangles showing intermediate goals and ellipses representing ultimate goals (Figure 2).

From a program logic map one can derive a succinct summary statement of the project's logical path. What follows is an example based upon the sample program logic map shown in Figure 3.

Copyright © 2004, Idea Group Inc. Copying or distributing in print or electronic forms without written permission of Idea Group Inc. is prohibited.

Figure 2:   Program Logic Map Shapes

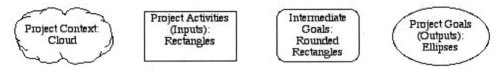

Given that it is difficult to engender a community of learners in geographically distributed courses using CSCL, a course offered to college students in geographically disparate sites, is theorized to operate as follows: a project-based community curriculum, coupled with curricular support will lead to increased engagement in the local community by students and increased collaboration among students across communities. Internet connectivity and technology support will lead to increased technology skills on the part of the student, thus increasing her or his ability to collaborate. Increased collaboration is theorized to lead to the creation of a learning community and, therefore, improved student outcomes.

Figure 3:   Sample Program Logic Map

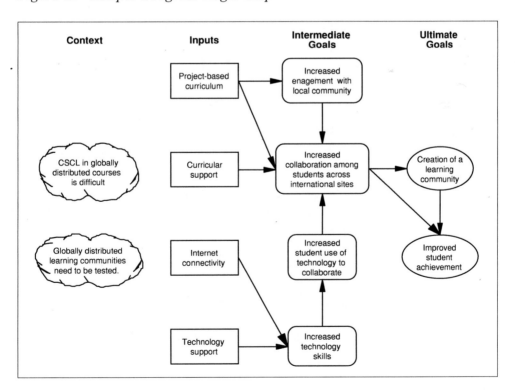

Copyright © 2004, Idea Group Inc. Copying or distributing in print or electronic forms without written permission of Idea Group Inc. is prohibited.

Developing the statement is merely a process of linking the elements of one's map in a way that makes sense to the reader. Developing a statement of the project's logical path provides a checking mechanism on the design of the initiative.

EXAMPLES OF SCENARIOS AND PROGRAM THEORY IN CONTEXT

To illustrate these approaches, we highlight their use via a case study of a CSCL project. The authors met with the project's investigator to develop the project's scenarios and program theory (the scenarios and program theory were developed in separate sessions). The mode of inquiry went as follows:

- Discussion with the investigator about his project, its design and ultimate goals;
- Development of either a scenario or program theory (depending on the session) with the investigator; and
- Collection of data on:
  - differences in how the project is perceived after having developed scenarios and a program theory;
  - questions that arise regarding project direction, goals and quality that were not evident prior to the process; and
  - matters related to the quality of operational definitions of key variables in the project, before and after the development of scenarios and program theory.

Case: The Modular Content Archives Project

Modular content archives (MoCA) project is a sub-project within the Personalized Access to Distributed Learning Repositories (PADLR) project at the University of Hannover in Germany. MoCA is a server and client-side tools project, focusing on modular learning environments and modular material collections, as well as tools for capturing video and audio and annotating the modular content using meta-data. Modular content refers to lecture slides, presentations, scientific graphics and texts, description of experiments, software, animations, simulations and so on.

In the MoCA project, software tools are under development that are designed to support intelligent and flexible archiving, management, allocation and distribution of modular content. The intended software tools will help to simplify the re-use of content for different purposes and audiences. The designers in this project needed to be aware of potential problems to create intelligent archiving and flexible and intuitive access to modularized content. For example:

Copyright © 2004, Idea Group Inc. Copying or distributing in print or electronic forms without written permission of Idea Group Inc. is prohibited.

- Content modules are often detached from context and are hard to find;
- Content modules can be of different file types; and
- There is a need for version lists (for more details, see Personalized Access to Distributed Learning Repositories (PADLR), 2001).

Act I: Using Scenarios in the Modular Content Archives Project

The two scenarios presented here were written in a very early phase of the project and are a sample of six scenarios. Of the six scenarios developed, three scenarios dealt with problems that occur in typical university teaching and learning situations without the presence of a content browser. Three other scenarios describe how the content browser can help to solve these problems (see Painter, 2002).

First Scenario: Responding to Students' Questions Without the Content Browser[1]

Professor Patao is the instructor of the course Digital Communications. He teaches students key issues of the design of digital communication systems, which involves a lot of math. Patao knows that some concepts are not easy to understand. To help students with the concepts, one of his assistants has developed some simulations that are installed on a PC dedicated for use in lectures and seminars. The students attending his lecture have heterogeneous backgrounds, coming from five different programs of study. Their prerequisite knowledge of signal and system theory, which is essential for understanding in this course, is very uneven. One day during a lecture, a student asks a question about material that is a prerequisite for this course. Patao imagines that, in order to answer that question with appropriate and instructive material, he would have to access his PC's hard drive for a simulation that will give an answer very quickly. But he does not have access to his PC in that right moment. He has to use the chalkboard to draw an outline. With the simulation, the student would have gained better understanding.

Second Scenario: Preparing for the Exam with the Content Browser

While preparing for an exam in Digital Communications, Eric remembers he has integrated the model to simulate the 64-QAM several weeks ago in his personal portfolio. He starts his computer and accesses his personal portfolio on the server. There he has organized all different kinds of material he obtained during this lecture. He immediately finds the simulation, since he organized everything properly using the supported meta-data. The search function allows him to tailor his search with only the meta-data

Copyright © 2004, Idea Group Inc. Copying or distributing in print or electronic forms without written permission of Idea Group Inc. is prohibited.

fields he needs at the time, for example, the Format field that is included in the Technical category of the Learning Object Metadata (LOM) standard. After the tool presents him a list of choices, he downloads a copy of the simulation model and opens it with its associated simulation application.

The purpose of writing scenarios at the proposal stage of the project is to describe the motivation and need for the project. This is but one possible range of use for scenarios. They can also be used by an investigator to guide design and evaluation.

Detecting Supplementary Scenarios

The first scenario refers to the course in Digital Communications, raising the question: "What are the unique and common aspects of this course?" The scenario includes additional hints that give a first impression of the characteristics of this lecture, for example: "To help students with the concepts, one of his assistants has developed some simulations that are installed on a PC dedicated for use in lectures and seminars." Can project stakeholders assume that for every class topic simulations or other electronic resources are available? Do similar problems also arise in seminars, discussion sections, practica, etc.?

The second scenario can also be used to detect additional scenarios. Scenarios that focus on the characteristics of preparing for exams might lead to a broader understanding of the situation addressed in the given scenario. On the other hand, the project team can also think about other student tasks, such as collaborative problem solving, and reflect on the special needs of such tasks and how they could be supported by the content browser. The detection of additional scenarios helps to prevent the project from focusing on special situations and neglect others also of potential importance.

Identifying Underlying Assumptions and Hypothesis

Assumptions about learning and teaching guide the design of both, technology as well as the context as a whole. One of the assumptions that can be identified in the second scenario is: "It is useful for students to have access to additional electronic resources while preparing for exams, and they will actually use them appropriately." On the one hand, it can be argued that the additional resources help to achieve a better understanding of the topic. On the other hand, by using information spaces, learners must integrate units of information into a coherent mental representation. This coherence formation process makes great demand on learners' cognitive and meta-cognitive skills. They must orient themselves and build up connections among single concepts, learning objects, units and courses. They have to relate important items of content. In navigation in non-linear data bases, learners suffer from conflicting and competing goal

Copyright © 2004, Idea Group Inc. Copying or distributing in print or electronic forms without written permission of Idea Group Inc. is prohibited.

intentions, as well as from cognitive overload, if the navigational task consumes too much of their resources. Students therefore may want to focus on some recommended basic literature.

An assumption that is made in the first scenario is "With the simulation, the student would have gained better understanding." This is an assumption made in contrast to the understanding gained by the student from an outline drawn on the chalkboard. By having project members discuss the pros and cons of both approaches, they are led to a deeper understanding of the situation and a better array of design solutions for the problem at hand. The identification of underlying assumptions and hypothesis helps to avoid bias. And, after all, only identified assumptions and hypothesis can be tested.

Identifying Pros and Cons of the Proposed Solution

Any proposed as well as implemented solution does not only entail advantages but also disadvantages. Referring to the given scenario, the use of electronic resources in the classroom can be helpful because information stored in the database is carefully elaborated. On the other hand, prefabricated information units might only roughly fit into the concrete learning situation and might fail to answer the given question. Chalkboard drawings are often not so well elaborated, but they can be adapted to the concrete situation more easily. On the basis of identifying pros and cons, the project team can decide if they only want to promote one alternative, or if they will look for a solution that combines the advantages of both approaches.

Requirements Elicitation

The second scenario addresses another important aspect: "The search functionality allows him to filter only specific meta-data fields, for example the Format field that is included in the Technical category of the Learning Object Metadata (LOM) standard." While both topics "managing electronic resources" and "meta-data" are explicitly mentioned in the technical report (Painter, 2002), the scenario focuses on the interrelation of both topics. As a consequence it appears to be relevant to work out a solution of how the students will get familiar with educational meta-data and can make adequate queries. While requirements derived from different sources are often presented in an unconnected manner, scenarios facilitate the reflection on the interrelation of different requirements.

Evaluation

The questions raised above might be seen as an integral part of project evaluation. Within this very early stage of the project, relevant aspects for evaluation are not yet identified. The stakeholders of the project might be interested in evaluating whether the content browser is used as it is hypothesized

Copyright © 2004, Idea Group Inc. Copying or distributing in print or electronic forms without written permission of Idea Group Inc. is prohibited.

in the scenarios. A further elaboration of the scenarios might also help to identify what variables could mediate the use of the content browser. Scenarios can be a starting point for formative as well as summative evaluations.

Reflecting on the Problems Addressed by the Project

While an additional scenario points out how the problem described in the first scenario can be solved by the use of the content browser, the scenario can also be a starting point to reflect on the projects genuine objectives. This can be done by asking if there are alternative ways to cope with the identified problem: Are there alternative solutions to dealing with students of heterogeneous backgrounds and questions that are beyond the scope of the actual course? This might help to prevent the so-called "garbage in, garbage out" situation.

General Issues the Use of Scenarios Reveals

The scenarios were written in a very early project stage. Therefore the set of scenarios as shown above is not complete, and additional scenarios might lead to further insights. Also a more detailed analysis of the scenarios would be helpful. While we recognize these shortcomings, several important things became obvious during this process.

First, even a small set of scenarios forces project staff into a mode of thinking about where developing additional scenarios is needed. Second, scenarios reveal, often in stark detail, underlying assumptions and hidden hypotheses held by the investigator or project staff. Third, by placing hypothetical users in a scenario with the computer support tools to be developed, pros and cons of the proposed solution can be discussed and possible effects can be evaluated. Fourth, previously unknown feature requirements can be revealed as scenarios are developed. Fifth, evaluation plans begin to take shape as early scenarios are "played out," and the expectations of the designers are made explicit.

Act II: Using Program Theory in the Modular Content Archives Project

A program theory is presented below for the Modular Content Archives project. Based on the map in Figure 4, the following theory of change was developed for the modular content archives project:

Given that:
- Instructors do not use electronic media in lectures;
- There is no good way for colleagues to develop instructional material together;
- Good animations and simulations can enhance the understanding students have about material;
- It's hard to share content;

Copyright © 2004, Idea Group Inc. Copying or distributing in print or electronic forms without written permission of Idea Group Inc. is prohibited.

- There's lots of interesting content being created;
- Students do not have access to "new" content;
- Time with students is limited for faculty;
- Time with faculty is limited for students; and
- It's hard to get access to the newest content for teaching (few professional distributions)

we believe that developing software that functions as a repository for modular content will influence:
- The creation of content archives;
- Instructors accessing more content;
- The exchange of content data over Edutella;
- The creation of individual repositories; and
- 24-hour access to material and content

which will influence the attainment of:
- Greater time efficiency;
- Enhanced traditional lectures;
- Increased opportunity to learn; and
- Storage of content for later use.

How the Map was Developed

This initial program theory represented by the program logic map was elicited over the course of approximately one hour from the project's leader. A facilitator (one of the authors) stood between the project leader and a white board. As the project leader and facilitator talked, the facilitator began to diagram the project's theory of change in the form of a program logic map. In the beginning of the process, the facilitator attempts to "surround" the project by first eliciting the presumed ultimate goals of the project on the right side of the white board, with the project needs on the left. This leaves a large white space in the middle of the board. In a third phase of the discussion, this blank area is filled in with the intermediate goals that link the activities to the ultimate goal of the project.

Stating an Ultimate Goal

Weiss (1998) notes that a useful way to begin conceptualizing a program is by looking at what it is trying to accomplish, starting with its official goals. While official goals only represent one view, they are a sensible starting place. In the case of the MoCA program logic session, the facilitator asked the project leader to state what he believed the ultimate goal of the project was.

Copyright © 2004, Idea Group Inc. Copying or distributing in print or electronic forms without written permission of Idea Group Inc. is prohibited.

Figure 4: Program Logic Map for the Modular Content Archives Project

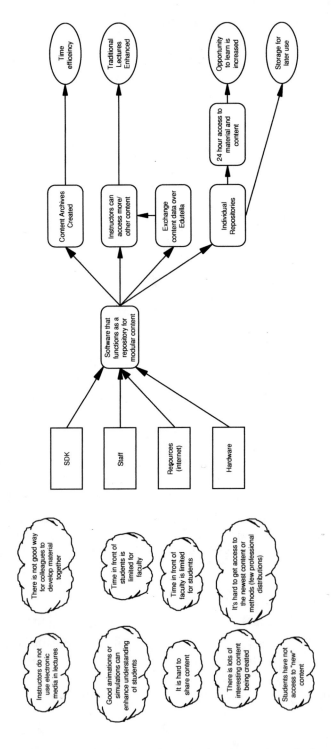

Copyright © 2004, Idea Group Inc. Copying or distributing in print or electronic forms without written permission of Idea Group Inc. is prohibited.

The project leader indicated that the "ultimate goal of the project is to develop software that facilitates the exchange and access of data." The project leader is very clear, in his mind, about the solution as a physical manifestation (software). At this early stage of the development of the logic map, the facilitator writes "Software" in an ellipse on the far right of the white board. As one can see from Figure 3, the ultimate goal in the final version of the map (represented by ellipses) is not a physical, tangible artifact (such as software), but rather a pedagogically related goal.

Defining Need

Working only with the knowledge given so far about the project (that the goal of the project is to develop software), the project leader is asked why this initiative is needed and to define the problems bringing about the need. Essentially the facilitator asked: "You've decided to provide resources for the creation of this key bit of software that doesn't exist today. Why? What are the problems you've identified that suggest you should develop this software?"

Initially the project leader found it difficult to provide an answer. In many applied development projects, the project members tacitly hold the reasons or needs for the project; they may be deemed too obvious to mention. Therefore, citing them concisely can often be a challenge for project designers. This was the case here. But after some silent thought a conversation ensued and a large list of needs emerged. This list of needs is represented on the left of the map in the cloud formations and is referred to as the contextual cloud.

Tackling the Middle of the Map

The project leader is asked to list the activities (referred to as "inputs") needed in the project to reach the ultimate goal. In this case, the answer was easy for the project member. He essentially responded, "It's software development! We will need things like a software development kit, programming staff, you know, the usual stuff."

At this point in the process, project members in the room may have begun to wonder what was so revealing about this entire exercise. After all, on the board before them is a diagram suggesting, "If one hires software developers, you get software." But something deeper is revealed at this point: after 20 minutes of discussion about a project, the most that is known is that if you hire software developers, you get software. "Is that just it, then?" asks the facilitator provocatively. "Your software's not supposed to result in something good happening for students or learners? Is your software supposed to have some kind of intended effect?"

Suddenly a great deal of tacit thinking is revealed. "Oh, yes. Of course," the project developer says. "We expect it to lead to greater time efficiency;

Copyright © 2004, Idea Group Inc. Copying or distributing in print or electronic forms without written permission of Idea Group Inc. is prohibited.

enhancement of traditional lectures; increased opportunity to learn for students and provide storage of content for later use."

A basic gap in the project's theory of change is now revealed; and the facilitator redraws the map, now looking very different from before. The ellipse "Software" is changed to a rounded rectangle to reflect its new status as an intermediate goal, and the right side of the board is populated with the new ultimate goals. We refer to this as the "ultimate goal shift," and in developing a project's program theory, this happens quite often. In an ultimate goal shift, the goal of ultimate interest is most likely to be revealed.

CSCL designers need to keep in mind that the ultimate goal of an initiative goes beyond the delivery of a fully functioning technical system. Designers need to determine the ultimate goal of interest for the CSCL system. In determining such, Mohr (1995) argues that the ultimate goal of interest should be the goal that is "inherently valued." The idea here is that the educational relevance of a CSCL project will be enhanced if the outcome of interest is inherently valued. How does a project team know if they have inherently valued ultimate goals? Inherently valued ultimate goals are those in which there is an interest for its own sake rather than for the sake of achieving something further. For instance, according to Mohr (1995), outcome Y is said to be inherently valued as follows:

- If Y is attained, the attainment of outcomes to the right is immaterial — one does not particularly care to learn whether they occurred or even what they are.
- If Y is attained, one is willing to assume that the specified outcomes further to the right will also be attained at a satisfactory level.

While the development of an innovative technical solution might be a challenging task, it is only one step on the way to create a computer-supported learning environment.

With this method evaluators, system designers, managers and clients via discussion select their own outcome. Furthermore, when the two above conditions are met, support for the project among stakeholders is significantly strengthened.

In any given project situation, solutions to perceived needs are generally articulated via the disciplinary lens of the respective stakeholders. The first thing a person usually starts to talk about is the implementation of well-known solutions within their field or discipline. Media people jump to media solutions. Technicians and computer scientists jump to software development. There's nothing bad about this. The key is to ask one's self if the solution proffered is the outcome of ultimate interest for the target users. Sometimes "new" ultimate goals are not new at all, but rather goals that were deemed "not this project's problem."

Copyright © 2004, Idea Group Inc. Copying or distributing in print or electronic forms without written permission of Idea Group Inc. is prohibited.

General Issues the Theory of Change Reveals

While there are areas where the articulation of the MoCA project can be improved through refined iterations of a program theory approach, several important things are revealed by this initial pass. First, instances where the principal investigator is very clearly set on creating a physical artifact as the solution to the problem are revealed. In this case, the physical artifact is a piece of software. The mere creation, and therefore empirical existence, of the software constituted a solution early on in the minds of the project participants. Second, an initial ultimate goal may not be the real (or even relevant) ultimate goal. Third, it may be revealed that the rationale for many attractive sounding projects eludes even the lead project members. Often the answers regarding "rationale for the project" are unclear. We find the reason for this is because the rationales are assumed or tacit. Fourth, it may also be revealed that a project is believed to solve many more problems that it actually can.

New Questions About the Project Revealed by Program Theory

The resultant "ultimate goal shift" in the program theory articulation paints a picture of the project that uncovers new questions that heretofore were not considered:

1. How will one know the ultimate goals, as mapped, when one sees them? What compelling evidence will exist to prove "time efficiency" has been created, that "traditional lectures" have really been enhanced, that "opportunity to learn" really increased and that "storage for later" has been defined in such a way that it can be measured?
2. How strong are the connections between the activities in the project and the ultimate goals?
3. Do the ultimate goals really represent a solution to the problems defined as the impetus of the project?

As a result of developing a program logic map and defining the project's program theory for the MoCA project, the following information, previously unknown to the MoCA investigator, was discovered:

*   The principle investigator was very clearly set on the creation of a physical artifact (the software) and less on the influence that artifact would have on the learning situation.
*   Creating a physical artifact (the software) was not the ultimate goal of the project, as previously believed. The creation of the software was an intermediate.
*   The evidence for detecting the attainment of the ultimate goals was unspecified. Operational definitions of what the software would enhance were often tacit or outright missing.

Copyright © 2004, Idea Group Inc. Copying or distributing in print or electronic forms without written permission of Idea Group Inc. is prohibited.

- It is possible that, in the initial formulation of the project, the goals that computer support is likely to influence do not necessarily represent solutions that meet defined need for the project.

Limitations Related to the Application of Both Methods in this Case

In spite of the rich information revealed in this case, the program logic of this project would be strengthened by having other stakeholders (a) in the room providing input at the time the first map was developed, or (b) providing their own theory of change separately and merging it with theories of change from other stakeholders. Theories of change developed with one project member are just the view of how a project works in the mind of one person. Adding other stakeholders' theories ensures the project is designed to meet the needs of all those involved.

This also holds for the use of scenarios. Having other stakeholders reading and providing feedback on the scenarios would strengthen the set of scenarios. Until the scenarios are discussed in a larger group, they lack evidence for their validity. To work effectively as tools, program theory, as well as scenario-based design, rely on the different perspectives provided by the stakeholder.

A necessary next step in the program logic approach not discussed in the context of the case above is a requirements review. In a requirements review, the facilitator and project team would determine what the requirements are for defining and completing all the tasks suggested by the program logic map. Initiating a requirements review is a good strategy to keep stakeholders from having a false sense of goal alignment. By engaging in a requirements review of the elements of the program logic map, project teams ensure there are no hidden assumptions about the elements of the initiative. Project planners should ask themselves, for every element (rectangle, rounded rectangle and ellipse): "What is the plan for this input or activity?" The more specific the answers to this question, the stronger the linkages become between the elements in the map.

COMPARING AND INTEGRATING THE APPROACHES

After having described scenario-based design and program theory and depicted the application in a concrete project, we now briefly compare both approaches, and sketch ways in which the two approaches can be used in combination to form a compelling approach to improving design and evaluation of CSCL experiences.

Copyright © 2004, Idea Group Inc. Copying or distributing in print or electronic forms without written permission of Idea Group Inc. is prohibited.

Comparison of Scenario-Based Design and Program Theory

Both scenario-based design and program theory stress the importance of the social context while planning computer-supported environments. They also represent means to facilitate the communication among the stakeholders and urge the project team to reflect their underlying assumptions in order to discuss and test them. Furthermore both approaches are particularly suitable for multidisciplinary project teams. Scenarios and program logic maps are not static artifacts; they are starting point for discussion and have to be changed when necessary.

Beside these similarities, there are systematic differences between both approaches. The major difference between them is that program theory offers a goal oriented way to structure a project, while scenario-based design proffers an explorative approach that opens the mind to the complexity of the problem, alternatives and the diversity of theories that try to explain social and socio-technical process. That is scenario-based design highlights the divergent aspects of project planning, and evaluation program theory stresses the convergent aspects.

Scenarios provide a vivid description of the socio-technical system. They try to reflect the complexity of reality and contribute to a holistic picture. A broad range of variables affects the interactions within a socio-technical system and has to be taken into consideration while analyzing the scenarios. By drawing on examples, instead of addressing every imaginable situation, scenarios can be used as springboard to think about different situations and alternative approaches. In contrast, program theory concentrates attention and resources on key aspects of the project (Weiss, 1998). Program theory tries to identify the variables that are seen to be the most influential for the success of the project. The project logic map provides a framework of the hypothetical interrelations of the variables and elements.

Scenarios constitute no theoretical explanations why the depicted interactions take place. In fact, as a representation of assumed or observed interactions within a socio-technical system, they can be analyzed or interpreted according to diverse scientific theories. Even a scenario written from the point of view of a specific theory can be examined in the light of another theory. For example, a scenario that describes problem-based learning for ill structured problems might be interpreted from the perspective of theories used in software ergonomics or sociology. Thereby scenarios live up to the fact that rarely a single theory is able to explain all processes within a socio-technical system.

Program theory, on the other hand, represents the assumptions about how the planned program will reach the goals set out by the stakeholders. Ideally it reflects the shared understanding of how the most influential aspects of the

Copyright © 2004, Idea Group Inc. Copying or distributing in print or electronic forms without written permission of Idea Group Inc. is prohibited.

program interact. This shared understanding is an important guide in coordinating the efforts of the project team. A program theory nevertheless can be grounded in multiple theories and is more of a meta-model for the project.

Figure 5 summarizes the differences between scenario-based design and program theory.

Using Both Approaches

The differences between scenario-based design and program theory reveal that these approaches represent complementary views on the design and evaluation of computer-supported learning environments. Design covers planned as well as evolutionary aspects. Therefore, it is important that the project team uses methods that support divergent thinking, and methods that support convergent processes.

Program theory helps to integrate each scenario, decision and predefinition into the whole process. Scenarios force users not just to use terms but give meaningful descriptions. They force users to state how they actually want to instantiate an abstract theory of learning and teaching. This helps to implement the project within real situations of use, which are complex and ill structured. Program theory helps to focus on core aspects of design, so that stakeholders don't get lost in the scenarios.

Figure 5:   Differences Between Scenario-Based Design and Program Theory

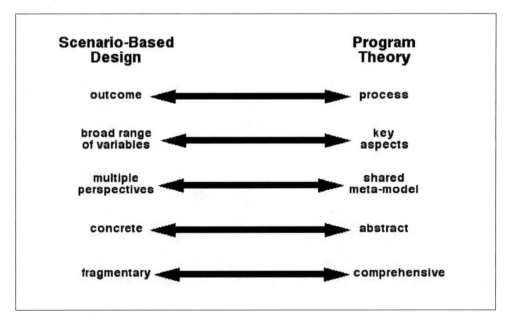

Copyright © 2004, Idea Group Inc. Copying or distributing in print or electronic forms without written permission of Idea Group Inc. is prohibited.

Scenarios and project logic maps can be used in an alternating way. Thereby it's possible to use both approaches and improve the overall development process.

The project logic map can be a starting point for writing scenarios. Especially the interrelations between the goals and ultimate goal; and inputs can be described with a scenario. The scenario shows how this interrelation works and how it will look like in a concrete situation.

Scenarios, on the other hand, can be used to create program logic maps by pointing out the main elements of the intended program. They can also be used to complete already existing program logic maps, by presenting alternative situations.

For CSCL researchers and developers, scenario-based design and program theory represent complementary approaches that when used together or separately can add strength to the implementation and success of CSCL projects.

CONCLUSION

This chapter addressed theoretical frameworks of the evaluation of learning technologies. We examined scenario-based design and program theory in the design and evaluation of CSCL, and then suggested ways in which the two approaches could be used to form a compelling approach to improving design and evaluation of CSCL experiences. In sum, scenario-based design and program theory hold many similarities. The major difference is that program theory offers a goal oriented way to structure a project, while scenario-based design provides an explorative approach that opens the mind to the complexity of the problem, alternatives and the diversity of theories that try to explain the social and socio-technical process.

Scenario-based design highlights the divergent aspects of project planning, and evaluation program theory stresses the convergent aspects. For CSCL researchers and developers, scenario-based design and program theory represent complementary approaches that when used together or separately can add strength to the implementation and success of CSCL projects.

ACKNOWLEDGMENTS

The authors wish to acknowledge Mark Painter of Technische Universität Braunschweig for agreeing to offer his project, MoCA, as a case study for this chapter.

Copyright © 2004, Idea Group Inc. Copying or distributing in print or electronic forms without written permission of Idea Group Inc. is prohibited.

REFERENCES

Baumgarnter, P. (1997). Didaktische Anforderungen an (multimediale) Lernsoftware. In L. J. Issing & P. Klimsa (Hrsg.), *Information und Lernen mit Multimedia* (2nd ed.), pp.240-252, Weinheim, Germany: PVU.

Benner, K. M., Feather, M. S., Johnson, W. L., & Zorman, L. A. (1993). Utilizing scenarios in the software development process. In N. Prakash, C. Rolland & B. Pernici (Eds.), *Information System Development Process, Proceedings of the IFIP WG8.1 Working Conference on Information System Development Process, Como, Italy, September 1-3, 1993.* (IFIP Transactions A-30) (pp. 117-134). Amsterdam, North-Holland: Elsevier Science Publishers B.V.

Bødker, S., & Christiansen, E. (1997). Scenarios as springboards in design. In G. Bowker, L. Gaser, S. L. Star, & W. Turner (Eds.), *Social Science Research, Technical Systems and Cooperative Work* (pp. 217-234). Mahwah, NJ: Erlbaum.

Bødker, S., Christiansen, E., & Thüring, M. (1995). A conceptual toolbox for designing CSCW applications. *COOP '95, Proceedings of the First International Workshop on the Design of Cooperative Systems, Juan-les-Pins, France,* January, pp. 266-284. Rocquencourt, France: INRIA Press.

Breitman, K., & Leite, J. (2001, August). *Requirements elicitation through scenarios – a hands-on tutorial.* Retrieved on December 12, 2002 from the Fifth IEEE International Symposium on Requirements Engineering web site: http://www.re01.org/program.html#Tutorials.

Carroll, J. M. (2000). *Making Use: Scenario-Based Design of Human-Computer Interactions.* Cambridge, MA: MIT Press.

Chen, H. T., & Rossi, P. (1989). Issues in the theory-driven perspective. *Evaluation and Program Planning, 12,* 299-306.

Connell, J. P., & Kubisch, A. (1998). Applying a theory of change approach to the evaluation of comprehensive community initiatives: Progress, prospects, and problems. In K. Fulbright-Anderson, A. Kubisch & J. Connell (Eds.), *New Approaches to Evaluating Community Initiatives, Vol. 2: Theory, Measurement, and Analysis.* Washington, DC: Aspen Institute, http://www.apseninstitute.org/Programt3.asp?bid=1278.

Dörner, D. (1993). *Die Logik des Mißlingens: Strategisches Denken in komplexen Situationen.* Reinbek, Germany: Rowohlt.

Granger, R. (1998). Establishing causality in evaluations of comprehensive community initiatives. In K. Fullbright-Anderson, A. Kubisch, & J. Connell (Eds.), *New Approaches to Evaluating Community Initiatives, Vol. 2: Theory, Measurement, and Analysis.* Washington, D.C.: Aspen Institute, http://www.aspeninstitute.org/Programt3.asp?bid=1286.

Copyright © 2004, Idea Group Inc. Copying or distributing in print or electronic forms without written permission of Idea Group Inc. is prohibited.

Janneck, M. (2002). *Der Szenarienansatz in WISSPRO*. Retrieved on February 26, 2002 from the web site: http://mind.wisspro.de/materialdateien/szenarien-in-wisspro.pdf.

Jonassen, D. H. (1997). Instructional design models for well-structured and ill-structured problem-solving learning outcomes. *Educational Technology: Research and Development, 45*(1), S65-95.

Kahane, A. (2000, July). How to change the world: Lessons from entrepreneurs from activists. Global Business Network Publications. Retrieved July 18, 2003 from http://www.gbn.org/GBNDocumentDisplayServlet.srv%3Fid%3D12754.

Keil-Slawik, R. (1999). Evaluation als evolutionäre Systemgestaltung. Aufbau und Weiterentwicklung der Paderborner DISCO (Digitale Infrastruktur für computerunterstütztes kooperatives Lernen). In M. Kindt (Ed.), *Projektevaluation in der Lehre – Multimedia an Hochschulen zeigt Profil(e)*, pp.11-36. Münster, Germany: Waxmann.

Koch, M., Reiterer, H., & Tjoa, A. M. (1991). *Software-Ergonomie: Gestaltung von EDV-Systemen; Kriterien, Methoden und Werkzeuge*. Wien, Austria: Springer.

Lehman, M. M. (1980). Program, life cycles, and laws of software evolution. *Proceedings of the IEEE, 68*(9), 1060-1076.

Leite, J. C. S. P., Hadad, G. D. S., Doorn, J. H., & Kaplan, G. N. (2000). A scenario construction process. *Requirements Engineering, 5*, 38-61.

Mertens, D. (1998). *Research Methods in Education and Psychology: Integrating Diversity with Quantitative and Qualitative Approaches*. Thousand Oaks, CA: Sage Publications.

Mohr, L. (1995). *Impact Analysis for Program Evaluation*. Thousand Oaks, CA: Sage Publications.

Nash, J. B., Plugge, L., & Eurlings, A. (2001). Defining and evaluating CSCL evaluations. In A. Eurlings & P. Dillenbourg (Eds.), *Proceedings of the European Conference on Computer-Supported Collaborative Learning* (pp. 120-128). Maastricht, The Netherlands: Universiteit Maastricht.

Nygaard, K. (1986). Program development as a social activity. *Information Processing, 86*. In H.-J. Kugler (Ed.), *Proceedings from the IFIP 10th World Computer Congress, Dublin, Ireland, September 1-5*, pp. 189-198. Amsterdam, North-Holland: Elsevier Science Publishers B.V.

Painter, M. (2002). *PADLR submodule: Modular Content Archives, first technical report*. Retrieved on June 27, 2002 from the web site: http://padlr.kbs.uni-hannover.de/bscw/bscw.cgi/d7164/.

Personalized Access to Distributed Learning Repositories (PADLR). (2001). *Personalized Access to Distributed Learning Repositories – PADLR – final proposal*. Retrieved on January 9, 2002 from the web site: http://projekte.learninglab.uni-hannover.de/bscw/bscw.cgi/d710/.

Copyright © 2004, Idea Group Inc. Copying or distributing in print or electronic forms without written permission of Idea Group Inc. is prohibited.

Pfister, H.-R., & Wessner, M. (2000). Evaluation von CSCL-Umgebungen. In H. Krahn & J. Wedekind (Eds.), *Virtueller Campus '99. Heute Experiment – morgen Alltag? Medien in der Wissenschaft* (pp. 139-149). Münster, Germany: Waxmann.

Rolland, C., Achour, C. B., Cauvet, C., Ralyté, J., Sutcliffe, A., Maiden, N. A. M., et al. (1996). *A proposal for a scenario classification framework* (CREWS Rep. No. 96-01). Retrieved on June 5, 2002 from ftp://sunsite.informatik.rwth-aachen.de/pub/CREWS/CREWS-96-01.pdf.

Rosson, M. B., & Carroll, J. M. (2002). *Usability Engineering: Scenario-Based Development of Human-Computer Interaction.* San Francisco, CA: Morgan Kaufmann.

Strömdahl, H., & Langerth-Zetterman, M. (2000). *On theory-anchored evaluation research of educational settings especially those supported by information and communication technologies (ICT)* (Submitted to Evaluation and Program Planning). Uppsala, Sweden: Swedish Learning Lab.

Stufflebeam, D. L. (2000). The CIPP model for evaluation. In D. L. Stufflebeam, G. F. Madaus, & T. Kellaghan (Eds.), *Evaluation Models: Viewpoints on Educational and Human Services Evaluation* (2nd ed., pp. 279-318). Boston, MA: Kluwer.

Weiss, C. (1995). Nothing as practical as good theory: Exploring theory-based evaluation for comprehensive community initiatives for children and families. In J. Connell et al. (Eds.), *New Approaches to Evaluating Community Initiatives: Concepts, Methods, and Contexts.* Washington, DC: Aspen Institute.

Weiss, C. (1998). *Evaluation Research: Methods for Studying Programs and Policies.* Englewood Cliffs, NJ: Prentice-Hall.

Wottawa, H., & Thierau, H. (1998). *Lehrbuch Evaluation* (2nd ed.). Bern, Switzerland: Huber.

ENDNOTES

[1]   The titles were not part of the original scenarios. We also made minor changes to the form of the scenarios.

Copyright © 2004, Idea Group Inc. Copying or distributing in print or electronic forms without written permission of Idea Group Inc. is prohibited.

About the Authors

Tim S. Roberts is a senior lecturer with the Faculty of Informatics and Communication at the Bundaberg campus of Central Queensland University, Australia. He teaches a variety of computer science subjects, including Programming A, which he teaches to more than 1,000 students located throughout Australia and overseas — many of them studying entirely online. In 2001, together with Lissa McNamee and Sallyanne Williams, he developed the Online Collaborative Learning in Higher Education web site at http://musgrave.cqu.edu.au/clp. He was awarded the Bundaberg City Council's prize for excellence in research in 2001, and won the Dean's Award for Quality Research in 2002.

* * * *

Heidrun Allert is a research assistant at the Learning Lab Lower Saxony at the University of Hannover in Hannover, Germany. Her research interests are in computer support for collaborative learning and educational metadata. She has a background in communication science and media education. Currently she is working on a doctorate in computer science at the University of Hannover.

Sue Bennett is a lecturer in the Faculty of Education at the University of Wollongong, Australia. She is an active member of the Centre for Research in Interactive Learning Environments. Bennett's interest in use of online technolo-

Copyright © 2004, Idea Group Inc. Copying or distributing in print or electronic forms without written permission of Idea Group Inc. is prohibited.

gies to support collaboration stems from her research into authentic learning environments and her experiences as a tertiary teacher of on-campus and distance-learning students.

Curtis J. Bonk is professor of educational psychology as well as instructional systems technology at Indiana University (IU), USA. He is a core member of the Center for Research on Learning and Technology at IU and a senior research fellow with the Army Research Institute. Bonk received the Burton Gorman Teaching Award in 1999, the Wilbert Hites Mentoring Award in 2000, the CyberStar Award from the Indiana Information Technology Association in 2002, and the Most Outstanding Achievement by an Individual in Higher Education Award from the U.S. Distance Learning Association, as well as a State of Indiana Award for Innovative Teaching in a Distance Education Program in 2003. He has published widely on e-learning and is in demand as a conference keynote speaker. He is president and founder of CourseShare and SurveyShare.

John M. Dirkx is associate professor of higher, adult and lifelong education and co-director of the Michigan Center for Career and Technical Education at Michigan State University, USA. He received his doctorate in continuing and vocational education in 1987 from the University of Wisconsin - Madison. Most of his work has focused on the education, training and professional development of persons who work with adult learners in various settings. He is the author of *A Guide to Planning and Implementing Instruction for Adults: A Theme-Based Approach*, published in 1997 by Jossey-Bass. He has also published numerous articles and book chapters on group dynamics, the psychosocial aspects of teaching and learning, workplace learning and the ways in which teachers and learners make sense of their experiences in adult and postsecondary education contexts.

Charles R. Graham is an assistant professor of instructional psychology and technology at Brigham Young University, Utah (USA), with a focus on distance teaching and learning. He earned his doctorate in instructional systems technology at Indiana University, where he worked for the Center for Research on Learning and Technology. He also has a master's degree in electrical and computer engineering from the University of Illinois, where he helped to develop an asynchronous learning environment used in many undergraduate engineering courses. Graham's current research interests include the study of online collaborative learning environments and computer-mediated learning teams.

Kai Hakkarainen, who has a doctorate, is working as research fellow of the Academy of Finland. Currently he is the director of the Centre for Research on Networked Learning and Knowledge Building (www.helsinki.fi/science/

Copyright © 2004, Idea Group Inc. Copying or distributing in print or electronic forms without written permission of Idea Group Inc. is prohibited.

networkedlearning) in the Department of Psychology, University of Helsinki, Finland. He investigates socio-cognitive aspects and theoretical foundations of computer-supported collaborative learning and working; and he has produced a number of articles about the topic. His research interests focus on dynamic theories of learning and inquiry that help to explain the knowledge-creation processes. He is particularly interested in empirically and theoretically analyzing complex reciprocal relations between individual, socially distributed and cultural-historical cognitions. Together with his colleagues, Hakkarainen has also organized several national and European level research projects about computer-supported collaborative inquiry learning.

Lesley G. Hathorn graduated with a master's degree in instructional technology from Kent State University, Ohio (USA), in 2000. Her master's thesis was "Collaboration and Cooperation in Online Communication." She is currently pursuing a doctorate in cognitive psychology, studying spoken language and reading. Her research uses an eyetracker to measure precise reading patterns. She is also studying situation models and the spatial distance effect. Her goal is to bridge the theory of cognitive psychology with its practical application to education. She has published papers in several educational journals.

Annette Hillers is a researcher in the Department of Instructional Psychology at the University of Heidelberg, Germany. She is just finishing her diploma and working on her thesis in clinical psychology. Her areas of interest are research methodology and psychotherapy.

Albert L. Ingram is associate professor of instructional technology at Kent State University, Ohio, USA. He received his doctorate in educational technology from Arizona State University in 1984. He has designed and developed instructional systems for a variety of organizations, including the Digital Equipment Corp., the Army Research Institute, The American College and the Software Engineering Institute. He has taught at Governors State University and directed state-wide instructional technology efforts at the University of Medicine and Dentistry of New Jersey. He is the author of papers in a variety of journals, as well as the co-author of two books in the field.

Agnes Kukulska-Hulme is a senior lecturer in educational technology at the United Kingdom Open University. She is academic chair of an online master's level course, Applications of Information Technology in Open and Distance Education, and a member of the team that won a Teaching Fellowship Award in 2001 for innovation and excellence in global online course delivery. She is also the author of a book on language and communication concepts for user interface design, and has written numerous papers and articles on aspects of online

Copyright © 2004, Idea Group Inc. Copying or distributing in print or electronic forms without written permission of Idea Group Inc. is prohibited.

teaching and learning, focusing on the design and evaluation of e-learning systems and learning resources.

Minna Lakkala has a background in psychology and computer science. She has extensive teachers' training experience in the educational use of ICTs. Her main research interest at present is teachers' pedagogical expertise in relation to collaborative inquiry learning. Lakkala has participated in large research projects concerning the use of ICT at schools. Further, she has been responsible for coordinating progressive inquiry courses for teachers and has investigated tutors' practices of guiding students in the context of networked learning. A consultant and educator since the 1980s, she has participated in the development of educational ICT and ICT-related user training. She has a master's degree and is currently pursuing her doctorate at the Department of Psychology in University of Helsinki, Finland.

Ji-Yeon Lee is assistant professor in Department of Educational Psychology and currently teaches graduate courses for the newly created Educational Technology Program, a joint master's degree program between Columbia and Aiken campuses of The University of South Carolina (USA). She joined the university in August of 2002, after receiving her doctorate in instructional systems technology at Indiana University, Bloomington. Her research interests revolve around the instructional use of Web-based technology (i.e., design and development of pedagogically sound and accessible Web-based instruction), faculty/learner support in distance learning environments and heuristic task analysis (HTA). She is a member of the Association for Educational Communications and Technology (AECT) and the American Educational Research Association (AERA).

Joanne M. McInnerney has two Bachelor of Arts degrees, the first in communication from Central Queensland University, Australia, and the second in anthropology from Curtin University of Technology, Australia. She is currently working as a research assistant at Central Queensland University, helping to maintain the Online Collaborative Learning in Higher Education web site at http://musgrave.cqu.edu.au/clp, and has a strong interest in how people can communicate effectively online.

Melanie Misanchuk is a doctoral candidate in instructional systems technology at Indiana University, USA. Her research interests include online learning communities, collaborative learning, distance learning tools, and distributed and hybrid education in general.

Copyright © 2004, Idea Group Inc. Copying or distributing in print or electronic forms without written permission of Idea Group Inc. is prohibited.

Hanni Muukkonen, who has a master's degree, is a researcher in psychology, completing her thesis in a doctoral program at the Department of Psychology, University of Helsinki (Finland), on the socio-cognitive effects of computer-mediated inquiry in higher education. Her interests include the development of academic literacy, meta-cognitive skills and processes involved in creating knowledge. The foci of her research include the roles of collaboration, multi-professional teamwork and the use of artifacts and tools. Her current interest lies in understanding the demands and competencies emerging in innovative knowledge-work, and whether and how these changes should be reflected in higher education.

John B. Nash is social research scientist at Stanford University, USA, director of the International Office of Evaluation for the Wallenberg Global Learning Network and associate director of evaluation at the Stanford Center for Innovations in Learning. He has a background in educational administration, educational research and program evaluation. His research interests are in the areas of evaluation of complex initiatives and the role of technology in education reform.

Rod Nason is a senior lecturer based in the Centre for Mathematics, Science and Technology Education at the Queensland University of Technology in Brisbane, Australia. His research interests are in the fields of mathematics education and computer-mediated education, and how these two fields of study can be utilized to improve the quality of student learning and teacher education. Since 1995, he has conducted collaborative research in the field of computer-supported collaborative education with Professor Earl Woodruff at the University of Toronto, Canada, and with Professor Richard Lesh at Purdue University, Indianna.

Peter Reimann is professor of educational psychology at the University of Sydney, Australia, specializing in instructional psychology, i.e., the psychology of learning and teaching. He holds a doctorate in psychology form the University of Freiburg, Germany. His primary research areas are learning and educational psychology, with a focus on new educational technologies, multimedia-based and knowledge-based learning environments and the development of evaluation and assessment methods for the effectiveness of computer-based technologies, both on the individual and the organizational level.

Christoph Richter is a research assistant at the Learning Lab Lower Saxony at the University of Hannover in Hannover, Germany. His research interests are scenario-based design, as well as prospective and formative evaluation. He has a background in psychology. Currently he is working on a doctorate in computer science at the University of Hannover.

Copyright © 2004, Idea Group Inc. Copying or distributing in print or electronic forms without written permission of Idea Group Inc. is prohibited.

Regina O. Smith is a doctoral candidate in higher, adult and lifelong education at Michigan State University, USA. Her dissertation is "The Struggle for Voice: Student Experiences in Collaborative Online Groups." She will become an assistant professor of postsecondary, adult and continuing education at Portland State University, USA. Smith has a master's degree in instructional design/ educational technology from Michigan State University, Oregon, as well as a masters' degree in Christian education. During her doctoral program, she presented a number of papers, which are published in conference proceedings on various aspects of online learning.

Elsebeth Korsgaard Sorensen, who has a doctorate, is associate professor in ICT and learning at the Institute of Communication, Aalborg University, Denmark. She is one of the designers behind a Web-based MS in ICT and learning. Sorensen is engaged in national and international research activities within design, delivery and evaluation of net-based learning. Her research centers on computer-supported collaborative learning and distance education, focusing on pedagogical aspects of establishment, reflection and evaluation of collaborative knowledge building. Currently, she is focusing on two themes: (1) qualification of online dialogue (she recently received a Best Paper Award for an international research paper on this issue), and (2) implementation of electronic portfolios as reflective tools.

Lesley Treleaven is a senior lecturer in the School of Management, University of Western Sydney (UWS), Australia, where she leads the Information Systems Knowledge Management Research Group. She received her doctorate from the University of Technology, Sydney. In teaching large numbers of undergraduates, she established a learning partnership with professionals across UWS to develop and facilitate Web-enhanced collaborative learning that supported experiential workshops. This collaborative action research created design and delivery developments commended in the 2002 UWS Vice Chancellor's Teaching Excellence Awards. Treleaven's other research interests are in managerialism, knowledge-based approaches to organizational change and application of Foucauldian perspectives on power relations in organizations.

Robert A. Wisher is the director of the advanced distributed learning initiative within the U.S. Department of Defense. Wisher has more than 20 years of experience as a research psychologist, examining the training effectiveness of emerging distributed learning technologies. He received a bachelor's degree in mathematics from Purdue University and a doctoral degree in cognitive psychology from the University of California, San Diego. He has published more than 90 technical reports, book chapters and journal articles related to training

Copyright © 2004, Idea Group Inc. Copying or distributing in print or electronic forms without written permission of Idea Group Inc. is prohibited.

technologies and the learning sciences. In 1999, he received the Most Outstanding Achievement Award by an Individual from the U.S. Distance Learning Association.

Earl Woodruff is an associate professor at OISE-University of Toronto, Canada. He has been involved in the production of cognitively based educational software for the last two decades. Woodruff has been at the forefront of research into computer-supported collaborative learning. He is regarded as being one of the most influential theory builders within this field. With Marlene Scardamalia and Carl Bereiter, he was a major conceptualizer and developer of CSILE, the predecessor of Knowledge Forum. Since then, he has pioneered the use of computer-supported collaborative learning in areas such as math education, teacher education, science education, nursing education and ESL education.

Joerg Zumbach is lecturer in the Department of Instructional Psychology at the University of Heidelberg, Germany. He holds a diploma in psychology from Heidelberg University. His current research focuses on teaching and learning with computers and computer networks, as well as collaborative learning with and without technology, especially analyzing problem-based learning. Most of his book and paper publications are in the fields of cognitive and instructional psychology, examining learning processes in technology-based situated learning environments.

Copyright © 2004, Idea Group Inc. Copying or distributing in print or electronic forms without written permission of Idea Group Inc. is prohibited.

Index

Copyright © 2004, Idea Group Inc. Copying or distributing in print or electronic forms without written permission of Idea Group Inc. is prohibited.

Copyright © 2004, Idea Group Inc. Copying or distributing in print or electronic forms without written permission of Idea Group Inc. is prohibited.

Copyright © 2004, Idea Group Inc. Copying or distributing in print or electronic forms without written permission of Idea Group Inc. is prohibited.

V

W

Copyright © 2004, Idea Group Inc. Copying or distributing in print or electronic forms without written permission of Idea Group Inc. is prohibited.

NEW Titles
from Information Science Publishing

- **Instructional Design in the Real World: A View from the Trenches**
  Anne-Marie Armstrong
  ISBN: 1-59140-150-X: eISBN 1-59140-151-8, © 2004
- **Personal Web Usage in the Workplace: A Guide to Effective Human Resources Management**
  Murugan Anandarajan & Claire Simmers
  ISBN: 1-59140-148-8; eISBN 1-59140-149-6, © 2004
- **Social, Ethical and Policy Implications of Information Technology**
  Linda L. Brennan & Victoria Johnson
  ISBN: 1-59140-168-2; eISBN 1-59140-169-0, © 2004
- **Readings in Virtual Research Ethics: Issues and Controversies**
  Elizabeth A. Buchanan
  ISBN: 1-59140-152-6; eISBN 1-59140-153-4, © 2004
- **E-ffective Writing for e-Learning Environments**
  Katy Campbell
  ISBN: 1-59140-124-0; eISBN 1-59140-125-9, © 2004
- **Development and Management of Virtual Schools: Issues and Trends**
  Catherine Cavanaugh
  ISBN: 1-59140-154-2; eISBN 1-59140-155-0, © 2004
- **The Distance Education Evolution: Issues and Case Studies**
  Dominique Monolescu, Catherine Schifter & Linda Greenwood
  ISBN: 1-59140-120-8; eISBN 1-59140-121-6, © 2004
- **Distance Learning and University Effectiveness: Changing Educational Paradigms for Online Learning**
  Caroline Howard, Karen Schenk & Richard Discenza
  ISBN: 1-59140-178-X; eISBN 1-59140-179-8, © 2004
- **Managing Psychological Factors in Information Systems Work: An Orientation to Emotional Intelligence**
  Eugene Kaluzniacky
  ISBN: 1-59140-198-4; eISBN 1-59140-199-2, © 2004
- **Developing an Online Curriculum: Technologies and Techniques**
  Lynnette R. Porter
  ISBN: 1-59140-136-4; eISBN 1-59140-137-2, © 2004
- **Online Collaborative Learning: Theory and Practice**
  Tim S. Roberts
  ISBN: 1-59140-174-7; eISBN 1-59140-175-5, © 2004

Excellent additions to your institution's library! Recommend these titles to your librarian!

To receive a copy of the Idea Group Inc. catalog, please contact 1/717-533-8845, fax 1/717-533-8661, or visit the IGI Online Bookstore at: http://www.idea-group.com!

Note: All IGI books are also available as ebooks on netlibrary.com as well as other ebook sources. Contact Ms. Carrie Skovrinskie at <cskovrinskie@idea-group.com> to receive a complete list of sources where you can obtain ebook information or IGP titles.

InfoSci-Online
Database

30-Day free trial!

www.infosci-online.com

Provide instant access to the latest offerings of Idea Group Inc. publications in the fields of INFORMATION SCIENCE, TECHNOLOGY and MANAGEMENT

During the past decade, with the advent of telecommunications and the availability of distance learning opportunities, more college and university libraries can now provide access to comprehensive collections of research literature through access to online databases.

The InfoSci-Online database is the most comprehensive collection of *full-text* literature regarding research, trends, technologies, and challenges in the fields of information science, technology and management. This online database consists of over 3000 book chapters, 200+ journal articles, 200+ case studies and over 1,000+ conference proceedings papers from IGI's three imprints (Idea Group Publishing, Information Science Publishing and IRM Press) that can be accessed by users of this database through identifying areas of research interest and keywords.

Contents & Latest Additions:
Unlike the delay that readers face when waiting for the release of print publications, users will find this online database updated as soon as the material becomes available for distribution, providing instant access to the latest literature and research findings published by Idea Group Inc. in the field of information science and technology, in which emerging technologies and innovations are constantly taking place, and where time is of the essence.

The content within this database will be updated by IGI with 1300 new book chapters, 250+ journal articles and case studies and 250+ conference proceedings papers per year, all related to aspects of information, science, technology and management, published by Idea Group Inc. The updates will occur as soon as the material becomes available, even before the publications are sent to print.

InfoSci-Online pricing flexibility allows this database to be an excellent addition to your library, regardless of the size of your institution.

Contact: Ms. Carrie Skovrinskie, InfoSci-Online Project Coordinator, 717-533-8845 (Ext. 14), cskovrinskie@idea-group.com for a 30-day trial subscription to InfoSci-Online.

A product of:

INFORMATION SCIENCE PUBLISHING*
Enhancing Knowledge Through Information Science
http://www.info-sci-pub.com

an imprint of Idea Group Inc.

Just Released!

Designing Instruction for Technology-Enhanced Learning

Patricia Rogers
Bemidji State University, USA

When faced with the challenge of designing instruction for technology-enhanced education, many good teachers find great difficulty in connecting pedagogy with technology. While following instructional design practices can help, most teachers are either unfamiliar with the field or are unable to translate the formal design process for use in their own classroom. *Designing Instruction for Technology Enhanced Learning* is focused on the practical application of instructional design practices for teachers at all levels, and is intended to help the reader "walk through" designing instruction for e-learning.

The goal of *Designing Instruction for Technology Enhanced Learning* is to pool the expertise of many practitioners and instructional designers and to present that information in such a way that teachers will have useful and relevant references and guidance for using technology to enhance teaching and learning, rather than simply adding technology to prepared lectures. The chapters, taken together, make the connection between intended learning outcomes, teachings strategies, and instructional media.

ISBN 1-930708-28-9 (h/c) • US$74.95 • 286 pages • Copyright © 2002

"**Most often, when forced to use new technologies in teaching, teachers will default to a technology-enhanced lecture method, rather than take advantage of the variety of media characteristics that expand the teaching and learning experience.**"
–Patricia Rogers, Bemidji State University, USA

**It's Easy to Order! Order online at www.idea-group.com
or call 717/533-8845 x10!
Mon-Fri 8:30 am-5:00 pm (est) or fax 24 hours a day 717/533-8661**

Idea Group Publishing
Hershey • London • Melbourne • Singapore • Beijing

An excellent addition to your library